Life of Octavia Hill as Told in Her Letters

LIFE OF OCTAVIA HILL

MACMILLAN AND CO., Limited
LONDON . BOMBAY . CALCUTTA
MELBOURNE

THE MACMILLAN COMPANY
NEW YORK . BOSTON . CHICAGO
DALLAS . SAN FRANCISCO

THE MACMILLAN CO. OF CANADA, Ltd
TORONTO

LIFE OF
OCTAVIA HILL

AS TOLD IN HER LETTERS

EDITED BY

C. EDMUND MAURICE

" *The Holy Supper is kept indeed*
In whatso we share with another's need.
Not what we give, but what we share;
For the gift without the giver is bare."
VISION OF SIR LAUNFAL.

MACMILLAN AND CO., LIMITED
ST. MARTIN'S STREET, LONDON
1913

MACMILLAN AND CO., LIMITED
BOMBAY · CALCUTTA
MELBOURNE

THE MACMILLAN CO.
NEW YORK · BOSTON · CHICAGO
DALLAS · SAN FRANCISCO

THE MACMILLAN CO. OF CANADA

LIFE OF
OCTAVIA HILL

AS TOLD IN HER LETTERS

EDITED BY

C. EDMUND MAURICE

" *The Holy Supper is kept indeed*
In whatso we share with another's need.
Not what we give, but what we share,
For the gift without the giver is bare."
VISION OF SIR LAUNFAL.

MACMILLAN AND CO., LIMITED
ST. MARTIN'S STREET, LONDON

1913

PREFACE

It was but a short time before the death of Miss Octavia Hill that one of her sisters succeeded, with much difficulty, in convincing her that some account of her life would be necessary to satisfy the public demand.

On realising this fact, she expressed a strong wish that the family should keep the details of such a memoir in their own hands; and she afterwards made a special request that the final decision as to what should be published, and what suppressed, should rest with me.

It will, therefore, be understood that I am rather the editor than the author of this book. The most important part of this Memoir will be found in the letters; and it is by my express wish that they are printed in larger type than the explanations which link them together.

But even those explanations are only in a limited sense my own work. All I have done is to weave together statements made by my wife and her sisters, a paper left by their Mother, and, in the very early part, the recollections of Octavia's early playmate, Miss Margaret Howitt.

Only in those chapters which cover the period from 1866 to 1877 have I trusted, to any considerable extent, to my own memory; for it was in those years that I was most closely associated with some parts of Octavia's work

With regard to the letters, there are two points to note. First, I have endeavoured, as far as possible, to arrange them chronologically; not separating the special subjects, in which Octavia was interested, from each other, but rather suggesting the variety of interests which were occupying her mind at the same time. Secondly, I have endeavoured to emphasise the human and family sympathy, and not merely her business capacity.

There was an outcry in the papers a little time ago, with regard to Florence Nightingale, which took a rather peculiar form. These writers said that there had been too much sentimental talk about the "lady of the lamp" bending over the sick bed; and that this picture had obscured Miss Nightingale's real power of organisation and practical reform. Perhaps twentieth century hardness may be as blinding as nineteenth century sentiment. At any rate, the danger with regard to Octavia Hill is precisely of the opposite kind to that which was supposed to threaten the fame of Florence Nightingale.

Octavia's power of organisation, and her principles of discipline, have been allowed by many critics to thrust into the background her human sympathies. The figure of the landlady sternly exacting her rents seems to stand rather on the opposite side to the "lady of the lamp"

"Miss Hill," said a critic in the early days of her fame, "I was puzzled to make out how you succeeded in your work, till I realised that the broker was always in the background."

This statement represents the view of her work which was always most distasteful to Octavia She disliked extremely the phrase "rent collector" as summing up the essential character of that work.   She maintained, as strongly as did Carlyle, that "cash payment was not the sole nexus between man and man," not, as another critic supposed, because she held that "the poor were there for the rich to do good to"; but because she realised that each had to learn from the other by common sympathy with each other's needs, and not by a hard enforcement of claims, or a careless belief in the power of money giving.   It is this wider and more human aspect of her life, which I hope these letters will bring home to their readers.   Perhaps the point of view, on which I am insisting, can be best summed up in Canon Barnett's words, "She brought the force of religion into the cause of wisdom, and gave emotion to justice."

I need only add my most hearty thanks to the friends who have helped me, either by sending Miss Hill's letters, or by hints derived from their own recollections, or by enabling us to use the pictures which appear in this volume.

C. E. MAURICE.

1913.

CONTENTS

CONTENTS

CHAPTER IX

CHAPTER X

CHAPTER XI

LIFE OF OCTAVIA HILL

CHAPTER I

EARLY in the nineteenth century Mr. James Hill was carrying on in Peterborough a business as corn merchant which his father had made very successful, and to which was added a banking business   Later on he removed to Wisbeach with his brother Thomas   James Hill showed much of his father's business capacity, though sometimes carried away by an over-sanguine temperament.   Both his ability and his hopefulness were to be put to a severe test, when in 1825 England suffered from a general banking panic, and Mr. Hill failed in company with other bankers of greater note.   But he roused himself to meet the emergency, and to a great extent retrieved his fortunes, for a time.

His troubles, however, were increased in 1832 by the loss of his second wife, and, as a widower with six children, he found himself in an anxious and difficult position.   He had always been a very affectionate husband and father, and he was most desirous to find some one who would help him in the care of his children.   While thinking over this problem, his attention was attracted by some articles on education, which had lately appeared in *The Monthly Repository*; with these articles he was so much impressed that he obtained from the Editor the name and address of the writer.   She proved to be Miss Caroline Southwood Smith, the daughter of Dr Southwood Smith, the celebrated Sanitary Reformer.

Mr. Hill called on the writer at Wimbledon, and found that she was already engaged in teaching in a private family.

When that engagement had ended, Mr. Hill persuaded Miss Smith to undertake the teaching of his children. How heartily they responded to her care will be shown by two letters given later on. and when, in 1835, she became the wife of Mr. Hill, she received a welcome from her step-children such as few step-mothers can have experienced. The marriage took place at St. Botolph's, Bishopsgate.

She assisted her husband in every way, and entered most sympathetically into his patriotic efforts to reform public abuses   He had been most successful in reforming the corruption in the Wisbeach municipal government, and had succeeded in excluding any claim for church rates from his parish   The extraordinary physical energy which he threw into all his work is well illustrated by his riding fifty miles to secure the pardon of the last man who was condemned to death for sheep stealing. This excessive energy was facilitated by a life of great self-restraint and devotion to study. He read much and accumulated a very fine library. Nor even in this matter did he limit his aims to mere self-improvement   He wished to extend to others, as far as possible, his own advantages, and he founded in Wisbeach an Infant School, which should introduce sounder methods of education. It was one of the first Infant Schools built. With a characteristic audacity he chose for the motto of this school the words in which Wordsworth embodied the advice which he sarcastically suggests that Rob Roy would have given to Napoleon, had they been contemporaries :

> " Of old things all are over-old,
>   Of good things none are good enough ,
>   We'll try if we can help to mould
>   A world of better stuff " [1]

He also started a penny paper to advocate various reforms, and at one time he bought the local theatre and invited celebrated actors to perform there   Later on he co-operated most earnestly with the advocates of Free Trade.

Into this energetic life at Wisbeach three daughters were born

[1] Wordsworth wrote "frame," but Mr Hill altered it.

Miranda, January 1st, 1836,
Gertrude, July 28th, 1837,
Octavia, December 3rd, 1838.

The name given to the third child marks the close connection always recognised between Mr. Hill's different families.
Octavia was his eighth daughter, and the half sisters welcomed
the new comers as heartily as they had done their mother.
Octavia's elder sisters were Julia and Louisa, the children of
Mr. Hill's first wife, Margaret, Ida, and Kate, daughters by
the second wife. There was only one son, Arthur, who proved
himself a most affectionate and generous brother. Later on he
built up a business for himself in Reading, where, as Mayor,
he did much for the improvement of the town, showing the
same public spirit which animated his father. And when he
became a rich man, he welcomed to his beautiful grounds on
many occasions the poor people in whom Octavia was interested.

But in 1840 a great change fell on the outward life of the
family. There came another bank panic, and, though Mr. Hill
tried to struggle against his difficulties, they proved too much
for him. The house at Wisbeach was given up and the children
of the earlier marriage were taken by their maternal grandmother; and Gertrude was adopted by her grandfather, Dr
Southwood Smith. Mrs. Hill was complimented by the Bankruptcy Commissioners on the economical way in which she had
managed the household expenses, which had facilitated a settlement of her husband's affairs; and Mr. Hill tried for some years
to fulfil all his obligations to his creditors

In the year of the bankruptcy, another daughter, Emily
Southwood, was born in her grandfather's cottage in Epping
Forest, and in 1843 Florence the youngest child was born at
Leeds.

For some years the family moved about from place to place.
At one time they were in lodgings in Pond Street, Hampstead,
where the house was discovered by an artist friend who was
convinced that the children dancing round a rose-bush must be
the daughters of Mrs. Hill.

At last the strain of anxiety became too much for Mr Hill
He broke down physically and mentally, and became

incapable of supporting his family   Under these circumstances, Dr Southwood Smith became responsible for the care of his daughter and her children, and placed them in a little cottage at Finchley.   Mrs Hill maintained that it had been a great advantage to her daughters and herself that poverty had deprived her of the help of servants, and compelled her to do everything for the children herself, and they heartily responded to her care   Her daughter Miranda in later years wrote as follows   " It is difficult to express to those who never knew Mrs. Hill what her influence was on those who came in contact with her.   On her children it left an indelible impression as deep as life itself, and as lasting   From her book ' Notes on Education ' it will be seen how entirely she felt the *spirit* to be everything in education.   She seldom gave a distinct order or made a rule , but her children felt that she lived continually in the presence of God, and that in her there was an atmosphere of goodness, and that moral beauty was a delight to her in the same way that outward beauty is to so many people.   She was ardent and yet so serene that to come into her room was like entering a haven of peace where evil and bitterness could not live.   Her children also learned from early infancy, from her attitude of mind, that if a thing was right it must be done , there ceased to be any question about it, and how great a help that feeling is to timid natures or weak wills only those know who have experienced it "

The children spent nearly all their time out of doors in the meadows, and on the common, and were described by one of the villagers as " the young ladies who are always up in the hedges "

Octavia early developed presence of mind and resourcefulness. One day she and Emily were sailing walnut-shell boats in a large water butt, when Emily fell in head foremost   Octavia instantly ran back to the other end of the garden to give impulse to her jump, and then, leaping on to the butt, pulled it over, so that she was able to drag her sister out   At an even earlier age, she saved another sister, who had fallen into a deep stream in Epping Forest   The nurse-maid ran away screaming, but Octavia stepped down the bank and held out a stick to her

sister and so pulled her out.   She was always overflowing with
energy which showed itself in various ways.   When about eight
years old she was climbing on a high fence and fell on the
back of her head; so that for some time she was forbidden to
do any lessons; but her mother found that she was playing at
keeping a school, and was learning long pieces of poetry, French
grammar, and doing sums for the pretence children, so that she
was working her brain more than she would have done in the
school room.

Her love of learning and writing poetry was great; and it was
about this time that she wrote the following elegy on a young
pigeon :

> " Little one thou liest deep,
> Buried in eternal sleep,
> And we oft for thee repine,
> While thy grave with flowers we twine
> Thou didst not live to see the sun,
> For thy short life was but begun,
> When silent death took all away,
> Thou lovely little flower of May." [1]

As some of the letters given in this book will show, Octavia
was somewhat inclined to exaggerate the practical as opposed
to the imaginative part of her nature   As a fact the imaginative
and even fanciful side of her was apparent at an early age; for
on one occasion she was found to have left a party at her grandfather's and to have seated herself on the steps in the garden.
When asked what she was doing, she answered, " I am looking
for the fairies!"   " Have you seen any?" asked her friend,
" No," replied Octavia, and added with the cheery confidence
which distinguished her, " but I am *sure* I *shall* see them."

This imaginative side of her must have been greatly stimu-
lated by the only young companions with whom she and her
sisters were brought into contact.   These were the younger son
and daughter of William and Mary Howitt, the well-known
writers   Miss Margaret Howitt writes, " The kind wish of my
elder sister Anna Mary to afford pleasure to her small brother

---

[1] Octavia called the mother pigeon "May," and the young one had
been hatched in a dark loft,

and sister led to a children's party being given to celebrate her twenty-second birthday on January 15th, 1846. The five little grandchildren of Dr. Southwood Smith were amongst the guests, henceforward to become our cherished friends for life. It was simply owing to suitability of age that Octavia became immediately the chosen playmate of my brother Charlton and myself, she was his junior by eleven months, my senior by eight. Although she was a very ardent, eager child, with a quick sense of the ludicrous that was partially hidden under a precise determined manner, she never forgot a smile of sympathy or a word of kindness bestowed upon her. . . On her two play-mates, though quite unconsciously to herself, Octavia enforced an exacting discipline of high aims and self-improvement, against which, I, being of a more ordinary mould than Charlton, often chafed, and more especially because her lofty standard was coupled with a quite startling humility

"I had secretly parcelled out the house to spirits both good and bad, and I think now it must have been to humour me that Octavia joined in my daily rites of propitiation to those invisibles I can see her now in the dim light of the cellar, the domain of hob-goblins, following Charlton who led the way, whilst I brought up the rear, with an awe-inspiring countenance either induced by some preoccupation, or by the thoroughness with which she would join in any pastime

"When Octavia visited us later on, her sense of humour was as keen as ever, but life seemed already to have for her a set purpose. . . . At the beginning of the 'fifties, awakening one night, I saw by the light of a lamp in the road a young statuesque figure seated with folded hands in the sister bed.

"'What are you about, Ockey?' I said.

"'Praying for Poland,' was the reply."

This last story was, in one way, less characteristic of Octavia than it would have been of Miranda, but the wave of feeling about such subjects, which passed over her friends and relations, was often reflected in Octavia both then and in later times.

At this time, however, her chief contact with those problems of public life which were afterwards most to interest her was confined to her visits to her grandfather, where she occasionally assisted Gertrude in copying Dr. Smith's papers on Sanitary

Reform.[1] It was in connection with this work that she gave a remarkable proof of that power of concentrating her mind on, and utilising effectively any important fact affecting the matter with which she was concerned, which afterwards stood her in good stead. Among the papers which she copied was an Order in Council, freeing tenement houses from a certain tax which had hitherto been exacted from them Years after, when she was beginning the work of superintending the houses, she remembered this Order in Council. She made inquiries and found that it was still in force, but that it was entirely unknown to many owners of tenement houses She was therefore able to free the tenants under her care from an undue burden.

Her visits to her grandfather also brought her into touch, unconsciously sometimes, with several distinguished men, one of whom remembered the meeting at a later period. Long after the time of which I am writing, on meeting the poet Browning at dinner, he informed her that he had seen her as a child at Highgate. She remarked that it was probably her sister Gertrude. "I remember her too," said Browning. "I was calling on R H. Horne, the author of *Orion*, who was on a visit there; and, when you and your sister had left the room, he said, 'Those are wonderful children, you can talk to them about anything.'"

The training which Mrs. Hill gave her children produced a certain independence and originality which was noticed at a later time of life, when a friend, commenting on a special little device, produced in an emergency, remarked, "I knew it must be done by a Hill; all you do is so original."

But this bright and free country life was soon to be exchanged for new experiences, the account of which needs another chapter.

Letter from Louisa Hill to her Stepmother.

Norwich, July 19th, 1840.

My Darling Mama,

I am so delighted to know that you will soon be well and strong again, and able to lend the strength

---

[1] *See* "Dr. Southwood Smith, a Retrospect." By Mis C. L Lewis 1898.

and assistance which you always have in trying circumstances.

How happy you will be, when the little ones are older, when you get beyond the merely physical part of their education. I am sure your children will all be beautiful, good and wise, for they come into the world finely organized and are watched and trained under your gentle and elevating influence

I heartily rejoice that the baby is a girl ; you will give her strength to endure and struggle with the evils which are the birthright of her sex She will add to the number of well educated women, who, I am afraid form but a very small portion of humanity. But I forget the difference in age. This little baby belongs almost to the third generation. She will be in her bloom, when we shall be old women, if not dead. Great changes may take place before she attains womanhood.

Very affectionately yours,

LOUISA HILL.

MRS HILL to her little daughter GERTRUDE.

81, St. Mark's Place, Leeds.
September 1st, 1843.

Ockey can now read quite well, and spends a great deal of time every day in reading to herself. Do you know she can scarcely walk, she goes leaping as if she were a little kangaroo—that is because she is such a merry little girl

(Undated, probably 1843).

Ockey speaks to everything that is said to her and corrects or makes fun of any mistake. She is

JAMES HILL.
Father of Octavia Hill.

always ready for a joke.   To-day her Papa said, "Take care or you will have a downfall." "That I should not mind," said Ockey, "if the down was there when I fell," and then she laughed.

Leeds, 1843.

Ockey learns to read very nicely. She is a very funny little girl; this is the way she talks. "Mama, I am as hot as if I were on the fire." "Mama, I shall never button this shoe if I were to try till the world is knocked down." She says things are as ugly as coal. The other day she told Minnie that she should "like to have a field so large that she could run about in it for ever."

From OCTAVIA (at the age of four).

This letter shows her early love of colour, especially red.

We have a box full of silks. I gave Miranda a beautiful piece, it was velvet and the colours were black, purple, yellow and white and green   Miranda gave me a beautiful piece of crimson plush.   Miranda has a book called The Peacock at Home and it has three stories in it.

MRS HILL to GERTRUDE.

November, 1845.

On Monday it is Ockey's birthday. She will be seven years old. She intends to give me a patchwork bag on that day—and she sits on a play box placed on a window-board, and looks so pretty, sewing earnestly away, never thinking that I am watching her. Every now and then she looks out at the passers by . they know every boy and girl, cat, dog, and donkey in the village by sight, and a good many of them by name, and for those whose name they do not know they invent one.

From Mrs. Howitt to Mrs. Hill.

February, 1846.

I am quite anxious to hear something about Maggie. I hope she has been as good a child, and may have left half as sweet a memory as dear Ockey.

Mrs. Howitt to Miss Mary Gillies.[1]

1846.

Ockey goes on beautifully. We are all charmed with her; and know not how we shall part with her again.

In another letter about February, 1846

I brought Miranda home with Maggie yesterday. We are all greatly pleased with her. She is a dear sweet creature; different from Ockey, but, in her way, quite as lovable. We find Maggie much improved by Mrs. Hill's kind care of her, and by her intercourse with those dear little children.

In March, 1846, Mrs. Howitt writes again :

Miranda and Maggie go on charmingly. Miranda is very sweet and much more cheerful than I expected to find her. She is full of life and fun, and has the same kind of ringing joyous laugh as Ockey. The same in spirit, though not in degree. Ockey's laugh is the happiest, sweetest I ever heard.

---

[1] Miss Gillies and her sister Margaret were Mrs Hill's bridesmaids, and became life-long friends of her and her children.

About 1849.

OCTAVIA to HER MOTHER.

June 10th, no year
(evidently a very early one).

We had a delicious sail yesterday. We were out for two hours, and it was so lovely; the sun shone warm and clear upon the calm blue waters; and the waves, and the bells were very pretty and made sweet music.

It is so delicious bathing; we stay in so long, and try to float and splash and dash and prance and dance.

I am so happy; you don't know how happy. They are all so sweet and kind to me, and it is so beautiful here.

Give my love to the little ones, and tell them (be sure to tell them) that I did mean to bid them good bye. It was not out of anger; but I forgot in my hurry; and though that was bad enough it was not as bad as they thought it was.

Ponney wants you and we all want you to try to get Mrs. Bugden to allow Miranda to come to the carting of the hay at Hillside, which will be about Thursday week.

From KATE HILL to MIRANDA.

Uttoxeter,
February 2nd, 1850.

I shall have great pleasure in working for the Peace Society; but I want you to tell me when the Bazaar is to be held, because if soon, I must not make anything too large to be sent in a letter. I hope it will not be before my holidays for I like best to do coarse work. Will you tell me, too, what are the doctrines of the Peace Society ? I know very little about it though still enough to engage my sympathies

Will you give the enclosed collar to dear Mamma with my love, and ask whether I shall make some like it for the bazaar ?

But Mamma is to be sure and keep this one for herself because I have made it for her, and I like my work to be round her neck, as my arms cannot be there."

OCTAVIA HILL AS A CHILD.

From an Oil Painting by Margaret Gillies.

CHAPTER II

1851—APRIL, 1856

THROUGH all the bright and free life at Finchley, Mrs. Hill had never forgotten that her daughters would have to earn their living. Miranda, indeed, at the age of thirteen, had begun to earn as a pupil teacher in the private school of a friend; and her sister Margaret mentions in a letter the characteristic fact that Miranda had wished to give some of her first earnings to her half-sisters, who were starting a school. When, then, these sisters realised that Mrs Hill was considering Octavia's future work, they, in their turn, offered to give her a free education, as a start in life. On the other hand, Octavia's artistic talent had already attracted the attention of Mrs. Hill's friend, Miss Margaret Gillies; and she offered to train Octavia in her studio. Both these offers attracted Octavia herself, but Mrs. Hill did not wish to part with her. Whilst she was still hesitating, her attention was drawn to the notice of an Exhibition, to be held at 4 Russell Place, Fitzroy Square, of special preparations of painted glass, consolidated so as to make it suitable for tables and other purposes. She found that Miss Wallace, the patentee, was promoting the Exhibition, partly to secure work for some Polish exiles, in whom she was interested, partly with the more general aim of finding regular suitable paying employment for ladies.

Mrs. Hill mentions that her first thought was that Miranda, whose overflowing fancy seemed to her dangerously unpractical, might be roused to more steady work by such an occupation as this. But it was natural that it soon occurred to her that Octavia's admitted artistic talent might also be utilised in this

13

way. So she applied for admission for both her daughters to this work. But, as Miss Wallace was unable to carry on the business, Mr Vansittart Neale most generously came forward with the capital, in order to carry it on on a co-operative basis He asked Mrs Hill to become the manager, which she very gladly consented to do, as she was much interested in co-operation and in the employment of women.

Such was Octavia's first introduction to London. The change from the healthy open-air life at Finchley, and from the beauty of the country, to the ugliness of her new surroundings told heavily on her spirits; and this depression was increased by the sudden sense of the evil and misery in the world Among the workers at the Guild was a Miss Joanna Graham, who rapidly became a warm friend of Miranda's. She introduced both sisters to the " London Labour and the London Poor," then just brought out by Mayhew, also to the pamphlets and other essays written by the Christian Socialist leaders of the movement with which Mr Neale had already brought them into contact The pictures given by Mayhew of the life of the London poor, and the desire awakened by the Christian Socialists to struggle against evils, which seemed to her irresistible, produced in Octavia such a state of mind that she began to think that all laughter or amusement was wicked. Miranda, always able to see the humorous side of a question, tried to laugh her out of this extreme depression, and, when Octavia persisted, the elder sister composed an imaginary epitaph on herself, supposed to be written by Octavia ·

" Her foibles were many, her virtues were few ;
And the more that she laughed, the more stern the world grew."

This produced a most startling letter of stern remonstrance from Octavia, so stern that one is relieved to find it closed by a loving message and followed by a P.S " Love to all Thank you for the apples."

Of course, this extreme gloom, unnatural in any young girl, was especially out of keeping with anyone of Octavia's buoyant temperament, and the happy busy life at the Ladies' Guild soon had its effect.

The following account given by Mrs. Hill in April, 1856, shows somewhat of the social life. "The ladies used to go to lectures together. In this case, the subject of the lecture became, next day, that of the conversation in the workroom. The conversation in general fell on interesting subjects, the favourite subjects being politics, religion, art, news, the country and its scenery, poverty and wages, etc. A very favourite subject was the derivation and definition of words; then the ladies would join their voices in chorus, taking different parts. Indeed a merrier company, 'within the limits of becoming mirth,' the writer never chanced to see. There was generally some joke in hand. In the winter, they often assembled in the evening at the Guild. Sometimes they drank tea together, and afterwards sang and danced joyously."

The artistic work at the Guild brought Octavia into contact with the Rogers family. Mr. G. Rogers was wood carver to the Queen, and produced some very interesting work. All his family had artistic leanings; but it was his daughter, who is best known by her writings on Palestine, who specially attracted Octavia, and for whom she formed one of those enthusiastic friendships which exercised so marked an influence on her life. A younger friend, whose name was afterwards to be so closely associated with Octavia's, was Miss Emma Cons. She, like Octavia, was much interested in art; and, on the other hand, her high girlish spirits called out in Octavia again the old love of exercise and fun that had shown itself so strongly in the Finchley days. Indeed Miss Cons was so much given to romps that Octavia's fellow workers (including her sisters) were rather startled at the attraction which her new friend had for her. But it is clear from the letters, produced here, that Octavia saw the real power concealed for the time under these hoydenish ways, and she marked her as one on whom she could rely, and from whom she expected much.

But it must not be forgotten that among the most important of these influences, then at work on Octavia, were the characters and teaching of the Christian Socialist leaders. Soon after joining the Guild she had begun to attend the lectures at the Hall of Association; and her attendance at Lincoln's Inn Chapel brought her in 1852 under the influence of my father, Rev. F. D Maurice. She and Emily attended the daily morning service, and, after a time, my father used often to let them walk back with him, and he would answer many of Octavia's difficulties about religious and social questions. On one occasion she asked him if it would not be very nice if one could get rid of all responsibility. He laughed and said it would indeed be very comfortable. But that she did not shirk responsibility is shown by the following incident. It was in the early days of the Guild, when Octavia was only about fourteen, that she was alone in the house with the exception of Mrs Horne,[1] who was at the top of the house. It was Sunday, and everyone else had gone to Church On coming out of a second-floor room she saw a man standing near the door of a large cupboard, in which she supposed he must have hidden "How did you come up here?" she asked "I came up the stairs," replied the man "Then you will please to walk down again," said Octavia in a quiet tone. He obeyed her, and she walked behind him down three long flights of stairs, and saw him out at the front door Her sense of responsibility was the greater because some money, belonging to the Guild, had been paid late on Saturday and was in the office

After the Guild had been carried on for some time, Mr. Neale was asked to take over a new kind of work, which a lady had started in order to employ some Ragged School children This was the making of a special kind of toy which she had invented, and Mr Neale appointed Octavia head of the work-room The following account is given by my wife and her sister Miranda The management of the toy-making helped to "develop Octavia's business faculties She had to pass the children's work, which was paid by the piece, to assign the various processes to each child, to choose the shapes and colours of the toy furniture, to price it, and to see that, when the suites were finished, they were neatly packed in boxes and sent over to the show room, where the ladies' glass work was also exhibited. From time to time she had to take stock, and to see if the sales justified the expenditure

[1] Wife of R H Horne.

" Her daily intercourse with the girls taught her to know intimately the life of the poor. Most of the children came from very poor homes, and had, though so young, experienced great hardships. There was Louisa, an emotional, affectionate girl who had lost both parents, and helped to support herself and the aunt with whom she lived She had worked at artificial flower-making, and told us how, when trade was busy, she had been kept late into the night, and had had to run frightened through the streets in the small hours of the morning, and tap at the window to wake her aunt There was poor Denis whose face and neck were terribly disfigured with burns, but who had such a sweet pathetic voice that, when she sang, one forgot her ugliness. There was Clara, a tall, over-grown girl from a dirty home, who was half-starved and cruelly treated She wore a low dress and short sleeves, and one could see her bones almost coming through her skin On one occasion when her work was too slovenly to be passed, she burst into tears, and said that her mother would beat her if she did not take back the money expected of her There was little Elizabeth, a stunted child of about nine, with so fierce a look that Octavia, in loving raillery, called her her little wild beast. She had never come with us on the Saturday-afternoon walks to Hampstead, but used to look wistfully after us. Once we pressed her very much to come, and then she exclaimed 'I cannot, I have to nurse the baby.'

" Another child was R. who was lost sight of, and later on was found in a dark cellar into which one descended by a ladder, where she sat all day to sell pennyworths of coal. She was half-starved and unkindly treated, but she seemed to take that as a matter of course ; what she *did* resent was that her cat was starved. Later on Octavia sent her to an Industrial School , and after some years she emigrated, and wrote to tell of her happy married life.

" Harriet and her sister were of a higher class, and had a clean, respectable home. They were earnest Methodists. We lost sight of Harriet for forty years, and then found her very happily married. She had remembered Octavia with the deepest affection, and had preserved all her letters.

" The girls were in the habit of bringing their dinners to eat

C

in the work-room, and what they brought was very poor fare. Octavia suggested that they should club together to buy their food, and that each girl in turn should cook it   The long table was cleared, and a white cloth laid, and the food served nicely. Octavia brought over her own luncheon to eat with the girls, and, after the Grace had been sung, it was a pretty sight to see the sad, careworn faces of the children light up, as they sat round the table while she talked to them   Among other things, she learnt to scrub the floor, in order to teach the children to keep the work-room clean

"A good many of the girls were older than Octavia and inclined to be insubordinate, but she very soon established order, and that without recourse to punishment.   The girls had been accustomed to be fined for offences, and they were quite amazed when they found this was no longer the case.   On one occasion they refused to scrub the work-tables, which was part of their daily duty   Immediately Octavia and her two younger sisters set to work to do the scrubbing, and soon the girls gave in   They had been fined for swearing, but the swearing soon ceased, and they sang hymns or nice songs.   Octavia was their leader and companion in all that they did, and this sharing in their work, and yet leading the way, won them all to obey as well as to love her   Sometimes, on a Saturday afternoon, she would take her little group of workers for a walk to Hampstead Heath or Bishop's Wood   Her sister Gertrude remembers walking in Highgate Lane on a spring afternoon with Professor Owen, who was quietly explaining something about the mosses on Lord Mansfield's fence—all being very still—when, to her surprise, the hedge was broken open, and, with a burst of joy, who should leap down from the bank with a staff in her hand and a straw hat torn by the thicket but Octavia, followed by a troop of ragged toy-workers, happy and flushed, each with a lap full of blue-bells   Octavia stayed for a minute to speak to her sister and the Professor, then off they all went back into the wood and away towards Finchley.

"Schools were not what they are now, and Octavia was amazed at the ignorance of these girls.   They quite believed that wolves and bears might be lurking in the woods, and they did not know the names of any of the flowers. It was afterwards arranged that Miranda should give the girls lessons for an hour or so each afternoon." [1]

In 1854 Dr. Southwood Smith left Hillside and moved to Weybridge, where his grandchildren were always welcomed in the same loving way that they had been at Highgate.

But, before he could move, he was seized with a severe illness which necessitated an operation. A few weeks later his granddaughter Emily was attacked by scarlet fever, and her life was despaired of by two doctors. Then her grandfather, in spite of his weak state, came back to London, and saved her life ; and when she could be removed, took her to Weybridge to watch over her convalescence   This of course withdrew her from the toy work, and threw more of the burden on Octavia. A year later her youngest sister Florence was also withdrawn from the work by ill-health, and taken to Italy by her aunt, Miss Emily Smith, who gave her loving care for six years. It was in the summer of 1855 that an expedition of the toy-workers into the country led to the formation of some important friendships. Mrs. Harrison, to whose house at Romford they were invited, was the sister of Mrs. Howitt, and she and her family became warm friends of Octavia's. Some of the letters given further on were written to Mary, the eldest daughter, who was very artistic.

But even more important was the friendship then formed with Miss Mary Harris, a member of the Society of Friends, who was a great deal older than Octavia, and whose calm, loving nature was a great rest to her. From the time they first met till 1893, when Miss Harris died, Octavia poured out more of her secret thoughts to her than to anyone else, and when they were away from each other wrote to her constantly.

On the occasion of this visit to Romford another guest was Mr. Ellis Yarnall, the American, whose letters to Lord Coleridge have lately been published. He recorded in his diary the following description of Miranda and Octavia.

"Some young ladies were expected, and with them about

---

[1] A vivid account of the life of the toy-workers appeared on May 17th, 1856, in *Household Words*, under the title of "Ragged Robin."

twenty children, girls to whom they are teaching some
decorative arts. The children played in the grounds, the
young ladies (Miranda and Octavia) were with us at luncheon;
and we had a great deal of talk about Mr Ruskin, who is a
friend of theirs They described his eloquence as a speaker,
his earnestness of manner, his changing countenance, even
when he was silent, as though thoughts grave and gay were
passing through his mind. It was plain to me that his strong
intellect and bright fancy were having their true influence on
these young persons, themselves highly gifted and altogether
like-minded, eighteen and sixteen or thereabouts—sisters. I was
astonished at the strength of intellect which they displayed.
The talk of the elder one especially was, I think, more
striking than that of any person of her age I ever knew. She
reminded me of Corinne and other women of renown. What a
pleasure it was to look at her fine face with the glow of
enthusiasm upon it, and to wonder whether gifts like hers
would not one day produce fruits which the world would value.
Her description of the effect which the hearing of Beethoven's
music on some late occasion had had upon her was an utterance
of passionate feeling showing true poetic susceptibility.

" They are the granddaughters of Dr. Southwood Smith "

Towards the end of 1855 an important event took place,
which led to Mrs. Hill's withdrawal from the Ladies' Guild.
My father had been interested in Octavia's work for the Toy
workers, and offered to take a Bible Class for them. The
Theological Essays controversy was just then at burning point;
and the ladies who had handed over the business part of the
toy work, still considered that they had a right to interfere
about the religious instruction of the children These ladies
were very Evangelical (as Evangelicalism went in those days)
and they threatened to withdraw all pecuniary help and the
support of the Ragged School Union, if my father was allowed
to teach the girls The managers of the business were so much
alarmed at this threat that they asked my father to withdraw
his offer. Mrs Hill and her daughters were naturally very
indignant at this, and Mrs Hill's protests led to her losing

the post of Manager at the Guild. She and Emily went to Weybridge. Miranda and Octavia continued to work for a time; but when it seemed likely that the Guild would fail, Miranda obtained daily teaching and Octavia applied to Ruskin to learn from him if there would be any chance of her supporting herself by painting. He replied most kindly, and asked her to let him have a table-top designed and painted by herself. This design [1] was a spray of bramble leaves in all their brilliant autumn colours, encircling the centre space which formed a background that was dark at one part and gradually grew lighter, and finally changed into soft blue, suggesting storm clouds passing away, and leaving a bright sky. Round the edge, among the leaves, were the words of the Psalm, "He brought them out of darkness and out of the shadow of death, and brake their bonds in sunder."

This led to Ruskin's undertaking to train Octavia and give her work. Soon after this came the final crisis at the Guild; and Octavia obtained the appointment mentioned in the last letter of this chapter.

June 14th, 1852.

To MIRANDA.

Thank you many many times for your sweet letter. It was such a comfort to me.

I am very well indeed now. I do not know when I have been better, except that I am rather weak. I am at Finchley with Minnie. I long dreadfully to go to town; but I think I can wait patiently till Wednesday.

I have been very unfortunate in being away from the Guild just at this time. Do you know Mr. Walter Cooper has been there? and Mr. Lewis and the trustees (Mr. Furnivall) go there so often; and all the bustle, and trying to feel Christian-like to Mr. and Miss ——. O, would it not have been delightful!

I have Miss Graham's books here; they are so interest-

---

[1] Mentioned in the letter of February 27th, 1856

ing.   I am so very happy when I am reading them.   My interest gets deeper and stronger every day.   I wish, oh ! I so long, to do something, and I cannot.   Andy ! do you think I ever shall be able to do anything really useful ?

I do not at all like Mr. ——, or rather I entirely despise and dislike his opinions.   I will tell you all about it when I see you.   I will only tell you now that he likes " the subordination of the employed to the employer " ; and he thinks " there is no tribunal so proper as the discretion of the employer to decide those delicate questions of the personal conduct of the employed."   Did you ever hear of such a thing ?   Is it not horrible ?

Mr. Furnivall I admire more and more the more I know and read of him , and, as to Mr. Ludlow, certainly there is not (excepting Mr. Furnivall) such a person in the whole world.   He has the largest, clearest, best-balanced mind joined to the truest most earnest wish to help the working classes I ever met with (of course excepting Mr. Furnivall's).

I have read to-day his " Christian Socialism and its Opponents."   All I can say of it, and all he writes is that it is grand, and that I never can forget it, or cease to be grateful for it.   His lectures have sunk deeper into my heart than anything else ; one reason is, I dare say, that they were the first ; but they were most noble and grand ; his own great soul seemed to breathe itself into his works.   But I forget—I shall get no sympathy from you.   I must tell Miss Graham.   Andy, do you think Mr. Furnivall will bring him to the Guild ? Do you think he meant it ; or, if not, do you think we ever shall know him ?

The Festival will be on Monday.   I am looking forward to it with such pleasure   I do so long to see you ; it seems ages since I did , I want to know

what you think about the 'Guild'; I do so want your
advice, too, upon a thousand subjects. I have a good
deal to read to you, which I have written since you
were away. Give my dearest love to Miss Graham.
Tell her I never can thank her enough for all the noble
and beautiful books she has lent me; that, as to the
Christian Socialist, I never never before read anything
which inspired such earnest longing to do *something*
for the cause of association; and it interested me so
very much that the hours I have spent in reading *that*
are never to be forgotten; they were unequalled in
pleasure to any that I have ever spent in reading;
and that, if I live years and years, I shall never forget,
or cease to remember with gratitude that it was to her
that I owe the great happiness of first reading a Socialist
book, which I consider one of the greatest happinesses
any one can have. Thank her, also, for the other books;
tell her the "Cheap Clothes and Nasty" and "Labour
and the Poor" are some of the most dreadful things I
ever read. They have made a deep impression on
me. How delightful the History of the Working
Tailors' Association is!

Do you know I have a post at the Guild? I have
to give out the stores and am responsible for them
The ladies have all sent me a book as a testimony
of their gratitude to me for reading to them. How
very kind it is of them! Dear Laura has written
me such a sweet letter. I love to think of you
among those lovely scenes by the beautiful sea, with
dear Miss Graham. . . .

Your own loving little sister, OCKEY.

I am sadly afraid the Journal[1] will stop at Midsummer. What is to become of me? ? ?

[1] Journal of Association.

Ladies' Guild,
July 27th, 1852

MIRANDA TO JOANNA GRAHAM,

We all declare that we have never spent a more
glorious evening   I think I never saw such a face as
Mr. Kingsley's   That face was the chief pleasure of
all, though there was a most splendid collection of people
there.   We went a party of six, Ockey, Mama, Mary,
I, Mr. Rogers, and Miss Cons.   We met Walter Cooper
at the door, and he was very kind and seemed glad to
see us.   The Hall was very crowded but he got seats
for us.   Mama and I were together   We looked round
and got glimpses of the Promoters [1]   Mary fixed on
Mr. Neale at once and was delighted with him.   She
noticed his head among all the rest and admired it
almost more than any. . . . Suddenly, amongst a great
crowd of faces, Mary pointed out one to me and asked
if that was Mr Kingsley, and it was.   Mary thought it
noble.   Mr. Neale introduced Kingsley to Mama, and
he talked to her for some time . . . and Mr. Neale
introduced Mr. Ludlow to Mama, much to Ockey's
delight. . . . I think Mr. Kingsley's face extremely
suffering and full of the deepest feeling.   But there is
such a sublime spirituality ; he looks so far above this
earth, as if he were rapt up in grand reveries ; one feels
such *intense* humility and awe of him.   I hardly dared
look at him ; and the more I looked, the more I felt
what a grand thing the human soul is when developed as
it is in him.   Professor Maurice was called to the chair,
and he made a nice speech.   He seemed as if he felt
a great deal more than he could express, and therefore
left feelings rather than ideas in one's mind.   He said a

---

[1] Promoters of Working Men's Association.

great deal about self-sacrifice; though he said he felt
almost ashamed to speak of self-sacrifice to working
men, while he himself was in possession of all the
comforts of life. He had to leave after he had made
his speech; and, just as he was about to leave the platform, Mr. Cooper said that the Manager of the Builders'
Association, Mr. Pickard, would read an address to
Professor Maurice as an embodiment of the sentiments
of the Associations, and that the Manager of the Printers
would present him with a testimonial, the exclusive
gift of the working men. The address of thanks was
very nicely expressed; and then the testimonial, a
silver inkstand, was presented. It was so touching
to think of all those poor working men, who had
worked so hard to earn the money to make the
testimonial, and the beautiful spirit of gratitude.
I could not restrain my tears. Professor Maurice
answered the address and thanked them in the most
heartfelt manner. After he left, Mr. Hansard was put
in the chair, and Lloyd Jones spoke on Cooperative
Stores. Mr. Newton spoke on Mechanics' Institutes, and
said they were not at all satisfactory as far as they
professed to educate the working men. Someone in
the Hall got up and said that he knew of one gentleman on the Committee of these Institutes, who, in
opposition to the majority of the Committee, threatened
to resign if "Alton Locke" was allowed in the Library.
I could not see Mr. Kingsley's face. . . . The next
subject was the Industrial and Provident Societies Bill
which had just been passed. Mr Kingsley then made
a short speech; one knew at once that it was a poet
who was speaking. . . . Gerald Massey's is a very fine
face. He has dreamy eyes and wild looking hair; but,
after the others, he's not to be thought of.

Ladies' Guild,
October 22nd, 1852.

To GERTRUDE.

Oh Gertrude! I am so happy, so very very happy I wish you were with me. You would so love all my beautiful things. I will tell you about them when you come. I have a little room, all to myself. When anything is wrong or unjust down stairs, I have only to come up into my own little room, and it is so still. It is full of such happy recollections. I have my *nice* books; all my great soul-inspiring books are here. Then I have all my writing things I write a great deal now. I have such a beautiful book of extracts that I have made. I have usually some flowers; for the ladies are very kind in bringing me them. I have a few poor little plants that I am fond of. Then I have eleven dear little snails. They are such darlings. And then, Gertrude, I have my drawing things. I do not let anyone see my drawings. I do not do much. It is sad to think, after I have done anything, " And, after all your visions of grandeur and beauty, is this all you can produce ? " I believe I am very wrong about my drawing; I never draw things for the sake of learning. I try things above me. I have such dreams, both day and night, of what I would do, and when I try what do I see ? A little miserable scrap that is not worth looking at Once I tried a figure. Of course it was frightful. . . . We have returned Ruskin. I do so miss it. It was so very beautiful. This evening I have found such an extract from " Modern Painters " that I shall copy it for you

Do you go on with your drawing ? I hope you do. Oh Gertrude! is it not a glorious thing to think that a divine thought should descend for ages and ages ?

Think of Raphael and Michael Angelo! (though I know but little of them).—To think that every grand feeling they had they could preserve for centuries! Oh what an influence they must have! Think of the thousands of great thoughts they must have created in people's minds; the millions of sorrow that one great picture (one truly great picture) would calm and comfort. Will that never be painted again? Do you think there will? And when? I am going to see the Dulwich Gallery soon. Is it not glorious? I wish you could see a bit of hawthorn I have here, such colours! I am writing a curious letter; just what comes foremost in my mind. . . . When I have finished work and go up to tea, if any one is out of spirits, it makes me so; and I feel (do you know what I mean?) a tear in my throat.

Ladies' Guild,
July 13th, /53.

To GERTRUDE.

I write to you because I wish to give you a happier impression of me than you can have from Tuesday. I am all alone; it is so still; and I am very happy; now I will try and account for the strange state I was in last night.

When I got into the country I felt that, if I stayed looking at sky and trees and flowers,[1] my friends would think me dull and become dull themselves and spoil all enjoyment. So all the day my whole energies were " stretched " to be merry and lively. I felt that if I waited one moment to look at anything, I should

---

[1] A party of four people.

never tear myself away, and I got into a wild state. I did enjoy very much the mere exercise, and the mirth, and happiness of every one. I hardly thought all this; I only felt it Then, at the singing class, the strain being over, and having nothing to sustain me, I sank into low spirits. As we were singing "Oh come ye into the summer woods," a longing came over me to be there; a dim recollection of tops of the trees with the evening sun upon them, a panting desire to sit there, and cry myself quiet . . .

But it is all too beautiful now, I could almost fancy myself at home . . . As to my drawing, whether I will or no I must go on with that; and, though I do not hope, I trust. . .

September 18th, /53.

DEAR SISTERS,

I fully intended to come over to you to-day, but I have a sore foot, and can only limp to the classes. *Private.* On Wednesday evening I went to see Miss Cooper, and spent the whole evening there. Just as I was going William Cooper came in and told me (don't tell *anyone*) that they have discovered heresy in Professor Maurice's last book, and he will probably be expelled from the Church. I had not time to ask any questions, as Miss Cooper returned, and she is not to know. Professor Maurice came to town on Monday night, went to Walter Cooper on Tuesday before Miss Cooper was out of bed, and returned to the country in the evening. . . . On Thursday there was a Council. Walter Cooper looks very grave and rather ill and anxious. What all this betokens, I cannot guess; but I fear something sad.

I have been reading "The Message of the Church to

the Labouring Men"; it is so beautiful; also "The Duty of the Age." I did not think Lord Goderich [1] was so nice; it would just suit Andy.

Mr. Edwards will give us a large order for a skirting board of marble if we can do it for 8d. a foot; also an order for a painted glass conservatory.

If any of you love me, see if you can't send me a piece of Indian ink and a paint brush, and "The Land we live in," and look out for some toys, or books that you don't want—the latter two for the little child at the needlewoman's.

November 27th, 1853.

To Gertrude.

About Ruskin, it matters very little to me what *The Times*, or anything else, says of him. I see much, very very much, to admire in him, and several things which I could wish different. If, as I suppose, *The Times* accuses him of affectation of style and want of humility, I entirely deny the first charge; as I think there is never a single word he writes, which could have been left out without loss, or changed without spoiling the idea; and, if it means that each sentence of his has a beauty of sound as well as of meaning, I say that it is to me all the more right for that; and that to be able to reproduce that sound is a gift not to be neglected. . . . As to the second objection I say, if Ruskin sees a truth which is generally denied, he is right to proclaim it with his whole strength. He says *not* " I see it is so because I am a higher creature than you," *but* " I see it, because I have gone to God, and His works for it. You may all see it, if you will look,

---

[1] Afterwards Lord Ripon.

using the powers He has given you; only look in sincerity and humility. It is only because I am humble, because I am content to give up my own ideas and notions, to take the truth because it is God's, to believe that it is good and right. It is only so I can discover harmony in this universe, and I am sent (he says) with a loud voice to proclaim this to you."

Ladies' Guild,
December 5th, 1853.

To Gertrude.

Ruskin has been here. All went as well as I could possibly wish. He was most delighted with the things, as showing the wonderful power we possess of introducing and preserving colour. He gave us some most interesting and useful hints about colour, and ordered five slabs to be painted for him; adapting two of the designs he wanted from some we had, which Mr. Terry was to go to his house to do on Monday. He offered to lend us some things to copy. If you had seen the kind, gentle way in which he spoke, the interest he showed, the noble way in which he treated every subject, the pretty way in which he gave the order, and lastly, if you had seen him as he said on going away, his eyes full of tears, "I wish you all success with all my heart," you would have said with me that it was utterly wonderful to think that that was the man who was accused of being mad, presumptuous, conceited and prejudiced. If it be prejudice to love right and beauty, if it be conceited to declare that God had revealed them to you, to endeavour to make your voice heard in their defence, if it be mad to believe in their triumph, and that we must work to make them triumph, then he is all four, and may God make us all so ! . . . . All my sisters, Kitty and Mama, have given me Mr. Maurice's "Ancient Philosophy" and have written in it "From her sisters in affection and work." This sentence makes me very happy. I know it is true. I know our work has bound us together. . . . Another thing happened on Sunday which pleased me very much. Mr. Neale heard Miranda talking about my birthday; and he said he was going to give me Mr. Maurice's "Prophets and Kings of the Old Testament." He came on Sunday on purpose to bring it. It seems such a glory that he does look upon us as related to him, not merely as receivers of wages, that he considers us workers with him. All that I have struggled to accomplish, so long and so wearily, seems just now to be succeeding, all fruitless as the work has seemed; the seeds buried, dead as I thought them, have sprung above the ground.

Ladies' Guild,
January 10th, 1854.

To GERTRUDE.

Mr. Cooper gave me last night a copy of the Address of the congregation at Lincoln's Inn to Mr. Maurice. He had asked Mr. Ludlow for it on purpose for me, and Mr. Ludlow had written my name on it.

I got "Yeast" for Miranda. Have you ever read it, and do you remember that Barnakill forbids Launcelot to be an artist? It has made a great impression on me.

Hillside,
February 10th, 1854.

MIRANDA TO MISS JOANNA GRAHAM.

You have not heard yet that there is great thought of enrolling the Guild as an Industrial Society,

under the new Act   Would it not be very nice ?   Mr.
Neale had drawn out a set of rules ; and he sent
them to Mama for her to approve or make her
remarks upon.   There are however some difficulties
in the way.

I have not yet been able to write a recollection of
that very beautiful class at Mr Maurice's ; but I hope
to do it.

Ladies' Guild,
June 11th, 1854.

To GERTRUDE.

(Speaking of Hillside.)

I hope that I may never, as long as I live,
forget the sunny, bright happy hours I have passed
there   There remains in my mind a recollection, a
vision of beauty connected with it, which can never be
effaced. . . .

Mr. Maurice has been speaking to-day of sacrifice
as the link between man and man, and man and God.
It was such a sermon !   One feels as if all peace and
quiet holiness were around one ; everything appears to
have a beauty and calm in it, to which we can turn
back in times of storm and wild noisy rivalries, as to
the memory of sunny days, and to shed a light on all
dark and difficult things, on sorrow and loneliness. . . .

It is so still !   A garnet coloured glass is on the table
full of bright golden buttercups, and grass ; now the
door is open they tremble in the wind, carrying one
back to slopes of long grass full of buttercups and
sorrel, as the evening wind sweeps over it.

September 17th, 1854.

To MIRANDA.

(In the Lake Country.)

I have spent three happy evenings with Miss Rogers. I have had a very interesting conversation on religion with Charlie Bennett, Harry and Mr. Rogers. . . . You cannot think what pleasure your notes have been, telling us, as they do, of a life of rest and beauty. One doesn't seem to know much about that sort of thing, and yet they seem to speak of home to you, as not many things do. One thing will be that you will be able to understand Ruskin infinitely better than you would have done. I imagine that some of the descriptions, that appear to us bright images of things almost vague at times (they are so far off), will remind you of actual beauties that you have really seen, memories connected with life. Ruskin has done something to rescue many things from vagueness. He has embodied them in words which will convey these impressions they gave you, as nobody else ever has, I believe. . . .

I have been to Westminster Abbey with Miss Cons, have I ever spoken about her to you? It seems to me that she is capable of a very great deal. She said something the other day about Mr. Maurice and Walter Cooper that made me very angry. I told her I would never tell her anything again; however, instead of that, I told her a great deal more than I ever did before. I told her that it was he who had led me to the Church, who had shown me a life in the creeds, the services and the Bible; who had interpreted for me much that was dark and puzzling in life; how the belief in a Father, a Son and a Holy Ghost might be the most real

D

faith, not a dead notion; that I might believe, not only that God was manifesting himself to each man in the inward consciousness of light and beauty in himself and all around; that those had led to infinite perplexities and doubts, but that a real person had come amongst us, who had known the Father, whose will had been brought into harmony with His; that He was stronger than doubts and sorrow and had overcome them; that He had declared that we might have life, that life was knowledge of God. From this conversation came a determination that Miss Cons and I should read the Theological Essays together.

. . . Oh if you could but see my ferns and all my things here. I have so many things I want to do in this room, but they all want money, sometimes as little as threepence, sometimes several pounds. It is perfect, because everything is progressing. The ivy will some day creep around the windows. I shall some day know my books better, and perhaps at last the room will be all grey stone, the window Gothic, and there may be pictures of my own painting; and the stony walls may be covered with wild masses of leaves standing out boldly in the sunlight, with their shadows sharp and dark on the grey background.

I began this letter to-day, as the first sunbeam fell on my flowers. Nobody could have been happier. Now I have run up from work to finish it, feeling very cross. Kitty has complained to Mama that Miss Cons and I make a great deal of noise. We never do anything but talk. Never mind! she'll find me silent enough.

Ladies' Guild,
March 14th, 1855.

To Emily.

I find on reflection that it will be a rather more difficult undertaking than I imagined to write to you every two days. However I will do my best.

You will have seen, by this time, what a wonderful event is about to take place in my life, and will, no doubt, have realized what it will be to me. But, however wonderfully you may all enter into my feelings, or even discover them, I do not think any of you can really understand what this is to me, unless you could have looked into my heart continually for three years, and seen how at first he was only a friend of Mr. Furnivall's [1]; then how his books were everything and he nothing; then how his name suggested a vision of vague beauty and distant and indefinite glory. . . . Still he was distant, almost unreal. He might be in Italy, or Palestine, or he might be passing me at that moment. . . . Perhaps in a year or two hence I may tell you what my thoughts were, and are at this period;—but, all this time I was learning to admire him more and more, and now leave the rest till after Friday.

I send you a prospectus of the College, which I beg you will return. Walter Cooper was with us last night; but I don't think we heard any news.

Anna Mary (Howitt) has fulfilled her promise to lend me "Modern Painters." She sent them yesterday; I leave you to put in all the marks of admiration and the "oh how delightfuls!" according to your own fancies; working people have no time for anything but facts,

---

[1] Three years earlier Dr Furnivall lent Mrs. Hill Ruskin's "Modern Painters," and Octavia read it then for the first time

(not that the delight of reading "Modern Painters" is less a fact than that the book is in this house), but——

I am very bright to-night. as you may perceive, and am writing this in the most comfortable way, in bed. Tell F. that I expect she is quite a woman, and is quite independent of my letters, and, as I promised to write to you, she must not expect letters from me; but she must accept my kindness to Pussie, and my care of her plants, as the affectionate proof of my remembrance and friendship. Will you, dear children, think of me very earnestly on Friday at two; and try to see poor Mansfield's[1] grave? I suppose there is not a single fern. You know how much I want them.

I'm getting a toothache with sitting up in the cold; so I must lie down and read. I've written to accept Ruskin's invitation.

Ladies' Guild,
March 16th, 1855.

To EMILY.

There is only one thing to speak about just now, Ruskin. I have been,—fancy! We could not get an omnibus which would pass the door, without waiting till it would be too late. We took one which brought us to Camberwell Gate; we tore along, thinking we were late, and too much engrossed by that idea, to see or think of anything else. At last we arrived at a green gate with a lodge. We asked for Mr. Ruskin, and were sent on to the house. Imagine a handsome mansion or large villa, a broad sweep of gravel road leading to it, bordered by a lawn, on which stood an

---

[1] Charles Mansfield, author of "Letters from Paraguay, and one of the Christian Socialist leaders

immense cedar of Lebanon, on the other a bank covered
with golden celandines in full flower, and shaded by
immense elms. Ascending a flight of steps leading to
a glass door, we looked into a handsome hall; a
footman came and showed us upstairs; we entered
Mr. Ruskin's study, and he was there. He received
us very warmly, asked us about our journey there, and
about the weather, which I then for the first time
perceived. The room was lofty, the furniture dark, the
table covered with papers, the walls rich with pictures,
a cabinet full of shells, with a dead fern or two; and
looking out of the window over a garden (I never
looked at it) on to a field which sloped very gently,
more like a bit of park, large trees on it, with their
shadows strongly marked by the bright sun, and very
still; beyond, slopes of meadow and woodland, over
which the shadows of large white clouds kept passing.
Mr. Ruskin was very kind, and showed us numbers
of manuscripts, which I admired more than I had any
idea of, and sketches. He evidently thought my design
well done, admired the fir and bramble, blamed my not
knowing exactly what colours I should put everywhere,
and illustrated these things—that in a fine design
each thing is of importance, that the effect of the whole
would be spoilt by the alteration of any part; that
simplicity of form is needful to show colour; that no
colour is precious till it is gradated; that grass is more
yellow than we think; that holly is not green (made
only with blue and yellow) (*sic*) but with crimson and
white in it; that it is impossible to have colour on
paper so light and so living as in nature; that, in
the fourteenth and fifteenth centuries, work becomes
coarser, more floral, less grotesque than in the thirteenth.
We had a delightful conversation about one thing. I

remarked what a world of beauty he was surrounded
with; and he answered that, if I could change places
with him, I should be no happier than I am now.
I said I knew that very well; but I affirmed there was
a positive pleasure in a beautiful thing. He said he
was very covetous, always wanting more, and that
he desired happiness, but from the success of what he
was doing; that he would part with all he possessed,
if he could thereby insure that some real illuminators
would arise. We then, though quite consistent, appeared to change sides in the argument. I said that
there was as much pleasure to be found in London
as in the country; that the beauties were more valued
when seen, and the scraps of beauty more loved. He
said that man was not meant to be in a constant state
of enthusiasm (of which by the way we stand in no
danger), that the blessing of the country was more
negative; that brick walls were a positive pain. I
said that I was very glad to say that, although sometimes feeling crushed by the ugliness, I could forget it.
He ended by saying that, as I was fond of the country,
he hoped after May, when the weather was warm, I
should often go down there; and then, altering the
reason of the invitation, he said that, if I wanted to
refresh my memory and come to see his MSS., I could
come any day and chance finding him at home; or, if
I would send a line the day before, he would try and be
at home This is not half of this conversation, and we
had several others, to say nothing of illustrations and
propositions.

And now, M., do you, or do you not wish to hear
what I think of it; that *that* which is asked for is
given; that, well-used, this friendship (?), so happily
begun, may be a long and growing one; that I have

seen a world of beauty; and that this might ·be the opening to a more glorious path; and that I would give years, if I could bring to Ruskin "the peace which passeth all understanding"?

Ladies' Guild,
March 19th, 1855.

To EMILY.

I ought to have written yesterday; but, as I cannot write on Saturdays, I thought it was well to get to the right days again. You must not think it unkind, if I do not write to you again, as Mr. Ruskin has lately sent us some work to do. Of course I wish to do it; so, as there is other work wanted, I shall have to do it in the evening. Mr. Maurice also will be home on Wednesday; and I am not sure that we shall not be admitted to two meetings there are to be . . . Tell F. her kettle mourns day and night at its loneliness, and muses over its utter uselessness; and the book-case looks sadly dejected, but it has not told me the reason.

Don't expect a merry letter to-night. I am rather dejected. . . . I often wish now I were quite free and could work at what I liked. . . . It requires a strong heart to go on working, without anyone caring whether you are longing to do anything else. I am going to work all the Fast [1] day at Ruskin's things; and God give me a brave heart, for I am sure nothing else can.

Dear child, I hope you are happy and enjoying the country very much. I long to see Mr. Maurice again. When I do, I shall have more to tell you, if I have time to write. I am very wretched. I am not to

---

[1] During the Crimean War.

begin Ruskin's work to-morrow· . . . I am trying very hard not to complain If I have attained so far thro' all obstacles of three long years, surely I shall be helped to go farther; and surely there is a reward, there is a use in all the long hours I have worked, all the energy I have given; surely there is a brighter day coming He who works for man must look to man for his reward; but we have worked for God, and He will reward us.

Ladies' Guild,
March 21st, 1855.

To EMILY.

Thank you very much for your letter. I am very much interested by your account of that clergyman. I should think from what you say, that his influence must be very good The mere fact of the congregation being so poor and degraded would seem to shew it. It is very difficult to tell what the doctrines of a man are from one sermon and very likely you heard the worst side of them

I have been to Lincoln's Inn to-day, and have heard Mr. Maurice, and have seen Mr. Hughes, Mr. Kingsley and Mr. Ludlow. Mr Cooper advises me to go and see whether we shall be admitted at the meeting. Mr. Kingsley will preach at Bethnal Green on Sunday evening. I am in the very heart of painting Ruskin's designs, really enjoying it.

I have a copy of the form of prayer for to-day, which you will like to read when you return. Mr. Maurice preached such a beautiful sermon about it.[1] The text was the 1st to 8th verses of 1st Chapter of S. Luke.

---

[1] Octavia never took any notes Her recollections of the sermons are wholly from memory

He said that, three weeks ago all England was startled
by the news that the man [1] whom she had looked upon
as her most deadly enemy was dead ; that whatever
hopes statesmen or merchants might entertain of the
result, had proved wrong ; that many people said there
must be a purpose in this event ; that however sinful it
might be to rejoice over it, they could not but believe
that it was working towards some good end.   To such
people, he continued, I would answer, "assuredly not
an emperor falls (because not a sparrow falls) without
our Father in Heaven ; and to Him who wills it every
event will bring a blessing." And what should we learn
from this ?   In the first place, we have all of us fancied
that we were fighting against a man ; whereas the fact
is we are fighting against a principle, which is represented, perhaps in a nobler form than usual, in this
man.   People objecting to this say, " no, we are fighting
against flesh and blood ; we leave all abstractions to
philosophers." I agree with them thus far.   We *are*
engaged with realities ; if a principle be a mere theory,
to be disputed about in books, it is nothing to living
men ; but, if it be that which gives energy and motive
to action, then it has everything to do with them.   We
are fighting against that arbitrary power, which treats
men as mere machines or tools, and is utterly indifferent
to national life.   There is great danger connected with
the belief that our enemies are men, not principles.
We are likely, we are almost sure, not to see the same
enemy at home.   We are all too much inclined to think
that we live only to carry on our separate trades
and professions.   We happen, indeed, to carry them on
together in a certain geographical position, which has
been for some years called the island of Great Britain.

[1] The Czar Nicholas.

We have, it is true, a common language. It is very convenient it should be so, just as it is very convenient to have a medium of exchange. It would hinder our buying and selling very much, if it were not so It is also very important to have laws to punish those who injure their neighbours. These laws must be general, lest one class should gain the ascendency. We must also have a doctrine preached about future rewards and punishments. Of course about such an uncertain subject there can be little agreement; and therefore, if all compete in preaching, it will suit all tastes. We do not want a sense of national life It is this indifference to it which we have been striving against thro' all generations. This common enemy unites us to all past ages; if we have lost sight of it, we lose the meaning of history And this is the meaning of a Fast day. It speaks to us all as members of a nation; it tells us of a stronger bond than that of possessing a common enemy; that we possess a common Father; this gives prayer a meaning, and national life a reality. And this speaks to us individually. So long as we look upon the Emperor of Russia as our enemy we cannot expect to have to conquer him; (*sic*), and we cannot ask for help to do so " . . . . Thank you for the promise of ferns. Bring several. Numbers here will be glad of them. We are having the garden dug, and shall be glad of all contributions. Can you bring a stone *and* a root from Mr. Mansfield's grave ? . . . . It is *very* late, past twelve (long)

Ladies' Guild,
March 27th, 1855.

To Emily

Thank you for your two dear letters. They interested me very much indeed. Have you read

"Brave Words" ?[1]   I think G. and you might like to
read it together.   Mr. Maurice preached at Lincoln's
Inn on Sunday morning.   I did not know of it.   Since
I have known him[2] I have missed hearing him four
times, Stepney, Whitechapel, lecture on Newspapers,
and last Sunday.   It was a funeral sermon for Mr.
Mansfield ; and all his friends met together afterwards.
They are going to have it every year.   Mama went
with me in the afternoon.   The text was the 27th verse
of the fourteenth of St. John.   Mr. Maurice began by
saying that these words were not understood at the
time they were spoken.   The events which followed
them seemed the most awful contradiction of them ;
for even He who had spoken them appeared to have
lost then the gift which He promised.   The question
was, What peace was it which He gave ?   It could not
be peace in the world ; the wars, the contentions
showed that *that* had not been given.   The Gospel
which they brought to the world seemed to bring
divisions not unity, strife not peace.   It could not be
peace in the Church ; for a few weeks it seemed as if
this might be the gift which Christ had left.   They
had all things in common ; and then arose contentions,
people pretending to have sold their possessions, and
given the whole value of them to the Church, when
they had retained half.   Paul rebuking Peter ; discussions about circumcision.   Was it outward peace for
themselves ?   Never had any set of men experienced so
little as the Apostles.   Was it inward peace, a cessation
of all fierce war with evil, of all conflict ?   Surely not.
For that which Christ promised He must have realised
Himself.   They had heard the cry on the Cross, and

[1] By Charles Kingsley.
[2] 1851 or 1852, certainly not later.

seen the agony in the garden; surely there never was a
more awful fight with evil than that which He had
carried on. Above all, they had forsaken Him themselves. If anything would add to their sense that they
had no peace, it would be that when they thought they
were ready to die for Him, they had left Him; the
cross and death did not divide Him from them so much
as their unfaithfulness. But all this showed that the
peace which He promised could be no outward peace;
that it could not be felt till they were ready to give
up that The sense of a friend, a deliverer, the revelation of a Father, would give them really a peace which
the world did not give, and could not take away. I
forget how it came in, but Mr. Maurice mentioned
Christ's look to Peter which made him weep, and
contrasted that with Judas's remorse. I would give
you a better account of this sermon, but I ought to
have written it before It is now confused in my mind
with Kingsley's, the one I heard on Wednesday, and
with several things I have been reading.

We are not to execute our own designs for Ruskin, at
any rate yet. I have been doing his letters in the work
hours. . . . About what you and G. have been saying,
I should answer, that I think you are quite right in
maintaining that, if the war is right, we must be right
in praying to God to help us in it; but I think there is
a certain cowardice, a shrinking from looking facts in
the face, when people say that they are not asking God
to help them to kill men That is not the end, but it is
the means What I think we want to see is that all
things are as nothing in comparison with right; that
we have no business to calculate results; that we are to
give up comfort, homes, those who are dearest to us,
life, everything, to defend right. I wish very much to

have time to think what a nationality is, that it should be worth so much. I feel that it *is* worth everything. I suppose every nation has a separate work to do, which would be left undone were it extinct I think a nation can never perish till it has so far neglected its mission that its existence has no more meaning. If it has fulfilled its work it will be given more to do; so with the Jews; they had borne witness to a living Ruler, a King of the people; they had had glimpses that the King would be more fully revealed; they believed that it was He who had brought them out of captivity, had strengthened them in battle. They had forgotten Him, and asked for a visible king like the other nations, when their glory was to be different from them, those other nations. The king was given; the prophet saw that there was a divine meaning in the cry for one; but Saul was the representative of the people, he was a mere general. He was wrecked; and yet there *was* a meaning in the offer. The earthly king might set himself up, might tyrannize over the people; but he was the continual witness of a power, which he might recognize and bow before; life was as nothing to the Israelites, nationality everything. And they did not fall because they thought so little of life; they thought too much of it, if you look upon life as merely the breath. But if life is the light of men, we have no evidence, we can have none, that it is in the power of man to take it away. They did not give it, and they cannot destroy it. If in Him was the life, in Him it is, and ever will be; we may surely trust to Him those whom He has made. The light which shined in the darkness was surely that which has been in our soldiers, in the long suffering they have had; their breath, their bodies man can destroy; but that which

has given them strength is still theirs, when their last
struggle on earth has ended, and they go perhaps to a
more awful fight; but with a peace which cannot leave
them   The Jews fell, they thought they were different
from all the world, when they were most like it.   They
were boasting of their privileges, trusting in themselves; they evidently thought the highest sign of
godliness was utter selfishness.   They would have
thought it a triumph for Christ, if He had saved
Himself.   He died that death might have no more
darkness for us, no more loneliness; for He was light
and life, that He might bear witness that breath is not
the most precious thing; that there is One Who is
always trying to destroy that higher life, but that it is
His gift and He will preserve it.   . .

Mr. Maurice preaches next Sunday at Mile End.

It is very late, so good night . .   Mr. Maurice
asked very kindly how you were.   He does not
appreciate the noble patience with which you are
waiting at Weybridge; but, if he does not understand
it, we do sympathise.

Ladies' Guild,
April 19th, 1855.

EMILY to FLORENCE.

I have such a great deal to tell you that I don't
know what to put first.   You must know that Ruskin
appointed to see Mr. Pickard[1] at 2 o'clock at his house;
and he was to take the letters that they have done as
specimens at about half past twelve.   Ockey came
running into the work-room, half crying, half laughing,
and came and whispered something to Miranda who left
the room with her   Presently Miranda came back

---

[1] Builder connected with Co-operative Society

laughing, and saying that she had succeeded. . . . It came out that this was the case. . . . Ockey had wanted very much to go with Mr. Pickard; but he was going in his cart; and Ockey could not go in an omnibus and meet him there, because it would offend him; so Miranda persuaded Mama to let Ockey go in the cart. She says that she enjoyed it so much; Mr. Pickard was so kind and thoughtful. He did not drive up to the door in the cart, but left it at some distance. Ruskin received them very kindly and was very much pleased with the letters, and has given an order for two more to be done. When they left Ruskin, Mr. Pickard seemed determined that they should enjoy themselves. He wanted to explore a pretty road that there was; and soon he set his heart on going to the Crystal Palace; so he took Ockey there, and showed her all over the gardens which she had never seen before, and led her about from room to room. . . . At last Ockey began to fear that he would never leave, and that she should be late for the meeting at the Agency. However, she got back in time.

Ladies' Guild,
July 6th, 1855.

To Miss Harrison.

We shall be very happy to see your friends and your uncle, who I think I have had the pleasure of meeting at Mrs. Howitt's.

It gives us very great pleasure to see anyone who is really interested in our work. Sympathy is very precious, and the knowledge that we are not working utterly alone; it is a wonderfully interesting work, at times a difficult one; thrown so much together as we all are, we have to ask ourselves what it is that unites

us, now that we have at last broken thro' the wall of ice
that has surrounded these children's hearts, threatening
to shape them into machines, not to educate them
as human beings, having individuality, powers of perception and reflection ; tho', thank God ! it never could
have achieved its work entirely because they would
always have had power of loving, however blunted it
might have been. . . . I do not think the influence that
the rich and poor might have upon one another has
been at all understood by either. I think we have all
taken it too much for granted—a great deal more than
we should have done—that the giving is all on one side,
the receiving on the other. . . . I have had a great
success to-day, in destroying, I trust for ever, a six
years' quarrel between two of the children. But a long
work lies before us ; and to-day's victory is but a small
emblem of what must be. There must be many a cloud,
and many a storm, and many an earthquake ; and
yet we must rise victorious, to lead these children
to love truth, to realize it as more eternal, more real
than any material substances ; to teach them that in the
principle of a sacrifice lies all strength ; to open their
hearts and eyes to all beauty ; to bring out the principle
of obedience and sacrifice, as opposed to selfishness and
lawlessness. This is not a small work, and they must
learn to do that which lies before them, to look upon the
fulfilment of the duties which God has given them,
in whatever position they may be, as that which will
open to them the Kingdom of Heaven. This is a work
which we must ask to be able to undertake in all
humility, all energy, all earnestness, all faith , feeling
that our *only* strength, our *sufficient* strength is that
God is working with us.

I do not know whether I ought to apologise for writing

such a long letter; but I hardly remembered what I was doing.

Ladies' Guild,
4, Russell Place,
Fitzroy Square,
July 16th, 1855.

To MISS HARRISON.

It has given me much pleasure to receive your very kind letter. I thank you in my own name and in that of the children for your welcome invitation. It will give us very great pleasure to accept it. . . . Your letters have given me much pleasure because they are assurances that we are not working utterly alone; because we want this assurance; because the evil which is so great, and so near, is almost crushing, without a consciousness of having fellow labourers. It is such a very small number that can come within our reach; our influence is so limited even on those with whom we have most to do; there is ·so much in ourselves that hinders us from understanding and loving these children as we should do; so much in them that hinders them from caring for our love. Fancy appealing to a child's sense of duty to do something which will delay her work, prevent her earning so much as she would otherwise have done, perhaps deprive her of a meal, very often of a new pair of shoes! How strong her sense of duty must be, how real right must seem to her (if she is to prevail), to counterbalance the reality of the dinner and clothes! How dare I hope, I very often ask myself, to awaken this sense? And yet I do go on acting as if it were existing; appealing to it, and receiving proofs of its existence continually. I dare not hope that I shall have the power of creating it. I dare not dis-

E

believe that I ought to be the agent in awakening
it. It is a very wonderful work in which we are
engaged. It is a very awful work, when you feel how
easily you can reach their hearts, how hard it is to
reach their consciences ; they will do anything *for you*,
they will do hardly anything because it is right. And
tho' this is dangerous, because so false a ground to stand
upon, yet this inclination testifies of a precious truth.
It might teach us, if we would only learn, how much all
human beings must crave for personality ; how cold,
how dead, how distant are all abstractions. A soul
diffused thro' nature, an ideal, an essence, a principle,
may seem to satisfy a comfortably situated philosopher.
It is sufficient to dream and speculate about ; it is not
enough to live upon   Even in his most easy moments,
there will be strange questionings in him as to what
connection this God of his bears to life ; and there will
come a time when the ground beneath him shall be
shaken ; when he shall ask what he is standing upon ;
when evil shall rise before him as something very real,
very near ; then he will have to ask whether there
is nothing nearer, nothing more real ; yes ! in his old
creeds (if they deserve the name) there is an essence
pervading all things. An essence, when this is a real
battle, when evil is gathered up in some person, is felt
to be most terribly personal. If evil is all vague, all
mysterious, and yet most real, is there no Person
stronger than it, mysterious through His divinity ?
Yes ! then all history, all life will testify there is such a
one. Man has been trying to bow down even to himself ; he has longed to worship, but it must be something
definite, something eternal , such a one has been shown.
Every man is to act as if it were so. You are all
to speak to those around you, as if they had that

in them which would recognise and reverence this Conqueror, this Knight; and yet as if they knew that He could only be God's warrior, because He came not to crush but to raise; and yet that, just because of this, He was bound to fight with evil, bound to destroy; and I do hope we may be able to awaken in the hearts of these children a knowledge that they are called soldiers of Christ, in whatever place they may find themselves; that it is their duty not to speak or act or think as if there were no evil; that it is no proof of trust in God to shut their eyes. They *do* see evil, they do feel it in themselves, they are bound to testify that God is stronger than the devil, light than darkness, life than death. There is all danger of our disbelieving this. I feel it in myself. I am frequently inclined to act as if I believed that another than a righteous God was ruling, especially in the hearts of others; as if there was nothing so strong as selfishness, nothing so mighty as self interest; and yet I *am* bound to claim for these children, to claim for all of us, the name of Christians, children of God, inheritors of His Kingdom.

Ladies' Guild,
July 24th, 1855

To Miss Harrison.

. . . And now I must thank you all very very much for your kindness, which I am sure we shall never any of us forget. I am sure you will be glad to hear how much we all enjoyed the whole day. I am sure that it was to many of us a revelation not only of beauty and comfort, but of gentleness and generosity, which we have cause to be very grateful for. The children have never ceased talking about it, the boat, the water, the garden, the flowers are continual sources

E 2

of delight. I asked them to-day if they had any message to you, as I was going to write. They seemed oppressed by a sense of wanting to say something. One of them said she had plenty to say, if she was going to write herself. There was an eager discussion in one corner as to whether it would be proper to send their love ; but they ended by asking me to thank you all for them, as they did not know how. I felt very much inclined to tell them how very little I knew how ; except that I thought the very love, which they seemed to think it would be shocking to express, was the only thanks which you would care anything about.

I have had a very sad day to-day A scene with the children, bringing up old quarrels, repeating unkind things which should have been forgotten long ago ; a recommencement of a feud, which I had so rashly hoped was destroyed for ever I spoke to them very earnestly ; there was not a dry eye in all the room ; but I fear that very little lasting good has been done. I do not see what to do about it.

I went yesterday to Epping Forest with both the Tailors' Associations. There were eighty of us at tea ; and, as they sat in the long room, covered with beech boughs, some of us were called upon to sing " Now pray we for our Country ! " and I could not help thinking how real the prayers of the workers are, because their lives are so much together. With no doubt that the prayer would be answered, I could sing " Who blesseth her is blessed," and think of all those dear children at home, who are trying, and will, I trust, try more to Bless England ; and I could thank God for such as you, because I am sure that, if England has not devoted children, and faithful servants, she must perish ;

and I could ask that such days as this may not be very rare, because the only meaning of our life, like the only meaning of her life, is union.

On Saturday the children were talking about their visit to you; and one of them said : "Ah ! I should like to live there always." "So should I !" and "Oh that would be nice !" echoed round the room. They then said to me, "Should you not like to live there always ? "

I was conscious of a very strong impulse urging me to answer "Yes." An idea of quiet (which has lately been *occasionally* my ideal of happiness) came over me, more especially a vision of your uncle's face, which always seemed to me to possess a divine expression of rest. I saw the danger; I yielded to the fear too much ; I feared I was shrinking from work ; and I said : "Do you want me to go? Do not you see there is work to be done here? I am of use." I saw the mistake in a moment; but something interrupted me, and I forgot the conversation. In about half an hour, I felt a little hand slide into mine, and hold it very tight. Harriet's large eyes fixed themselves on me, and she said in a trembling voice : "But, Miss Ockey, isn't there work to be done *there*, if one is willing to do it ? "

I felt the rebuke very much. It spoke to a very strong tendency in me ; and I told her that there was in all positions some work to be done, for which the world would be nobler ; that we must all try to see the good which others were doing ; but that I was sure we never could do any work well, until we were content to do our own well ; that, until we had cultivated to the utmost the little garden in which our house stood, we must not cry for acres of distant land ; that no change of circumstances, before death or after it, could ever make us conscientious or zealous, or gentle ; and that I was quite sure that, if any one of them could have done more good in any other position, they would have been there

Mama has asked me to be sure to say that **Mr. Vansittart Neale** is very much interested in your uncle's plan, and that he is here on Tuesdays, Wednesdays and Fridays. . . I am very sorry that I cannot send the plan of the Ladies' College in this letter ; I will do so on the first opportunity. I send you two addresses which I wish you would read, as I should like you to know something of Mr. Maurice. If you could know, as I know, the unwearied energy, the untiring devotion with which he works ; how he has established the Associations, the Working Men's College, and now the College for Working Women, you could not fail to respect him. But, if to this was added the consciousness that he had been the agent of showing you the ground on which you were standing, the sun by whose light alone you could work ! It has been my very earnest prayer that I may be able to prevent some from living on speculations, even as long as I lived on them. When first I met your uncle, I had just begun to know Mr. Maurice, apart from the band with whom he was working,—just begun to long for the certainty of which he spoke ;— to be utterly weary of conjecturing ; and I think I owe a great deal to the impression of your uncle's face and voice. They seemed so calm, so fixed ; but nothing except real work, real intercourse with people who needed comfort, could ever have given me strength. Again, after three years, we have met ; and I am still crying for more earnest faith, but only for others now. I do thank him. I do thank you and every one who has helped me to make their lives more blessed and happy. I hope they may learn to work for one another in fellowship.

Ladies' Guild,
August 1st, 1855.

To Miss Harrison.

Thank you very much for your long, kind letter. It did my heart good to receive it.

You may indeed call me " Miss Ockie " if it pleases you ; but I shall be glad if you will leave out the " Miss " altogether, if you like.

" Ockie " is a very familiar name associated in my mind with most of my sisters, and with the times when I ran wild in the country ; a name which binds the past and the present together, which bears a continual protest against my tendency to forget my childhood.

" Loke " is my name with which is associated all my strength ; it is Florence's own invention ; whenever my sisters call me their brother, then I am " Loke." " Octavia " is Mama's name for me, whenever I am working with her. Whenever I am steady, I have a right to it. " Miss Hill " is bound up with very precious recollections, very happy associations. Mr. Maurice, Mr. Ruskin, and one or two others use it principally.

But I now think I see in the children's name for me the union of all, the gathering up of the essence of each,—the casting away of its evil. It must bear witness, as the first does, that, however changed, I was once passionate, lonely. It must remind me of scenes long past; it must comprehend the strength of the second, the energy and perseverance of the third; it can do so because it is a working name ; because there is no motive of strength or energy, without affection ;

it must be connected with the last name, because there
is no sure ground for it, except in the words "This is
My commandment that ye love one another."

This name is indeed dear to me now. I never can
forget (I do not think the recollection will ever grow
fainter) the way they received me on Saturday. I had been
ill, but insisted upon working   One of them suggested
that they should be quiet; and I never had such complete
silence, although I did not once tell them to be quiet.
because I thought it hard to cramp them simply because
I chose to work ; and the next morning when I returned
from my early walk, they were all over the house, to
catch the first sight of me.   Four of them had been
here since before seven, nine being their usual time
Those who lived near together arranged that whoever
woke early should go to call all the others   Every one
had something for me—flowers, books, fruit; they
brought me the footstool ; they anticipated every want
that I had.   I never saw such bountiful unconscious
love and attention . . . I should never have done telling you how kind they are . . . I began reading out to
them to-day; it succeeded admirably   I only wish I
knew more people to do it.   I can only give them three
hours in a week, and *that* only during the autumn.

August 5th

I do not know what you will say to me, dear Miss
Harrison, for not sending this letter, but I have been
very busy and much excited

I have been, since I wrote it, to Mr. Ruskin's for
the third time.   But still it is a very wonderful event
for me ; and, I think, always will be ; for not only is
everything which he says precious—all opening new
fields of thought and lighting them,—but also his

house is full of the most wonderful pictures that I ever dreamed of. Not fifty Royal Academies could be worth one rough sketch in that house; and he is so inexpressibly kind, so earnest to help everyone, and so generous that one comes home inclined to say to everything, " Hush while I think about it " ; and then to continue, " Whirl on ! for I have a quietness, which has another Source than you, and which is given to influence you."

I go to-day to see the Sunday School, which most of my children attend ; they press me very much to teach in it. Would to God that I could show them the deeper, mightier foundation than that they are standing on ! I believe I am doing so in a way. I believe that, when I first came to them, I took the right ground. I was bound to assume, and I have assumed, that justice, truth, and self-sacrifice, are the principles that hold Society together; that its existence testifies to their strength ; that what is true of Society at large is true of our Society ; that it does not and cannot stand, except in proportion to their strength. I believe that this is the great Christian principle—that there is no might nor greatness in Christ's life, no saving power in His death, no triumph in His resurrection, unless it is the eternal witness that obedience and self-sacrifice give to victory over lawlessness and selfishness.

I believe that, in so far as I am acting as if this were true, I am teaching them to be followers of Christ. What I wish I could teach them is to have a more personal religion. This I believe to be the great work that Sunday schools have done ; they have little scope for teaching the other truths, even if they recognise them. Daily life must teach that. We are teaching it to one another here. They are making it a much more living faith for me than it has ever been before.

May the God of England strengthen us all, to trust that
He is King and that He is righteous.

Thank your sisters very much for the prospect of
the leaves; they will indeed be treasures to all of us.

                              Ladies' Guild,
                                   4, Russell Place,
                              September 21st, 1855.

MARGARET—A TOY-WORKER—TO EMILY HILL.

I hope you are enjoying yourself. . . . We had
such a beautiful lesson to-day about the world.   I miss
you very.   I wish you would come back again.   It is
now twenty-five minutes to eight; it was very dark,
and I and Harriet put a farthing together, and sent
L. and S. out for a halfpenny candle. . . . Oh! our
gardens are getting on so badly!   We had an Irish
stew for dinner to-day.   Do come back as soon as you
can; and I daresay you see numbers of snakes and
snails, and glow-worms, and beautiful caterpillars and
all sorts of insects.   I daresay the leaves are falling
fast.   I daresay you are very happy together.   When
you went away, Louisa, Sarah, and Dennis did sob and
cry so.   I daresay when you are alone by yourself you
are thinking of home, and it makes you very sad; but
never mind, cheer up.   S earned two shillings and a
farthing, and L two shillings and two pence; and
I earned two and twopence yesterday.   Were we not
good girls? and Miss Ockey was very pleased with us
We have finished that splendid, oh beautiful! book,
"Steadfast Gabriel"; and I never saw such a beautiful
book in my life.   Sarah is always thinking of you, and
I too.   The account this week comes to £19 all but

fourpence. We have most splendid boxes of toys in the show room, beautiful, elegant.

I am writing the poetry that you like very much in my copy book. Good night. I must depart from the workshop.

Marshals, Romford,
October 16, 1855.

To EMILY.

Tell Miss Cons that I often wish she were here; she would appreciate so much the beauty of everything. She would rejoice to look at the gigantic trees holding themselves so still, with, here and there, a branch all gold or copper coloured, and the brilliant berries; to trace the light wreaths of briony not yet transformed into streams of gold, but just changed enough from their summer green to tell you their own individual story, how they grew deep down in the hedge, and then climbed up clinging for strength even to thorny branches, even to leafless ones; they tell how they trust themselves, and tangle and knot themselves closer and closer; one wreath only impatient for light and *sunlight*, running up some spray of rose or bramble; and then, as if content to be made more and more like that sun, rests on its thorny pillar and stretches down its golden arms to its friends below, every leaf telling the same story as the whole plant; beginning in darkness, ending in light; beginning in life, ending in glorified death; beginning in green, ending in gold; beginning in massive strength, ending in spiritual power. But it is of you and A. I think, when, gathered round the fire in an evening, we talk of the Guild, of Ruskin, of the poor, of education, of politics and history.

Marshals,
October 19th, 1855.

To Miss Howitt

Will you tell your Mama that I shall have great pleasure in writing to Maggie . . . How many days we have spent together! She remembers them, I find, with as much pleasure as I do. I do wonder whether we shall ever know each other better! Has she many friends of her own age? I have not very much time. Still there are some things (and this certainly one of them) which are well worth devoting time to

I am very happy here. The country is very beautiful. The gold and red and purple leaves are very precious— partly because of their rarity There are, as yet, no masses of colour,—no leaves of autumn foliage,—only single boughs, and sprays and leaves, standing out from among the green. The sunlight comes and goes, like one who knows the innermost soul of those around him, and loves to pierce into their mystery. The purple distance is, however, so far, so lovely, that it seems as if the sun even could not penetrate it ;—like those sad, solitary beings whom one sometimes meets, who have no fellowship with those around ;—still, in the darkness of night, there is union between them and the world that is nearer ; and, as the sun is leaving the earth, and the twilight gathers in the East, the whole earth will be lighted by a wonderful mist of light— lighted and wrapped in it.

I must thank you again for the " Modern Painters " It has been a very great pleasure to me to have it.   I grow to value it more and more every day

As I daresay you would have heard from Charlton, we acted the " Bondmaid " yesterday. All the children came to see it. It was the only play that they had ever seen. I have not seen them since, and am very anxious to hear what they thought of it. It must have been a wonderful event in their lives. They are (as indeed I think we all are) a great deal too much wrapped up in our own affairs; and it must be very much because we know ourselves so much better than others. Therefore I do not fear to give way to what I know is a preference that the children feel for story-books. They have even expressed it; and I reserve to myself the choice of books.

I would rather that they had a strong sympathy with men than with birds; therefore I would prefer them to read about men, particularly if they will learn to study the characters more than the events. Yet I value all natural history, all science, as bringing them to realities, saving them from dreams and visions. But I would have them to look upon all strong feeling, love, hate, gentleness, reverence, as being as real as stones and trees and stars. They are very suspicious. Now in books there can be no suspicion. All is declared to be good or evil. Deceit may be shown indeed, but devotion is shown also. I would not have them to believe all around them to be what it appears; for it is not so; but I must get them to believe that, in the deep souls of those even who appear the worst, there is a spark of nobleness, which it is in their power to reach, with which they are to claim fellowship, which they are to look upon as the only eternal part of men. It is for this reason that I do not fear, day after day, to read stories to those who are in the midst of hard work, poverty, sickness, hundreds of people, trials, hopes and deaths. Therefore I have asked you for those books, which are among the very few which I would let these dear children read.

Ladies' Guild,
December 2nd (1855?).

To EMILY.

I am writing with my consolidated [1] table before
me.   I do hope you will be able to see it before it goes
to Ruskin's.   Mama will I daresay tell you how I
intend to spend my birthday.   Do think of me at half
past one, if you know in time.

Mr. Maurice asks how you are continually, and is
very kind.   He is gone to Cambridge, and will not be
at Lincoln's Inn to-morrow   Is it not a pity?   All
goes on very well here; the children are very dear.
I wish you could be with us to-morrow.   I want you to
see Ruskin.   I trust it will be a fine day. . . . I have
undertaken to teach the two C.'s writing and arithmetic.
It is so nice.   I am very happy, everyone is so kind.   I
am delighting in the thought of to-morrow.   I do not
know whether any other day would be the same, if one
thought about it; but it does seem to me as if one's
birthday held the same relation to other days that
Mr Maurice says a ruler does to his people,—as if it
gathered up all the meaning of those other days,
embodied the meaning of all of them; and so, if things
happen, as it seems probable they will, I shall feel that,
as, last year, I had to learn the value of the Church
service read by Mr. Maurice, so this year I have to
learn how precious it is when read by anyone, now
that he is away; as last year I was to feel what a
blessed thing a home was, where all members of it were

---

[1] After the glass had been painted, a hard composition was put at the
back to make it solid enough to bear a weight.   Sometimes it broke in
the process, and the painting had to be done over again

together, so this year I must learn how much of the real
spirit of home, unity, cheerfulness, may be brought out
when many members of a family are scattered. . . .
Many of the workers are coming to Lincoln's Inn.   If I
do not *see* Ruskin I shall think that it represents
the past year.   I have had intercourse with him on
all subjects connected with art.   If I do see him, I
shall hope that it is emblematic of the coming
year ; . . . it is a strange thing that the sad, hard-
working, selfish should cling to the bright, radiant,
generous.

Ladies' Guild,
December 3rd, 1855.

To MISS HARRIS.

Miss Harrison tells me that she thinks I may
write to you.—I need not tell you how much pleasure
it gives me to do so, especially to-day, as it is my
birthday.

All is quiet, everyone asleep, the room empty, the
fire out ; but I never knew a more cheerful scene
Everything seems bright and blessed, to-day, for me.   I
trust that it is so, and always will be, for you ; that,
after many dark shadows, fearful changes, hard work,
(if you ever know such) there shall come calm joy like
this.   And not only after, but *in* the darkness.   You
have heard about those last strange changes that have
taken place among us.   In the very heart of them, I
felt most deeply conscious how very mighty all good
must be ; how little our weakness would hinder God's
work.   This conviction gave me whatever strength,
courage, power, I have had.   In proportion as I lost
light of it, I have been weak, timid, and wavering.

They may chain our tongues and hands to a great
degree, forbid us to read the Bible together, &c , but no
human power can check the influence which continual
sacrifice has ; no one can hinder the conviction that
these children are gaining,—all Love can overcome
Evil.   This is a Gospel which will prepare them
for that more personal one, which these people will
teach !

You ask what Miranda and I intend to do.   Andy is
teaching in the morning, and teaching my children in
the afternoon.   I am working here, where I will continue, as long as ever I have any strength, or as long as
I am permitted to do so.   My whole life is bound in
with this Society.   Every energy I possess belongs to
it.   If I leave here, I intend to continue to support
myself if possible, if I can keep body and soul together.
I have just completed some work for Ruskin.   When I
take it home, I intend to learn whether he thinks it of
any use for me to go on drawing ; whether there is any
hope of employment , if so, I shall devote all spare time
to it.   If *not*, I intend to begin to study with all
energy, to qualify myself as a governess ; resting sure
that whatever work offers itself may be done well, may
become a blessed, noble, occupation

I wish I could convey to you any impression of the
picture [1] I have seen to-day.   Yes, if I could impart to
anyone my own perception of the picture, could only
let them have an opportunity of looking at it for as
long as I did, I should have done something worth
living for.   That union of the truth with the ideal is
perfect, solemn, glorious, awful and mighty.   It will I
trust never fade from my memory.

---

[1] Turner's " Old Temèraire "

December 4th, 1855.

Thank you for all kind messages about us, or to us. I wish I could tell you about my children, of the blessed spirit which they are beginning to show continually. I wish I could tell you of the kindness of all our friends; above all I hope that you do possess that strong confidence in a great spirit of love, that you do see the effects of its strength in those, whoever they may be, for whom and with whom you have worked, a confidence not based on fiction or fancy, but on experience, on a clear perception of motives. I have had that faith for some years; but I am sure we shall all look back to this crisis as to a time which has tried, proved, and strengthened it. No one need suspect us of blinding ourselves to the existence of selfishness; our life would not permit it; but oh the joy, after a life of many sorrows, many changes, in which either no friends did stand by us, or we had not the power to see that they did, to see at last the time arrived when numbers of arms are stretched out to save us,—this is glorious! But, above and beyond the delight of gratitude for sympathy, what a blessing it is to feel how much there is in men that is generous, affectionate, sympathetic; to know that, if you are no longer to encourage this spirit among those with whom you have lived so long, God can and will strengthen it. If you may no longer bow before those with whom you live, when you see their wonderful nobleness, struggling with adverse circumstances, no longer learn humility from them, God himself will teach you in other places, and by other means. You dare leave all your labour to Him, because He has given you whatever of a right spirit you have exercised in it.

F

Ladies' Guild,
December 7th, 1855.

To EMILY.

I have been trying to write to you every night, but have been too sleepy. It is now luncheon time, so I must not write much . . . I did indeed spend a glorious day on Monday. Emma Cons and I walked to Dulwich. Oh the delight of the frosty morning! the beautiful leaves as they peeped out from the banks! As we passed Ruskin's house, it seemed wrapped in mist; just as we came up, the sun broke out behind the house, which, however, quite shaded the garden, except that one ray darted thro' the glass doors of the hall, and pierced the darkest depths of the steady cedars; then on to Dulwich, where we met Miss Harris I wrote a letter asking Ruskin to let us see his pictures. We drove to his house, sent the letter in; the answer was that the ladies were to be shown in. "Crawley" took us into the dining room and stirred the fire; the room was papered with red flock paper, and there were a number of *almost* purple leather chairs and a number of pictures. Crawley led us up to one saying, "This is the Slave Ship." Oh, you do not know how often I have read Ruskin's description of this picture, and have hoped that it was in his possession: I had not remembered it, however, since I had heard of this promised visit. It was such a surprise. I looked at it for some time; then I just looked at the other pictures in the room; one was the " Grand Canal at Venice " by Turner, which I hardly saw. There was a sketch by Tintoret of a doge at his prayers, *very beautiful*, with a picture of the second coming of Christ; the large picture, for which this was a study, is now in Venice. There were two or three William Hunts, two or three

by Prout, who you know now paints architecture so
beautifully. Crawley said, "Perhaps you can find
enough to amuse (! ! !) you for twenty minutes, until
our other rooms are disengaged." Of course I was
delighted; but, having once really looked at the Slave
Ship, it was impossible to turn to anything else. I must
not attempt to describe it, Ruskin having done so;
. . . Crawley returned but too soon; told us about the
other pictures, pointed out a figure of "our Saviour
which Mr. Ruskin thinks a great deal of." Had he not
done so, I should be standing before the Slave Ship
now. Ruskin sent down a very kind message. I did
not hear whether it was "his kind regards" as I was
thinking; but the end of the message was "he would
have been very glad to have come down to shew us the
pictures himself, were it not that he was correcting his
book, and had been much delayed by a severe cold."
And then we went thro' three more rooms, and the hall
full of pictures, which I had not time to see properly,
but which remain in my memory like a bright vivid
dream; quiet lakes with a glow of colour, cities in
moonlight, and lighted with a wonderful glow of furnace
light; emerging, wild, fantastically shaped grey clouds,
blown by evening winds leaving the sky one glow of
sunset light; fairs all bright; with an old cathedral
quietly watching impetuous waves dancing against lonely
rocks; solemn bays of massy rocks with a darkened
line of evening sun against the sky; the sweep of the
river beside rounded hills; but all done by an eye which
sought for true beauty, not a line out of harmony, or
that does not tell some precious tale. When I reached
home W. said that Miss Sterling had called . . . "She
said she was very glad you had taken a holiday." Well
what do you suppose I did? I had dinner and set off

to Queen's Square, where I was most kindly received. Mr. Maurice had just returned from Cambridge and had four gentlemen with him ; so I did not see him or Mrs. Maurice. Kate[1] was busy making ornaments for a Christmas-tree " for the boys." I was there a long time, and it was a complete success. Miss Sterling grows every day kinder.

(Then follows a list of the little presents given to her on her birthday by the toy-workers)   .

Ladies' Guild,
December 19th, 1855.

To her Mother

I have received your letter and will attend to the business . . . About coming to Weybridge. . . . Mr. Maurice tells me that he will preach at Lincoln's Inn on Tuesday morning. Of course I *cannot* miss *that* ; but I will, if necessary, as a great sacrifice, give up the morning service, on one condition, that it is not made a precedent for expecting it again. . . . I very much wish to spend some part of Christmas with you, and to see you again ; but I very much wish you would all be contented, if I spent Christmas Eve with you, as I would much value to do so. See how people feel about it, and let me know.

Ladies' Guild,
4, Russell Place,
December 24th, 1855

To Miss Harris,

I know very well that you will like to hear of my little darlings. For some time past I have written but little about them, because I have been much

---

[1] Kate Sterling, afterwards Mrs Ross

interested about other things; and they have been but
little to me, except that I have treasured their affection
much.   I know now how much I have neglected them,
and am at last thoroughly awakened from my dream.
But I very much regret to say that a spirit has entered
into the work-room which I do not think healthy.
When I was with you, I think I must have spoken of
the hardness of working when one is suspected, and not
steadily cared for.   Now I have a far different cause of
complaint;—an exaggerated admiration, an immovable
belief that all I do is perfect, a dislike of anyone who
even tells me to do anything which they see I do not
wish to do.   But I trust soon to bring this also to
reason.   I care little for what is called a merry Christmas; but it made me very sad to hear all last week
calculations about puddings, discussions as to whether
they could not manage to come in for two Christmas
dinners, mixed with laments that they should have to
nurse a baby all day; no real pleasure to look forward
to, with a very strong feeling that they had a right to
some.   I could bear it no longer.   I proposed that we
should have a snapdragon all together some evening
They were overjoyed.   We found we could have a grand
one by paying twopence each.   Still I found that it
was but little, as it would last so short a time.   I
then thought of a Christmas tree.   I am going to
Grandpapa's to-morrow, and shall endeavour to get a
little fir or holly.   All the children bought small things
for it last Saturday, and will I daresay, do so next;—
tapers, apples, oranges, nuts, &c.   I then asked them
to bring all their sisters, and all their brothers under
twelve.   Many did not wish for the trouble of taking
care of the little ones; but I have insisted, and I
believe prevailed.   Of course we shall have grand

games, sea's rough, hunt the slipper, old coach, frog in
the middle, blind man's buff, &c.　The children must
all have tea before they come.　Fortunately there is no
ice to break.　We all know one another.　Andy is going
to write a little play for them to act ; and I shall teach
them it during work.　This is a great delight to them.
Another thing which I anticipate great pleasure from
is dancing.　They will enjoy it much.　Really the spirit
shown has been beautiful.　One of the girls has asked
her mother to make a cake and send it　One great
distress is that some of them have nothing but heavy
boots, and so will not be able to dance.　Poor little
things !　I wish I could do for them all which I have it
in my heart to do.　It will be a strange party ; there
will be no hostess ; or rather, we shall all be hostesses.
Each will have contributed what she could.　Another
thing which I mean to do, if I find it possible without
bringing ourselves into bondage, is to ask for contributions from the richer members of the Guild.　I am sure
it will do both them and us good.　But I trust to show
to others and to myself, how much of what is precious
in a party is entirely independent of any expenditure,
and eating , how possible it is to have much fellowship
and gaiety without large outlay of money.　I have
renounced parties myself.　There is no longer any
pleasure to be found in them, which may not be found
better elsewhere.　This love of immense gatherings is
unmeaning.　The love of show is detestable.　There is
no time for conversation, no place for affection, no
purpose in them, or none which I can understand.
And yet I do feel that this party will be a very nice
one.　I do believe it will succeed.　I have renounced
parties, above all I have renounced Christmas parties.
It is now certainly a time for rejoicing.　I believe it ;

but, as one grows and lives, above all as year follows year, and there is removed from one's side one whose blessed smile has lighted our Christmas hearth, as the vacant chair becomes a witness of the lost one, as one is conscious of the "one mute presence watching all," when one has said in one's heart, "Why should we keep Christmas at all ; witness as it is of change?" and one has answered, "Would the sense of change forsake you if you had no such time ? Do you wish that it should leave you ? Or has it taught you to put all trust in One who is unchanging, Who gives to all their work, Who binds ‑all in one?" When one has felt all this, the mirth of Christmas is gone but not its value ; witness, as it is, of that inward union of which we vainly strive to hold the outward symbol. We may spend it in the truest sense *with* those who have been called to other lands.

But these, my children, to whom care and anxiety are so familiar, and to whom all the beauty and poetry of life are so strange, so new,—I must bring home to them some of the gladness which they see around them ; their only Christmas trees must not be those in confectioners' windows, at which they gaze with longing eyes. There is time enough for Christmas to become solemn, when it has become joyful and dear.

I thought that I loved these children when I was with you. I did not know how much it was possible to love them. I am very much pleased about another person, with whom I have been so long,—Miss Cons. She has now thoroughly established herself, and has begun to study, walk, think, draw, be entirely independent of me. More than this, when she came here, she had not a single person in the world to love or be loved by except her own family. . . . Our Miss Cons,

however, has got to know friends ; and whoever cares to
break through her shell will be well rewarded.   I am
most pleased to find that there are several who have
done so, and that she is gaining warm friends.   I find
in her a strength and energy which is quite refreshing,
and consign to her much which I should otherwise
undertake myself.   I feel, in Miss Cons, whose growth
I have watched eagerly, an amazing perseverance, a
calmness, a power, and a glorious humility before which
I bow, and which I feel may be destined to carry out
great works more nobly.   I am particularly glad that
she has friends, as I find that now instead of giving her
my society, I can only give her my friendship and
sympathy.

Now dear Miss Harris good night.   I do most fervently
hope that you may have a blessed Christmas and a
Happy New Year.

January 11th, 1856.

To Mary Harris.

It is on loving, infinitely more than on being
loved, that happiness depends.   I feel how little the
reception of one's services or love has to do with their
power of giving joy.   However, yesterday the children
were particularly kind, dear little things !   To-morrow
the College begins again.   Oh I am so glad the holidays
are over !   I have not heard from Ruskin.   Perhaps I
shall find a letter to-day.   Shall I, I wonder, go to him
to-morrow ?

I am reading aloud to the children a very beautiful
book by Miss Gillies ; and it was so strange to meet
with real things that I had done and said and heard
said, long, long ago, when I used to stay there.

The Men's College is to be moved to Great Ormond

Street; but whether our classes are going too I do not know. I hear that at one meeting it was proposed that women should be admitted to the General Meeting. The idea was laughed at. Someone then proposed that the women's classes should be held in the evening; and the question was referred to the Council.

Ladies' Guild,
January 27th, 1856.

MIRANDA TO JOANNA DURRANT *née* GRAHAM.

Ockey is so accurate and so certain in her statements that she has been able to refute all aspersions; and her excellent management of the toy work is so evident; all the details are so perfect, which is what Mr. Neale thinks so much of, that it is clear he is entirely on Ockey's side in the matter; though she has a good deal of pain, and has still some anxiety about it. As for her influence over the children, it strengthens day by day; those who have been constantly with us are so much impressed.

Ladies' Guild,
February 18th, 1856.

TO EMILY.

. . . . My own plans are very uncertain; my own wish is to find such work as can be done in the workroom, so that I may superintend the children without receiving remuneration, but which may at the same time be sufficiently remunerative to allow me to earn more, and yet continue my studies. I shall speak to D. to-morrow to find out whether colouring photographs would meet these conditions, and whether I can get work at it. Another plan is to learn watch engraving. Bennett promises work to us, but cannot teach. I cling to the idea, as it affords a prospect of establishing a Guild gradually ; the objection is the time which would probably intervene before I should acquire skill. I do not at all enter into D.'s plan of designing. I do not believe in it as remunerative ; and it would separate me from that social work which I have learned to prize so highly. One other path is open. I have to write to Ruskin this week, and you will hear from me after I have done so. I ought to say that I told Mr. Neale my plans on Saturday ; and he said he was very glad that I should get other work, the employment here being so uncertain. . . .

I speak (perhaps it may seem indifferently) of the utter failure of that for which we have all struggled so long and so hard I do so, partly because I believe that what we have asked for has not failed , but I am not to speak of that now. I do so, because, although at present I am much bent upon securing a living for ourselves, I intend to accept no work however delightful, however remunerative (except as a temporary thing), which would deprive me of the power of working for others. I care but little for any system of division of profits, although it may bear witness for a great truth, and be the means of equalising remunerations, and avoiding disputes. That which I *do* care for is the intercourse, sympathy, self-sacrifice, and mutual help which are called out in fellow-workers ; and this I believe to be worth striving for ; this I mean to work for. I may seem to turn out of the path in this wearying wood ; but it will only be a walk round a thicket, which hindered my progress ; and free from debt, and with a clear conscience, I will work, even if I have (which, however, I do not believe) to work in another way for a short time.

Ladies' Guild,
February 27th, 1856.

MIRANDA TO MRS. DURRANT.

There are many events going on here ; but I do not wish to speak of them till they are certain. It is indeed delightful that Mama has found some one to take her articles. I long to read them.

Thank you for the present for the Scripture prints. I have refrained from at all touching on the subject of religion with the children, since Miss C.'s affair ; because I thought Mr. Neale would not wish it introduced as a lesson. Miss C. did not approve of my reading the Bible with the children. They have often begged me to do so since ; but I felt I had no right to do it in lesson time without Mr. Neale's permission ; but I shall ask him now whether he objects. . . . Ruskin is delighted with Ockey's table, and means to give her employment in illumination, if she will learn it, and if she has the powers he believes she has ; and she means to give an hour or two to the Toy superintendence, and the rest to illumination. Is not this *very very* good news ? Ruskin has been so exceedingly kind to Ockey about it. She received to-day a present of a beautiful paint-box and all other materials she can want. I think she must be very happy. She has just completed some work. I mean the moral training of the Industrial children ; so she can now leave the chief superintendence to another person, in the full confidence that all will go well, and she is just beginning another work that is delightful to her. And she has so many friends. The Sterlings, Mr. Maurice, Miss Rogers, Ruskin and nice Miss Harrison all seem so fond of her. She is very successful and deserves to be so, for she does everything so well.

Ladies' Guild.

March 18th, 1856.

To EMILY.

We shall indeed be glad to see you. Come as early as ever you can on Thursday. I have succeeded in avoiding going to Pentonville. At present the arrangement is that Mr. P. has no connection with us, except that Kitty or any of us can cut and inlay for him in a workroom at our own house; that our house is to be entirely separate from the children's workroom; the former being cheaper if situated nearer Camden Town, and it being essential that the latter should be easy of access for Mr. Neale and others. We shall probably get it somewhere near Red Lion Square, Queen's Square and Lincoln's Inn. Hurrah! This morning all was doubtful, to-night all is going right. . . .

Dear Minnie, think well before you decide to come, whether you will choose to do so now, while all is bustle, change, confusion, and contention, or after we are settled We long very much to see you; and you would be of *great* use, and it would be a great comfort to have you with me to " baffle " everyone. Could you manage to stay till Tuesday, and go with me to Ruskin's? We would stay afterwards and see his pictures; and I could leave you at the Waterloo Station as we passed, coming home? You will hear Mr. Maurice too. I never can find time to-night to tell you all or one half of that which has happened only to-day. How much less then, that which has happened during the last week! Already I have more to do this week, than I could possibly do, if it were not absolutely necessary that it should be done. Mr Neale has found a house, which he thinks would suit us; it must, however, be taken on lease; of course we can be neither legally nor morally bound to remain there. Our work may call us in other directions. I go to look for a toy-room to-morrow. Do come, darling

Tell my own Mamma that we feel with her how terribly painful this scene would be to her; but we hope she will soon come to us. Ask her not to think me unkind or thoughtless for not writing oftener. I really cannot. I work almost without intermission, giving up Lincoln's Inn [1] even, continually. Also when one has some great purpose to carry out, some great struggle to go through, or some things troubling one, one cannot write to any to whom it would seem strange —not to mention that which is going on within one. If she could see what we go through, at every crisis of such a change as this, how one is one day triumphant, another uncertain, a third uneasy; and if there is momentary rest, the reaction is so strong that one is bound down by it, she would not wonder. Give my dear love to her.

Harry Rogers has been here to-night, to tell me about gold, outlines, brushes, pens, burnishing, etc.

I trust soon to send Mamma my first balance sheet! Do come, come early, but be prepared, if you come, to work.

If I find that I have time on Saturday or Monday to go to Ruskin, without an appointment, we will perhaps run the risk of not seeing him, as we can probably see the pictures.

Give my dear love to Mamma; tell her I hope not to fail, and ask her to believe me to be for ever her fellow-worker and disciple.

[1] The morning daily service to which she was accustomed to go

March 29th, 1856.

To Miss Harris.

I have seen your cousin to-day, as perhaps you may have heard, and am very much pleased with him and all that he says I am very, very sorry now that we did not keep to the subject, in which I suppose his principal interest lies, the employment of women. But somehow one so naturally speaks of that which one is doing ; and so the conversation naturally turned to the employment and education of children ; though I think you may have seen how conscious I have been lately of the intimate connection between the two subjects , principally because, unless you can develop the minds of your workers, they never can become intelligent, or qualify themselves to fill better situations

Have you (and has Mrs. Simpson) seen Mrs. Jameson's "Sisters of Mercy" ? It is a book in which I feel a great interest ; and which I value, particularly as showing how women and men ought to work together.

Octavia to Miss Harris.

I am out of spirits to-day , because we had already succeeded in making a profit of twelve shillings a week—instead of a loss of two pounds—when Mr. —— came to-day and gave orders for really unnecessary fittings which will cost a good deal. It is more than any mortal (or at least, more than I) can bear ; it is really no use working. Yes it *is* though

13, Francis Street,
April 6th, 1856.

Mrs. Hill to Emily.

I write to tell you what I am sure you will consider very good news Mr. Maurice has given

Ockey the Secretaryship at the Women's College at a salary of £26 a year. She has to be there two hours only every afternoon ; and, as the children [1] cannot be left, you are to come and take her place in her absence. It is all settled ; but you must come on Monday, that you may go on Tuesday to Ruskin with Ockey. . . .

Now are you not a happy child ? . . .

Mr. Neale is so glad you are coming.

[1] The Toy-workers.

CHAPTER III

THE appointment mentioned in the last letter of the previous chapter must have been surprising to some of those interested in the classes. It was certainly a most responsible position for a girl not much over seventeen. Not only had Octavia to superintend the business arrangements of the classes, but also to advise the women attending as to the subjects that would be most useful to them. And she was even expected to step into the place of any teacher who happened to be absent from her class. This was a sufficiently trying demand, even when the class dealt with subjects with which she was tolerably well acquainted, but on one occasion, at any rate, she found herself required to teach botany, and, as she explained to her sister Gertrude, " I knew nothing of botany, but a great deal about flowers, and as there happened to be a bunch of flowers in the room, I talked to the women about them, and I do not think the time was wasted " When the Ladies' Guild was broken up the toy work was continued by Mr. Neale for a time, in a room at Devonshire Street, which, being near the working women's classes, was convenient for Octavia She and her mother and sisters were in lodgings at Francis Street, and then moved back to 4, Russell Place, which was let out in furnished apartments, after the Guild left

In 1857 a scholarship at Queen's College, Harley Street, was founded in honour of Mr Maurice, who was given the choice of the first scholar, in recognition of the time and money that he had devoted to the College. He knew that Emily was very anxious to become a teacher, and he offered the scholarship to her, partly out of sympathy with this wish, and partly out of regard to Octavia. Thus when, later on, the school was started, Emily was able to help Octavia in a way she could not possibly have done otherwise.

In 1868, Miranda's health began to fail. She had begun work very early, and had found the strain of so many hours' teaching, added to the long walk, and exposure to weather, more than she could bear. It was therefore arranged that she should join her aunt and Florence in Italy, and obtain teaching there, while Mrs. Hill took over her English pupils.

May 1st, 1856.

From one of the Toy-workers.

DEAREST MISS OCKEY,

I hope you arrived at Plaistow quite safely on Monday. Dear Miss Ockey I hope you are quite well and very happy ; but I suppose that you are very happy with your dear friends.

Dear Miss Ockey we do miss you so dreadfully. I do so long to see you and hear your voice again. The place is so dull without you, and to me seems like a prison. I have been agoing to say so often—" Miss Ockey repeat some poetry (*sic*) or talk about birds, or do something."

Dear Miss Ockey, will you, if you please if it will not be too much trouble, get me a furn (*sic*) ; only gather it yourself, or else it will not do. Dear Miss Ockey I have thought so often of what you said on Saturday that two people could hardly work for one year without owing each other something ; and I am ashamed and very very sorry to be obliged to come to the conclusion that all you owe me is the recollection of many unhappy days, and the great trouble and anxiety that I have been to you ; for you said yourself that, when you were in bed of a night you used to think what could you do to

me to alter me, while on my part I owe you that no
one on earth can ever repay you. Dear Miss Ockey
your Mama as been reading to us out of Howitt's
"Boys' Country Book," and teaching us poetry. I hope
you are not working, for I am sure Mr Ruskin would
not wish you.

How is dear little Emma ?[1] I hope you have some
fun with her, and you will be able to tell us of the fun
which you had with her. How does the beautiful
celandine and violets and primroses look ? On Tuesday
I saw Mr. Morris running so quickly. Dear Miss Ockey
do you know that I knew a person who was afraid to
speak to there (*sic*) friends, what do you think of them ?
Do please come home on Saturday, and if you write to
anyone will you tell them at what time you will be there
dear Miss Ockey. I do not mean this for a hint, but if
you take it for one I shall be very glad indeed. Will
you give my love to the flowers ?

I am yours ever truly and affectionately,

LOUISA.

No date (1856).

To MISS MARGARET HARRISON.

Well! if I had power, I certainly would write or
draw something very bitter, *sad*, and severe about
people; but it ought to go hand in hand with something deep, pathetic, and reverent about them. I wish
I could draw or write; for I believe that I feel people's
characters to my very fingers. I long to draw them as
I see them, both when my spirit mourns over them, and
when it bows before them. I say I feel their characters;
and so I do, just as one *feels* the beauty or harshness of
a colour or line.

---

[1] Presumably Miss Emma Cons.

39, Devonshire Street, Queen's Square,
July 5th, 1856.

To the Mother of one of the Toy-makers.

Dear Mrs J.,

I regret to have to tell Harriet not to return to work till Thursday next, as I have said that those children who do not earn five shillings in a week should lose three days' work. I am very sorry to be obliged to say this, but I hope it, or a sense of the necessity of being industrious, will soon render any such law unnecessary. I shall be as pleased as proud when the day arrives, when I see all the children steady, earnest, and eager to do all they can to help those near and dear to them. I am sure their idleness results more from want of thought than anything else; but they must try to overcome this; and if they fail to do this because it is right to do so, they must be taught to do so by other means.

However, I ought to say that Harriet has improved very much indeed lately; she has been so much more gentle and steady, and more earnest about her lessons. It is therefore with much pleasure that I give her Mr. Neale's invitation to spend a day at his house, and hope that she may grow more and more good, gentle, generous, and earnest, working for you, herself and all whom she can benefit, not only willingly but unceasingly; and I am sure she will find in quiet earnest work a happiness and peace which are far more joyous than giddiness. I ought to tell you how much I love her, and how much life and pleasure she gives to all here. I am pleased to see her take a deeper interest in things, because I am sure we all care too little, and not too much for things; and rightly directed, her love for

G 2

all she cares for may be a constant source of joy to herself and others. I wish she would draw more. I am sure she would do it well.

With many thanks to you for all the pleasure she has given us, believe me, dear Mrs. J., yours very truly,

OCTAVIA HILL

The Cedars,
July 24th, 1856.

" Let earnest work for ever show
　Our willing service to our God ,
Let peace and grace like flowers grow,
　Beside the path that we have trod

Let them be watered by that rain
　Which from strong trees is wont to fall ;
Which they themselves receive again
　From Heaven which bendeth over all

For not so much a flower depends
　Upon the rain on which it lives,
As men do on the love of friends,—
　The trust, the hope, which that love gives

Yet if the rain is like man's love,
　Like God's love is the blessed earth ,
The one refreshing from above,
　The other giving beings birth.

That which on God's love does not stand
　No might of human love can plant.
God grant us rain ! oh let us stand !
　A root in Thee to all men grant ! "

For dear little Harriet from her friend Octavia Hill, with earnest hope that neither summer drought nor winter frost may ever deprive her of the rain, and that her trust, like the roots of the flowers she loves, may ever take more firm hold of God, as their little fibres do of the strong nourishing dear old earth.

31, Red Lion Square,
August 19th, 1856.

To MISS ANNIE HARRISON.

Do you remember a long time ago when you were at Marshals, taking a great interest in all that I told you of a little girl, called Elizabeth. I had not been able to find her house, and so had not seen or heard anything of her for many months—last night, however, as we were sitting expecting Mr. Simpson, some one came up and said, " Miss Ockey a little girl of the name of Elizabeth wants you." I ran down and led up the little girl. She is not much grown, has still a pale but pretty face ; and her dark hair and eye-lashes make her look quite southern ; she speaks in a raised voice, and like a child ; she is very small, but is, I believe, thirteen years old. She was so glad to see us. I asked her how she found us out. She had been first to the Guild, and was told, as she said, " That no such name lived there." She then determined to go to the other children's houses, to which she had been once last summer. She went to Clara's. She had moved ; she went to Margaret's, she was out ; but her mother directed her to Harriet's, and she is one of the girls who now works for us, so she told Elizabeth we now worked in Devonshire Street. " I told her she had better tell me your residence ; for that Devonshire Street was such a long way. I thought so because of its name, but I must have come by the end of it, if it leads into Theobald's Road. I said the number of the house all the way for fear I forgot it." She said she has " been at service in a large *gentleman's* family at King's Cross where I did all the washing ; I kep' it (meaning the situation) six months but I was forced to give it up, it was too hard, for I had all the work to do, they didn't keep no other servant." "Have you seen anything of the country lately ? " I asked. " Oh no Miss, I haven't seen it since you took me ; oh, don't I remember Romford ! " I had seen her large bright eyes looking earnestly at a bunch of glorious purple flowers I had brought with me, and I could not help giving her one piece to carry back to the miserable home she had left. Her father has lost his work through drinking, her mother has but little washing to do, and has two children younger than Elizabeth, and a baby. The eldest boy has work at 4/6 a week but he has to walk an immense way to it. They lived in Clerkenwell, over a rag-shop, where this little girl used to sleep in a back-parlour, but could not go to bed till after eleven or later, because the girl she slept with always kept the key ; " for there was lots of rags there." And this is a child who seems meant to live wherever beauty may be found, comparatively without affection, utterly indifferent to home. She is hardly touched by kindness ; but at the sight of flowers her face lights up, her eyebrows rise, her whole being seems expanded. I never, never shall forget her in the fields at Hampstead. She is high-spirited ; and I trust she may not be crushed by sorrow   Energetic and persevering to the extreme, I think she will make herself master of events by submitting to their laws. She, alone of all my children, worked beautifully when I doomed her to do anything. "It is no use, it must be done," said in an unsympathetic tone, acted like magic   Indeed, she was altogether indifferent to sympathy. When I had to go and help and teach and encourage others, Elizabeth struggled on alone. She is gloriously proud, can stand alone, and say candidly to us

what she thinks. There is not one-half the feeling
about equality in classes in any of the others, notwith-
standing all their talk, that there is in her, with her
free, independent spirit. Twice, and twice only, have I
seen it broken, and then but for a short time ; once
because she came late and I ordered her to leave work.
Her mother it seems would not let her come without
breakfast; her father had been out all night drinking,
and had not returned with the money. And again
when she heard she was to leave, she cried as though
her little strong heart would break ;—still, unlike the
others, not complaining, but passionately. When the
last day of work came, and the others were all miserable,
she was laughing, calling it the day of judgment, and
hopping about like a little spirit of evil. And, when the
last moment came, she only made a bow, and said
good-bye like a little cockatoo, and left us. Left us ;
and went where no mother's love was strong enough to
call forth love which ought to direct that strong will,
and mighty energy,—to Clerkenwell, where no gleam
of beauty should gladden, and so soften, her little
heart ; where the angel face, that I have seen smile
forth from below wreaths of flowers instinctively
arranged, and most beautifully so, should cease to
be beautiful because children's faces are often like deep
water, reflecting only the images of what they see. The
strength of her nature will not leave her ; but to what
will it be applied ? who will direct the strong will ? who
will cultivate the latent powers? who will call forth the
spirit of love ?

I have written more than I intended, I only meant to
let you know we had seen Elizabeth as you seemed to
take an interest in her. She is coming to me on Thursday
at Devonshire Street.

September 10th, 1856.

Louisa to Emily.

It was such a pretty little cottage where I went. It has a thatched roof with pretty green creepers all over it, and the birds come and build their nests there, and bees and wasps make nests there. At the back of this house there are some beautiful fields, and into these I went, and all round was the garlands of bright night-shade. The field looked one glow of scarlet berries, and of course I gathered some for my dear Miss Ockey, and I put some nightshade and some of Miss Ockey's own thistles and some buttercups together. The butter-cups always remind me of dear Miss Florence. I never see one without thinking of the day I first went with her in the fields, how she jumped up those banks! I think she sprang up them like the silvery-footed Antelope does about the rocks. Miss Ockey was at Miss Harris's on Sunday and Monday and she did some photographs of leaves, and Miss Harris is agoing to do us each one of our favourite leaves. Mr. Furnivall came on Saturday to see the drawing class given, was not that a gloriously beautiful thing ? . . . Mr. Evans the toy dealer has gave us an order of a pound's worth of things, and when they were taken in, he gave another order for another nine shillings' worth of things. Is not that good news ? I think we all go on better with our work. Last week I earned ten shillings at ring stands, which I think was wonderful, because I never did any before. . . . Please come back soon. You have got four weeks longer to stay now. It seems as if you had been away two years

October, 1856.

To MARY HARRIS.

Oh, about Tom Brown! No it is not by Arthur Hughes, the artist, but by Thos. Hughes, the barrister, the friend of Mr. Maurice, teacher of gymnastics at the College, co-worker with Mr. Furnivall in establishing social meetings, etc. ; one of the brightest, best men in the world. *I* think the book one of the noblest works I have read, possessing the first element one looks for in a great book, namely progress—a book, too, opposed to the evil of the age, as I think, sadness. I know you may say, " Oh! that is the fault of the bit of the world you see as a worker, one who sees the poor, and who knows earnest people." There is a sorrow which I honour; and I believe Mr. Hughes would too; but I speak of that sorrow which eats into their warmest heart, and fights ever against their energy, urging them to hopelessness and despair, the selfish sadness that asks itself continually, "What have I of joy ? " I speak of the sadness pervading all classes, which rushes with sickening force on the young lady who has danced most gaily at the ball, when she begins to unfasten her sash in her own room ; which weighs heavily on the comfortable old lady as she sits in her drawing room, to receive guests ; which makes the worker gaze in gloomy despondency on the long long wearying days of toil, and makes the poor man say, "Nothing but care and trouble, and hard work, and the workhouse at last,"— each and all saying, "What is the end and purpose of all this ?"—I feel the book is a healthy blow at all this way of looking at things ; and, as such, I hold it to possess the second element of a great book, namely fitness, for the age in which it is written. Then I feel that shadow of Dr. Arnold thro'out the book, the presence and

work felt, the form so rarely seen, both beautiful and
life-like.   Then I think the instance of the ennobling
influence of having someone depending on one is most
valuable.   Then see how the truly great nature gathers
good from all things thro' life.   And imagine how I
delight in the athletic games, and try to feel how I
prize the book   I know you will feel all the objections
to it quite strongly enough ; and I won't try to say
anything about them except ; Don't hastily believe that
the author advocates all he paints.   There are few
things in the world (are there any ?) from which a great
nature won't glean some good.

4, Russell Place,
October 21st, 1856.

To Mary Harris.

Oh, Mary, money *is* very powerful.   I have
just came in from paying several people for some work
done, for the execution of an order which we accepted
to give them employment.   Many of them are old
Guild people, who arranged to wait till the things were
paid for ; the payment has been a little delayed, and
so it was unexpected by them ; and there they were,
educated and uneducated, living in nice streets renting
the whole house, or in little back attics in small streets,
—all glad to see me ; but still more so when I told my
errand ; and the relieved look that for a few moments
lighted up their care-worn faces touched me very much.
To think of the power of those small pieces of money,
to think of the thankfulness they caused !   But what
struck me especially was that to one the shilling was of
as much importance as the pound to another ; and so it
was ; one set had learned by hard experience not to
expect the little luxuries of eating.   Butter, sugar, and
even meat are rarely used by them ; but, more than

that, they have less of an appearance to keep up. Are
they better for it ? Does that effort to appear something not help to keep up self-respect ? I rather
think it does. But in all classes there is the same
care ; all thought bent upon that which must be paid
for, whether to-morrow's dinner, or neat gloves in
which to go to church next Sunday. But God be
thanked for English home life ! say I, whenever I come
in from visiting anywhere. See how, if one is ill, all
the calculations are gone and forgotten in a moment ;
and the full ardour of love is given with a depth of
tenderness that withers in a moment all worldly considerations.—I saw Louisa to-night set out to walk
about four miles home, after coming from Notting Hill
this morning,—walking twice from here to Devonshire
Street, and I do not know how many miles yesterday.
I stood and watched her among the hurrying crowd
She was walking slowly, for her feet were terribly sore,
and as she was lost to view, I noticed how the gas-light
flared in the foggy night on the worn faces near me.

October 27th, 1856.

To MARY HARRIS.

I am so much disappointed not to finish the
illumination. But what a day I have had ! One continual whirl of doing and remembering, taking
addresses, examining pupils, covering books, sorting
copy-books, but (most tiring of all) trying to attend to
fifty people at once, with the knowledge that at least
five of them will be offended if they think themselves
the least in the world slighted, and that they think I
have no right to be indifferent to what they think. I
am so glad to-morrow night I shall see Mr. Maurice.
Oh ! Mary, think of that !

I don't know what there is in the word "lady" which will connect itself with all kinds of things I despise and hate ; first and most universally it suggests a want of perseverance, and bending before small obstacles, a continual "I would if——"

October 29th, 1856.

To MARY HARRIS

I can scarcely see because of the terrible fog, but I must tell you what I know you will be very glad to hear ;—all my immediate fear about the toys is over, as I have this morning received an order from the same wholesale house to which we had furnished specimens of the toys some time ago. This will not, I think, necessitate my taking an additional worker, as the Bazaar gets on so very badly just now ; but only fancy how delightful it would be to have the business steadily increase. These wholesale dealers, too, are so delightful to do business with, as they always pay ready money, order things in large quantities, and never change their minds when things are half done.

4, Russell Place,
November 4th, 1856.

To MARY HARRIS,

I have left off learning my Latin as I walk to Devonshire Street, and get a little time to think. I wish the children were better. They have not at all gone back, but I should like to be able to try them by a higher standard. I think they grow mentally and morally lazy They care about history, natural history, geography and many other things, if once I begin to talk till they are thoroughly interested, and go on without giving them trouble; and I—yes the fault always finds its way home—I get lazy and would rather dream and think, rather be silent than sing or talk; and so we very often stagnate, except as far as our hands are concerned. I must study something for them—but when? . . . Andy says she is quite as ignorant about dress as you can possibly be. She thanks you very much for the lace, which she thinks beautiful. I say *she* because *I* know nothing about it, but do thank you very heartily, as far as I am capable of thinking on the subject.

November 9th, 1856

To Mary Harris, who was visiting in Newgate.

If you knew or could imagine what effect the presence of a noble soul can have on those usually surrounded by a hurrying struggling crowd; what it is to be taught to look at spiritual beauty; what to a much worn care-pressed being it is to know at last that, shut out tho' she has seemed from all the best and most honourable around her, borne downwards as she has been by the weight of many sorrows, much anguish and inward evil, there is yet left, even on this earth, one who will take her as she is, and love her because she has that in her which is God given. This last she will learn afterwards, and I know that, deep in those hearts hardened by crime and degraded, there yet is human feeling to be called out by nothing so much as trust and love.

39, Devonshire Street,
November 9th, 1856.

To Mary Harris.

I thank God for work, and for so blessing our work. I believe I might often say with Ruskin the first clause of the sentence, certainly always the last, "I am happy while I work; when I play I am miserable."

Is it not strange that tho' I have an unusually clear idea of the sermon, the only impression last Sunday afternoon is one of complete quiet? It was no effort to understand, nor was I, as usual, dreadfully tired in church; but I had the consciousness, not of peace nor of rest, but of quiet, such as when one sits out of doors in the country, not thinking, only seeing.

4, Russell Place,
January 17th, 1857.

To MARY HARRIS.

On Wednesday evening we went to hear Ruskin give a lecture on the occasion of the presentation of some money offered by him as a prize; but, owing to the imperfection of the work, the money was divided between the competitors, as some compensation for their loss of time. Their failure, he explained, was mainly owing to his having set them to work which was not possible for them to do well,—the carving of a panel, the subject to be taken from some historical event of the year. Apparently both parties took it for granted that it was to be about the Crimean War; for Ruskin said that he had overlooked the fact that no one could represent that which he had never seen; and, when the old builders lived, happily for art, but unhappily for the nations, wars were continually fought within sight, their scenes were present with the workman; they haunted him; he dreamed of them by night, and could not help carving them. Ruskin had expected better things of the workmen, because he saw with what spirit cheap periodicals were illustrated; really we see quite wonderful things in them. He had expected, too, that there would have been many competitors, and there were only two. He felt sorry for the failure ; but not so sorry as he would have been, had he not noticed that things which begin too swimmingly do not always succeed so well as those which fail at first. The workmen would not be altogether pleased that instead of a prize, he gave them a lecture. " Last year," he said, " while travelling in the North of Scotland I was very painfully impressed by the absence of any art—amongst grand natural scenery ; the inhabitants seem to be utterly without any art-expression of their perception of it ; no buildings rise, no pictures are painted ; truly the huts of grey stone are roofed with the peat, set picturesquely in oblique lines, which seem to have been marked by the stroke of some gigantic claymore. The only evidence of any power of design among them is the arrangement of the lines of colour in the tartan. And in Inverness, a city built on the shore of the most beautiful estuary in the world, at the foot of the Grampians, set as it were like a jewel to clasp the folds of the mountains to the blue zone of the sea—the only building which has evidence of any recognition of art is the modern decorated prison."

4, Russell Place,
March 19th, 1857.

To Mary Harris.

Some time ago Miss Sterling had a very long conversation with me on the way I am ruining my health, but especially about Sunday work ; and I told her just what I have felt about it—that to leave off working was a privilege, to continue a duty—that I *dared* not claim *any* time as my own ; that I had sometimes felt as if I had earned a time to rest or enjoy leisure ; and then had been convinced that all time was God's and to be used for Him.

Miss Sterling mentioned it to Mr. Maurice, and in consequence he asked me to go to his house this evening, to talk to him about it. He spoke very beautifully indeed about it, and of course very kindly to me. He thought that rest was as much a part of God's order as work was ; that we have no right to put ourselves out of that order, as if we were above it. He told me that the division of things into duties and privileges was an arbitrary one ; there is no such broad distinction, every privilege involves a duty ; our highest privilege is to perform our duty ; rest is as much a duty as work ; it is very self-willed to try to do without it ; it is really hopeless to try to exist, if one is for ever giving out, and never receiving ; nor does he think that the doing of actions rightly, brings with it enough of this receiving. He also advised that I should go to church every Sunday morning [1] with Mama, as he believed it would be a great bond of union.

And, Mary, I could not help the tears coming into my eyes, and my voice being choked at feeling so cared for by one so noble, so infinitely strong, so perfectly calm ; and a strange sense of perfect peace, such as I have not felt since I saw you, stole over me. And yet I was so hard, so unconvinced, and so strangely bitter ; bitter with myself in feeling how much of pride had made me think I could stand without help ; and we sat quite silent for a few moments. At last Mr. Maurice spoke in a deep full voice, you felt what a depth of human sympathy was in it. " Will you think about it then, Miss Hill ? "

[1] She went every *afternoon* to Lincoln's Inn

I felt how I trusted him; and told him that I did not see clearly about it, but would do what he advised, and then perhaps all would be plainer to me. " I am quite sure it will," he said; and wishing him good-bye I came away.

45, Great Ormond St.,
July 1st, 1857.

To EMILY.

I did not go to Mr. Neale's and the children made a horrid mess of it. Miss C. forgot the name of the station; and they went to *Beddington* and had to walk eight miles, and other absurdities.

I saw Rossetti last night, and learned that Ruskin is not going abroad, but to Manchester, Oxford, etc., to lecture. He starts to-day. He was at Russell Place, to see the pictures; but did not see any of us. Rossetti was *so* friendly, I could not hate him, with his bright bright eyes, and recalling, as he did, dear people; and he was so kind too. . . . Miss R. has heard of our being confirmed.[1] . . . Mr. Maurice has been lecturing on Milton before the Royal Society.

45, Great Ormond St.,
July 8th, 1857.

To FLORENCE.

. . . What fine efforts you are making about the toys! They quite put me to shame. How nice it is tho', that we can work together, tho' we are so far apart, is it not? . . . I hope you will get to know Mrs. Browning some day. How glorious that thunder-storm

---

[1] Octavia was confirmed at Christ Church, Marylebone, by Tait, then Bishop of London.

H

must have been ! Do you know I am to teach all the classes this autumn, except singing,—(*all* is not many— reading, writing and arithmetic). The ladies are all going out of town . . . Do you know I so enjoyed my visit to Weybridge last April. I have never enjoyed a visit there so much. I enjoyed the riding so, and how beautiful the country is ! . . . (Of a visit to Bucking- hamshire she writes) : You know there are acres and acres and acres of beech woods, valleys and hills clothed and covered with them, and there are rounded hills with most beautiful slopes ; and from little cleared spaces in the woods one catches a glimpse of far off purple hills, and nearer hills covered with wood, and farm-houses with their great barns golden-roofed, with lichen lying in a sheltered hollow ; and the great bare head of some uncovered hill, cut with clear outline against the sky ; and then perhaps we plunged into the depths of the woods again, where the sunlight fell between the fan- like branches of the beeches and thro' their leaves like a green mist, on to the silver stems, and on to the ground russet with last year's fallen leaves, perhaps upon the crest of some tall fern, or upon a sheet of blue speed- wells, or on some little wood sorrel plant, or a grey tree stump, touched with golden lichen, or gold-green moss. And then the larks, cuckoos, and nightingales seemed hardly to stop by night or day, but kept up a glad sweet chorus —The classes will be over in a minute, and then I must go. Forgive this short letter. I will try to write more next time I often think of you, dear dear little Flo, and love to see " Loke " at the beginning of a letter. It is your own name, and no one else uses it, so it always reminds me of you.

4, Russell Place, Fitzroy Square,
July 17th, 1857.

To GERTRUDE.

If you could bring me anything at any time to draw I should be so glad. I am so tired of privet, and dusty hornbeam,—especially when I have drawn one piece several times, and don't the least know when I shall get a fresh one ; and if, moreover, the things you brought told me a little about far, fair places, where they grew, they would help me.

The following letter refers to the building of a school at All Saints', Suffolk.

4, Russell Place, Fitzroy Square, W.,
August 14th, 1857.

To EMILY.

I return the tracings. I decidedly prefer No. 3 to any which you can choose. I mean I approve of your choice entirely, under the circumstances. At the same time, I enclose a small extract from Ruskin, bearing on the subject. Now I should not propose altering any but the *entirely* square windows. But, if that were possible, they would be much more beautiful. I am afraid they would have to be a little lower down, to make room for the shield, as they call it (namely, you understand, the solid block of stone), which need not, I think, necessarily be carved at all, though it would be more beautiful, of course. One or two words, or even letters, that were appropriate, might perhaps be found and placed on the shields. At any rate the Committee could hardly object, could they? The opening, you understand, would be square as ever. I suppose each window would require

three little shields. I think you will quite understand
about them from the drawing I send you. It is the
window Ruskin refers to (thirteenth century, Oakham
Castle). I could not resist doing a little towards
beginning to shade it; but, in spite of that, I think
you'll understand it. I leave it entirely to you to
apply the suggestion, if practicable. Tell Mr. Durrant
I admire the arrangement of large square panes very
much. I *think* I even prefer it to the *quarries*. I
am very glad indeed to have influenced, in the least
degree, his wish to have Gothic windows. I'll make
a finished drawing, or clear tracing of this window,
if you want it; but yours will be so simple that this
will not be of any use, I think, except to explain the
plan, which my rough sketch will do

I have seen Ruskin's manager to-day, and had a long
talk about Ruskin, which I enjoyed much . . .

P.S.—There is not the smallest necessity for the
aperture of the window being of a pointed shape.
Make the uppermost arch pointed only, and make the
top of the window square, filling the interval with a
stone shield, and you may have a perfect school of
architecture, not only consistent with, but eminently
conducive to every comfort of your daily life The
window in Oakham Castle is an example of such a
form actually employed in the thirteenth century.

4, Russell Place, W.,
September 22nd, 1857.

MRS. HILL TO EMILY.

Amelia[1] has taken the toys, and in a rather
different spirit from Mr. P. She said to Miranda,

---

[1] Formerly nurse to Octavia and her elder sisters at Wisbeach, then
married to a tailor in London.

"Well, Miss Miranda, I shall expect of course to be
paid for my time bye and bye; but more than that I
don't want for myself. If I fail, I shall think others
have failed before me; and I may perhaps have done
a little good." This being her tone, I am proud of her,
and look upon her as a fellow-worker in the cause, who
has come in by God's providence to relieve Ockey of a
burden, and so setting her free to work her higher
influence all the more. I am to go and teach as usual;
and Ockey will keep the accounts for Amelia. Amelia
said to M., "You know, Miss M., I shall want your
Mamma to come and give the spirit." The debt on the
toys is £25, which Amelia is to repay, as she can—
half to us and half to Mr. Neale. He did not wish to
take any, and entered with zeal into the new plan.
Ockey seemed quite touched. . . . He seemed most
anxious that the teaching should go on. The children
are quite in love with his Geography lessons, and won't
hear a word against him. On the morning of the day
it was all settled, Ockey received the sweetest letter
from Miss Harris, asking what sum it would require to
carry on the toys for another year; but dear O. very
properly, I believe, was firm to carry out the change.
We must give all our influence now to the new phase
of things, since the spirit is the same. . . . Ockey
begins to-morrow to work at home. I mean to read
some nice book to her, and do all I can to make her
happy. She is my own brave, beautiful, good tender
Ockey; and it's a hard trial to lose one's post in a
Cause; but the Cause itself (that being God's) can
never be lost.

November 22nd, 1857.

To FLORENCE

I don't know whether you will receive this letter, or the box that was despatched yesterday, first. So I must tell you that in it you will find a very few drawings of mine. I will tell you a little about them. I have selected them from a great many that I have done, for I have been at work at that kind of drawing all the summer I am speaking of the flowers. You will see we chose to send you the water forget-me-not, cranes-bill and lady's-finger, all of which were old favourites of yours. There is one page of virginian creeper and creeping jenny which I send, partly because they are of London growth; and when I had no fresh bright wild country things, day after day did I persevere in drawing the dirty little fellows from the black wall and dirty earth; so they seem to me rather characteristic of my work The dear buglos is one of my friends; the bramble you know I always loved; and so I have sent you a little piece shaded. I am rather proud of the stalk of the highest leaf; indeed I like it all. Then those drawings on note-paper are copies from Albert Durer. Is not that a beautiful little piece with the thistle and grass, and stones? How do you like my old donkey's head? It is nearly the first animal I have ever drawn. In the picture, which is one of Joseph and Mary taking Christ, when a little child, down into Egypt, the donkey is being led by Joseph, and he is just looking out of the corner of his eye in that odd way at the thistle, evidently thinking if his rein is long enough for him to snatch at it; but he is nearly past it, and clearly will have to go without the treat Down below two little lizards are at play; on a log a little bird is perched. I hope you will receive the drawings on my birthday.

They are the only things I have to give you, dear one ; but I like to think you know what I have been doing.— I had not seen Ruskin all the summer and autumn, but he just came, on Friday, in time to see my work; so that I could send it to you. He is busy in town every day, so that he could not see me at Denmark Hill ; but he came here. You do not know how pleased he was with all I had done, or how happy I was that he was pleased. He said I had done an immense quantity of work, and that I was far more accurate than any of his men at the College, whom, you know, he teaches every week. He said of one of my drawings, "This is quite a marvellous piece of drawing, Octavia." And when I showed him one of my Albert Dürers he exclaimed, "Is that yours? I was going to say you had been cutting up my print."

"Ah," I said, "you won't find it so accurate when you look nearer." He then said that it was as accurate as it was possible to be without absolutely tracing it. He told me he saw with what spirit I had worked. He is going to take me to Marlboro' House on Friday, and give me a student's ticket ; for he wants me to copy some Turners for him in outline. He says he must give me more teaching, which he can do when I am working at Marlboro' House, where he will come and superintend me, when he has time. I felt altogether so delighted. Ruskin is so kind and beautiful. You know he is coming to keep my birthday with us. . . . He has been very busy, so that his looking over my work has been delayed. He sent me the Albert Durer four weeks ago, saying, "Copy this, bit by bit, till I see you." At last I had done it so long that I was sure he could not want me to go on longer. So I hit on this odd plan. I wrote to him something in this style : " My dear Mr.

Ruskin, there was once a shepherd's dog, who was ordered by his master to watch a flock of sheep. His master forgot to call him away, and went home. Surprised at the dog's absence, he returned after two days, and found the poor fellow still watching his sheep. And the dog, who now addresses you, would be very glad to be thus patient and obedient, if she were sure that she was really doing the work her master most wanted done ; but a great doubt has arisen in her mind as to it. She would not venture to set up her ideas of what is best or most necessary above her master's. If he does want her to go on with the work, well and good. If not, can he write ? If he cannot, she has done all she could, and will remain obedient to his words." Was it not fun ? He answered by return of post beginning, "My poor little doggie, I really will come to-morrow." We are going to Lincoln's Inn to-morrow, and then I am going to hear Spurgeon. Do you know who he is ?

4, Russell Place,
November 22nd, 1857.

EMILY TO FLORENCE.

I told you that Ruskin had promised to come the evening before Ockey's birthday. She wanted to give him some present, so this is what we have thought of. Do you remember a little stand Ockey was going to paint for a chamois with the words[1] .—

> " We see our skies thro' clouds of smoke
>   Theirs bends o'er wastes of sunlit snow
> God leads us all in different ways,
>   His hand to see, His will to know "

We have just thought that she might finish that for him. But we were at a loss how to get a Swiss

[1] Composed by Octavia.

chamois. Well! you remember you had one given to you by Joanna, and they appealed to me as to whether I thought you would like to give it to Ruskin; and, as it is only ten days before the time, we could not hear from you; so I have ventured to take the responsibility of Ockey's giving it, feeling sure what you would say if you were here. I hope I have done right, but I cannot bear that you should not join us in doing nice things of the kind, because you are at a distance. I know that your heart is in them. If she has an opportunity, Ockey means to say that it is your chamois. Ruskin will be pleased at its coming from you too. He always asks so kindly and sympathetically about you. When he was here on Friday he asked about you, before he looked at any of Ockey's work. . . . Our reading in the evenings goes on delightfully. We have finished that beautiful book of Myers, " Lives of Great Men," and are reading Mr. Maurice's " Philosophy."

4, Russell Place,
November 27th, 1857.

To Gertrude.

I have been to Marlboro' House to-day with Ruskin, and of course greatly enjoyed it. He showed me the work he wants done; but he wishes me to copy, this week, an etching of Turner's, that he may see if I can do the work. It is not what you would call high art, I think. I do not yet at all know if he still means me for an illuminator or not. He does not say; but wishes me to copy these sketches in pen and ink, because they will be of use to him too. He wants me, after that, to copy some pencil drawings of Turner's, but says it may possibly be six months before I can do them   I don't *think* he still does mean me for an illuminator; but I feel, as Dawie[1] says, it is altogether his doing, and I have no responsibility. He was so kind to-day.   We are looking forward to his visit with great delight.   He has lent me 3rd and 4th vols. of "Modern Painters" to read aloud in the evenings, at my request.

December 10th, 1857.

EMILY TO FLORENCE.

    Ruskin came a little before his time.   Mama, Ockey and I were in the room ready to receive him. He came in, looking kind and bright; and the first thing he asked, before he sat down, was, how you were.   Mama read him Aunt Emily's letter about you, and one of your letters.   Andy soon came in, and we had a great deal of most interesting conversation—on the respective influences of town and country—on French, English, and Americans—on animals, of which Ruskin is very fond—on Reserve and Cordelia.   When Ruskin said something about reserve, Andy and Ockey exclaimed, laughing, "Oh you should ask Minnie," which made me feel very hot and blush.   Ruskin took my part and was very kind.   He agrees with me in thinking it so much more easy to write than to speak about anything one feels.   Andy and Ockey disagreed about it.   He agreed very much with all Mama's remarks.   After tea we sang to Ruskin, which he liked, I think; and it was very interesting to hear his remarks on the different songs.   He always chose out some point which he liked and which he could praise, which was very pretty of him.

----

[1] Miss Margaret Gillies.

After that we spoke about poetry. He does not think anyone but a great poet, who gives up his life to it, should attempt to write any. He says there is always a good deal of vanity in it; and it spoils one's ear for good poetry to compose bad. Mama had been speaking of our poetry; Ruskin asked Andy to repeat some, saying it would be very pretty of her to do so, after all he had been saying against it. She did so, and I think he was pleased with it, and the more so when he heard it had taken a long time to write. He said that he could not judge of it by hearing it in that way, and he should like a copy.

Ockey is drawing at Marlboro' House, and Ruskin is at work in another room; so he comes up once or twice to look at her work.

January 5th, 1858.

RUSKIN TO OCTAVIA.

MY DEAR OCTAVIA,

I am very glad you and your sisters and friend enjoyed the pictures, and that you see how beautiful they are. They are quite infinite. I cannot understand how any human work can possess so much of the inexhaustibleness of nature.

Do not be sorry that you cannot see beautiful places at present. The first sensation is a thing to look forward to with hope. It cannot be had twice—it does not not much matter whether it comes sooner or later.

My lecture is at Kensington on the 13th of this month. If you find difficulties in getting admission, write to me, and I will get you a ticket or two.

I send you a new etching, and the print finished.

I only want the etching copied, but thought you would like to see how Turner prepares in it for his light and shade.

Yours always most truly,

J. RUSKIN.

Kind regards to Mama, Miranda, and Minnie.

That story about the Fisherman always puzzled me sadly to know who the Fish was. How could *he* do so many things for the Fisherman?

Florence,

January 9th, 1858.

FLORENCE TO OCTAVIA.

I have spent an evening with Mrs. Browning. I will tell you all about it; but first I must say how delighted I am with her. I felt from the first minute how *simpatica* she was to me, a woman one could love dearly and admire. Last Tuesday B [1] met Browning (who is always very friendly), and he said " Will you come and take tea with us to-morrow night ? " Of course she accepted, and I was most delighted. Accordingly the next evening we went. As we went in, I felt so excited ; it is so long that I have wanted to see her, and I said to myself that I should be disappointed Mr. Browning came forward cordially to welcome us ; and then came Mrs. Browning. She is very short indeed ; but one does not observe the shortness. She has long black curls, and large eyes ; one can hardly say what colour ; in some lights they look a beautiful brown ; in others a dark grey ; as for the other features they are not pretty ; in fact I suppose she would not be considered at all pretty ; but to me

----

[1] Miss Emily Smith.

she is a great deal more. She shook hands very kindly
and made me sit on the sofa by her. There was also
Mrs. Jameson. She is quite an old lady with mild blue
eyes. There was also Mr. Tennyson, Alfred Tennyson's
brother. There was a good deal of small talk, and there
was a discussion about places. Mrs. Jameson asked a
good deal about Viareggio. At last the conversation
turned towards England. It is evident neither Mrs.
Browning nor her husband like England much.

She began abusing it, saying she always felt so
downcast when there, that the sky felt as if it was
falling down, and the rooms were so small; she finished
by saying, " I do not sympathise with those who have
yearnings after England." Then she turned to me and
said, " Perhaps you can tell me something about yearnings after England. Do you yearn after it?" " Oh
yes," I said, " very much indeed; I love England, and
would not live out of it for long for anything." " Why
not?" said Mrs. Jameson in her quiet yet energetic
way. So I said, " Firstly Mama and all my sisters
are there," and I was going to say more, when other
visitors were announced and there was a general stir.
Mrs. Browning said to me, with a very sweet smile,
" I am sure it is a very good reason." . . . There was
a great deal of very interesting conversation about
women, with regard to their right to property when
married. Mrs. Jameson was very energetic about it,
though I did not think her reasoning was good; also
Mrs. Browning talked very nicely about it; but I could
not hear all that she said, because I had changed places,
and was not near her; and she has such a small voice,
that it is difficult to hear what she says. They wanted
to get Mr. Browning to sign a petition to Parliament,
showing the injustice done to women, according to the

present law, about their property. I liked what he said very much. He has very liberal ideas about it, and was quite willing to sign; only he did not know how the law could be altered without entailing other greater injustices. However, at the end, he said he would sign. I think he does everything that his wife wishes. It is so nice to see them together; they are so exceedingly fond of one another, and he is so attentive to her. There was a great deal of merry conversation. When we were leaving Mrs. Browning said, " This is the first time you have spent the evening here; but I hope it won't be the last."

April 21st, 1858.

To Mrs. Howitt.

My dearest Mrs Howitt,

How glorious this weather is! To-day I saw, in a little back street near Soho, two little golden-haired children, leaning out of a window in the early sunlight, gazing intently into a bird's cage, hanging on the wall,—the poor little prisoner singing as if his little heart would break. Just so, I thought, the children here may want *us*; but we must break our hearts in longing for the distant glories of hill and wood. In a moment, one felt that it ought rather to teach that even here Spring brought joys—that we have visions and witnesses of brighter lands and fairer lives than we can see around us.

Derwent Bank,
July 4th, 1858.

To a Friend.

To me the whole world is so full of things crying out to be done, each one of which would be sufficient

for a lifetime's heart and thought, I think.   In fact
each work seems to be interesting in almost exact proportion to the amount I can devote to it, capable of
infinite expansion in breadth or depth.   For my part I
would always rather choose the latter, would rather
take up wholly a few individuals or pictures or books,
and love and know and study them deeply, than have
any more superficial (though wider) sympathies ; and
my trial is, and has always been, that I have to tear
myself away from this intense grasp and absorbing
interest, to love and know and help in fresh and fresh
directions.   I have often felt like a perpetually up-
rooted plant.   Only somehow in looking back, I find
continuity and deep inner relation between the various
works and times of my life, and always find the past a
possession because in memory I have it still. . . .

I am so glad you will not turn the ignorant ones out
of the class, at any rate yet.   I know well one weakens
one's hands by not keeping one distinct aim before
one ; but then one never likes not to meet any effort,
however small, on the part of people under one's charge.
I have not always the courage to give myself pain of
that kind, I believe.

How very beautiful the lines on the Supper are !

4, Russell Place,
August 1st, 1858.

To MIRANDA AND EMILY.

Take dearest Mama under your special care, for
she will not take care of herself under her own.   Send
her back stronger, I charge you.   Also think of your
old sister here, and how she loves you both, and thinks
of you.   You won't think her unkind not to come,
knowing what prevents her, and she hopes her previous

consent proves to you that work and whims wouldn't have detained her.   Be merry, be happy, be free ; send for anything conveyable that you want, and trust to Aladdin's lamp.   See what grand things it has done already, and have faith

August 8th, 1858.

To Gertrude.

If we were all less self-occupied, what a depth of beauty and order we should see in the influence of persons and things on people, traced in the momentary lighting up of an eye, or the slight quiver of a lip, which we lose perhaps in a fit of self-contemplation ; and *that* revelation of God's purpose and way of work passes unnoticed, a cause of praise and power lost to us. And then I would wish most lovingly to grasp the whole purpose of each life, and influence of details on it, to see all the strong impulses leading to selfishness or pride, or any form of evil; to watch, not unaiding, the struggle with them ; to contemplate with intense sympathy and reverence every purifying affection, stimulating hope, earnest purpose, self-control, and every form of good ; to look at all, not as one standing aloof or above , but as fellow-worker, fellow-sufferer ; to trace the same tendency to evil and good in myself ; to find the point or points, as one always does, in which everyone is so much greater than oneself, that one bows before it in joy and cries, " Thank God for it."

4, Russell Place,
August 15th, 1858.

To Mrs. Hill.

R.[1] went on Wednesday.   Her mother was much nicer at the last.   I hear from Brighton that the child

---

[1] The little toy-worker who had cared so much for the cat.

is very happy. It would have done you good to see her delight at her new clothes, and the care with which she went to a clean crossing, tho' the roads were not very muddy. Her indifference about leaving home was, of course, very sad. But just as we were going away, one of those immense Irish women one sometimes sees, who was selling apples in the Old Bailey, called her back, and giving her a kiss said, " God bless you, child. Be a good girl."

I have wished Mary good-bye. . . . We spoke about my going back with her, which is a relief. I don't like a thing which both people know the other is thinking of not spoken of and explained, and so I was very glad she mentioned it. . . . *Private.* Would you ferret out for me whether A. is looking forward to her half holiday for going to see people ? and if she is, say nothing ; but, if she isn't, ask her not to make any engagements to go away, at first, out of charity or acquiescence, as I shall like very much to have her at home. *Public again.* I have some more flowers which are a great pleasure. Everyone is *very* kind, that is to say everyone I hear of or see ; there are not many.

It seems so strange to feel the piano had not been opened for so long. This morning I sang all our sacred music,—some that I am fond of and did not know, I *spelt* out on the piano. It reminded me, by contrast more than by likeness, of the Sunday music we sometimes used to have. I have invitations from Margaret and Gertrude which I shall accept, if I can, after I know that Mary is gone ; but next week my College opens. However, considering that I have Wednesday free, I hope to get away. I do not seem of any use to anyone, but I hope I shall do all the better when work begins . . . . Thank you for all your long, most welcome,

letters. . . . In constant thought of you, Yours
Octavia.

August 19th, 1858.

To EMILY.

(Tho' this is for all of you.)   It is but right and
nice that, having known of my long waiting, you should
know now that I am quite satisfied.   Dear Mary has been
here; and really, I don't know how to be thankful
enough for having seen her so long and so delightfully.
I waited all the morning, getting more distracted and
disappointed every quarter of an hour; for I knew she
must be back at Elmhurst at 6.30, and leave Camden
Road at 4.30; and 1, 2, 3 o'clock came.   Before 3, however, I had quite made up my mind to it.   I did this the
more easily, because I was sure that, when she did
come, if I had been repining and longing before, I should
be selfish and covetous then.   Well, at 3.10 she
arrived with such a headache she could hardly stand.
. . . In a very few minutes her head grew better, and
she resolved to go by the 5 50 train.   And oh ! we had
such an afternoon !   It is worth more than many weeks
with her in society. . . . She asked to hear Andy's
song "Wilt Thou not visit me ? " . . . . She promises
that if she comes to London next year she will come to
stay here, if we still want her !   At last we parted, not
at all sadly.   She is so sweet and good. . . . Her heart
was open as usual to hear all about everyone,—Ruskin,
Mr. Maurice and the children, in fact every person and
thing we care for.

August 17th, 1858.

To MIRANDA.

Tell Minnie I have just finished Maurice's
" Ecclesiastical History "   I am so very much interested in

it, and think she would be even more so, knowing so much about all the people. I should very much like to have a talk with her about them, especially Polycarp, Clemens of Alexandria, Irenaeus and Ignatius. I should like to know if she has been taught to like Tertullian or not. . . . Ruskin's work seems to take nearly all day. My own needlework has hardly been touched since Mama left. Certainly I have despatched R. I think singing and reading have flourished most. I can't consider Ruskin's work has got on, because I was not at Marlboro' House last week, tho' in other respects it's all right. I think, most of my time *seems* spent in putting the room neat.

4, Russell Place,
August 26th, 1858.

To Miss Harris.

Margaret[1] has been kindness itself. . . . She urges that Andy should take a resident situation on account of her health. But Andy's heart is so clinging, and wound so fast round her home, her health even would suffer. . . . Her influence on the children is the fruit of three years' work. . . . Andy is the sunshine of her home.

4, Russell Place,
December 3rd, 1858.

Emily to Miranda.

Mr. Maurice talked to Ockey a good deal about the Bible Class at the College. He wanted to know who some of the pupils were; and Ockey said it was so interesting to hear his descriptions of the people,

---

[1] Octavia's half-sister, Mrs Whelpdale

and see the kinds of things he had noticed. One woman he said he met very often; he fancied she was a milliner; and then he was so distressed lest this little theory of his should have misled Ockey in any way; and he said he was sure he did not know why he thought so.

45, Great Ormond Street,
December 8th, 1858.

To Miranda, who was in Italy.

I am doing some work for "Modern Painters." Ruskin is coming on Friday to spend the evening with us. Dearest thing, I wish you knew how much I feel your sweetness. Now I must tell you some news. Ruskin is most kind. He called the Prouts "quite admirable," the tones so even and pure; "some of them," he continued, "I like better than the originals. But I think you might make your work more accurate!" Is not the last an odd remark? He was so delighted with the progress of my Portman Hall pupils, quite astonished. He writes: "I wish I had seen Miranda before she went. But I can't do a tenth of the things I want to do"

4, Russell Place,
December 12th, 1858.

Emily to Florence.

When Ockey saw Ruskin, he said that he should be sure to come, unless his father should propose for them to go to the play that night, in which case, he must put off almost any engagement.

On Friday we got all the room beautifully neat, and decorated with sprays and leaves that dear Gertrude had sent us from Weybridge. Ockey and I were in

white with black ribbons, and dear Mama looked very
nice in her black dress with white collar and sleeves.
There was a splendid fire, and tea very prettily set out,
and all looked cheerful and nice. When we were all
ready and seven o'clock came, Ockey and I began to
get very anxious lest he should not come; listening
most intently to all the carriages, and sitting with the
door open, and candle ready to light him upstairs. A
quarter past seven came, and Ockey said, "Well at
half-past I shall give up all hope and begin to cry.
The only thing that makes me think he is coming is,
that the lamp burns so remarkably well." A carriage
stopped; a knock at the door came. Ockey, much to
my surprise, would run down to meet him. Mama
and I sat demurely on the sofa, and waited till he
came in. He had brought a number of sketches to
show us—all his summer's work. Was it not kind?
When we were all seated, he asked directly about
Andy. How she had got on, on her journey, and how
she had found you. When Mama began talking about
you both, he said so sweetly and sympathetically, "I
hope it does not pain you to talk about these things."

He explained to Ockey, one of the first things, that
he had not brought her any birthday present; that it
must be a Christmas present, as he had wanted to know
what books she had. Ockey said something about "Oh
no! he did so much"; and Mama said that when we
were children, she had introduced the practice of our
giving presents on our birthdays, rather than receiving
them, because she had wished to impress on us that we
were born to give, rather than to receive. Ruskin said
that he thought it was very ungracious that friends
should come to a person, and expect them to give them
presents, because it was their birthday, as much as to

say, "You came into the world to give to us.   Prove to us that you are of some good."

Then Ruskin made a remark about the cream and said that the difficulty people had in getting cream in London was a proof that it was growing too large. Ockey said that so much milk and cream came from the country, and asked Mama if she remembered the cans they had seen the morning they came from Cambridge.   This led to their speaking of the pleasure of their visit, and, among other things, Ockey spoke of the sunlight dying away from the stained glass windows in King's College chapel, when they were at the service there.   Ruskin said there was hardly anything more solemnly impressive than the death of a stained glass window; and then he said how very little influence the beauty of the Universities had on the men.   He says they are proud of them, but nothing more; that when he first went to College he thought it very grand and fine; but soon lost all the impression of solemnity, and looked on the gowns as so many black rags, and the service in the chapel as a daily punishment; and he found that it was the case with all the young men he met   Only perhaps Tennyson or other poets care for it.   Ockey said, "Well! people don't feel it at the time, I think they do afterwards.   I know many people who speak with such great pleasure of their University. I am sure it is quite beautiful to hear Mr. Maurice speak of it."   Ruskin said, "Well! but Mr Maurice is a poet"   At which Mama and Ockey said they thought him anything but that.   Mama said how very seldom he made any similes, Ruskin said, "But I do not look upon it that a poet's work is to make similes; but to make things."   He said he did not know much about Mr. Maurice; he had not read much of his, he found it such hard work. He could not follow him. He seemed like a man who did not see clearly, and was always stretching out, moving on in the right direction, but in a fog.

Ockey said, " No! I don't believe it is so at all. Mr. Maurice quite understands what he means himself; and the difficulty which people find in understanding him, arises partly from his style, and partly that people require to understand his way of putting things." Ruskin said, " I'm very glad to hear you say that you think Mr. Maurice knows what he means himself; but I had always thought that the very greatest men were essentially simple. The only great man I know who is not, Dante, throws out a word or two quite knowing what he means, and says, ' Think out that,' and people do not know which end of the thing they have got, and so quarrel over what he does mean. But when he says anything directly, it is very clear and simple. And so with *all really* great men."

I said that Mr. Maurice had a wonderful power of understanding his pupils' answers, of finding out what they meant by confused answers, of getting at the truth they wished to bring out, and of putting it so clearly to them. Ruskin replied that *that* was a very great thing. Ockey said yes it was very beautiful; and that she could not understand how it was he had such a knowledge of human nature, when he had no knowledge of individuals. I said, "Perhaps he has more than you think." Ockey said, " Of course *you* would solve the matter in that way." Ruskin asked why, and O. said, " Because Minnie has such an admiration for Mr. Maurice."— Ruskin said, " Well, Minnie, as you admire Mr. Maurice so much, can you explain why it is that he is so pained at being misunderstood ? " Ockey answered for me, to

my relief and said, " Oh, you refer to the Preface of the
' Doctrine of Sacrifice.' I think it is because he longs
so much for Union." Ruskin said that was a very good
answer. He repeated again that he was glad we thought
Mr. Maurice knew what he meant. O. said, " O yes, and I
would engage to make anyone who took the trouble to read
a small piece of his writing carefully, master the style
and understand him, in three-quarters of an hour."
Ruskin said he would take her at her word ; for he
wished to understand Mr. Maurice, and that he would
make out clearly, as his tutor used to say, what he did
and what he did not understand, and ask her about any
difficulty he had. So O. said, would he read the
sermon on Mr Mansfield's death ? And he said he did
not want to read anything about death ; it made him
so very sad. O. said she did not think it would make
him sad to read what Mr. Maurice said about death,
and explained who Mr. Mansfield was. When Ruskin
remembered, he was interested, and took the sermon.
They were talking about the want of music in Mr.
Maurice's writings ; and O. asked Ruskin what he
thought of Kingsley's poems. Ruskin had not read
them ; but he did not like hexameters, he could not
read them, even for the sake of a fine thought ; for
perhaps the thought would make him remember the
hexameter, which would be too great a punishment.
O. said she thought the ballads very beautiful,—R. said
he only knew the poems in " Alton Locke," and he liked
those very much Mama asked if he knew the "Three
Fishers," and asked us to sing it, which we did, without
the music of course. Ruskin was pleased both with
words and music. But he said that in general he
thought Kingsley too sad, and that he injured the
purpose for which he wrote by being exaggerated and

not correct in his facts. We were talking about happiness, and Kingsley's suffering so much when he came to town. Ruskin said for his part he was never happy except when he was selfish, when he shut himself up, and read only the books he liked, or enjoyed the sunshine and nature. He did not know how it was that, whenever he did what he believed to be right, he suffered for it; that it seemed like his unlucky star. O. said, "Don't talk about stars. What do you mean by it?" R. said, "Well, I will give you a small crumb of an instance. When I was travelling a great many years ago, at a time my father was ill, I met with a picture of Turner's, one of the finest he ever did. I did not quite know the value of it myself; and I knew that it would vex my father if I bought it without his leave; so I wrote back to him. Meanwhile the picture was bought by some one, who utterly destroyed it. Now if I had bought it, it might have made my father lose his appetite for a day, but nothing more. And this is only one small instance. It is always the way when I do right. Miss Edgeworth would have made the picture go to a round of people, converting them to Turner, and come back to me crowned with laurel. I was brought up on Miss Edgeworth's principles; but I have not found them at all true in my case." Mama said there was a truth in them, but that in some respects they were very false; that she believed that every one had to suffer very much in doing right; that she had felt it so particularly about Ruskin himself; that the brave and true things he said were often misunderstood; but that she always felt her heart warm towards him, and she thought to herself,—if only people would receive them as they were meant. "But," she said, "I think you may be very happy that you do excite the kind of admiration that you do, in many people; and that you have the power of exciting the noble and beautiful emotions which your words and writings do." Ruskin said that he would wish his word about art to be taken just in the same way that a physician's or lawyer's would be about medicine or law. O. said she was sure it was so, more than he thought; and that it was a growing thing. That a lady had said to her the other day, that a word from him would be enough to ruin her; and O. added, "At which I felt very proud." She said that she thought when people did right, the good they expected very often did *not* come, because they were not perfectly wise, as well as perfectly right; but that, tho' they had to suffer for want of judgment, in the end they were always blessed; but in different ways from those they had expected; that, as long as people calculated results, they could not do right; they must do right for right's sake.

Ruskin said, "Do you mean to say that a man, who had been very selfish, and thought he would make himself happy by going out and giving to all the beggars he met, would not succeed?" O. said, "No! he might at first, but he would find afterwards that he had gathered around him many people who only cared for his money. Whereas, if a man did the same thing from a sincere love for his fellow creatures, he would not have the pain of suspecting the motives of all around him, and he would have the sympathy of those engaged in the same good work." They were speaking of the blessing of having the sympathy of people, and R. said he had some people who understood him. O. said, with a very bright smile, "Oh have you?" R. said, "Yes. I think you do pretty well."

Then Mama read Miranda's letter about her voyage

from Marseilles, with which R. was much pleased, and
said it recalled all the scenery to him; and when she
came to the part about the red sail, he told O. to
remind him to show her a small Turner in the National
Gallery which showed the wonderful beauty of a red
sail. He asked if there were part of another letter he
might hear, and anything about Florence. I brought
Andy's to me, and while it was being read I turned my
face away for fear of its telling too much, as I could
hardly bear it; but when the thought of you both
changed into joy, I lifted my face and met such a look
of tenderness and sympathy. When the letter was
finished, R. said to Mama, "How happy you must be
in them all!" "Thank you. It is very beautiful."

Then he showed us the sketches. I don't think I shall
ever forget them. I see them constantly at night when
I shut my eyes. They have given me most beautiful
visions of lovely scenery. One of the things which
gave me the most pleasure was to hear R. talk about
them with such perfect humility, condemning or praising
them, just as if they had been another person's work,
no false shame in admiring them, and entering with such
hearty sympathy into our pleasure in them. Then
came a quiet talk, which I think R. quite enjoyed. I
felt as if we had come nearer to him than ever; as if he
were opening something of his heart, and asking for
help. He said once, "I do not say any of these things
to make you sad, but because I think you may say
something to make me happier." He was regretting
that the colours of a sunset faded; and I said I thought
the changefulness of nature was one of its greatest
beauties. At first he agreed; and then he said, "No, it
reminded him how all things must pass away." Then
we had a very solemn talk about good being continued

in another world, and the purpose of sorrow. I said that it was most comforting to me to look back, and see how things which had seemed so sad turned out as blessings. R. said, " It may be so with you good people ; but if I look back it is to find blunders.   To remember the past is like Purgatory " O. said that the past interpreted the present, and made her hopeful for the future.   I think some of the things we said (especially what Mama said) may have made him happier.   When he heard that his carriage had come, he said something about its being sad that evenings went so fast.   Indeed he stayed long after his carriage had come, and when he was half down stairs, returned to look at O.'s pupils' drawings of his own accord, and said he was in no hurry if she had anything else to tell him.   When we thanked him for coming, he said that he ought not to be thanked, as he had so much enjoyed himself.

December 19th, 1858.

EMILY TO MIRANDA.

Dear Ockey has had rather a disappointment lately about her work,—that is to say she has been awakened to the sense of its not being as accurate as she had hoped it was.   She wrote to Ruskin to ask about his employing a young artist.   He wrote back very kindly saying he could employ two or three girls, supposing they could copy accurately ; but accuracy meant so much.   " Even you are nothing near the mark yet, tho' the Claude foreground is a step in advance."   Of course O. knew that the things she had done in water colour were very far from right ; but she had thought that her pencil and pen work was very nearly so.   In the same letter he said that he always had a chivalrous desire to help women, but he began to think his old lady friends were right when they cautioned him against it, as he had found all his girl protegées, with the exception of Ockey, "very sufficiently troublesome." She met him the same day at Dulwich, and he was very kind ; and if she can have a little bright weather, so as to get on with her Dulwich work, she will be in good spirits again, I think.

4, Russell Place,
December 19th, 1858.

To MIRANDA.

Now for Ruskin. Minnie has told you something about the evening ; but nothing about the sketches. The first we saw was one of an old walled and fortified town in Switzerland, with little arched gateway guarded by towers and wall ; the moat is dried up and filled up ; long grass and buttercups grow there. Then he showed us a view of the cliffs which form the banks of Lake Lucerne ; their tops are for the most part inaccessible, quite lonely, haunted only by the eagle. "Fancy, Octavia," Ruskin said, "walking up there, where one can get among chestnut glades, along winding paths, bringing you suddenly to the edge, and looking down on the blue water." He showed us two sketches of Morgarten. Then he showed us exquisite sketches of Bellinzona, where the three Forest Cantons had each a castle built on a high rock. He has done the whole thing in the loveliest way, making a kind of plan of the whole, and sketching large and carefully in colour each bit of it, even the little rows of leaves on a bank. But nothing can explain to you the sense of size and space and grandeur conveyed by the drawing of hundreds of pines, chestnuts and poplars, yet each seen as part

of an enormous whole. The sketch of Bellinzona Ruskin
had drawn from the priest's garden, a lovely spot on a
rock near the chapel and house, on the side of a steep
craggy cliff, the little posts carefully bricked up to
support a patch of mould here and there, on one of
which was planted corn. Among it grew white lilies
seen against a further piece of brightest green grass;
beyond lay the ravine of the Ticino, and beyond again
the mountains. . . . Miss B. has been offered the
Secretaryship of the Children's Hospital; but her father
and mother say that no daughter ought to leave home
except to be married, or to earn her own living, witness
Florence Nightingale, who has returned a mere wreck.
Why if ever there was an example fitted to stir up
heroism it might be hers! I wonder if her mother
were asked whether she was prouder and fonder of her
before her work or after? or whether she grudged the
health which she herself has sacrificed so willingly? I
am going daily to Dulwich. It is a long walk even if I
take omnibus between Charing Cross and Camberwell
Gate.

CHAPTER IV

WHEN Miranda went to Italy, in 1858, Octavia suggested to her grandfather that it would be more economical, as well as more comfortable, if she and her mother and Emily could move into *un*furnished rooms. Octavia said that, if he would lend the money for furniture, she would be able to repay him out of what would be saved on rent. He kindly undertook to lend the required amount, and, after the rooms had been secured, Octavia made out a list of necessary furniture, with approximate prices. Then after her day's work, she visited various shops, and with Gertrude's and Emily's help chose what was required. If she spent more on one thing, she took the amount off something else, and she determined that she would keep to the fixed sum. This was achieved. Then she planned and cut the carpet, and each evening she and Emily sat on the floor sewing it. One night they worked till 12 o'clock. All this time Octavia was going each morning to Dulwich, where she stood drawing for about four hours, then she went to Great Ormond Street to the Women's Classes, and walked from there to Milton Street, Dorset Square. Yet she was as merry as possible, and sang and repeated poetry while she and Emily were at work. And in due time she repaid the money that she had borrowed

> 103, Milton St., Dorset Sq.,
> January 4th, 1859.

MRS. HILL TO HER DAUGHTER MIRANDA.

I only came to this house to-day. It is so very pretty; you and Florence would be enchanted with it.

Dear Ockey and Minnie must have worked so hard ;
they would not let me have any trouble, but arranged it
all, and beautiful indeed it looks · the crimson table
cover and chair cover and green carpet and white muslin
curtains and white walls with roses, make such a lovely
combination, and I enjoy the nice square high rooms.
Miss Sterling, who called yesterday, exclaimed, " What a
dainty room you have." It certainly does give one a
most pleasant sense of simplicity, cleanliness, and
beautiful colour.

January 25th, 1859.

OCTAVIA TO MIRANDA.

. I think you will like our dear new home ;
the prettiness of it is a continual delight to me, and I
am most thankful for its order and cleanliness. . . . I
am so fond of it. . . . I was amazed to find how much
you had all thought of Ruskin's statement about my
accuracy. Of course I was disappointed, because I
thought the battle was won , but you see it referred to
pencil and colour sketches, in which I had not tried
mainly for accuracy, believing that I need not try, that
the amount of measurement I gave it secured it ; and I
had other things to aim at. It was not colour or pencil
sketches that he ever praised for accuracy (Oh yes, the
first coloured one ; but then it had so little colour). I
never thought for a moment my eye was accurate about
anything, unless it were matching colours   I only
thought that, by some miracle, the things I had done
were as accurate as human work need be ; and that all
would continue so, if I worked in the same way. Now
that I know where I am, I don't doubt I can win the
battle in time by steady work ; and I have not been

the least cast down about it, since the first 'hour I knew it. I am very impatient to get home and see how Minnie is. I didn't like leaving the darling all alone.

To her Sisters.

. . . Don't let anyone frighten you about my health ; I think they none of them are frightened now ; but, whether or no, I am resolved to take the most immense care ; for I think it probable this will be required for a little time, and that it is very important that I should preserve both health and strength. . . . I enjoy Dulwich[1] extremely ; you know it is so nice to · see a little country. I only go three days in the week now, because of fatigue and expense. . . . I have such lovely walks home past trees with rooks' nests, you remember them. Our home is in such exquisite order ; for dear M. has the housekeeping and everything is as orderly and noiseless and comfortable as can be. I hope she won't find it too much for her . . . the rooms are very pretty and comfortable. For my part I greatly fear I'm growing idle, I never seem hard worked now, and I never seem to do needlework or anything. I take it however very quietly, and don't mean to exert myself just now unless I need. . . . Ruskin was so kind when he heard I had been ill. He wrote to tell me to write and let him know whether I ought not to stop working for some time. . . .

February 7th.—We went to a Pre-Raph. Exhib., and saw the loveliest wood in Spring, full of harebells, a thorn tree casting a shadow over some of the flowers

---

[1] She was drawing for Ruskin and walking a great part of the way to Dulwich and back and standing there for five or six hours

K

February 27th, 1859.

EMILY TO HER SISTER MIRANDA.

. . . Ockey has just received another Veronese
to copy for her work at home. She has begun doing
it so beautifully. She is distressed at only working three hours on Dulwich days ; so she has begun
working in her spare time at the College, and by that
she will manage six hours *every* day. . . .

We are very regular with our reading three evenings
a week from nine to ten. Mama reads and Ockey and
I work. . . . I think Ockey is becoming converted to
Shakespeare. Dear Mama reads it so beautifully.

February, 1859.

MY DEAR MR. RUSKIN,

I thank you for your letter. " What has been
the matter ? " you ask. Physically, only this, I have
severe pains in walking distances that I used to manage
easily. But you would quite laugh if you saw me, to
hear me speak of want of strength.

But the truth is that, if enough is as good as a feast,
too little must be as bad as a famine ; and I feared that
I had just too little for my work   But everyone agrees
that it isn't fatigue that has made me ill, but responsibility and worry and want of change. It's my own
fault. I ought to take things more quietly and not
think that so very much depends on my deciding
wisely, and not nearly break my heart if things go
wrong for a time.

I think you're mistaken about the teaching, which
is hopeful and refreshing. As to sentiment there are
few people who have not stronger feelings than I have.
I assure you, I am considered *the* person in the family,

who is without imagination, poetry, feeling, affection. Good only to do a sum, carry a weight, go a long walk in the rain, or decide any difficult question about tangible things. You happen to know the other side of me. All *that's* kept in, that I may do my work ; and you don't know what a life of calculation and routine and steadiness mine is. I'm told that the best developed organ that I have is that of caution.

However, thank you, I hope I haven't "come to a smash." I'm gloriously well to-day, and I've done my full work ; perhaps I may manage five days at Dulwich after all. I think I wrote too seriously, and I beg your pardon. You can imagine the horror of being ill, to a person whose whole heart is in what they do, and who has never been obliged to calculate strength, but only time.

Never mind, I'm in glorious spirits now. The Salvator is going on well. I'm not the least afraid of anything. I will conscientiously take care of my health ; and, if I lose it then, I can't help it. I should like to leave them all comfortable, and learn to love them, and to live to do some drawing worth doing and to see the Alps ; and then I'd leave the world in God's hands who made it. In the meantime I'll order the dinners, and try to be quiet and sensible, if you will go on having patience with me. You'll see me rational and quiet some day. You mustn't expect a great deal of wisdom, in spite of my having begun with hard experiences so young. You know I'm only a little more than twenty ; and it takes a long time and a great deal to teach me anything. I assure you I try to be calm and sensible about all things, and if I say foolish things, I don't often do them, as our condition here shows. I never, but for two days in my life, felt so strongly about anything as to prevent my working and both times I think you would admit that I had sufficient cause. So neither feelings nor excitement do anyone very much harm

Most sincere thanks for your letter. You won't forget the out-of-the-way ways that I can help you. I will be sure not to overwork myself; and it would be a great pleasure to me to help you more.

I am,

Yours affectionately,

OCTAVIA HILL.

103, Milton Street, Dorset Square,
March 6th, 1859.

To MIRANDA.

. . . Ruskin has written me such a kind letter telling me to take as long a holiday as I like. . . . I am to do "such a difficult thing from Turner" at South Kensington soon. I was much puzzled, knowing *that* would prevent my beginning work till ten o'clock any day; so after much thought I meant to give up the College. I mentioned it to Miss Sterling, who seemed quite dismayed, said I must know they could not possibly supply my place; it was impossible; the whole flourishing or decay of the classes depended on whom they had in my place; my value could not be calculated in £. s d., or in any number of mechanical performances. So after calculating that I could get at the worst thirty or thirty-three hours' work weekly, I resolved to remain. I had no idea Miss Sterling cared so much about it. . . . To-morrow we have a grand tea-meeting at the Young Women's; Lord Shaftesbury will be there. . . . I draw at the College daily now. I have such nice expeditions to Dulwich, I go over the fields, and now the leaves are coming out it is most lovely.

Minnie and I never sing here now at all, we haven't time.

March 27th, 1859.

To MIRANDA.

I really could not write last Sunday. I am now writing in the lovely early morning, before setting off to go to the eight o'clock Communion service at Lincoln's Inn. We shall think of you both. . . . I have nearly finished the cloud I have been copying at Dulwich, and am anxiously expecting Ruskin's criticism on it. You know I am going to Normandy on or about the 16th; fortunately I do not yet realise it, except as a point before which certain works must be done and preparations made; but when I am fairly off I suppose I shall believe it; and not until then. I think you would be very much interested in some of my drawing pupils. One little boy, James, is my great favourite. He is ten years old, and tells me he has lived in Worcestershire until last September; but he is not like a country child, he is so intelligent. He has bright beautiful eyes, and I like to see his queer little figure in his pretty white blouse waiting for me at the door. He is so earnest and interested in his drawing, and works so very hard at it, it is quite delightful to teach him. Then there is a little girl, Annie, who is now so good and attentive. I like to see her dear pretty little head, bent down over her drawing. She has a beautifully fair skin, and when I find fault with her, all her face colours; and she has large blue eyes with long lashes and soft fair hair. She hasn't special talent

for drawing like James, but I like her personally so
much.   My women are progressing surely and steadily.
They're getting the right spirit and aims.   I take them
leaves and sprays to show them their beauties and teach
them their names.   . . I am reading the first volume
of "Modern Painters."   I thought you would like to
look at these pictures in the light of his words . . .
I am so very much wrapped up in my drawing I seem
to think of little else ; and yet I do manage somehow to
remember and dwell on a great deal besides.   I often
think of you both.

103, Milton Street,
April 3rd, 1859.

To Miranda.

I have been suffering with severe pains in my
back, but else I am quite well and I hope Normandy will
set me up in health.   It will seem very strange to you,
but I dread it.   I have been working so long, I don't
feel as if I knew how to stop.   I am afraid I shall be in
everyone's way, and do everything awkwardly and ill.
Mary [1] will forgive me however.   Dear Mary !   Mrs.
Harrison writes that she is looking forward to my visit
most eagerly ; and she thinks it will do her a great deal
of good.

You will know how thankful I am that we shall stay
in this dear little home   I need not tell you how kind
everyone is, you know they always were, but it seems to
me as if people even increased in kindness wherever
I go, from the old man who takes care of the pictures at
Dulwich, and brings me his first wallflowers and spray
of sweet-briar, to Mr. Maurice's ready advice ; poor and

---

[1] Miss Harrison, with whom she was to travel.

rich, learned and unlearned, old foe and new friend seem to help us ; when I am good and humble and walk home watching the sunset or rooks' nests against the night sky, I often repeat the Magnificat and think thankfully of all people's kindness   Sometimes I look back thro' the strange long years and trace the growth of things and people. Then, dears, I think of you both.

Via della Scala,
April 5th, 1859.

FLORENCE TO OCTAVIA.

You ask me if there is any danger for English at Florence. Everyone says that as long as the English minister is here, we are perfectly safe ; but, if England takes any decided part in the war, if the minister goes, and it is not safe for the English to remain, they will be ordered to go, and a certain time allowed them ; but people seem to think it very unlikely. . . . There is a great deal of excitement among the Italians, and a great deal of fine feeling. I heard an anecdote the other day which pleased me very much, particularly as it was about a Leghorn boatman, which I had always thought to be the most horrid class possible. There were two young men volunteers, who had to cross in a boat to go somewhere ; on landing, they gave the boatman 5 pauls ; he still held out his hand ; they thought he was not contented, and gave him a Napoleon ; he continued to hold out his hand, " What is it ? " they said.— " Take your money back," he replied. " I never have taken any from volunteers, and hope never to do so ; but if you would shake hands with me, I *should* like to shake hands with any one who is going to fight for Italy."

45, Great Ormond St.
April 16th, 1859.

EMILY TO HER SISTER MIRANDA.

You will be glad to hear that Ockey has really gone to Dieppe . . . It seemed a great pity to shorten her holiday by two days, because of her college work this afternoon, which I was fortunately able to take. . . . She saw Ruskin yesterday. She went to Dulwich and took her work from there to Denmark Hill. Ruskin had said in his letter that he had only a quarter of an hour to spare ; so of course she was careful to go away after a quarter of an hour ; but altho' her visit was so very short, it seems to have been very nice. Ruskin was very pleased with all her work. The cloud is to be left till his return in the autumn ; and O. is to draw other things at Dulwich, which Ruskin wants for the " Modern Painters." She is also to copy Turners at South Kensington, directly the pictures go there from Marlborough House ; so this summer she will have three days at Dulwich and three at Kensington.

In speaking of the cloud, O. said that it was all wrong ; why did Ruskin praise it ? And he said he knew it was wrong, but that it was very difficult indeed. Salvator had a great deal of power, and what he blamed him for was for misdirecting it.

The Veronese which O. had been doing at home, Ruskin was delighted with. He said he wanted to keep it, to show some people what girls could do. You may think what a state of excitement dear Ockey was in yesterday with seeing Ruskin and with the thought of her journey. . . . Her costume looked so pretty and suitable. Gertrude made her a present of such a

beautiful black silk dress, so nicely made that it has
disclosed to me, what I did not know before, that Ockey
has an extremely pretty figure.

27, Faubourg de la Barre, Dieppe.
April 18th, 1859.

To her Mother.

I am quietly, splendidly happy; everyone is
kindness itself. I had a very rough passage indeed,
but the wind was favourable and never shall I forget
the vanishing of the cliffs of England in a deep intense
blue mist of cloud, as the storms came on. I stayed on
deck all the six hours we were on board, standing on a
bench looking over the changing space of waters; the
fresh free wind blowing delightfully. The old look of
all things is enchanting; high flint walls are built up
the hills, out of which grow hundreds of wallflowers.
The large old church, with its time-eaten stones and
boldly carved gargoyles, delights me more than anything; its pinnacles rise up in the sunny air; and its
lovely flying buttresses against the blue sky, all crested
and crowned with wallflowers and ferns; and all the
grey stone mellowed and toned by thousands of gold
and silver lichens.

I hope you are all comfortable and have all that you
want. Tell Minnie that, though I gave her directions
about what she was to do, she is not to think that I
mean to bind her to do these things if circumstances
alter. She will use her own judgment.

I took a vehement determination to have nothing to
do with a short stout repulsive foreigner, who sat in
the railway carriage opposite to me, and who, to my
consternation, was most polite and attentive.

Tell Minnie this, it will amuse her.   He was a man
of immense curiosity ; and, I must in justice allow, he
gave me no cause whatever for my aversion to him
unless it were that, though he was willing enough to
discourse about France, Switzerland, etc., or open and
shut windows when he had nothing else to do, he took
good care to keep all his energies for himself at any
time of bustle ; and, after chattering nearly three hours
to me, directly we reached Dieppe he never even
looked round to see if I'd met my friends, or told or
showed me anything, though he knew the regulations
of the city well—which would have surprised me if
I'd trusted his nasty eye, and would have made me
feel desolate, if I hadn't been who I am, and in a state
of happy and independent resolution (which, perhaps, I
ought to give him credit for perceiving).   I was really
glad of his chatter at last, for I thought the voyage
long.

April 24th, 1859.

To EMILY

It has seemed to me so wonderful really to see
large spaces of almost uninhabited country ; they give
me a sense of loneliness and quiet, quite unequalled
and delightful.   We came to a large lonely château,
surrounded with firs, just as the sun sank behind a low
hill, towards which it looked.   The hill, the firs, the
birches opposite stood up dark against the sunset.   Oh !
it was so lovely !   That night (Thursday) we slept at
Houden in a room with great white-washed beams,
looking out over the yard.   We didn't sleep, we were
so cold ; and we got up only just in time for the
diligence to Rambouillet.   The country was flattish,

and very like Weybridge in soil and trees and plants; only the poplars were exquisitely graceful. I never knew what avenues were till now. They are lovely, and seem to me to be particularly interesting in being so orderly; yet the order was only discerned, the beauty only felt, from one spot. . . .

We could hardly bear the suspense of climbing the hill, on which it[1] stood. We wanted to see the carving, and could hardly have borne the time, but that we saw its spires. At last we stood at its foot, and saw the great thing towering in the sunlighted blue vault. We could not tear ourselves away from the rich old porches at the north end; tho' we were sinking with hunger;—one exclaiming, "Oh this is St. Peter— his key! look!" Another discovering, with delight, that there was the Virgin, or there was the Righteous Judgment. At last we went and had dinner, and on returning, entered.

I think you will be greatly amused to hear of our adventures, and all the people we have seen. I have to do all the talking to people, I'm getting quite ready to ask questions, and it increases the fun very much.[2] We have been in the most complete country and among quite rustic things; and I have laughed more since I came to France, than I have done for years, I think. I can't say that I think the people very nice; they are extremely polite, except the soldiers, but are wretched beggars. . . . I hope, dear people, that all goes on well with you, and that all is comfortable. Pray tell me if it is not.

---

[1] Chartres Cathedral

[2] Octavia had only learned a little French from her mother, and had had no practice in speaking except a *very* little to the refugee Poles, who worked at the Ladies' Guild, eight years previously.

Via della Scala,
Tuesday, April 24th, 1859.

FLORENCE TO OCTAVIA.

There is great excitement in the town ; a great many people about, and a great many gens d'armes. It seems the troops here want to go off to the war ; and the Grand Duke does not know what to do ; the soldiers are in great excitement, and it was said if he did not let them go there would be a revolution, or something or other to-day.

The poor old Hyena does not know what to do, he has too many keepers *I believe* the end will be he will abdicate, and leave the management of affairs to his sons. Many people are going · and still more are talking about it, because of the war and the unsettled state of affairs. I cannot say I feel at all afraid, I feel so perfectly safe. I am in the hands of One who knows what is best. In case of a revolution, everyone seems to think there would be no danger for private individuals. The Italians, especially the Florentines, are a good people, passionate, but not bloodthirsty and savage like the French. It would certainly be very shocking to be among scenes of violence ; and I do hope the *French* will not come here, on any excuse. Of course there is no knowing.

Wednesday, April 25th, 1859.

Well here we are without a government ! Old Hyena has decamped, and all the family. The accounts at present are rather confused ; but it seems the troops said they *would* go to the war, and it would be the worse for the Grand Duke if he did not let them ; so he was obliged to consent : but then the people wanted a

constitution, and he was to tell them his decision at the
Pitti Palace this afternoon; I do not know if he
appeared; but at six he was gone.   To-morrow General
something or other from the King of Sardinia comes.
You have no idea of the happy wild excitement the
town has been in all day; everywhere the Italian
colours, troops of men, with bright coloured flags, going
about the streets, crying "Viva l'Italia!" "Viva il re
Vittorio Emanucle!" "Viva l'independenza Italiana!";
at the cafés and hotels great flags up, and hardly a man
without a bow or feather or something of Italian
colours.   It is very impressive and exciting; there is
something so beautiful in *unity*, in men forgetting for a
time their petty cares and dislikes, enmities, passions,
interests, uniting in the great common feeling.   *Coach-
men* seem especially patriotic.   I have not seen *one*
without the Italian colours; perhaps it may be that,
being mezza festa, and many people wanting carriages,
in the present state of feeling a coachman who had the
colours would be preferred.   M. would call it very
wrong of me to be suspicious, and attribute bad motives
to people.

I cannot help pitying poor old Hyena; I hope he is
pretty comfortable.   No doubt he has been sending his
things off for a long time.   He would not have been
bad, if he had been a private gentleman, poor fellow;
he was out of his place, like a poor old dog having
to draw a great cart.   There were great placards up
saying that the Grand Duke had gone, and that
General —— from Piedmont would come, and in the
meanwhile begging of the people to behave properly,
and not to make any disturbance.   But they were as
peaceable as possible; seemed as if they would like
to shake hands with everyone.   I never saw such a

happy expression on the Florentine faces; it was quite pleasant; even the little dust-heap boys had the colours on their ragged hats. I wonder how it will all end. What a terrible thing war is. A thing for the ninth and not the nineteenth century. . . .

B.[1] told me to say we have had a most peaceable revolution; and there is no danger. It seems the Grand Duke first refused *everything* that was demanded; but afterwards said he would do *anything*; but the people would not accept them.

Milton Street,
May 12th, 1859.

OCTAVIA TO GERTRUDE.

I've enjoyed all. It is right to let people hear of joy in this world. We were so delighted with Mortain, where there are immense grey granite rocks, and soft green dells of richest grass, bright with millions of flowers. . . . I saw showers of rain in the distance changed to bright mist, as they were between me and the sun, and the mist swept over the waves of blue hills, and from higher still among wastes of moor desolate with wind, tho' bright with furze and cranberry, to which I climbed with hands and feet. I saw the sea, nine miles away, one golden blaze, on which the motionless grey rock of Mt. St Michel stood faint and clear and firm. I delighted in the diligences. We always took the coupé, and there we were almost always alone. . . . The view from the top of the castle of Mt. St. Michel was magnificent, rising suddenly 300 feet out of the flat sand. This granite rock is very impressive; it had a wonderful tendency to become deep purple and has a look of solemn solitude which is rather increased than

---

[1] Miss Emily Smith

diminished by its one neighbour Tombe-lame. . . .
Light and shadow passed quickly over the immense
space now turning the grey sand to dazzling yellow
white, now lighting a silver thread of some far-off,
before unnoticed, stream ; now leaving some space of
water the brightest green, or purest blue ; while far in
the distance a long white line tells of the approach of
the tide of dashing waves and rushing waters, and
of the deep unfathomed ocean.

1859.

To Miss Sterling.

My own impression about the Library is that all
books may be read rightly or idly ; that, if the pupils
are inclined to choose the latter course, they will not
read " instructive books " and will get no good from
wise ones. I should choose books by great authors,
whether fiction, poetry or science ; because they will
repay earnest and careful reading ; and any which seem
to me likely to be delightful, because they treat truth-
fully anything that ought to interest people. I would
suggest a few books ; but they will probably be those
which have taught me much, and which other people
have been interested in, more because they knew them
better than other books than because they were naturally
suited to them. Longfellow, Wordsworth, Scott, George
Herbert (too difficult ?), Tennyson, Mrs. Gaskell's
" Moorland Cottage," " Lizzie Leigh and other Tales "
(cutting out " Lizzie Leigh ") and " Mary Barton "
(perhaps). For the girls " Moral Courage " and
" Steadfast Gabriel," published by Chambers. The
" Ocean Child," " Birds and Flowers," and some of Miss
Martineau's books are full of right and interesting
thoughts. Miss Bremer's " Strife and Peace " and

" The Home " always seemed to me very beautiful books. If we might add one copy of the " Lectures on Great Men " to the Library and one of the " Feats on the Fiord " I think it would be well ; the former would be a most valuable addition, and the more often it was read the better. I don't know the price of Kingsley's " Good News " nor whether it be much read, or if not whether or no it would be worth while to get it for Mary Moore's benefit. I know very well the harm that would be done by any one reading these books only ; and I would give you a far more serious list if I were able, provided always that they were great books of their kind. None of the books that I have read of a more studious kind seem to me the least suited to them ; and of course you will remember that, where study is voluntary, it is begun because something has become living and interesting to us, as poets and writers of fiction often can make things, and people who love actual fact, like Ruskin and Carlyle, so seldom do. I don't mean to exclude the two last from amongst the poets ; but there is a great deal of simple fact and logic, untouched by feeling, in both. It often seems to me that, if we all had more of the poet nature, we should get people much more interested in all things near and far ; and then, if we loved truth more, they would go thro' much otherwise dry hard work to know facts. And one thing more, we mustn't forget that reading forms but a small portion of a working woman's life.

103, Milton St., Dorset Sq.,
May 29th, 1859.

To MIRANDA.

I have Ruskin's notes ready to send you by the next opportunity ; and they will tell you far more

about the exhibition than I can. I saw him on Monday
week; and he told me that he saw from all I had done
that I had the power to become all he wanted of me,
namely a thoroughly good copyist. He wants me to
learn to copy in water-colours the great Venetian
masters. He asked me if I could be quite happy
to do this, and told me he could be quite happy to
spend his life thus, if he were in circumstances to do it.
He then said to me that he had thought of setting me
this summer to copy things for Mod. Paint. ; but that,
as that would not teach me much, it would be better
for him, if I could be happy not to do any work which
was to be used by him at once ; to get a greater power.
" In the one case," he said, " at the end of six or eight
months I should have several useful drawings, but *you*
would be of little more use than now ; whereas, in the
other, you would have attained considerable power." . . .

I believe it will be a real comfort to Ruskin, to feel
that I am going to copy the pictures that he feels to be
so precious, and that are being so destroyed. You see
no one is taught to be humble enough to give up setting
down their own fancies, that they may set down facts ;
and they deify these fancies and notions and imaginations of their own hearts, till they really think it a
mean thing to represent nature, or other men's works
simply and faithfully : people hate copying because
they do not copy simply, I believe. One tells me that
when she copies, she is striving to appropriate the
excellence of the picture ; another that she is not
wanting to copy the picture, but to sketch nature ;
she therefore will go so far off that she cannot see it
clearly. . . . One lady assures me she should despise a
person who paints exactly from nature, as she should
a person who copies pictures : that Art has a higher

L

function than either to delight or to teach ; it has to
remind us of our glory before the fall.　Mr. D. informs
me that in the time I take to copy a foreground, he
would get the essence of every picture in the Dulwich
collection.　It sets me wondering what the essence of a
picture is, that it can be got at so rapidly ; and whether,
if it is worth much, it may not also be worth much
labour to gain it, and require much of the much talked
of thought and spirit of man ; whether faithful and
earnest work may not be the only fit preparation for
perception of truth in picture or in life ; whether
before we can understand, much less embody, noble
truth, it may not be necessary firmly to believe day
after day, when it is inconvenient, and when it is
agreeable, that there really is a truth and a God of
Truth, distinct from the imaginations of men's hearts ;
whether simplicity is not much more necessary than
excitement, even in art.　So that I think one has reason
to be very thankful to have been taught to look at real
lines and colours and sizes, which one may not misrepre-
sent ; which don't change when we change, nor depend
for their power or beauty on our thoughts about them.

Milton Street,
June 26th, 1859.

To FLORENCE.

　　. . . I quite trust Ruskin about his plans for
me ; only I wonder why he should speak *so* despisingly
of all copies, and yet set me to do them ; but some day
I shall understand it.　I haven't any doubt that Mrs.
Browning feels passionately and intensely ; but probably her passion is both controlled and concealed.　I
think her turning away, when you spoke of England,

simply showed she saw you were feeling a great deal, and she meant to help you to conceal it. Ruskin says of her that she is the only entirely perfect example of womanhood he knows. You will see her again? I wish it were possible, or would be of any use, to thank her thro' you for all she has taught me. You know sometimes as I walk to Dulwich in the scorching sun and am doubtful, or as tiredly I return up the New Road, the sunset or moonlight speaking less to me than haunting uncertain fears about those I love, I begin repeating "Isabel's Child" to myself. The wonderful power of contrast of wild storm without, and dream within, the glory of the child's vision, the almost awful infinity of thought in every verse, the perfect reality of the whole, are fresh delights to me, and yet I forget them all in the perfect rest of the last verse.

> "Oh you
> Earth's tender and impassioned few!
> Take courage to entrust your love
> To Him so named, Who guards above
> Its ends, and shall fulfil,
> Breaking the narrow prayers that may
> Befit your narrow hearts, away
> In His broad loving will."

And numbers of other lines and verses and poems teach me day by day. Well! you ask what I mean about not singing. Simply that I sing out of tune and haven't time to learn not to do so, having a bad ear; and so I think I'd better make up my mind to the fact.

Thanks, dearest, for all your sympathy; but don't be unhappy about me for any reason. I am so happy; and more so day by day. Miss Rogers returns this week. Mrs. Yarnall[1] has a little daughter.

---

[1] The wife of Mr. Ellis Yarnall and sister of Miss Harrison.

103, Milton Street,
July 24th, 1859.

To Miranda.

I want to ensure giving you some account of a speech of Kingsley's. An Association of ladies has been formed to help sanitary reform; they have published tracts, etc. Their first public meeting was held on Thursday at Willis's Rooms. Lord Shaftesbury made a speech as chairman, and urged ladies to attend to all the details of the question, as men could not. The legislative and theoretical was to be done only by them; the minute and much of the practical by ladies. Mr. Kingsley said· "After the excellent résumé of your intentions which we have just heard in your report, there seems nothing left for me to say, except to ask you to consider what will be the result, if you succeed in accomplishing your aims. Now just consider ! very great aims, very important aims—very dangerous aims some people would tell you that they are; nothing less than saving alive of some four out of every five (?) children that die annually. If you believe the teaching of many great political economists, who think that England is in great danger of being over-populated, and who advocate preventive checks on the increase of population, you had better pause and think whether it wouldn't be better on the whole, just to let the children die; whether we mayn't have difficulty in finding work and food for them But if you hold, as I confess I do, that a human being is precisely the most precious thing the earth can have; if you think that the English race is the very noblest race the world contains; that it has, moreover, a greater power of adapting itself to every kind of climate and mode of life than any other, except the old Roman, ever had ; that, besides all this, it is, on the whole, a young race, showing no signs of decay ; you will see that it is worth while for political economists to look on the map, and see that at least four-fifths of the world is uninhabited, and not cultivated even in the most ordinary way."

I ought to tell you that, before this he had shown us how he expected women principally to be of use, by saying that he looked upon this Association most thankfully because, for reasons which he wasn't going to explain here, he looked upon the legislative part of sanitary reform with something more like despair than ever. They were not reasons connected with this Government, or with any possible Government, but resulted from his consideration of the character of the individuals, into whose possession small houses were passing more and more. He was not going into the question here ; it would have to be attended to, but it seemed a great way off. Therefore he hoped women would go, not only to the occupiers, but to the possessors of the house, and influence people of " our own class." " And it's so easy," he said ; " there isn't a woman in this room who couldn't save the lives of four or five children within the next six months ; and this, without giving up one of your daily duties, one of your pleasures, one even of your frivolities, if you choose.

" You ask me what is more terrible than a field of battle, and I tell you outraged nature. Nature issues no protocols, nor warning notes to bid you be on your guard. Silently, and without stepping out of her way, by the same laws by which she makes the grass grow, she will kill and kill and kill and kill. And more than this, we have our courtesies of war and our chivalries of war ; a soldier will not kill an unarmed man, a woman or a child ; but nature has no pity   By an awful law, but for some blessed purpose, she is allowed to have none ; and she will strike alike the child in its cradle, the strong man or woman.   I wish to God someone had pictorial power to set before the mothers of England what that means—100,000 (?) preventable deaths !   Oh be in earnest.   Remember that, as a live dog is better than a dead lion, so one of those little children in the kennel out there is worth saving. Try to remember that it is not the will of our Father that one of these little ones should perish."

> 103, Milton St., Dorset Sq.,
> August 14th, 1859.

To EMILY

I hope you haven't thought me unkind, which indeed I haven't meant to be, but only very busy, as assuredly I do mean to be all my life long, if I can contrive it.   Thanks for your sweet and welcome letters. You will have received the French lines, without accents.   I will neither vouch for spelling nor grammar, but you must treat them as if they were exercises in Chapsall.

The event of my life since I last saw you has been, as you know, an expedition last Sunday of which I would wish to speak reasonably and calmly if I can succeed. Indeed it was glorious !   I never saw a better friendship than that between the men and him (Mr. Furnivall). I'm a little weary of thinking over the Sunday question, and yet—lest you cast me off utterly, and Mr. Durrant ceases to send me kind messages, and Mary be shocked indeed—I must tell you a little how we stand here about it   Of course I told Mr. F. that I should never

dream of entering into a plan involving habitual
absence from church; tho' I didn't tell him how much I
can sympathise with the spirit of some people who do.
He goes with the men every Sunday; they, some of them
at least, remain at home to go to church each alternate
Sunday; but that is no part of his plan. His own faith
is just as deep and living as ever; but he has evidently
been disappointed with the amount or kind of union the
church gives. They go regularly and very happily
all together; he is ever ready to sympathise and enter
into all kinds of happiness from the greatest to the
least. He showed me where they walked, he told me
when we were coming to the loveliest groups of trees,
when to the creek where they bathe, how the park looked
at moonlight, and how they all enjoyed it. He wants
us to join them in an excursion to Leith Hill or Box
Hill in September. I asked if it must be a Sunday, and
he thought much about it, but says the men can't get
holidays. He talked about Rossiter, told me he heard
one of my sisters was down with Durrant. He amused
me vastly by saying, "Hoets, whom you saw at Cambridge, wants people to go and see his wife and children,
as he's thinking of going to Australia." As if one
could go and call on Mrs. Hoets without introduction, on
such a plea! Oh, Minnie, but it was so glorious! As
we walked through the park at Richmond at night, we
sang hymns, "No! never part again," "There is a happy
land," "Here we suffer grief and pain." In the chorus of
the last, a number of working, or rather loitering, men in
Richmond joined very earnestly. We saw the pictures
at Hampton Court with which I was much pleased. The
men were very nice; they are so learned about flowers,
etc., so respectful, so thoroughly happy. Several of our
own pupils were there; everyone behaved well.

103, Milton Street, Dorset Square,
August 20th, 1859.

To Rev. F. D. Maurice.

I hope that you will, in your great kindness, forgive my troubling you by asking whether you can give me a few words of advice on questions that are troubling me practically very much indeed.

1st. I have been very much impressed by the good and joy Mr. Furnivall's Sunday excursions seem to be giving to the men and to their wives, sisters, and friends, who from time to time accompany them. I have rarely seen a more respectful, intelligent, and happy party than they. Of course I shouldn't approve of members of the Church missing service habitually; but that doesn't seem to me to be at all necessary to the plan. I know some people, to whom such a refreshment after their week's work would be an inestimable good. It would give me a great delight to accept invitations for them; and have this opportunity of seeing them, and helping them; nor can I see any rule which can make it right for me to go and see my friends on Sunday, or go into the country, and yet makes it wrong for *them* to go all together. Ought I to give up my only day for seeing relations and friends? I shouldn't have hesitated about it, but that I imagine, perhaps incorrectly, that you disapprove of those excursions. May I ask if it is so? I have been trying to enter into the full purpose of Sunday, as you told me, quite giving up work, and, as you told me, everything that was an effort (except writing to my sisters, which ought to be none), and I do at last understand Sunday as a duty as well as privilege; but is not refreshment by seeing friends and change of scene right?

I wanted to ask two still more difficult questions but really ought not to trouble you more. Oh that you were in London that I might ask you! No! I am glad you are resting. And truly too, I don't depend on your advice, but I know our Father has thousands of ways to teach me, if only my stubborn will and foolish fancies don't blind me.

God bless you all. I hope Mrs. Maurice is better. Please don't answer if you are busy or tired. Is it really difficult to tell what is right? Or is it only that one will not see the truth? Or does one not pray trustfully enough?

The classes are going on steadily and well. I am very well too; and dear Mama and Minnie are having happy holidays. I am all alone.

OCTAVIA TO REV. F. D. MAURICE.

I cannot attempt to express the thankfulness I feel for your kindness in answering my letter, perhaps most of all for the first words, "You should never apologise for asking my opinion," because it seems as if it might be understood to have reference to our baptism; and although I quite feel the help you would give to everyone to be the most precious, and don't want any special right to more than you would give to others, yet I often feel as if I very much wanted to be sure that I was not wrong in asking you questions about our own life, which I do not feel wise enough, or old enough, to decide myself, and which I cannot trust, though I sometimes do leave, to the decision of others. It is not about questions referring to faith that I feel this most. I know always about this to Whom I can go, and thank God! for some years (until this question of Sunday) have felt His help all sufficient; and it has been, except for my own sin and weakness, but one long blessed revelation of His love, of the meaning of prayer and sacraments. It was not about them that I feel as if I wanted any more help than I have, seldom now (tho' most deeply when I feel it at all) about home-life; for we have learnt a good deal now about where we have been wrong about it; it is principally about the application of principles to other social questions; it is all very well for people to tell me not to trouble myself about them, but they are involved in every action of daily life. Earnest thought, life itself, and some words of your own and others, for whom I have a great respect, have led me to convictions which, as I say, would lead me to actions differing widely from yours, and, I suppose, proceeding from some difference in principle. Sometimes I act for a little while on my own convictions, and am very happy, till the recollection of how wrong I was, and how sure I was about other things which you have taught me, principally by advising my giving up a course of action and adopting another, or some partial failure, make me think I am arrogant and self-willed; and yet when I take the other course I am oppressed with a sense of neglected duties, fear of my own honesty, and confusion about how far I ought to trust people, and you specially. This produces inconsistency in action; tho', on the whole, I adopt the latter course for the questions relating principally to work at the College; I feel my position there implies very complete obedience. When I can see you (but that is so seldom now), I so try (indeed I try always) to understand the grounds on which you act; and I own myself fairly puzzled It was to this I referred.

Your letter has shown me a much deeper meaning in
Sunday than I had ever perceived in it; and I see the
difficulty about the excursions very clearly, as not
speaking to people as spiritual beings, called to full rest
in trust in God : I am not sure that I do not think that,
after the Church service has done this, the rest of the
day would not be better passed among God's works in
the country, and in friendly intercourse ; but I am less
sure of having entered into the teaching of the Bible on
the subject, than of setting a sufficient value on mere
cessation from toil and recreation ; and so I shall
decidedly give up these excursions, till I have thought
more about them.   And even then I hope I am not
wrong in feeling that I do not think, especially as
College people are concerned, I could feel it right to go
to them, when you feel as you do about it.

I am afraid this letter will give you the impression
that I am trusting far too much to you, far too little in
God ; tho' I have stated very frankly (it reads to me
almost unkindly), how fears that you may be wrong
about some things mingle with my sure knowledge how
wonderfully you have been proved right about others.
I accept both reproaches.   I am often tempted to trust
too much to you ; not, I think, to believe your wisdom,
and gentleness, and patience, and faith to be greater
than they are, but to think too much that I was to
trust to them in you, instead of in God, because I have
not felt Him to be an ever-present guide, not only into
the mysteries of His own Love, not only into the meaning of past wants, but into the grounds of all right and
all wise action.   This and this only has confused me ; all
has been ordered to teach me, all to strengthen me ; and
I alone am wrong.   Only with these thoughts others
mingle ; I must not, in order to recover faith in a

Director, give up the direction He places in my way ; I
must not mistake self-will for conscience, nor impatience
for honesty.   No one on earth can distinguish them for
me ; but He will.   It so often seems to me as if two
different courses of action were right or might be right ;
and this is what puzzles me, even tho' it is a blessing
as binding me to people of widely different opinions.
Thank you once more, dear Sir, for all teaching, given
now and before.

(Undated, probably August, 1859.)

To Miranda.

Thanks for your sweet letter received yesterday.
What have I been thinking and feeling about ?   Dear
me, that is a question.   Well, dear, of extra things, first
and foremost of a delightful dance Mr. Furnivall gave
to his friends among the men and their friends, and to
which he invited me.   I went with Louisa [1] and
Henrietta, [2] and a glorious evening we had !   Before
that, I had been one of their Sunday excursions with
them. . . .   I received, however, a letter from Mr.
Maurice in answer to my enquiries (oh such a beautiful
letter !), which makes me feel I have much to learn about
Sunday, and at any rate I could not go with College
people, his feeling being so strong on the subject,
I think.   This has been, as you may imagine, a great
effort to me ; for really my day refreshed me so entirely ;
and I was so happy.   Do you know perhaps I'm going
down to Godmanchester (where Cromwell was born) to
visit a new friend, Miss Baumgartner, during my next
holidays.

[1] One of the girls who made toys
[2] The daughter of a former nurse.

103, Milton Street,
September 11th, 1859.

To MIRANDA.

. . . . I have just begun the most wonderful piece of drapery, black and gold, copied from a Rubens at Dulwich. Neither Jupiter, nor any of my other Dulwich work, is finished ; they are waiting for Ruskin. . . . . Last night I had the glorious delight of looking over a sketch book of his, which Mr. Ward brought to 'Margy's. It was called " Notes by the Wayside, 1845–46." The things were exquisite ; some of Florence specially interested me of course. The original coloured sketches of the two engravings of sunset clouds behind mountains, and St. George of the Seaweed at Venice, which are published in the " Modern Painters," were there too. Oh so lovely !—Miss Sterling is now in Ireland. I begin to long dreadfully for their return. . . . While Gertrude is in Scotland, I have the use of her Library subscription. I have been revelling in Oliver Cromwell, and Ludlow's " India," and look forward to several delightful books, if only I can get a little time. . . . My drawing class for the Portman Hall children is going on so very well. I have had it all alone since July. Oh ! and they begin to draw so well ! T. is I think very pleased. I am teaching Mrs. W. and a new lady, illumination ; that is to say they come and draw here, while I am at work, two hours weekly. I've been writing an article for the College Magazine, at Mr. Litchfield's request.

103, Milton Street,
September 25th, 1859.

To MIRANDA.

Decidedly take lessons from Kraus. . . As to sending money home, dearest, don't think of it ; we have

ample, as my balance sheet next week will show you ;
spend it in any way that will be most useful to you in
promoting health, rest, and knowledge ; we are getting,
one way, or another, an immense amount of change and
rest here, and I earnestly hope you will do the same to
the best of your power. . . . I do indeed sympathise
with you about church ; it is a quite inexpressible
blessing, and must be specially so to you. . . . I have
read Tennyson's "Idylls of the King." I consider
the whole book glorified by Arthur's last speech to
Guenevere   Tennyson takes the view that, if she had
been pure and worked with Arthur, his noble efforts
and reforms would have lived and triumphed.   He goes
away to fight his best knight, all his hopes and
successes blighted.   I always did like Launcelot, in
spite of everything ; and I do still.   There is a lovely
character too, called Enid   But the whole book is
painfully impressed on my mind, as written by a man,
so vividly and perpetually conscious of sensuality, tho'
of so much that is noble ; but I should love to possess
the book.   Oh it is so real !   I am reading, too,
Carlyle's "Cromwell" with intensest interest.   Mama[1]
is so very very happy in her life, it is quite delightful.
I have answered your question briefly, because I'm so
sure of the answer. . . . We want to see that we and
our work are not essential to the world ; that, if we do
our work imperfectly, so that we love Him, that is
what He asks.   He can save and teach people without us.
. . . . . My own dearest, God will lead us all, will
He not ?   We know how our blunders of judgment,
and want of power can never hinder His work ; that
He asks us, not for great works, but self-forgetting
peaceful hearts ; that our wisdom at best can fathom

[1] She was teaching all day.

little of His purposes ; but that He reigns and sends His spirit to us. I fancy, if we saw God working and resting, instead of our own working, our faces would shine like that of Moses ; and we should care very little that we could not speak, but would trust Him to fill us with such love that it would breathe in all we did.

October 10th, 1859.

To MIRANDA.

I have a good deal to tell you to-day. On Saturday I saw Ruskin. I think he was very well satisfied with my work, tho' it was none of it finished, and none of it right ; still it was very satisfactory to me to find that it had none of the faults my work had last year, i.e., not being dark enough, nor massed enough. I returned, in spite of all this, in a horrid state of wretchedness ; but this I have got over now, as I will tell you. . . .

I believe what made me so wretched was the sudden vivid thought of how very little pleasure I could ever give Ruskin, even by the most conscientious work ; that one stanza of Tennyson's was better to him, would teach more that he wanted to teach, than all my life's work. I had thought that, by earnestness and humility, and sacrifice of other works and thoughts, I might really help him considerably. I have no doubt that an immense deal of thought of self is mixed with this notion ; but it has its root deeper than that ; and now I come to think over all Ruskin said, I see no reason to alter my conviction that I can do this work. The fact is, if one sits down to make a plan, it is often foolish and impracticable ; but the plans life reveals to us, which are unfolded to us, and which we are hardly conscious of,—these, I think, are usually God's plans, and He helps us to carry them out. If this is not what He means me to do, may He, for He alone can, help me to give it up; but if, as now I think, He has been prepaing me by multitudes of things, childhood in the country, girlhood in town, hard work, most precious and direct teaching of drawing, sympathy with people round, affection for and gratitude to Ruskin, and an ever deepening admiration for him, and knowledge of his plans,—if, I say, God has been preparing me by this, and much more, first to love Nature and Art, second, to care that all should love Nature and Art, and third to see how to help them to do so; will He not too give me humility to take the place He ordains for me in this great work, tho' it be the lowest of all,— faith to believe I can help, and oh such energy and earnestness? I am very happy indeed now. . . . Ruskin was particularly pleased with the bull's head. . . . I believe one of the things that made me so unhappy on Saturday was that I had been reading the "Political Economy of Art"; and I could not help thinking of the passage about the great man, beginning, "He can be kind to you, but you can never more be kind to him." And then too I had wanted to take home a very good account to dearest Mama and Minnie; and he did not criticise it altogether; and in spite of all the praise he gave it, I felt how miserably incomplete it was But I am sure I have progressed; and perhaps the dissatisfaction is also a gain. But this they could not feel, and all the way home, and even now, I can't help crying at the thought of it; and the less they show they're disappointed, the more I feel it; and sometimes Mama seems to think Ruskin capricious; and I am certain he is not. Well it is all over now.

Chivery, near Tring,
October 10th, 1859.

To HARRIET, A FORMER TOY-WORKER.

I had been thinking a good deal of our conversation about teaching. . . . I will just tell you a very little what I think of it,—I believe most people render their position a blessing, or otherwise, themselves good or wretched ; and that the post becomes one of interest and usefulness, according to the estimate of it held by her who occupies it ; in fact that all work done as routine without love, whether it be a queen's or a chimney-sweep's, is quite despicable, and *all* done with love most honourable. I know some works have greater responsibilities, and call for higher, or rather more, powers ; some works (writing poems for instance) are in themselves greater ; but I believe the noblest faculties of every human being are called for in her work. Conscientiousness — for instance — is wanted everywhere. Much intellect is not. But that which equalises the dignity of various works is, that all, or all that I can think of, are exercised either with people or for people. And people, being God's children, may be taught and influenced, unconsciously often to themselves, by every part of those round them. I believe this teaching to be the *most* precious part of all our lives. Those of us who are called to be teachers may, I believe, thank God that it is so with them so clearly, so definitely ; but I often think that the influence over us by those who are not definitely set to teach us is the most powerful. Love and mercy and gentleness and humility and thoughtfulness each of us needs equally in her work. And, as I said at first, people give us the work they find we can do. A nurse may wash and

M

dress children for many years in love and faithfulness ; but she can do more besides, sometimes. She can tell them stories and teach them, and in a thousand ways call out their powers. No one expects this in a nurse, because they cannot get it ; but once give it them, and you raise your position, probably in their eyes, at any rate in our Father's. We are not half ambitious enough ; we struggle for little honours, seldom for the far more difficult and far nobler ones. . . .

With most affectionate wishes for your future, dear, and love to Sarah and yourself, and in remembrance of old days, I am

Ever your loving friend,
OCTAVIA HILL.

I don't know when I felt so proudly pleased as when I gathered that you were trying to be cheerful and useful in your present work.

Godmanchester,
October 15th, 1859.

To EMILY.

Here I am, all safe and well. This is the loveliest, dearest old house. I never was in such a one before. Miss Baumgartner met me at the station, and we walked here. The house stands in a long old street, almost opposite the church. It is (the house is) old red brick, not very pretty, but quite old. The dining room is like a grand old hall ; the staircase, which is in the centre of the house, faces it, and is separated from it by three Gothic doors ; low steps, broad banisters, and a kind of gallery landing make it feel quite ancient ; the hall is hung with old pictures. The garden is not large, it consists of a glorious lawn of smooth bright green grass, a few brilliant flower borders, and a long bright old brick wall, a small cedar on the lawn ; but it is bounded at the bottom by the Ouse, a deep clear stream, across which is a pretty bridge leading to an embowered island, belonging to this house ; a water mill is above ; below the view of Hinchinbrook where Cromwell's uncle lived. The boat-house contains several boats ; one Miss B. pointed out to me as hers. She will teach me to row. She is very kind and interesting ; her mother, a nice old lady of whom I am rather afraid and rather fond. Her father very old. Her brother very fond of flowers, very nice, I think. They have lived here for years It is very nice.

103, Milton Street, Dorset Square,
October 23rd, 1859.

To Miranda.

Your letter of delight about the music lessons gives me great pleasure. I received it one morning in a large wood-panelled dining-room, looking out to a smooth field set with large elms. I had just entered the room thro' one of three Gothic doors, after descending a low-stepped staircase with massive oaken banisters, into a large wood-panelled hall hung with old pictures. Just as I had finished your note, an old lady entered by another door, whom you would not at all have known, if you had been watching in a magic mirror ; a tall stately old lady dressed all in black, with a quick step and very kind face, holding in one hand a basket of keys, and in the other some scented-leaved verbena and heliotrope, some of which she gave to me ; and some was laid on the bright breakfast table for someone who had not yet arrived. The door opened, and there came in

with springing step, and upright carriage, someone whom
you would have felt inclined now to call girl—now
woman. Her cheerfulness, and the air of one who has
long been the youngest of the house, and the darling of
many brothers, as well as of father and mother,—her
slight figure,—all seemed to give her the first name ; but
when you looked at her, there were older lines about her
face that made you say " 30 " ; and, as you knew the
face better, you would trace, under all that glad manner,
lines of deeply felt suffering ; and certain looks in the
deep softness of her grey eyes,—a certain calmness, even
in her enthusiasm, would have made you feel that the
best of womanhood and of girlhood were combined in
her　I suppose you have guessed long ago that I am
describing Emma Baumgartner, my new and very dear
friend. As I went down there a perfect stranger, having
only seen her twice, and her mother once, knowing
nothing about who they were, and we had no mutual
friends, we had to be specially communicative ; and so, I
suppose, our friendship sprang up more quickly than
otherwise it could have done. Then, except at meals,
we were quite alone, drawing, walking, rowing or resting.
But the principal thing that drew us together was my
delight in finding in her a great nobleness of judgment
and of sympathy, right views about work, and all
religious and social questions ; and I think she found a
great pleasure in my companionship. We taught her
night-school for men and boys together. We attended
her men's reading-room. We taught in the Sunday
school. We drew. We talked of Ruskin and Mr.
Maurice, as well as of her brothers, my sisters, architecture, and all kinds of things. I have had a delightful
visit , and she says she does not know when she has
enjoyed a week so much. She has no friends in London

now, and greatly longs to come up in the spring, to see the exhibitions, or earlier in order to see Ruskin.

When you can, will you look carefully at the tracery of the head window of the Campanile of Giotto at Florence, if you have an opportunity. I have the most splendid engraving by me in the "Seven Lamps." Also an arch from the façade of the Church of San Michele at Lucca. How you would delight in the book! I have not yet read it. He says the Gothic of Verona is far nobler than that of Venice, and that of Florence nobler than that of Verona. He says, that, in Italian traceries the whole proportion and power of the design is made to depend upon the dark forms.

November 20th, 1859.

To MIRANDA.

Thanks for your sweet sympathetic letter. I think Ruskin is right. First, about work in general, I think he wishes us to perceive the wide difference between that which shows moral rightness in the worker, and that which shows peculiar intellectual and other greatness. Then as to *my* work, Ruskin has set me to one which he believes to be the right training for an artist; and he would be glad that at present I did not look beyond it; first, because one must be contented to do a work before one can do it, and secondly, because he would then be sure I loved art, not only my own ambitious notions; in addition to which he really longs to have things well copied. This is what I think on the subject; but your letter was very delightful, dearest. . . .

Dearest Andy, how heartily I wish you all success in your work. It is just a year to-day since that terrible parting at London Bridge—a year not lost to any of us. I think we can feel something at least has been done, since then   We feel a little stronger, surer, better, fuller of hope, more able to bear patiently any shock or storm that may come. .   .

My love to little Florence, for whose dear sake I am kind to every dog and cat I see, and even love them a little   I protected a little cat from some teasing children on Tuesday, by nursing her for an hour !

November 21st, 1859.

To Miss Baumgartner.

You must not (in charity please, you must not) contrast your letters with mine.   Depend on it, those whose minds are most healthily toned write, more often, true and sympathetic accounts of facts than about faiths, principles and theories.   It is so invigorating to be brought in contact rather with God's facts than with men's fancies; and, though the question " What do all these things mean?" " What should they teach us?" is indeed a deeper one than " What are they?" yet one is too apt, if one asks the question too often, to lose sight of the facts in their simple existence; to see only their relation to men, at last only to oneself.

I spent an hour last Tuesday evening at the house of one of my pupils (W.M. College pupils).   Her mother had begged that I would go.   They live at the very top of a house near one of the London markets, rather a wretched neighbourhood.   Sarah, my pupil, a quiet girl of fourteen, walked with me   Her mother, prettily dressed, opened the door, carrying in her arms the baby, dressed in its little white frock, and coral fastening its little shoes. I had never been there before; and I was conducted up the dark staircase to the attics. Here I saw by the furniture that they had seen " better days." One tiny room was their sitting room, comfortably furnished; a bright clean fire, tea set, and the children's grandmother sitting primly attired to receive me. All this I saw, and it made me understand something more of the people at once. It would have done anyone's heart good to see the self-forgetfulness of these people; the five tiny little girls, the eldest only seven, each delighted to give place to one another; and as to Sarah, who is their half-sister, it was lovely to see how quietly she served everyone. They are earnest High-Church people; the baby is called Amy Herbert, after Miss Sewell's heroine, and also because Mrs. —— is so fond of George Herbert's poems. The tiny children all sang some hymns, " O let us be joyful," and others.

Sarah comes to my drawing class, and we had much talk about her lessons. Her mother means to read aloud to her these winter evenings, while she draws; and then she will read while her mother works. It is a brave faithful little home, and such as one loves to come upon; and I was much touched by their hospitable cordial reception of me. I thought you would like to hear thus much.

103, Milton Street, Dorset Square,
November 27th, 1859.

To Miss Baumgartner.

Mrs. Browning has taught me so very much, or rather has been such a friend to me, saying precisely what I wanted to hear (first expressing my own feelings so completely, and then carrying me on to the only hopes and thoughts that can satisfy one at such times), that it seems to me as if I knew her, and that she really had suffered and thought with me. . . .

Why is entering into other people's feelings, even sad, so restful ? Is it not because we are meant to bear one another's burdens ? So I've been reading authors who don't echo my own feelings so much, and trying more than ever to understand all kinds of people. . . .

I always feel so solemnly about my own birthday ; . . . . Your way of spending yours makes me ashamed, for . .   in the evening we shall have friends, who are far from being among the sad and poor. . . . I never have seen any but specially nice people on my birthday.

On the 5th, I shall take my drawing class to South Kensington which I shall consider also a kind of cele-bration of my birthday. About Arthur, I believe that the duty of a wife, even of a friend, is, with regard to a man's work, so terribly misunderstood. Mr. Ludlow says, " He sacrificed his wife to his Round Table," not seeing that, as he loved her, had she been anything worthy of the name of wife, her highest joy and duty should have been to work for it with him ; and that it was his great glory that he expected this of her. . . . And this is true, in part, of all relations and friends, the glory of each is not in demanding attention, but in love, sympathetic fellow-work, ready sympathy. . . .

Tried by the precious test of facts near home, I say my theory is right ; and I think you, of all people, believe it.

December 5th, 1859.

To MARGARET HOWITT.

Dear Miranda is deeply interested in her little Italian pupils, and longs much for nice English stories for them. She just wrote to beg us to send her all that remained of our childhood's stock. I never read them now ; they would be of real use there ; and I conquered my selfishness at last ; but I couldn't help a great pain in packing the dear books which Mrs. Howitt had given me so long ago I remember well the night she gave me " Fireside Verses," and the many many happy hours it gave us as children. And now the books are gone, to do a little more blessed work ; but I have instructed Miranda to bring them carefully back with her.

Milton Street,
December 5th, 1859.

To MISS BAUMGARTNER.

I am glad you have redeemed your birthday from melancholy, and consecrated it to charity, which, after all, is one of the most surely joyous things. I must read the St. Andrew's Day carefully ; but now I must give you an account of *my* birthday. It was a cold, bright day. I woke late ; it was post time as I left my room, no letters ; time went on, no letters. I was fairly disappointed ; but, half an hour too late, owing to frost, your letter and one from Miss Harris arrived. I was leaving the house for Dulwich, and so read them in the omnibus with thankful delight. I enjoyed my walk much ; the snow lay white on the long finger-like boughs of Ruskin's cedar, as I passed, and prayed God's blessing might rest on the house. I worked well, and then went to the College and did the same, thinking of many things. Dear Miss Sterling was most kind, and

allowed me to leave early. When I reached home thro'
long damp-aired gas-lighted windy streets, all looked
bright and warm. Gertrude had arrived bringing
presents,—one a pair of quaint, delightful, old silver
bracelets from an old lady, a friend of grandpapa's,
whom I had never seen, but who has heard of me.
When I entered the room I was amazed. It was
brightly lighted, and decorated with ivy a friend had
sent; another dear old lady had herself gathered me
the last roses and lauristinus, myrtle leaves and
chrysanthemums from her garden. One long table
was set for tea, but the other was covered with
presents. Mary Harris had sent me the "Idylls" and
the "Two Paths." One dear lady, whom I have never
seen but often written to (Mrs. Robins), had sent eleven
volumes of poems—Scott (who will be very valuable
to me) and Crabbe whom I don't yet know. I tell you
of the books, because they are such very precious things
to possess . . Miss Rogers read us the loveliest Arab
story. Gertrude, Minnie, and I sang, and all my best
available friends were here, and were delighted to make
one another's acquaintance. I was proudly delighted
with them all, and most humbly delighted by all their
kindness which I felt I had so very little deserved. It
was almost too much to bear. Once or twice I dwelt
thankfully on the thought that, except Mr. Maurice,
who was ill, I had seen or heard from everyone I cared
for specially, except Ruskin. When nearly everyone
had left, Gertrude rushed upstairs, handed me a parcel
saying, "Someone thinks it's from Mr. Ruskin." "No,"
I said quietly, looking at the unformed handwriting.
"Then what made the servant say so?" I sat down
on the stairs and tore it open. It was! I enclose his
letter, which specially pleased me, for its sympathy with

my work among people. The books are by Souvestre, an author whom I love already, from the little I know of him. It was very sweetly thoughtful of Ruskin to remember me. . . . Do you know the old Spanish proverb, "To him that watches, everything is revealed." It certainly is true ; and how glorious it is to gaze backward upon the past, which, be it ever so dark, is fact and therefore God-permitted. And as one gazes one sees gradually the unbroken way in which our Father leads us towards Him, unbroken save by our own rebellious wills and by many sharp rocks which seemed hindrances ; but now we see that they bridged for us many a dark gulf.

I have been reading the most beautiful book called " The Missing Link " It is an account of the Bible women of whom you may have heard. They are quite poor women, sent by ladies to sell Bibles, to teach and help and cheer the very poorest people. It is wonderful what they have done, and what lovely things they have seen. They have reached the very lowest class, seen and helped them in their homes. They give nothing away, but get people to buy beds and clothes, for which they pay gradually. They encourage women to take a pride in keeping their children and homes neat ; and, living among them, can do so much. Mr. and Mrs. Maurice are so deeply interested in the plan, that they have lent me the book, to see if we cannot help at all.

December 10th, 1859.

EMILY TO MIRANDA.

You cannot think how affectionately everyone at the Shaws[1] took leave of Mama, and how sorry

---

[1] Miranda's former pupils, whom Mrs. Hill was teaching

Emily and Willy were to lose their lessons   Willie
said, " Well, Baby, what *shall* we do without lessings ?
It's horrid ! "

103, Milton Street,
December 18th, 1859.

To Miss Baumgartner.

. .   Last night we had the second practice of
our men's and women's advanced singing class at the
College.   It was very delightful ; the mere singing
was *that ;* and then it was nearly the first united thing
we have had, and so full of promise.   When I contrasted the nervous shamefaced way our ladies behaved,
seeming to think it would kill them if they happened
to open the door of a room where there were only men,
etc., etc., with the natural, free noble way in which you
work among them, I was proud of you, and thankful
too. . . .

We go down to Grandpapa's at Weybridge.   But
many other things are Christmas celebrations too.   On
the 28th, I am to be at a " Musical Evening " at the Boys'
Home, where are about 50 destitute boys.   The singing
will delight them, I've no doubt.   Then on the 5th
we shall have a social party at the College ; Mr. Maurice
and Mr. Hughes will be there and many other good
and great people   Have you ever read Crabbe's life ?
I think nothing can be nobler than Burke's behaviour ;
and how fine Crabbe's letter to him is !

The Pines, Weybridge,
Christmas Day, 1859.

To Miranda.

. . . I am particularly happy about my work.
Ruskin is *so* pleased with it all.   My four Dulwich

DR. SOUTHWOOD SMITH.
Grandfather of Octavia Hill.

From a Chalk Drawing by Margaret Gillies.

drawings are now right and ready for use; in fact he wants them at once that they may be put into the hands of the engraver. I am to do four more, small, but, Ruskin says, difficult examples of inferior work— and one bit from Turner. . . I had a quite delicious hour and a quarter at Ruskin's on Friday. We talked on many interesting subjects. . . .

Snowball fell down yesterday when I was riding him. Mama and Minnie were being driven by Gertrude just behind. If anyone else had been driving, I must have been run over; but G., with her grand calmness and power, stopped Ariel at once, turning her to one side. I am only shaken, not hurt at all. I was not thrown, but fell with Snowball.

Christmas, 1859.

To MISS BAUMGARTNER.

On Friday I was shown into Ruskin's study. One window had the shutters shut; the table was covered with books and papers; the fire burned brightly; at one window Ruskin sat drawing from a Turner, all squared over that it might be reduced With his own exquisite elegance and ease, which enables him to do the oddest things in a way that one can't feel rude, instead of rising, he threw himself back in his chair and shook hands with me, as I stood behind; then he rose and giving me his chair walked to the fire—and then, Emma, he produced the loveliest drawings of boughs of oak to show me, one beautifully fore- shortened, and explained the growth of it to me; how every leaf sends down a little rib that thickens the stems —how the leaves grow in spirals of five. He got a bit, and showed me the section. They were lovely. Then he told me that he wanted me to do an example of *good* work for " Modern Painters," one he had meant to do himself but for which he will not now have time—a bit of the fir boughs in Turner's " Crossing the Brook," now at South Kensington.

I told him about you, about my visit, about your work among the men—how lovely I thought it, and how fresh. He was very much pleased, and told me about the daughter of a friend of his, who does much the same—to whom it seems he has sent several of my drawings for her men to use.

We got at last upon the subject of the education of working women; and he asked much about it, seemed greatly interested   I told him many anecdotes, and something of what I said in my article on the subject. He was much interested about the question of fiction. He hopes to publish the fifth volume in the spring.   I was with him an hour and a quarter.   When I came away he said, " We'd quite a nice chat "; he " wasn't so horridly busy as usual."

January 8th, 1860.

To MISS BAUMGARTNER.

In a description of a gathering at the Working Men's College she says · " I was much interested in an earnest young countryman of the name of Cooke, who had presented a collection of butterflies and moths, etc., to the College.   As every scrap of natural history is eagerly learnt by me, to be repeated wherever I go, and lovingly remembered, I got him to tell me some of their names and habits.   . .

" I was delighted to hear Mr. Dickinson (whose portrait of Mr. Maurice you may remember) praising Mr. Ward's drawings. .   It was very nice to see old faces back again and to feel as if I never should have done

shaking hands. . . . its joy consisted so much in the
momentary grasp of a hand, in the sudden sight of a
face which owed all its preciousness to the thought
of natures I had learnt to know in sad moments or
hard working days. . . . Does it not seem to you one
of the main things we long for in heaven that every
strong affection for visible things will have some
answer? . . . I often feel so sure that the love of
places, employments, books, as well as people, is not
to perish, but to be justified."

January 29th, 1860.

To MISS BAUMGARTNER.

Yesterday I saw Ruskin. "Do you come by
appointment?" the servant asked me, "because Mr.
Ruskin said he would see no one." "Mr. Ruskin fixed
the day, I named the hour; but if he is busy ——." The
servant, however, seemed sure that I was to be admitted, and I was shown into the study, where Ruskin
greeted me with the words, "I'm very glad to see
you." I saw he was ill, and found he had been suffering from toothache, and awake all night. I begged
him, therefore, not to attend to my work. However
he would do it. I shall not readily forget the afternoon. He was not busy, and showed me the loveliest
things, exquisite copies of illuminations, wonderful
sketches by Mr. Bunney (one of his College pupils),
sketches which Ruskin said he had seen nothing like
them except Turner. . . . And then Ruskin showed
me two of Turner's loveliest small drawings, one of
Solomon's pools, and beyond their square basins, and
the battlements, amidst which the light gleamed, the
sun was setting; and clouds gathered about him,
because, Ruskin said, the clouds gathered about

Solomon's wisdom. Oh that sky palpitating with colour, changing on every thousandth inch!

Ruskin asked me if I'd been reading anything lately; and we talked about Tennyson. I said he was so very sad. He said, " You see far more to make you sad than I do; but I don't think Tennyson a bit too sad. I haven't found that he sees far enough." " He knows, however," Ruskin said, " how far he does see, and that is more than other people do." I told him how years ago Tennyson's words had distressed me, because I believed that good was then and always, and that we it is who mar it all; I forgot that what had distressed me most of all was Tennyson's apparent uncertainty about the fact at all. " So runs my dream," etc.

Ruskin said, " Do you think that good is coming now to bad people?" " Yes," I replied, " and that their greatest sin is in refusing it." " But how much more *that* is than most people see," he went on. " Oh, yes, I see *that* now," I agreed, smiling; " I am amused now that I did not know that then."

We spoke about the wickedness of rich and poor people. Ruskin spoke of the little children like angels he saw running about the dirty streets, and thought how they were to be made wicked. I spoke about the frightful want of feeling in all classes; but added that I thought rich people were now waking up to a sense of their duties " Yes," he said, " I'm glad that you and I have probably a good deal of life still to come. I think we may live to see some great changes in society." " I hope at least," I said, " to see some great changes in individuals before I die." " Oh, no," he said, " that's quite hopeless; people are always the same. You can't alter natures "

We talked a good deal about it; but not quite

decisively. I see we quite agree that you can only call out and make living that which is in a nature. Ruskin meant a great truth when he said, " I can never alter myself. I think I had better make the best of myself as I am." When I said, "I am very much altered during the last few years," he laughed very kindly, saying, "Oh, no, you're not ; you're just the same as ever ; only you know more."

But it does make all the difference in the world whether we are fully developing all that we are meant to be, conquering all bad passions, or not.

103, Milton Street,
February 5th, 1860.

To her sisters Miranda and Florence.

I am afraid that it is long since I wrote to you ; but of course I am always thinking of you both, dears, and longing to have you home again, that you may really know all our doings and lives. Mine lately you would assuredly consider rather of the dissipated kind. I've been giving some book-keeping lessons to Miss J. B. She is a bright, spirited, brave, generous young lady living alone in true bachelor style. It took me three nights to teach her, and she begged me to come to dinner each time. . . . She has a friend, who is killing herself by hard work to support her younger sisters. . . . I gather she would gladly give her friend help, for she speaks most sadly of the "modern fallacy" "that the money must be earned." She thinks it might be given when people are dear friends ; she says they've given the most precious thing ; and what difference can a little money make ? I am so very happy about my work, now that I've finished nine drawings altogether for the "Modern Painters." Oh,

N

you old Mirry, what a person you are for a joke! I've found you out! How came you to write that I'd received 6d. from Lord Palmerston, and spent 6d. in seven birds' nests! Impertinent old thing! I came upon the entries in looking thro' my cash book; and I think Mama will never forget it.

February 26th, 1860.

MRS. HILL TO MIRANDA.

Gertrude, Octavia and Minnie went to a party at Mrs. Shaw's Gertrude and Minnie say Octavia looked "perfectly lovely." She had a high white dress, a grand scarlet sash and scarlet net. . . . Ockey, tho' looking so ill, is unusually nice, genial and merry. She has met with some amusing people lately, and it is as good as a play to hear her relate her dealings with them. She attracts an unusual share of confidence. Even strangers go to her for advice. Ladies at S. Kensington [1] read their letters to her—tell her their history. She could not help laughing one day; she said a lady, a perfect stranger, told her all about herself, even to the time she went to bed.

April 1st, 1860.

To MISS HOWITT,

MY DEAREST MAGGIE,

As to those old days—I owe more to those visits than I can ever express. I remember now that strange imagination of yours that peopled the world for us with wonderful and beautiful beings, and I am sure we always went on happily together.

(She also speaks of the impression of Mrs Howitt's loving, cheerful look.)

[1] Where Octavia was drawing

April 15th, 1860.

EMILY TO MIRANDA.

Yesterday we took Miss Baumgartner to see Ruskin's Turners. . . . Ruskin says he does not mean to write any more for ten years, but to teach more. . . . He said he did not want to write any letters to people. He wanted Ockey's advice, as to what excuse he should make. She said he should think what was the truth, and try if he could not say that. Then he began talking about truth, saying it was difficult to speak the truth; but to convey a truthful impression was almost impossible. That those who speak the truth are often the most misunderstood. O. asked him if he had read Mrs. Browning's new poems. He called them beautiful but absurd. O. said, "Why absurd? Because she trusts Louis Napoleon?" "No," he said; "I hold it is right to trust a man till he does something which proves him wrong. But mind, you're not to say I'm wrong if he turns out treacherous." Ruskin said that the taking of Savoy did not implicate Napoleon's character, because it was no pecuniary advantage to him, "not much larger than my garden and very poor." Do you think an ambitious man would spend thousands of men and money for that? He takes it just to pacify the French, who want some substantial proof that they were conquerors. To me personally it was a great blow, because it was so nice and dirty and tumble-down, and those wretched French will go and put it all to rights. It will be much better for the people, but I shall get no more sketching."

103, Milton Street,
April 29th, 1860.

To MIRANDA.

At last I've returned to my old proper habit of writing once a fortnight to you, I hope. I've been gadding about in the idlest way possible, and yet with my time quite full. You ask me about Good Friday. My dear sister, I'm far more afraid of your plaguing and torturing your conscience than of your doing wrong.

Mr. Maurice and Mr. Davies seem to me decidedly to think it a mistake to treat going to church as always a duty ; of course you must do whatever you think right. I shouldn't hesitate to give up going to church on one day, or even fifty, for one of you. You dear old thing, I wish I had you here to give you a thorough good rest, and rousing, and refreshing. How I should enjoy it ! I'm as merry as a grig. I greatly enjoyed Miss Baumgartner's visit. Miss J. B and I are great companions. I'm always doing things with her. You know she's teaching me Euclid. We went to see Holman Hunt's picture. It is very wonderful, in some respects extremely beautiful, exquisitely beautiful as to colour. But I don't feel as if the picture had thrown much light on the subject for me. I have taken a class in the night-school for girls here for three weeks, during the absence of Miss C. S. I am so glad at last to get into parish work. Miss Sterling and Miss J. B. give me almost unlimited money help for poor people ; the only question is how to use it wisely. . . .

We have been twice to Spitalfields and seen much poverty there among the weavers, besides making the acquaintance of a most nice Ragged School master there. He went round with us to the people's houses quite gladly, after his hard day's work ; and it was so very nice to see the welcome all the people gave him, but especially the children. He told us such an interesting story about a pupil of his, a very desperate bad character, about 16, who gambled in school, and only came with the avowed intention of having "a lark," *i.e.*, pouring out the ink, and upsetting the forms. At last this schoolmaster spoke to him, told him he had no children of his own, and that he should be one to him, if he would. The boy was deeply touched. He always sat by the master and studied hard. To quote Mr. S., " I assure you, and I'm not ashamed to own it, he distanced me out and out. He was a first-rate mathematician ; he solved some of the greatest problems of the age (?). 'There, old 'un,' he used to say, showing me his slate in triumph, ' do you know anything about that ? ' "

" And what became of him at last ? " we asked. " He died at twenty-one," Mr. S. answered, his eyes filling with tears as he went on " He died a peaceful and triumphant Christian. My wife and I never left his bed for three days and nights That's his portrait ; he'd long promised it to me, and on the Thursday (he died on Tuesday) he said, ' Old fellow, if you don't have it now, you'll never have it.' I never could break him of his rough way of speaking. He'd come in here to the last and say, ' Well, old 'un, have you got anything to eat ? ' He wanted to come over from his father's house, and die in my easy chair ; and the little wife and I would have given him his wish. But the doctor forbade it. Yes, I do miss him."

Maggie Yarnall is now on her voyage to England, which gives me the faintest most precious hope that Mary Harris may possibly come to London.

103, Milton Street, Dorset Square,
August 16th, 1860.

To MIRANDA.

Your sweet and kind letter gave me a great deal
of pleasure. I have written to Florence, as you will
probably see. I am glad that you asked me to do so.
I have a great deal to tell you. I do not know how
you think or feel about Portman Hall school. You
know that I do not think the omission of all religious
teaching a sufficient reason, for disapproval to counterbalance the immense good which I consider they are
doing there, especially as the teacher and three of the
monitors are earnest believers in our Lord; and I do
believe more is taught indirectly than directly. I
teach my drawing class there, and heartily wish the
school success; tho' I confess I look to a day when we
shall have as liberal views about education carried out
by members of the Church. I would not give my
whole or main strength to the school unless I were
obliged; but I would and do very willingly help You
will wonder why I write all this It is because they
are trying to find a lady to help there; and I have
mentioned you to them. They could not meet with
what they wanted, and had just made arrangements
for extra lessons instead until spring, when my note
proposing your taking the work next spring arrived.
I mentioned Mrs. Malleson as able to say what she
thought of your fitness for the post; and, since com-
municating with her, Mme. Bodichon is very anxious
to arrange it in the spring when she again returns
from Algiers. They first wanted a person's entire time
for £100; but now they have resolved to divide their
fund, and would probably like to have you for about
two or three hours daily except Saturday. I do think

that a permanent work of this sort, and among that class of children, would be deeply interesting; that it would make a nice change from private pupils; that you would find Mme. Bodichon and Mrs Malleson delightful people to work under; you would have such power to carry out what you thought best;—and, dearest Andy, it is not the least part of the pleasure of the thought to me that it does seem to me it would make it so safe for you both to return, so certain that you would, if you had the prospect of this daily work. I must tell you that Miss Sterling appears, from the short talk we have had, to think that it is not a good thing to do, only a nice thing to have a certainty; but she herself confesses, and I am sure it is true, she does not know about it. Nothing has to be, or can be, settled yet, but I should like to know how you feel about it. I mean to learn what Mr. Maurice thinks. Oh, darling, you must come home in spring somehow. We are on Mr. Davies' side of the street, two doors nearer to the New Road. I am doing such a glorious illumination round a photograph of Raphael's Madonna della Seggiola, with the words, "For unto us a child is born, etc." It reminds me of the glorious chorus.

Milton Street,
August 19th, 1860.

To Miss Baumgartner.

Yes, I am really back again, and so hard at work that our glorious tour [1] only comes to me at moments as a precious bright possession that nothing can take away, and interpreting splendidly one passage after another in this glorious volume of Ruskin (which I have at last obtained to read). . . .

[1] A visit to Wales, where she first saw mountains.

If you had any notion of my state of mind just now ! Everything I want to do seems delayed. One girl, a darling *protegée* of mine, says her mistress starves her, will not try another place, insists upon going home. Oh such a home ! irreligious, dirty, cruel, impoverished ; and the girl has just had two years' training. Well ! she must just try her home, and God bring her safe out of it. . . . We hope to have my dearest sisters home next spring. I have been offered some delicious teaching for Andy, in a school near here, Just the kind of work, and among the class of children that she would enjoy ; and the supporters of the school are earnest generous people. There is, however, no religious teaching given in the school ; wherefore, say many wise people to me, you as a Christian should not accept it at all. So I have *not* thought ; but I suppose I hardly feel sure enough about whether I ought to give my sister advice, however strong my conviction may be, when wise good people think differently. . . . I never have stopped, I hope I never shall stop, to consider what set or sect of people are at work, if I thoroughly and entirely approve of the work. I may think the work incomplete ; but, if it comes in my way, and I think it good, as far as it goes, I do help it with the little power I have. Above all I would not, in this age, refuse help to a society because it did not state that it was working in Christ's cause. I do believe we want all generous and good work recognised as Christ's, whether conscious or unconscious. I think the tendency is very much for doubters to think the best work is done by benevolent unbelievers ; to think our faith cramps our labours and narrows our hearts. I would like, so far as in me lies, to show them we care for men as men, we care for good as good. I never would deny

faith.   I care very little to express it anywhere but in
life. . . . How much these people lose by their omission
I believe they will one day know.   I think the time
will come when all this round world will seem to them
mainly precious, because it was made by a Father and
redeemed by His Son.

October 30th, 1860.

To Miss M. Howitt.

In these days, when so many conscientious
people seem to be seeking over the whole world for
some new good work, and cannot see the holiness of
that which lies near them, it is very delicious to find
people owning their home work as first and most blessed.
At the same time, I cannot feel that I should join your
Society further than I have joined it already.   It feels
to me that all people who are obeying the best part of
the nature that has been given them, do, more or less,
belong to it ;—that those, who know from Whom the
light proceeds " that lighteth every man that cometh
into the world," know themselves to be bound into
a society by that gift, by being children of God and
heirs of Christ.

Do, dear Maggie, believe that I feel it the greatest
honour to have been asked to join your Society, and
have great sympathy with you about it.

To Mary Harris.

How the real bond of family re-asserts itself,
dominant over fancy, attraction, yes even perhaps, in
a measure, over friendship itself ! as tho' it would teach
us how tremendous is the bond of duty.   Certainly we
have duties to our friends too ; but they seem to have
more relation to what we feel instinctive longing to do,

innate capacity for doing,—to stand more by virtue of relations we have chosen for ourselves, than solely, wholly on the command of God. I suppose it must be because He is our Father.

November 15th, 1860.

To MIRANDA.

I have spoken to Mr. Maurice about Portman Hall; and he decidedly thinks you ought *not* to undertake it. He says, what one sees at once, that you could not bind yourself not to speak to the children in any way that seemed best to you. He said that he believes those who are acting up to all they know will learn more; but those who habitually ignore what they know, lose it. He was so good, and took a great interest in all our plans.

November, 1860.

To GERTRUDE.

I begin not to wonder that men of business look forward to leaving off work, when they get old. I think it would be very delicious to have done with the bustle, and be able to see people one loves, and think a little in peace. However, I daresay it's all right; and it certainly is a glorious life; but lists of things one has to do, and machinery to keep things going, never can be as interesting as writing to my darling sister.

December 17th, 1860.

To MISS BAUMGARTNER,

Account of the taking of the lease of 14, Nottingham Place.

MY OWN DEAREST EMMA,

All has been arranged about the house at last. I am very thankful indeed about it; and we are all thoroughly pleased with the house. . . . Ruskin was very kind indeed about it.

We had a delicious talk afterwards about my life and life in general, and cultivated affection, its duties, practicability; whether or not the cultivation of it deteriorated natures and how.

Ruskin spoke of his own father and mother. He quite willingly wrote what he imagined would satisfy Mr. Harlowe,[1] and so did Mr. Maurice; but in the meantime Miss Wodehouse had most kindly offered a guarantee. She was perfectly convinced of the success of the plan, and was anxious that Miss Jex Blake should have her rooms.

I had such a glorious talk with Ruskin, stayed till 2.20; had to take a cab, and to drive furiously to College, where I was ten minutes late, and recovered from shame and remorse for it, by finding everyone in a state of alarm about me; only so thankful I was safe, my unpunctuality being unprecedented. I was a little proud, and vastly amused.

[1] The landlord of 14, Nottingham Place.

CHAPTER V

1860—1870

NOTTINGHAM PLACE SCHOOL. BEGINNING OF HOUSING WORK

THE removal to 14, Nottingham Place was one of the great crises in Octavia's life The housing work, with which her name is specially connected, was organised in this new home ; and here began the regular co-operation of the sisters in the educational work, which they felt to be so important in itself, and which, as will be seen from the letters, linked itself on so happily to the work among the poor tenants of the Marylebone courts.

On the other hand, this period was marked by special troubles , which, however, led to the formation of new friend-ships, and the strengthening of old Thus the value of her friend-ship with Mr William Shaen, which had been realised many years earlier, was yet more fully appreciated, in consequence of the difficulties connected with the purchase of Ruskin's houses , and the help, then begun, continued throughout his life. Her friendship with Mrs Nassau Senior, the sister of Mr. Thomas Hughes, was increased by the ability which she brought to bear in the arrangement of the accounts for the houses [1] A time of great despondency and pain, during Octavia's first visit to Italy, led her to appreciate the sympathy of her friend, Miss Mayo ;

---

[1] How difficult some of Octavia's zealous workers found this problem may be gathered from the following story —On one occasion she heard a stormy altercation going on between one of her collectors and a tenant, and found that the point at issue was whether the rent due was 6s 11d or 7s. all but a penny

and the rather dreary, commonplace life in the hydropathic establishment at Ben Rhydding, brought her in contact with Mr. Cockerell, who became one of her most helpful fellow-workers; while the need of assistance, caused by the turbulence of the children in the playground, made specially valuable the staunch fellow-work of Miss Harriet Harrison and her sister Emily.

Another friend, who came forward to help, when Octavia was obliged to go to Italy and Ben Rhydding on account of her health, was Mrs. Godwin, the sister-in-law of George MacDonald. The management of the houses had devolved on Emily, who found in Mrs. Godwin's firm and gentle influence the greatest assistance in those early difficult days in Freshwater Place. With regard to the housing problem, my wife gives the following account of the incident which first fixed Octavia's mind on the subject:

" When we went to Nottingham Place, Octavia arranged to have a weekly gathering in our kitchen, of the poor women whom we knew, to teach them to cut out and make clothes. One night, one of the women fainted, and we found out that she had been up all the previous night washing, while she rocked her baby's cradle with her foot. Next day, Octavia went to the woman's home, and found her living in a damp, unhealthy kitchen. Octavia was most anxious to help her to move into more healthy quarters, and spent a long time hunting for rooms, but could find none where the children would be taken. Then all she had heard as a child about the experiences of her grandfather, Dr. Southwood-Smith, in East London, and all she had known of the toy-workers' homes, rushed back on her mind, and she realised that even at her very doors there was the same great evil. With this in her mind, she went to take her drawings to Ruskin, not long after the death of his father. He was burdened by the responsibility of the fortune that he had just inherited, and told Octavia how puzzled he was as to the best use to make of it. She at once suggested the provision of better houses for the poor He replied that he had not time to see to such things, but asked whether, if he supplied the capital for buying a tenement house, she could undertake the management. He should like to receive five per cent. on his capital, not that he cared for the money; but that, if the scheme were placed on a business footing, others might follow the example.   Upon which, Octavia exclaimed, ' Who will ever hear of what *I* do ? '   Nevertheless, she admitted the justice of his criticism, and promised to use her best efforts to make the scheme a paying one, and so actually began the work which was to spread so far.

"When Octavia was searching for a suitable house to turn into tenements for the poor,—she was most anxious to find one with a garden.   We spent many days looking at empty houses, and seeing landlords and agents, but, whenever the purpose for which the house was required was understood, difficulties were at once raised   At last, after one of these refusals, Octavia exclaimed, ' Where *are* the poor to live ? ' Upon which the agent replied coldly.   ' *I* don't know; but they must keep off the St. John's Wood Estate ' "

With regard to the school, which was to supply so many zealous and sympathetic helpers for Octavia's work, it will be noted that all of the four sisters had shown an early interest in education ; and while Octavia and Emily carried on the teaching at Nottingham Place, in which Florence afterwards shared, Miranda was managing a day school for the children of small tradesmen and artizans   The Nottingham Place school was originally intended only for a few children of intimate friends. But the growth of the numbers, and Octavia's additional work in the management of the houses, induced Miranda, in 1866, to give up her separate teaching, and to become the head of the Nottingham Place school.

As will be seen from one or more of the letters, Octavia was disposed to emphasise the difference between her stern ideas of discipline, and Miranda's gentle persuasiveness, and, though this difference may have been exaggerated in Octavia's mind, something of the same feeling seems to be reflected in the accounts given by early pupils   On the other hand, that Octavia's readiness of resource and helpfulness in emergencies was specially impressed on the memories of the scholars, seems proved by an amusing story, which I remember hearing from one of the pupils.

One night, some of the girls suddenly awoke to the impression that some intruder had come into the room. Whether the newcomer was a ghost or a burglar, they were, of course, uncertain. (I forget whether a chest of drawers or a towel-horse was the real offender.) But after trying all sorts of remedies, one girl cried out triumphantly, "I'll tell Miss Octavia"; and this form of defiance seemed to restore the courage of the most timid.

But one would rather mention as the distinctive part in the management of the Nottingham Place school, not so much the differences of quality between any of the sisters as the way in which they all worked into each other's hands. Another old pupil, writing since Octavia's death, says, " I feel what a privilege I had in being one amongst you all—the little I do was first put into me in Nottingham Place days. I so admired you *all*, and the separate work you did "

Nor was Octavia's power over the young limited to those who were officially recognised as her pupils. Dr. Greville MacDonald, who has since made his mark in such different ways, writes:—
" Miss Octavia Hill had an extraordinary influence upon me in my boyhood, though she could have known nothing of it. She was the first person who taught me how to learn, and how to love learning In my youth, when I began to know a little of her social power and her personal sacrifice, she had more to do, I think, than even my father, in giving me a steadfast faith , which, thanks to her heart and life, became established amidst the ruins of conflicting questions, and has ever grown in stead-fastness."

But, besides the assistance which the school supplied in the development of Octavia's work among the poor, the home at Nottingham Place was connected in a more material way with the inhabitants of the Marylebone courts. The stables at the back of the house were turned into a room for the tenants' parties; the rooms above were let to a blind man and his family in whom Octavia was much interested , and, in order to prepare the place for habitation, Octavia and Miss Cons whitewashed and painted the rooms, and even glazed the windows. This practical knowledge of such work was a great help to her in carrying out the repairs of the houses, and training unskilled men, whom she wished to employ.

The rest of the development of this period may be gathered from the letters. There is one to Mrs Shaen, dwelling on her difficulties with the playground, and at first they were very great   When the ground was being enclosed, the wall was twice pulled down   And, when Octavia and Emily went into the court, they were pelted   At the time of the opening, to which I and my father went, we were warned by a policeman that the court was too bad for us to go down   How great a change was wrought the following letters will show

14, Nottingham Place, W.
December 13th, 1860.

EMILY TO MIRANDA.

We came here on Saturday ; and very delighted we are with our new quarters.   Poor Ockey had such difficulty about getting the house, because of being a lady without property, and so young ; they thought it mere speculation.   Mr. Maurice and Ruskin, who were her references, were so kind about it.   Ruskin saw the landlord at the College about it ; and Ockey received a letter to the effect that Mr. Ruskin had borne testimony to her "energy and every estimable quality," and, if he and Mr. Maurice would, without giving a formal guarantee, say as much in writing as that they believed Ockey capable of managing the affair, it would be sufficient.   These letters were written ; but, before they were both received, Miss Wodehouse had given a formal guarantee ; and O., to her delight, found that Mr. Shaen had arranged the matter.   Was it not nice of Miss Wodehouse ? She heard from Miss J. B. of the difficulty, and said that she had perfect confidence in O. and perfect confidence in the plan , and she would give the guarantee in a minute. . . . We did not know till nine o'clock that morning that we were to move; so you may think what a bustle we were in. . . . Ockey is immensely busy, and quite in her element, buying things, and reading over schedules of fixtures, and examining the plans, and carpentering. We have not yet fixed what rooms we are to keep; it must depend on the lodgers. . . . We are close to the park; so the air is very good; and we are about ten minutes' walk from Queen's College. The back of the house is delightfully quiet, because it looks out on Marylebone church and schools. The rooks in your favourite tree are so near that we often hear them cawing.

The Pines,
Christmas Day, 1860.

EMILY TO MIRANDA.

. . . Ockey came from Brighton yesterday. On Monday evening she proposes to start for Cumberland. She has to go up to town to-morrow, for Ruskin is going to attend to her work. She is much better than last week; and I never knew her sweeter. I can hardly bear her to leave the room, I have seen so little of her for so long, and I feel she is so soon going away.

14, Nottingham Place,
January 20th, 1861.

You need not be anxious about the house, every-one calculates to lose the first quarter. Ockey has all the money put aside for her first quarter's rent, in case we should not let. . . .

Is it not delightful that Ockey is so happy with Miss Harris? She seems not able to express half her joy; her letters are full of such expressions as "Oh, I am so happy!" "Oh, it is so delicious!"—and she thinks she shall go back there again and again.

O

Weybridge,
January 1st, 1861.

To Miranda.

. . . . I am just going to Cumberland for three weeks. Think of the glory of that! To-morrow I am to see Ruskin about my work. We had a very delightful evening on my birthday ; you know he sent me "The Angel in the House" and "Faithful for Ever." Ruskin and I had a delightful long talk on the 5th about all sorts of things. . . . This bright, beautiful Christmas, with all its glorious thoughts, makes one hope that next year we shall all be together. Dearest Andy, you know I would not urge you lightly to leave a work you had undertaken ; but I do feel that we ought to be all together again. Life is too short and precious for us to spend much of it separate ; and we do want all our strength for work here. . . . It's a miserable fact that I never write to you except about business ; but I should have liked to tell you about our new home, with its wide stone stairs, and large, light, quiet rooms. I am looking forward to your return with great longing. . . . It's striking twelve, so I must not write more ; but, dearest Andy, I do wish you all good birthday wishes, and that this year may be brighter than any before it. Give darling Flo a kiss for me ; how delicious it will be to see her again !

Hurstpierpoint,
Sussex.
May 18th, 1861.

To Miranda [1]

. . . I wish, dear Mir , that you were having a holiday ; it seems really hard for you alone to be work-

[1] After her return from Italy.

ing. I wonder when you will get some change and
refreshment. . . . I am grieved that Mama refused to
go to Cromer; I am really anxious about her getting
away somehow this summer; she seems to me to be
living too monotonous a life; so if you see anything
she would like to do, pray encourage it, regardless of
expense, and write and tell me about it at once. I
don't consider it an open question whether, if it is in
our power, we should send her anywhere she fancies
going. And will you remember that often the only
way to do this is to enter heart and soul into some
pleasure with her?

Written from Derwent Bank (undated, 1861).

To Miranda.

.... How well I remember coming suddenly
in upon you that last dreadful night, and finding you
hard at work on my skirt (which, by the way, has met
with unqualified admiration, darling), and how good
you were in never opposing my coming. Well, I've had
such a summer as I never shall forget. The unbroken
peace of it, like one long unclouded day! The merry
home life, and exquisite redundance of the perpetual
beauty. If I raise my eyes I see the mountains,
perhaps crowned and veiled in lighted cloud; if I walk
round the garden, the long sprays of rose, or delicate
green ferns, delight me; if, in the night, or rather early
dawn, I come into this room which adjoins mine, I see
the moonlight lying over the river, field and hills, or
the long cold level lake of mist lying in the valley,
breaking under the first ray of the sun, and rising
in wreathed pillars, covering the lowest end of the
village of Broughton, as it rises, but never, I under-

stand, rising as high as this house. Then we've read so ; the ignorant old thing is getting some glimmerings about history. I've left off walking again ; after the first fortnight I got more and more tired with it, but I persevered till the fever came, and have never resumed it ; but the terrace here is my continual haunt.

Ambleside,
June 10th, 1861.

To Florence.

I want to tell you something of all I have seen and felt, because . . . I fear you have had a sad house. I have been to Keswick We spent several delicious days there, sitting up on lovely hills overlooking Derwent Water, with all its wooded islands, and the blue valleys that part ridge beyond ridge of mountains ; and rowing in the evening on the smooth water watching the sun set, and mists gathering on the mountains, gathering in intensity of colour, minute by minute ; or driving far over the mountain passes to Buttermere, and Crummock, and learning about ferns and flowers. Then we drove to a lovely little village called Eamont Bridge ; it is rich in historic memories. . . . We saw a large Druid circle called Mayborough (of which Turner has made a lovely picture). Then we went to Lord Brougham's place, Brougham Hall. It is an old building which belonged to his ancestors genera- tions back. It is kept in the best possible taste ; there are fine old Norman rooms, with a well under one bed for supplying the castle in times of siege. There are beautiful pictures by Gainsborough, Reynolds, Holbein, —a most interesting collection of portraits. Then we saw a grand old ruined castle. Then the village where the rebels were taken in the rebellion against George, in favour of Charles Edward. Mary's aunt, a dear old lady who lived at Eamont Bridge, was the child of a man whose father has written a most interesting letter giving an account of their capture. The Duke of Cumberland came to his house; and Mrs. Mason's father, then a youth, was sent out to him to give him notice of an ambush. His mother hid in a wardrobe for fear.

We drove to the foot of Ullswater, and then rowed up it—nine miles; but it poured, which we thought fun.

Flimby, Maryport,
July 15, 1861.

To EMILY.

I wrote a few words to you to All Saints, as I didn't like your birthday to pass without one word from me; but now I write in answer to your dear little letter. . . . . .

We are so happy here, sitting out on the beach. Bathing, reading, and going to church are, I believe, our only employments, for I am often very very weary. The children[1] are running wild, as they always do here, it seems; so Mary and I sit in the sunlight in great peace. The children heard it was your birthday to-morrow; and, dear little things, they have come running in with their little treasures of seaweed and flowers begging me to send them; several offers have been made of various things which it was impossible to send by post; so I enclose lavender and heartsease, and some seaweed from them all, and my best love to you, darling. Shall I send the balance sheets to you in future, or will it be useless? Does A. understand them? I speak of returning in September, because A. cannot do

---

[1] Miss Harris's five nieces of whom she had charge.

my work and hers too ; also because I thought I'd like
to see you quietly before Sophy's return; but I don't want
the report spread ; besides, it's quite uncertain whether
I shall be well enough to return.   Do tell me whether
it could be anyhow easily arranged about the double
work without me till October.

Derwent Bank,
August 15, 1861.

To MIRANDA.

I went all over a coal pit yesterday.   It was
very impressive.   Of course the depth and darkness
and lowness one expected ; but I had not realised the
entire absence of all *native* life ; no rats or mice, or
even insects.   Of course there was no place for them to
be ; but, were the pit forsaken, there would be none at
all.   At present there are a few weak flies seen ; and
the rats are terrifically fierce, having so little food.
When caught in a trap they are usually found with
great pieces eaten out of them by their fellows.   They
are brought down sometimes in the bags brought with
food for the horses, who live in darkness, but in such an
equable temperature, and free from exposure to weather
that they look quite thriving.   Wood down there soon
rots, and is soon covered with white lichen like wool,
but exquisitely feathered.   The large furnace, kept
continually burning near the second shaft, to cause a
perpetual draught, looked so living and bright, after
the damp low dimly lighted passages.   The height of
these depends on the depth of the coal strata.   They
call the earth above it the roof.   The safety of a mine,
and the ease with which it is worked, much depends on
the material of the roof.   Here it is stone, which is nice
and firm.   The main roads are first cut out, from which

five yards apart are the cuttings. When these are
sufficiently worked, the spaces left between (called
pillars) are taken out, and the roof supported with
props, which soon give way, and the passages gradually
are closed.

April 27th, 1862.

To Miss Baumgartner.

Ruskin is coming to us on Wednesday. . . .
There is something almost solemn in the intense joy. . .
I can remember when he came to us when we were so
very very poor, and home was like a little raft in a dark
storm ; where the wonder every day was whether we
could live thro' it ; and now the sea looks calm, even if
there are waves ; and we have leisure to look at the
little boat in which we sail, and wonder if it will ever
be painted with bright colours. . . . I remember too
how once Ruskin's coming was like some strange joy ;
any little accident might have removed him for ever from
all connection with us. Now the silent work of years has
bound us together in a sort of friendship, which,
whether it leads to outward communication or not,
years, and separation, and silences will not touch ; and
this visit comes like the expression of a friendship
naturally, and like a bit of a whole.

14, Nottingham Place,
August 31st, 1862.

To Mrs. Shaen.

I am in town now to take care of the young
friends, who are to live with us. The work is extremely
interesting to me ; all the girls have some special
interest to me. Annie and Edith Harris from their
relationship to my best friend ; I. from her position ;

M. from her position, and for the sake of her family. Minnie's pupils, who are coming daily to be taught with the others, are the children of a widow who is working hard to educate them well to support themselves. They are dear, earnest, thoughtful, gentle, well-trained girls ; so that the work will be very nice, and supplies an object now that the home is rather broken up.

1862.

To Gertrude (about starting the School).

As to needlework, it is one of my great desires to teach it to those children thoroughly, as well as all habits of neatness, punctuality, self-reliance, and such practical power and forethought as will make them helpful in their homes. I think they may be taught to delight in them. When lessons are over, I hope to read to them, while they work ; or we will sing or talk together. If the children have time for study, work, walking, and play, I so much hope some of the elder ones will manage to spare some time for teaching quiet little children, either on Sunday or some other day. I think it would deepen their interest in their own studies so much ; but I do mean to be so very careful not to overwork them. I may find that one cannot set them to teach without overstraining them.

14, Nottingham Place,
(undated). Probably August 1862.

To her Mother.

I believe that I really have not written to you since you left us, which certainly is very shameful behaviour on my part. . . . A. is certainly infinitely better than she was, in mind and spirits, but just as foolish about overwork. It seems impossible to influence her about it. Annie and Edith are *very* fond of her; and this is good, I think. She will often sing to them in the evening, and read aloud to us all. I hope gradually, by these sort of things, to get her interested in finishing work early, and undertaking no more; but it is slow and difficult work. Her school is increasing, and her hope and delight in it too. You will easily imagine what a busy and merry household we are, with these young things laughing and playing like kittens. . . .

I take Annie and Edith to the Swimming Bath every week. . . . They are to join a gymnasium too, and always walk in the park. I hope we shall manage to keep, or rather make them well. I don't think they have strong constitutions. . . .

I am *very* glad that you are seeing so much that is beautiful and grand. It must be a great delight. . . . Now that teaching has fallen to my share, I regret very much my great ignorance. I want to work very hard at Latin. Minnie and I are thinking of trying whether Miss S., or some other good Christian, will read it with us. At present I work at it a little alone. . . . The Sintram is packed to go now. We miss it very much; but I have had the St. Michael framed, and think of putting it there. I often reproach myself so much, dear Mama, now that you are gone, with the way I never entered into your plans for joy. I tried latterly to do it, even then feeling my mistakes, which I suppose will all come more clearly before me as years go on; and perhaps it is no good dwelling too much on what is past recall. I wish this letter, or anything else I could do, would make you feel how entirely I rejoice with you in all you are seeing; but perhaps you do know it partly. I am trying now to make the house-

hold bright and sociable for all the children ; and I feel
more every day that every right healthy joy is a little
bit of true riches—the end for which really all work is
done. . . . Tell dear Flo. I will write next time, and
assure her I remember all her directions about half
hours after dinner very seriously and very tenderly,
because they remind me of her. I hope she'll find my
education improved on her return. Give her a kiss
for me.

January 18th, 1863.

To Miss Baumgartner.

We are all reassembled for work after Xmas
dispersion ; and my little troop occupy much of my time.
We are all well, and busy. I am succeeding capitally.
Ruskin, you know, perhaps, has gone, giving me the
grandest drawing lesson, an hour and a half quite alone,
—thorough teaching ; and then it is so nice ; I do feel
we are such thorough friends. He talks so quietly, so
trustfully, so (I had almost written) reverently ; and
then the thought made me laugh. But I think you'll
know what I mean. He saw me again the next day at
Burne-Jones's, introducing me to him and his wife ;
and after a little time, asking to speak with me on
business. We went into a quiet little room ; and, after
business was over, had the most delicious talk. He
asked me to write to him in Switzerland, saying that I
was " the one " (and then with his accustomed accuracy
correcting the statement to), " one of the few " people
from whom he wished to hear ; and then once more he
qualified it by saying, " You tell me just the things
I wish to hear." All this, however, this quiet acknowledged friendship can hardly be described even in
words, to me so precious, which expressed it, because it

depended on the way, and slight accents and actions impossible to describe. So to come to more important things; Ruskin was so delighted with the trumpet Fra Angelico, that I am to leave Turners and all else and devote myself to Fra Angelico and Orcagna, wherever I can find them; also a little water-colour drawing won the remark that now I had "delicacy" of touch for *anything*. Nevertheless Ruskin's heart is with social things; and I was earnestly charged to leave any drawing, if I saw what of help I could give any- where, believing (which is not difficult) that in doing *any* good, I was fulfilling Ruskin's wish and will as much as in drawing. "Never argue that it is not my work," he said; "I believe you have power among people, which I ought not to monopolise. I'm going away myself too; so just look upon it that I leave you charged to do anything you may see good to be done; only mind, Octavia! one way there is in which you may both grieve and vex me, namely by hurting yourself. Don't be proud and foolish; remember your strength is worth keeping. Rest for months or years, if you ought, but don't lose it." Rather a strange, rather a proud, a very thankful and glorious position,—isn't it, Emma? It doesn't make much practical change. The social work is best done by the way. He didn't mean "help people with money," for he didn't leave me any. I meant to rest a good deal; but the confidence and the freedom, if it is wanted,—*these* make a difference.

14, Nottingham Place, W.,
February 4th, 1863.

To FLORENCE.

    . . . . I only began my physiology yesterday, but have done a great deal since, and if Mrs. M. has the sense not to object to the children's learning it, I shall go on with it steadily, preparing a lesson for them each week, and so shall learn much myself.—I think you would think all our little flock very much improved, if you could see them . . .

. . . . You will have heard, I suppose, of our magnificent concert for the blind. It was one of the most splendid evenings of my life. . . . M.E. is so delightful a child to me. I can't tell you how I enjoy her. I often long for you, dear, with all your sympathy with people in general, and power of making children happy. You know I've a damping cool sort of way that just stabs all their enjoyment. I don't think I've any child nature left in me. However, it will injure them less, that what they all want is to grow up. I mean S. and I. and M.E. want qualities, that will fit them for early usefulness, developed.

July 25th, 1863.

Mrs. Hill to Miranda.

. . . . I think neither M. nor O. can have found time to tell you about their visit to Ruskin. He entertained them grandly at luncheon. They stayed two hours talking on all kinds of high subjects. It seems M. said some very pithy things, which delighted him extremely, and which he afterwards quoted. He spoke of O.'s painting powers *very* highly—he was all kindness. M. says he seems so impressed with O.'s greatness, and he told someone she was the best person he knew. . . . . He said to O., "I don't like to blame people for what they do, when they are mad with grief or terror; but I must say it was *cruel* of you to tell me about A.'s illness; I was very ill at the time; and it threw me back." She answered, "I didn't think——" "You didn't think I should care. I care very much for her sake, and very much for yours." He asked a great deal about it, and when they spoke of how we nursed you, the tears came into his eyes.

July, 1863.

To Miss Baumgartner.

Miranda's life has been in imminent danger; in fact, for some days the doctors gave us no hope. . . . You may imagine what the watching and nursing were. I can never tell; so awfully is every incident of those long days and nights burnt into my memory. But there is one thing you can't know. The infinite, the wonderful, the universal sympathy and desire to help; it was something triumphantly beautiful; one felt it even at the worst, only it felt so very far away, so helpless. Mr. Maurice was here daily, often twice or thrice. He used to come, like a great tender angel of strength, so infinitely pitiful, saying and reading to us things never to be forgotten, answering Miranda's questions unconsciously asked, so that they answered those deep down in us, thinking no service too small for him to render, none too arduous, startling me to a sense of my own existence by some tender bit of thought for me. And Miss Sterling, I don't know what we should have done without her. When danger was gone but anxiety remained, I sank down to a state of miserable weakness and low spirits; and she would come and take me out for drives. I couldn't stand or walk, so terribly fatiguing had the nursing been; why, the simple feeding was enough. Miranda was fed every half hour, and Mama and I did *very* nearly everything. Ruskin sent most kindly. And then the little children, who stole about the house and spoke in

whispers; and my children, who did their work quite
self-reliantly, and waited with gentlest service on us;
and poor old women who sent daily to ask, and teachers
who offered all service to set us free, and friends who
drove in to bring flowers and grapes, and servants who
were like rocks of strength : there wasn't one person,
who didn't show love and helpfulness far above what
one could have dreamed or hoped.

                                        July 25th, 1863.
To Miss Baumgartner.

   Minnie and I had been at Ruskin's, talking for
two hours about faith. It has left upon us both an
impression of the deepest solemnity. Minnie says joy.
Well yes, I say joy too. . . .
   I am sitting in the hush of an examination; the
children each at a separate table are deep in sums; so
strangely do the little things of this world blend themselves with the great, all these strange duties leading
one on to the great thoughts and facts that lie below.

                              14, Nottingham Place,
                              September 1st, 1863.
To Emily from her Mother.

   Dear Octa has just arrived. She has been so
happy at Leicester. She says she never had such a
fight to get away from any place. They were so happy
together, those girls. Octa spirited them up to all kinds
of things, made designs for L's carvings, inspired one
of them to come up to town and go in for a Latin
certificate at Queen's, gave A. hints about village
schools, etc.

November 29th, 1863.

To Miss Baumgartner.

We have all felt some time or other how much we owe to those who have consented to be served by us ; and I sometimes dream about the time that shall come when we shall try " to keep up the spirit of our poor," not by shutting up their hearts in cold dignified independence, but by giving them others to help, and thus rousing the deepest of all motives for self help, that which is the only foundation on which to build our services to others. How strangely then, when all confess mutual dependence, and glory in mutual service, will all our strange words sound about admiration for those who starve in silence ; as if that silent starvation were not the most awful protest against all who might have been near friends, who might have been noble Christian ministers. . . . I have been thinking very much of the past, because of the sad news from Australia of my dear old playfellow Charlton Howitt. They sent me a copy of the *Govt. Provincial Engineer*, saying it should be sent to me as " one of dear Charlton's old old friends" ; and they all seem to bear it as calmly and faithfully as they were sure to do.

Offley Cottage, Luton, Beds.,
December 22nd, 1863.

To Miss Baumgartner.

It happens that Andy's school has moved to the very room which, in the first old days of London work, Mama took as a workroom, now twelve years ago,

I had not been to the room till the day of this party, and Andy had not remembered it.

And there I stood again after twelve years, with a

deep sense of mighty love on all sides, to help me to do whatever I willed; friends and sisters, pupils and servants watched and waited for sign and look that they might know what I wanted done; and there was not one among the little pale faces lit up with unwonted joy, that I might not have committed to some strong friend to be cherished, if my own strength failed.

On the Sunday following I had eight young servants from different places, whom I have long known and watched, to go with me to receive the Communion, as we hope to do together each year.

As I came out, Mr. Hughes was waiting for me, asking, almost entreating, that one of us would teach his children. Finding that we really couldn't, he asked me to come to breakfast next day, and see Mrs. Hughes, to advise her about a governess.

They were extremely cordial and earnest,—said that for years they had been longing to get us, but that Miss Sterling had always told them that we were too busy, which indeed is true. I was much touched by Mr. Hughes' grief about the children's hatred of lessons; and finding that they wanted someone to take the children into the country for a month, till they could find a governess, I thought that I might take the work, and perhaps might get the little things thro' some difficulties, and so might make lessons pleasanter hereafter.

I gave my own pupils [1] three days' lessons. Minnie took the last three, after which they went in to the Cambridge Local Examinations.

I came down here at three days' notice, and have succeeded beyond my brightest hopes.

---

[1] At Nottingham Place.

Offley Cottage, Luton,
Christmas, 1863.

To MIRANDA.

Last night Mr. Hughes read some splendid Christmas thoughts about " Vie de Jésus " of Mr. Maurice's from " Macmillan." It was glorious. Mr. Hughes is cordiality and politeness itself, and does so like to talk about Co-operation. He speaks of Mr. Neale, but has not seen him lately.

December 31st, 1863.

I am *very* happy here, getting on capitally, especially with Mrs. Hughes, whom I like extremely. Mr. Hughes and I have very nice talks; and he is so entirely kind and considerate. The children are most delighted with the history poems.[1] Will you tell Mama I kept the " Education " because Mrs. Hughes was so interested in it; and I have read a bit to her each night after dinner, before Mr. Hughes joined us.

14, Nottingham Place,
February 18th, 1864.

To MISS DAVIES.

Re a petition to ask for the extension of University Exams. to girls.

I am really ashamed to have troubled you to write twice about the signatures, which we are heartily glad to forward.

I meant to write and ask whether signatures of private governesses in private families were needed. I gather from your last note that they are. I will obtain any that I can on the other paper, and forward

---

[1] Written by Miranda for her *little* pupils.

them to you, if I am not suddenly called from London. We are very anxious to learn the girls' fate ; though we feel sure none of our pupils have passed. I suppose, in that case, we shall receive no notice. If there is any chance of a formal or informal examination next term, we should like to know ; and every pupil *shall* pass. We shall know the standard, and have time to prepare, and shall send in those girls only who are just of the right age.

P.S.—I see you ask how I think the examinations told. I was *extremely* pleased with the effect on our pupils. I thought they were much invigorated by the examination ; it interested them much ; the intercourse with other students gave them a feeling of working with a large body of learners all over England, which was very good ; and I think the examination tended to raise their standard somewhat—which, I regret to say, I think is not high.

These like all other examinations require careful and noble use ; people must look beyond them, or they cannot look at them rightly. There are better things to be learnt than ever can come out in an examination. And to work for one is dangerous ; learning, for the sake of learning and knowing, is the only legitimate course ; but a standard, that will test our knowledge at last, is almost invaluable.

I hope to find these examinations quite consistent with real education of body, soul, and spirit. I would not give up an hour's rowing weekly, nor a single bit of reading to a blind old woman, nor any deeper study than would be tested in the examination, for the privilege of attending and passing ; but I believe the intellectual stimulus will be most valuable, and need interfere with nothing , and I quite expect to send up our pupils regularly, if you are able to obtain the privilege for us. But there is a still greater value in these examinations. Some such plan *must* be adopted before the education of our girls will improve. It is next to impossible for ladies to know what their governesses know; there is no recognised system of examining pupils. I am sure the want is a very great one, and very generally felt. I have had very much to do with finding governesses for people; and I feel the difficulty myself keenly, so keenly that I would not myself undertake pupils here, until I had organised a plan by which their parents might see something of their progress. I provided each girl with a book, in which her answers to the examination questions, each half year, might be written; and then her parents can see her progress. But of course this plan is clumsy. The questions are given by the teachers, who must necessarily know where the pupils are likely to fail, and who examine, in fact, on their own course of instruction; and we want just such a standard as this offers. I write in haste, but hope you will be able to understand, though I have expressed myself so badly.

April 17th, 1864.

To Mrs. Shaen.

As to myself, I can only say that every year adds more and more to the number of blessings I have to be thankful for,—friends, and knowledge, or rather sight, and power, and hope, all increasing steadily; rich and poor, young and old, teachers and taught, forming so bright a band of friends round us here I don't think anyone can be richer, and all our work opens before us calling for fresh energy and hope, while as I look back over the past years of those I love, as well as of mine, I see ever fresh proofs of a guiding love and wisdom. I am so happy!

March 11th, 1864.

To MISS BAUMGARTNER.

Florence is coming back to us after the Easter holidays. Will you be interested to know that I have got to know Holman Hunt very well, through the Hughes's, to whom I often go now? Two of their children come to us to learn drawing, arithmetic, and Latin. I like Mr. Hughes more and more.

We heard Kingsley the other day, such a splendid sermon.

Mary Eliza passed the Cambridge Local Examination, though two years under the age, and with six weeks' preparation. I have my certificate (*i.e.* from Queen's College) signed, amongst others, by Stanley.

14, Nottingham Place,
Sunday, April 19th, 1864.

To MRS. SHAEN.

I have long been wanting to gather near us my friends among the poor, in some house arranged for their health and convenience, in fact a small private model lodging-house, where I may know everyone, and do something towards making their lives healthier and happier; and to my intense joy Ruskin has promised to help me to work the plan. You see he feels his father's property implies an additional duty to help to alleviate the misery around him; and he seems to trust us about this work. He writes, "Believe me, you will give me one of the greatest pleasures yet possible to me, by enabling me to be of use in this particular manner, and to these ends." So we are to collect materials, and form our plans more definitely ; and tho' we shall begin very quietly, and I never wish the house to be very large, yet I see no end to what may grow out of it. Our present singing and work will, of course, be open to any of our tenants who like to come. We shall take the children out, and teach the girls; and many bright friendships, I hope, will grow up amongst us. The servants and children here are trained for the work and longing to co-operate. I saw Ruskin on Monday, and felt that the suggestion might be a blessing to him ; so I wrote on Wednesday, and received the grand promise of help by return of post, showing how entirely it met his own wishes. So now we are deep in studying details of model lodging-houses, and are so very happy.

May 19th, 1864.

FROM RUSKIN TO OCTAVIA.[1]

MY DEAR OCTAVIA,

Yes, it will delight me to help you in this ; but I should like to begin very quietly and temperately, and to go on gradually. My father's executors are old friends, and I don't want to discomfort them by lashing out suddenly into a number of plans,—in about three months from this time I shall know more precisely what I am about : meantime, get your ideas clear—and, believe me, you will give me one of the greatest pleasures yet possible to me, by enabling me to be of use in this particular manner, and to these ends.

Affectionately yours,

J. Ruskin.

Thank you for notes upon different people. I've got the plates for Miss B.

---

[1] First reference to the housing schemes.

Received May 24th, 1864.

To Miss Baumgartner.

I write expecting your warm sympathy in a much beloved plan that now Ruskin promises to help me to carry out. We are to have a house near here (with a little ground to make a playground and drying ground), and this house is to be put to rights, for letting to my poor friends among the working-class women. We are to begin very quietly, and go on gradually; but I see such bright things that may (that almost must) grow out of it. I hope much from the power the association of several families will give us of teaching and help. The large circle of helpful friends around us will be invaluable. I am so happy that I can hardly walk on the ground.

Egerton House,
Beckenham, July 11th, 1864.

To her Mother.

I think you will be interested to hear that we went to West Wickham church yesterday. It is the loveliest village church I ever saw, I think, standing near an old castle-like house, and far from the village. Evidently, at some time the chaplain of the lord of the manor has been the clergyman; and the chapel has been an appendage to the great house. . . We had not long sat down, when I saw Mr. Neale very near. His wife and two daughters were with him. He does not look one bit changed to me. . . . The service was very beautiful and set me thinking much about him, and his life, and its apparent failures and real successes. There was something very touching in the sight and thought of him. I had such a sense of his being looked upon by many people, if not as foolish, at least as having utterly failed. As if that unbounded, because entirely unselfish, generosity could fail to leave its impression on the world ! His own retreat from all the people who would have reverenced his spirit seems, too, as if he himself had a sense of utter failure. I would give a great deal, if I could know what may, indirectly, or rather untraced, grow out of such work as his.

14, Nottingham Place,
December 11th, 1864.

To MISS BAUMGARTNER.

The purchase of the house has been delayed by legal difficulties ; but, at last, Ruskin has placed the whole affair in my hands ; and when I am satisfied about the house, he will at once send me a cheque for the whole amount required. This enables me to employ our own lawyer,[1] who is, heart and soul, in the plan ; but, since I saw Ruskin, I could not attend to the matter at all ; for every moment of light time has been occupied by a drawing for the Society of Antiquaries ; and the dark has been little enough for teaching, accounts, and all my various extra work. This drawing I should like you to see ; it is a copy of the earliest dated portrait of an Englishman,—1446. It is of an ancestor of Lord Verulam ; one of the Grimstones ; such a quiet, stedfast face, looking out from under a perfectly black hat, with quiet thoughtful eyes, like a person who went slowly and steadily on his way, without either hurry or doubt. I should never have done, were I to tell you of all the importance attached to his shield and chain and necklace, and all the accessories of the picture ; how the antiquaries glory in each detail, and understand

---

[1] Mr. William Shaen.

from them each, who and what he was. To me his
quiet face comments in its silence on our hurry and
uncertainty; and, as I sit drawing him, I hope to
gather reproach enough from his still eyes to teach me
to live quietly. It is rather a grand piece of work; and
is to be kept in the gallery of the Society, after being
sent to Germany, to be chromo-lithographed for publi-
cation in their "Archæologia" The Secretary of the
National Gallery had noticed my work, and recommended
me to the Secretary of the National Portrait Gallery,
to do the work. It is expected by them, and by the
Director of Antiquaries, to lead to much more, and
would really make me rich, in spite of myself, but
there is small chance of time to do it in. I have also
two portraits waiting to be done, miniatures; but
happily I do them at home at odd half-hours.

I am also much interested in my large drawing-class
at the Working-women's College. Eighteen hardwork-
ing, intelligent women attend regularly. Our daily
pupils have increased to six, which, with six residents,
are as much as we can manage well, and we have refused
any more, daily or resident. When we once get the
tone up, the new pupils will fall into it naturally; but,
after increasing our number and parting from some, we
have had hard work this term to battle with the school-
girl element, which was strong in new-comers, and gained
strength from numbers. Our old pupils have come out
finely; but the experience has made it a difficult term.

And now for another side of our lives. We are every
moment expecting Mr. Maurice. He comes in now we
are such near neighbours, and sits and talks so very
delightfully. We hope he will spend an evening here,
while Mrs. Maurice is at Bath, and we should not be
robbing her of him. MacDonald is so kind and nice,

I am going there on Tuesday, when he gives a lecture on Sacred Poetry. Mr. Maurice is to be there. I have twice lately heard MacDonald read Chaucer and lecture on it.

Ruskin, whose lecture at Manchester you will probably hear, is coming to us on his return. He wrote such a delightful little note about it, and I had such a grand talk with him, quietly, just before he went.

April 2nd, 1865.

To Miss Baumgartner.

Our great event of the term has been the actual purchase for fifty-six years of three houses in a court close to us, which Ruskin has really achieved for us. We buy them full of tenants; but there is in each house at present a landlord, who comes between us and the weekly lodgers, and of whom we cannot get rid till Midsummer. All we can do, therefore, is to throw our classes open to the tenants, and to do much small personal work among them, so that we may get to know them. But all repairing, and preventing of over-crowding, and authority to exclude thoroughly disreputable lodgers, must wait till Midsummer. At that time we are to begin the alteration of our stables into one large room, which will enable us to get the tenants together for all sorts of purposes, much more easily than at present. I am taking my holidays now, that I may do with short ones after this additional work begins. . . . I feel that the work will be invaluable to my own girls here. They have each chosen one little child to work for. We are hoping to improve all the children's health by taking them to row, when we go into the park, and we are to try to get a playground for them. The plan promises to pay; but of this I say very little; so very much depends on management, and the possibility of avoiding bad debts. Did I tell you of the purchase of a chest of tea for selling to the women? They save much, and get very good tea. My hope is, however, not in this, nor any other outward arrangement; but in these as a means of knowing and training the people to work and to trust. It is with me entirely a question of education. My whole hope is in that I do care immensely, however, for just sufficient material power to be able to meet any efforts of theirs to manage better; and for the children to secure their health in some degree; but *this*, so much having been given, I confidently expect to receive, if there be a real need. My conscience smites me for calling the possession of these houses the event of the term for us. I ought to have spoken of Gertrude's marriage.[1] They are now in Florence, very bright and happy. We were all at the wedding; and very solemn and beautiful and bright it was.

Denmark Hill,
April 14th, 1866.

My Dear Octavia,

I am much obliged by, and interested in, your letter. That Friar's Crag! I was thankful to hear it is still there with its roots. Did I ever tell you my first memory of all life is looking down into the water there, holding my nurse's hand?

All that about the quiet children liking old things is delightful to me.

Is any part of the lakes likely to be left in any human quiet? and do you think there might be any

---

[1] The marriage of Gertrude to Charles Lewes, son of G. H. Lewes

possible chance of finding a purchaseable fragment of earth and ripple of stream anywhere? Sometimes I feel horror at calling *this*, or any place like it among these accursed suburbs, " home "—for ever.

My mother was saying—just before your letter came, " I wish you would ask Miss Hill if she has time to come out and sit with me for an hour—and talk to me."

So I said I thought you would when you came back. It will be nice—for I'm not well and I'm going away for a few weeks, to try if I can get just one more glance at Venice and Verona—before I am utterly old; but I haven't yet left my mother for any time since my father's death, and I shall be grateful to you if you can come to see her sometimes.

That is very lovely about your friend; it rejoices me to hear of your being so happy and having this utter peace, after your utter toil. But it is too soon over.

Ever affectionately yours,

J. RUSKIN.

The Crag, Maenporth, Falmouth,
April 15th, 1865.

To MRS. SHAEN.

The money part is very regular and simple, just so much paid into Ruskin's bank each quarter; but to me the work is of engrossing interest. We have three houses, each with six rooms; and we have managed gradually to get the people to take two rooms, in many cases. . . . When it was well started, we looked round for some opportunity to complete the original plan, by getting a playground, which we had failed to do with any available houses. I was so very happy at finding a bit of freehold ground, covered with old stables, to be sold with five cottages, in a very populous district near us, and a large house and pretty garden besides Ruskin has bought it, and it is this which just now is taking every thought and power that is available, to plan and bring into order. I dare not tell anyone the difficulty of this. When it is over, I may venture to speak of it ; *now* I should lose hope and courage if I dwelt on it much . . . We have made eighteen additional rooms available for the poor, and have given orders for four cottages, which are Ruskin's, but still in the hands of the middlemen, to be thoroughly repaired . . . . The children seen to have so few joys, and to spring to meet any suggestion of employment with such eagerness, instead of fighting and sitting in the gutter, with dirty faces and listless vacant expression. I found an eager little crowd threading beads, last time I was in the playground. We hope to get some tiny gardens there ; and Ruskin has promised some seats. I hope to teach them to draw a little ; singing we have already introduced. On the whole, I am so thankful, so glad, so hopeful in it all ; and, when I remember the old days when I seemed so powerless, I am almost awed.

Everything is so lovely here. Dear Miss Sterling ! is it not like her to give us all the opportunity for such a rest ?

About 1865.

To MR. RUSKIN.

This place may be considered as fairly started on a remunerative plan. I daresay you will be as pleased as I that this is so.

I told the tenants how difficult I found it to pay for all the use of the money,—an expense that they never realise ; and explained how the less they broke

the more they would have.   I told them what sum
I set apart for repairs; and that they were freely
welcome to the whole, and might have safes and
washing-stools and copper-lids, if the money would
buy them—since which time not one thing has been
broken in any house.

May 19th, 1866.

To Miss Baumgartner.

My work grows daily more interesting.   Ruskin
has bought six more houses, and in a densely populated
neighbourhood.   Some houses in the court were reported
unfit for human habitation, and have been converted
into warehouses; the rest are inhabited by a desperate
and forlorn set of people, wild, dirty, violent, ignorant
as ever I have seen.   Here, pulling down a few stables,
we have cleared a bit of ground, fenced it and gravelled
it; and on Tuesday last, opened it as a playground for
quite poor girls.   I worked on quite alone about it, pre-
ferring power and responsibility and work, to committees and their slow, dull movements; and when
nearly ready I mentioned the undertaking, and was quite
amazed at the interest and sympathy that it met with.
Mr. Maurice and Mr. L. Davies came to the meeting;
and numbers of ladies and gentlemen; and the whole
plan seems to meet with such approval that subscrip-
tions are offered, and I hope to make the place
really very efficient.   My girls are of course very helpful. . . .

My dear old houses contribute the aristocracy to all
our entertainments.   We took twenty of the children
from them, to make a leaven among the wilder
ones on Tuesday; and I hope much from them hereafter. . . .

Often it grieves me to find how much they preserve peace because they know I feel their disputes so sadly ; but I try to console myself, and to hope that beginning from this, they may at last learn how bitterly all their sin pains God who loves them better than I do, and works for them so much more wisely. I never speak to them of Him I think too much, not too little, is said about Him, to the poor especially ; but sometimes I do break through my rule, when I am urging them to *do* better, to live a little more nearly in accordance with the teaching of their hearts. . . .

Ruskin has lent me a Rossetti and two William Butts and a John Lewis for some weeks ; the colour of the first is a perpetual joy.

August, 1866

My work promises to lead to some drawing again now. I have commissions to make four large pictures from the old Masters to be fixed on the walls of a room like frescoes ; and Lady Ducie, to whose daughter I gave a few lessons, wants me to go down there some weeks in the autumn, to teach her again. As I should be living in their house, I should give all my time to drawing.

Perhaps Harriet will have told you that Andy is coming back to help us instead of teaching her own school ; and we are to take additional pupils. Until they come, Andy's return gives me time to draw.

I hope that, for the children, Andy's return may be an unmitigated gain ; for I hope much from her gentleness and tenderness, and her great power of interesting them in study , and all the strong stern rule may be in my hands still ; and, whatever else I feel I can do best for them, I shall continue to do. I should like to write to you of each of them, for the thought of them all haunts me continually ; they seem such a bright, strong, dear band of young things, better knit to me just now, on the whole, than ever they were before.

December 9th, 1865.

EMILY TO MRS. SHAEN.

Last week we gave a concert to upwards of a hundred poor people, eighty of whom were blind. It was a very pathetic sight ; but their great delight in the music, and the beautiful expressions of many of their faces, redeemed it. Some of the faces were continually turned upwards, and seemed as if they were drinking in every sound. One of the blind people, in speaking of music, said : " Why you know it is like meat and drink to us blind." Some of them had never had such an evening ; and did not even know what the word concert meant. We admitted a great number of guides this time, which we had not done before. The blind people seemed to care so much about having them, that we thought it better to let them come, even tho' it excluded more of the blind. One man spoke so nicely about it ; and said, " You see we feel so grateful to our guides ; they are like eyes to us, and we don't half enjoy it if they are shut out."

One of the blind men we know is teaching a poor crippled boy chair-mending ; and, when we asked how the boy was getting on, the man answered " Why he ought to learn to do it by feeling ; for it stands to reason his sight don't help him much. I don't think much of sight." The boy enjoys his work so much, and he says he dreams of it ; and if he had a chair at home he would practise all day.

The Crag, Maenporth,
July 29th, 1866.

FLORENCE TO EMILY.

There are great signs of cholera coming to London I have been administering Battey right and left with great efficiency. I was *very* sorry to leave at such a time, for one really was of use. I compiled a beautiful thing for Ruth, with Gertrude, from the cholera reports, and sent her the lecture on epidemics. What a good thing it is that they have the house to house visitation ! . . . Mama, A. and O. all seem to me gloomy ; they declare they are not. Ockey is rather like a *man* taking a holiday ; she thinks it her duty to be idle, and does not quite know what to do with herself ; but I am going to worry her down to the rocks to hunt for zoophites ; and she has promised to read " Modern Painters."

The Crag.[1]
August 2nd, 1866.

MRS. HILL TO EMILY.

. . . We are all very happy here.   A. and Octa bathe every day, and read Virgil together after break-fast. . . . After early dinner we all sit out of doors, and the others work while I read Spenser. . . . Octa paints the sunset every night from the field above the house. . . . at 9.30 we sing a hymn and read prayers and then separate, some to bed.   F. and I perhaps walk by starlight ,—some read in their own room till bedtime. They all go out at low tide to find things which have " suffered a sea change into something rich and strange " on the rocks ; and have been very successful, to F.'s

---

[1] Mrs Hill and her three daughters were staying near Falmouth in a cottage lent them by Miss Sterling

great delight. . . . We are very merry. O. thinks she
has laughed more this week than in a year at home;
but I don't think she knows what a frequent occur-
rence that is. . . . A. has written such a beautiful essay
on contentment for the Essay Meeting, and Octa a very
good one on tact. . . . Did you know Hugh[1] had
fought at Waterloo and in four battles in the Peninsular
War. He has medals for them. . . . Mr. Maurice took
away twenty-four photographs of him, so I suppose he
liked him—but Kattern[2] is *my* favourite. Hugh told
us "there was a very pretty chapter—Titus—it gave
advice to old men and young people—and was very
solemn at the end." He groans at prayers—but poor
fellow, I suppose he feels, and does not know how to
express that feeling.

Sarsden, Chipping Norton,
November 11th, 1866.

To MRS. SHAEN.

    To-morrow I return home, after a most happy
visit.

I go to take possession of the four very worst houses
of any I have ever had to deal with.

My dear pupils become more and more to me. I
cannot even express what their love and helpfulness
is to me.

January 4th, 1867.

To MRS. SHAEN.

    I return home on the 12th, to a very interesting
meeting at Mr. Maurice's, about forming an Industrial
School.[3]

---

[1] Miss Sterling's servant.   [2] Hugh's wife.
[3] This was afterwards known as the "Maurice Girls' Home."

January 14th, 1867.

To MRS. SHAEN.

Gardening is to me a great joy. I hate the trouble of going out, but when I *am* once there, I am as happy as it is possible to be. What a quantity one learns when one tries to do nothing.

14, Nottingham Place, W.
February 17th, 1867.

To MISS FLORENCE DAVENPORT HILL.

I am very sorry indeed to hear such a bad account of Mr. Hill. I hope, if this bright warm weather continues, it may do him good. It is sad for the Clifton time to have been spent in nursing instead of nice society.

About the reader, or about anything else, you need never think that I should ever suspect you or your sister of shrinking from effort, or of being anything but brave and generous; but one has to be brave in refusing as well as in accepting; and considerate towards those whose whole lives God has bound up with our own most nearly; as well as to the many pathetically forlorn of the great world family who cross our path. Each case can but be decided on its own merits. I quite see how in this one there may be many difficulties. If I did not, as I say, I should feel quite sure you had decided it as rightly as you could, and quite unselfishly. Do you not often feel (I do) as if people were often selfish in yielding to feeling instead of ruling it?

This brings me to the most interesting question about gifts, to which you allude. It is to me a puzzling one, not so much as regards the poor (there I can see

my way some distance, I think, and have written a few
words on the subject, which I hope some day to print).
I think that when gifts are given and received by the
same person, they are ennobling.   It is the greediness
of the recipient that is the awful result at present ; and
the helpless indolence of expectant selfishness.   Call
the man out of himself by letting him know the joy
of receiving and giving, and you may pour your gifts
upon him, even lavishly, and not corrupt him.   Besides
this, let us give better things ; sympathy, friendship,
intercourse ; let us be friends, and then we can give
with comparative impunity.   For the hearts of people
always feel the spiritual gift to be the greater if it be
genuine at all.   Where a material gift comes as a
witness of real love, it is the love that is the all-absorb-
ing thought, not the gift, be it ever so much needed.
All presents, too, should depend to some degree on
character ; we do not to one another select those
calculated to deepen any tendency we disapprove,
rather to awake fresh admiration of what is noble.

I cry out to myself in the courts every day, " What
a frightful confusion of chances we have here as to how
or whether there is to be food or not ! "   A man accepts
underpaid work ; a little is scraped up by one child,
a little begged by another ; a gigantic machinery of
complicated charities relieves a man of half his responsibilities, not once and for all clearly and definitely,
but—probably or possibly—he gets help here or there.
There is no certainty, no quiet, no order in his way of
subsisting.   And he has an innate sense that his most
natural wants ought to be supplied if he works ; so he
takes our gifts thanklessly ; and then we blame him or
despise him for his alternate servility and ingratitude ;
and we dare not use his large desires to urge him to

effort; and, if he will make none, let him suffer; but please God one day we shall arrange to be ready with work for every man, and give him nothing if he will not work; we cannot do the latter without the former, I believe.

Then, at last, will come the day when we shall be able to give at least to our friends among them as we give to one another, and not confuse still more hopelessly the complication of chances about the means of support, —nor have any doubt the giver is more than the gift, and be sure that he who gladly receives to-day will to-morrow give more gladly.

It is not often that I turn away from the very engrossing detail of work here, to think much about general questions; and I am afraid I have expressed myself very badly, and that you will hardly make out what I mean. It is with me here almost as with the poor themselves, a kind of fight for mere existence;— references, notices, rents, repairs, the dry necessary matters of business, take up almost all time and thought; only as, after all, we are human beings, and not machines, the people round, and all we see and hear, leave a kind of mark on us, an impression of awe, or pity and wonder, or sometimes love; and when we do pause, the manifold impressions start into life, and teach us so much, and all the business has to be ar- ranged in reference to these various people; and how hard it is to do justly and love mercy, and walk humbly.

March 8th, 1867.

To Florence.

They've just announced that there is space for half a sheet in this letter, but that it must be written

now or never; and indeed I am not fit to write to a
Christian. Here I am, head and ears deep in notices
about dustmen, requests for lawyers to send accounts,
etc., etc. ; and yet I am so glad to say a few words to
you, even if they're not of the brightest; and *that* they
can't be, for I've just come in from a round of visits to
the nine houses ; and somehow it's been a day of small
worries about all sorts of repairs, and things of that
kind. I was thinking when I came in that really it
would be a small cost in real *value* to pay any sum, however tremendous, to get rid of this annoying small
perpetual care, if the work could be done as well ; but
then it couldn't : it is only when the detail is really
managed on as great principles as the whole plan, that a
work becomes really good. And so, I suppose, being
really the school of training the tenants most effectually,
I must still keep it, and hope that it will not finally
make one either mean, or small or bitter. . . . I think
the playground is going very well now. Did I tell you
we have opened it during school hours as a drying
ground ? Oh, Florence, the court is so improved ! I
think you would be so pleased. We have broken out
windows on all the staircases, and cleaned all the rooms,
and put in a large clean cistern ; and oh ! it is so fresh
and neat compared with what it was. Do you hear
about our Girls' Home ? I hope it will soon be started.
God bless you, dear child !

Derwent Bank, Broughton, Carlisle.
June 14th, 1867.

To Miss Baumgartner.

　　. . . I have asked Miranda to send you a copy of
" All the Year Round " in which there is a short article
on the Playground. It seems Ruskin read an extract

from it at the lecture, of which I am not a little proud. It is however sadly cut up by the editor, which I am the more sorry for as there were parts with which I had taken the greatest pains, in order to express as clearly and concisely as possible my principles and experience about gifts. I cannot readily do the thing again ; and they have only printed a sentence here and there! That they have made the construction most awkward does not really matter. . . . I enjoy reading very much, and tho' I would rather read on the old subjects, and the dear old authors over again, I try to choose those newer ones, and get a little general information, to know a little about matters in which my whole heart is not bound up.

Sunday, June 16th, 1867.

Emily to Octavia.

On Florence's birthday we are going to have a concert and reading for the tenants, and I thought that it would be so nice if you would write a letter to them which we could read aloud. I think it so important that they should feel your sympathy and influence near them as much as possible.

The little Martins are going to school to-morrow. We have been very busy making their clothes. Isabel and Eliza (two of the Nottingham Place pupils) have been most helpful about it ; I sent for Mrs. Martin to speak to her about it ; and Mrs. Simeon said she set off to come and then turned back, saying that she could not go ; it seemed so much was being done for her that she felt like a regular cadger. She is a woman with a strong love of independence.

Then follows Octavia's letter to the tenants mentioned in the preceding letter.

June 23rd, 1867.

My dear Friends.

As you will be all together I take the opportunity of writing a few words to tell you how much I am thinking of you. I remember the many times we have met on such occasions before, and I long to be amongst you. I should so like to have a little chat with each of you, to hear how all the little ones are, and how you have been getting on all this long time. My sisters write and tell me how you are, more than once a week; but you know this is never quite the same as talking to you. Those are, however, my happiest days when I hear good news of you; and the best news I could hear is that you are trying to do what is right. You and I, my friends, each know how difficult this is; we have each our different temptations, but we will strive to do better than we have done. You will all know how I look for good news of you, how I have wished to see you make your homes better and happier, how I have felt that the places I possessed were given me to make them better; how I have loved my work, and now that I have only left it in the full hope of going back to it far better able to do it than I was. So you will understand that I hope we have a great deal to do together, in the glad time to come, when I shall be among you again.

I am in such a beautiful place, among such very kind people; and it is all so quiet and restful; how often I wish each of you could have a long complete rest.

And now I can only once more wish you God speed! thanking you for all the many kind things you did for me while I was with you, and asking you to help all those who are so very kindly doing my work for me, and to make their work easy, as you so often did mine.

There is little or nothing I can do for you now ; the old days of work are over for the present ; but I have a home for which I worked long ago, almost as hard as some of you have worked for yours, and which I love more than I could ever tell anyone ; and now I cannot help my sisters any more. Will you try, for my sake, to make their work happy and easy ? This you can do ; and you know, as well as I do, how happy helping people is.

I do not desire for myself, or you, or my sisters, pupils, servants, or any of the dear circle I have left, any better blessing than to have the joy of helping others. Oh ! my dear people, pray and hope for me that I may have it again soon amongst you all.

I am,
Always faithfully yours,
OCTAVIA HILL.

June 27th, 1867.

EMILY TO MRS SHAEN.

Octavia is starting on a three days' tour among the lakes with Miss Harris. On Monday evening we had a concert and reading for the tenants ; and a letter from Octavia was read to them, which they all responded to most beautifully ; one of the men made a most touching little speech in reply. Many of them said they had never enjoyed an evening so much in their lives ; and I have been so much touched and delighted at several little acts of kindness and consideration towards me ; their silent answer to Octavia's appeal that they would try to make the work easier for those who are carrying it on for her.

Heatherside, Wellington College,
Woking,
September 28th, 1867.

To Mrs. Nassau Senior.

Thank you so much for the accounts; how beautifully you have managed them. . . .

It is dreadfully tempting to be so near you all. I long to be amongst you, if it were only just to feel myself with you for an hour or two. You seem to me such a blessed company gathered round that dear old home of ours. But the time will not now seem long before I really see you, and am once more at work. Remember me to all the tenants. Tell Mrs. Moirey she must remember I don't mean to lose sight of her and hers. . . .

My love to Mrs. Hughes and the children. It is such a comfort to think of your being back to help them at home, and I like to think of your cheering them by your uniform brightness as you used to cheer me.

October 6th, 1867.

Emily to Octavia.

We had a very nice work class. Andy reads while I attend to the people. They were anxious to hear about you, and were touched at your sending the little presents to the children. . . . I think I have got a much better set of tenants. M. is very anxious to pay; still I feel it so uncertain with his health in that state. You know he was a year without work; and when he got it, he was too weak and gave himself an internal strain. . . .

It was so nice to see how the pupils had thought

of the poor children, and had brought little presents. Mary had brought an ivy root and fern roots, and clothes for the work class. Louisa had cut out and made entirely a lovely dress and jacket for Alice P., and had dressed some very pretty dolls, and brought some splendid flowers. Harriet had gathered black-berries and made them into jam. It is so nice that they remembered and cared for these things in their holidays.

20, Via dei Serragli, Florence,
October 10th, 1867.

To EMILY.

Here I am safe and sound at last, and very cheery and bright   Dear Aunt Emily is so kind; and there is something genial and homelike about being here. The journey from Chambery was very interest-ing, the Mt Cenis was so impressive; it was too dark for me really to see it, and perhaps I a good deal misunderstood the things I did see; but it was very quiet and awful and solemn, sitting up in the banquette, so wholly alone as I felt, in the near presence of the great peaks and gulfs and winds and snow; sometimes foaming streams glittered for a few minutes far below; sometimes a great cloud of mist came slowly down and wrapped us round; the horses were many of them grey, and looked very ghostly and unreal under the lamp-light; but their shadows looked like real black horses tearing along. Altogether, it was weird and wild, and I liked it. I had a very stupid companion; but happily he relapsed into perfect silence during the whole time   He was such a forlorn and stupid young Irishman whom I had picked up. He had been travel-ling with two companions, had got out of the train, and it had gone on without him. He could not speak one word of either French or Italian, and was going to Rome; they had his luggage and his passport. He was very tall, and very miserable, and I had to take pity on him, and do everything for him; but he certainly was very cowardly. At Turin I was weary, and did not want to have any breakfast; and I asked an energetic Prussian lady, who spoke English and Italian, to take him, and see to him, but he wouldn't go for a long time; and then, just as all the time was over, he returned and said he thought he'd better stay by me; so, to my no small disgust, I had to rouse myself and take him to his breakfast at Alessandria. However, the best of him was he didn't speak at all, but only clung piteously to my heels. By the way, writing of travelling companions, Aunt Emily just suggests you would be amused to hear that at Turin I fell in with such a polite and attentive Italian officer, who travelled with me all the way. He surprised me so much by his penetration about everything. You know it is rather troublesome to have an expressive kind of face; and yet it is, I suppose, helpful too. He was extremely kind about the window, tho' he was very cold; and I didn't say a word, for I knew it was unreasonable to have it open; but he saw in a moment what I wished, and wouldn't let me even half shut it. Then we had a great deal of talk about cities and countries; and I asked him if he knew London. Long afterwards he said to me, "You asked me if I knew London; and it was with an accent which told me you love it much, tho' you do call it an ugly and dirty city.' I told him that the worse it was, the more one was bound to help it; and the more one tried to help it, the more one loved it. He said, "We soldiers have to leave our country to serve it." And I said, " Yes, it did not matter how, but we must all do it." I kept catching glimpses of the mountains in the distance, and presently he said, " There is something out there which pleases you from time to time." So I told him what it was ; and after that he was so kind in warning me to look here or there, for the mountains would be in sight. . . . He behaved extremely well, and I think he thought I was the queerest creature he ever saw. . . . He was rather sneering at the Prussian lady for being *une savante* and for travelling alone. I was looking out of the window and thinking. He said, " You smile continually ; one sees that you think of what is dear to you. Are you thinking of your country ? " So I just told him I was thinking one could travel alone or do this or that or anything when one was really sure that God was with one ; and that one often knew it best when one was alone. Then I said all things, all people, help one. " But," he persisted, " those who really are brave because they know this, they do all things with a different manner, such a manner that all who meet them feel too that they are in His presence and under His protection."

Well, I was very thankful for the dear home letters. . . . I have seen literally nothing of the city as yet. I am to do the picture for Lady Abercrombie. Was it not fortunate I did not go on Saturday from Chambery ? A portion of the Mt. Cenis fell and blocked up the road ; the diligences had all to be unloaded, and people and luggage carried across a torrent and past the blocked portion of the road to other vehicles beyond.

October 18th, 1867.

MIRANDA TO OCTAVIA.

The houses in Freshwater Place seem getting into much better order now that Minnie is in town again. The P.'s are *so* energetic about the playground, so anxious to make it succeed. P. has been painting the swings (for which he would only take a trifle). He says a ground like that is a Godsend to the neighbourhood; and he proposes putting up a little direction board outside the court that people may find the way. . . . Minnie wants to know if she may admit P.'s children on Sunday. He longs so much for quiet to read his newspaper. I suppose the playground would be like a garden to the cottage.

Florence,
November 2nd, 1867.

TO EMILY.

The galleries were closed yesterday, as it was All Saints' Day; so I wanted to have a long bright day at Fiesole, or somewhere in the country, which is my great joy. But it was not to be; we did not get off till about three, and went to Certosa. Ask F. to tell you what a lovely place it is; and it looked so lovely in the autumn afternoon and evening light. A convent on a hill, the approach almost like that to a castle, so straight and steep, and bounded by such high walls. But the loveliest view was when we ascended a steep road to the south of it, and looked beyond it to the setting sun, the great couchant hills purple and grey beyond its own battle-mented wall,—campanile, and cypresses all dark against the sky; but Florence and the mountains beyond Florence were bathed in rose mist. Gradually as the light left the valley it became pale misty blue, the shadow creeping up till it veiled even the snow-covered peaks themselves. Tell dear A. I am not, and never have been, disappointed with anything, except a little perhaps with having to work, after all ; but this is very unreasonable I have no anxiety, and possibly I am after all better for a little compulsory action ; or I might go to sleep altogether, or take to thinking too much. As to the country, it might grow upon me ; but it hardly seems to me as if it could, it is so supremely perfectly beautiful. I have not even missed my beloved grass ; for first it would not fit in with the rest ; and second there seems to me to be a kind of uncultivation or perhaps rather of mountain character given to the landscape by its absence which has a peculiar charm. I daresay this is an unreasonable fancy, based on my northern associations of grass with richness of soil ; but it is involuntary and to me specially delightful, partly as being different, and *so not* touching me too much, partly as giving a sense of freedom and air for which I pant. Then it is quite delicious to an eye that glories so in colour, to see the great masses of earth, ready to turn to gold or purple or red, or all these in infinite combinations with brown, and over all the silver network of the weird olive trees. I fancy I should rather miss the grass increasingly than decreasingly. . . .

Remember me affectionately to Mrs. P.[1] ; dear, good, bright little George ! to think I shall not see him again, and that he is to do no more service here below ;—all young lives that go out so, hint so distinctly of the life that is to be—I do think of you all so. Has anyone

[1] One of the first tenants Her only boy died in hospital She was a widow who went very early to work Octavia and her sisters went every morning for some weeks to get the children ready for school, until they had learnt to do it themselves.

thanked dear Mrs. Nassau Senior for her letter? and told her of the pleasure it gave and brought me? . . . . I take the opportunity of writing when B. is out. I like to be ready to chat and walk with her when she is here. . . . .

Florence.

To EMILY.

I joined the Cherubini Choral Society here; we are singing some lovely things of Bach's and one of Mozart's. I believe we are to give our first concert on the 18th. . . . The anemones are quite wonderful. I gathered on Sunday every imaginable shade of purple, from blue to crimson ; such a bunch they made, so soft and deep in their gradations.

I hardly dare, even now, to write of home. I think of it as little as I can ; the abiding sense of it in all its preciousness, and the heart-hunger for it never leaves me for a moment, but I try to pretend to myself that the things here are very engrossing and sufficient ; and in a way they are. I have put aside the question of possible wants of one and another which I might satisfy, sure that I shall some day have a richer store of help to pour out for them, if I am (as I now believe I am) gathering strength. Every word mentioning the dear English people is precious. I glance down the letters for proper names very eagerly ; you are all too good about writing, but there are necessarily so many you never mention . . . and oh so many of the tenants and playground children . . . and I always want more and more about the people you mention. Do you not mean to send me Ruskin's letters to you ? I should like to see them. I fancied perhaps you did not send them, because you thought they would make me gloomy ; if they are gloomy—or might somehow pain me ;—but they would not. I know him too well for that, and I should like to see them.

I have been reading Browning's "Rabbi Ben Ezra." I think it one of the truest things he, or anyone else, has ever written.

Miranda's letters are so delightful. Her fun always touches me somehow, and never too much. . . . So my pride is to be broken every way, and even those proudly triumphant P. P. accounts are to get into a mess.

I am much honoured by dear Mr. Maurice's interest about my return ; I see S. Ursula [1] never got back ; but I think I must give up all claim to the name, if it depended on the 11,000 virgins ; tho' the number swells now even here.

Via de Serragli,
January 24th, 1868.

To EMILY.

I seize the time when I am bright and hopeful to write to you dear ones at home ; and for once will tell you facts not feelings. I have just returned from my visit to the S.'s. It has been very delightful. . . . M. is full of will and temper, and, not understanding any English, would be wholly unmanageable by me ; and I keep a good deal away from her. But the others, strangely enough, have attached themselves warmly to me ; and there seems no end to the amusements I can think of for them ; and I have so enjoyed it. They are not the least tiring children, partly because they are quiet ; partly, I fancy, because I have not to try to do other things too, but give my whole thought to them It is so soothing to feel the dear little hands in mine,

---

[1] A name her sister Miranda gave her, because she attracted so many persons to join her in all she did

and see the sweet upturned faces. Besides, it is nice to get on with children. I don't like the things I can't do. We three wandered out into the quiet *poderes* which are all round. We turned even away from the view of Florence over to the quiet distances. I set the children gathering daisies to make chains to decorate the dolls' house for a doll's birthday which I proposed ; and suddenly we came upon a large purple wild anemone. The view was English in colouring, for it has been grey and rainy, but all so wholly different on earth that no sameness of sky or light made it speak to one even in the same language, of which I am always glad. The children were full of delight with their walk. It was so nice going with me, they said.

Now good bye, dearest sister.

March 1st, 1868.

EMILY TO OCTAVIA.

It is wonderful how smoothly things go on, and I am able to do the most important part of the work. The thing I have most to neglect is going to see the people ; but I spent nearly two hours with them ; and they all welcomed me. Poor Alice[1] had scalded her hand and was very suffering ; but, after I had talked to her a little she said, with tears in her eyes, " Somehow before you came in I was so down-hearted, but telling you my troubles eases my heart, it does indeed."

20, Via de Serragli,
March 1st, 1868.

To EMILY.

. . . As to me I am thriving in the most unaccountable way. . . . This week I really *have* had

---

[1] Mentioned in the " Homes of the London Poor."

dissipation, and it has done me all the good in the world. . . .

There was some masquerading at Mrs. Taylor's, and we were asked to come in costume. I was gloomy and unwilling; but, seeing "B" "in for a spree," entered into it. I wrote to Mrs. Ross for an Eastern dress; she sent such a magnificent one. It was the admiration of the whole company; in fact, I am never to hear the last of it, I think. It was pronounced very becoming. . . . Then we went to the Corso. It has been very grand this year; for there is a Society which has offered large prizes, and done a great deal to promote the matter. It was very silly, you know; but I tried to forget *that*, and managed pretty well. The Turkish Ambassador sent Mrs. Ross his carriage. She did not know he was going to send it, and it came too late for her to send to ask me to go with her; so I went with Mrs. Taylor; but we saw Mrs. Ross looking so lovely and queenly, and childlike, with little Alick by her. I am to dine with her some day soon, and go to the French play afterwards. On Friday I fancy we (Miss Mayo and I) start for Pisa; next week I shall probably spend at Bello Sguardo with the Starks. They have kept asking me to go; but I have deferred it till the Orcagna is finished.

14, Nottingham Place,
April 5th, 1868.

To Miss Mayo.

After mentioning a failure to see Ruskin, and George Macdonald (the latter failure partly due to her painting and partly to her ill-health), she adds, " But you will know that I am prouder and more thankful for the special place amongst (and love of) the many

who have few to love them and few to help them, than
even for the friendship of the greatly good; and of
these among all classes I have found so many.   Monday,
I collected rents, and had such happy talks with the
people. . . . When people are kind now, it is a great
pleasure, but when, my power of physical effort being
all gone, they seem to feel as if I might yet help them
by presence and care, it makes me thankful to God who
has left me some small work to do for Him; it is
almost too much.   This I had half hoped to feel in
returning.   I have far more than realised the hope that
I had." . . .

(Speaking warmly of Mr. Watson of the Society of
Antiquaries and his wife she says) They are very High
Church, but not foolishly so.   I fancy it is the refine-
ment and beauty which attract them.

My sisters have asked me so earnestly to leave the
main work for the pupils in their hands that I have
done so.   All is going on so beautifully that I have
little temptation to meddle either.   It seems a little
strange, most so in the mornings, when I no longer
read; but the sense of perfect harmony with them all
takes away any kind of regret from the change.

. . . (Speaking of the houses she says), " I have now
drifted past the triumphant meeting into full work
there, and all its tiresome details; but with the refreshment of seeing people I love, and the stimulus of
other minds occupied with other thoughts, I meet these
details with less intensity of thought than of old.   My
sisters are such a rest and joy to me; I could never tell
anyone what they are. . . .

. . . I have drifted into the old state of intense
interest and joy in all the little world I love and work
in; it seems like native air to me; and it seems to me,

in what Matthew Arnold would call my provincialism, much more interesting (if not important) to see whether a few words will obtain a holiday for the over-worked teacher whom I love, and who is wearing herself out for her family, than to know what Louis Napoleon is doing."

Probably May, 1868.

To Octavia from her Mother.

Altho' I was not there I have volunteered (like many other reporters) to describe yesterday's gala. It was a complete success; the prettiest fête that has yet been given; and your sisters were delighted with the improvement in the children compared with last year. On Monday evening Minnie and most of the pupils went up to 207 [1] to make wreaths. They found Mr. Ruskin's and Mrs. Gillum's flowers there—both most beautiful in their way. Eliza said the gardener had asked to deposit them himself in the kitchen, and had laid them down so carefully, and as if he were so fond of them—worthy servant of his master! Andy spent the whole day there, and the pupils went up, as they finished work, to help The result was splendid; numbers of lovely wreaths, and a throne made of a chair shape with three steps. The blind fiddler *non est inventus*; so they got an organ man, which did quite as well. Your sisters were delighted with Mr. and Mrs. Howard . . . their sympathy was so genuine—they left with tears in their eyes. Well, the ceremony began by drawing lots for the queen, and it fell on Nelly Kinaly. The child took out the wreaths from the basket; and Florence called the child whom she thought they would suit, and one of our girls in turn crowned them. Andy says the children

[1] Marylebone Road.

looked so pretty—their untidiness only went for picturesqueness. They had cakes, biscuits and oranges; but except one or two boys, the flowers interested them more than the cake. Florence played at trap with the boys and Mr. Smale.

Derwent Bank,
July 22nd, 1868.

OCTAVIA TO MISS MAYO.

The time of my leaving here draws sadly near and I have done so little—mostly weeding I think, and that is so interesting, it keeps me out of doors, not standing or walking and yet gives me something to do. It is quiet and nice and I like the smell of the earth and the soothing monotony of the movement and thought. We have not been reading anything of any depth or weight; usually we do here, but somehow this time we have read scraps of things, and what I should call decidedly light reading. . "Scenes in Clerical Life," part of Chaucer, the "Story of Doom" (I am *delighted* with Laurence), a good deal of Browning, and a little of Thackeray.

Ben Rhydding, Leeds,
August 3rd, 1868.

To MISS MAYO.

I want Dr. Macleod to let me leave, as I am so without definite illness now; and it hardly seems right to stay here merely to gain strength; but they won't even let me speak on the subject yet; and nothing is so provoking as to leave things half done; so I must let the matter be finally decided by them.

(Very warm expressions of admiration and gratitude for Dr. Macleod.)

2, Ashfield House, Harrogate,
September 20th, 1868.

I came here on Wednesday to see Miss Harris, who has been seriously ill but is now rapidly gaining strength. . . .

I should like to have seen you while I am still in overflowing health and so merry; it seems too bad to go to one's best friends always when one is broken.

(Description of Turner's Norham and Melrose.)

We are reading the Spanish Gipsy aloud. I wonder what you think of it. To me it seems full of wonderful passages expressive of fresh fact, and so exquisitely expressed that one longs to remember the exact words; but the whole thing is disjointed; the story improbable. I always find it impossible to believe people would have acted as she makes them. I suppose I am mistaken; but I can never feel the things the least natural; and yet I should find it hard to say on what ground I disbelieved them. To me the power of looking all round questions, and seeing how all view them, is not specially delightful, unless at the end there comes some deliberate or distinctive sense of reverence or sympathy with the most right. The perpetual suspense is painful to me. I feel as if I would say, "See as much, judge as mercifully, as you can; but show just so much enthusiasm on one side or another, as would lead to action in real life." The other temperament seems always either weak and irresolute, or likely to lead to wrong action.

Now Browning, with all his dramatic power, and turning it upon such various (and often such low) people, has yet distinct love or scorn, has definite grasp of some positive good.

14, Nottingham Place,
October 4th, 1868.

To a Friend.

We three sisters have had a jolly meeting; and we are anticipating the arrival of our dear pupils, Mama and Florence, to-morrow.

Dear Alice Collingwood[1] has done wonders; I never knew the business half so well managed when my sisters were away; and she has been so happy in the work, and has learnt to know and care for the people so much.

Have you read Morris's "Jason"? I have been reading it for the second time. I am increasingly impressed by it. It is marvellous to me how any one can so throw himself into so noble a time without Christianity; the hint of deeper meaning is so telling, and goes so home, because it is only suggested and kept subservient to the intense realism of the scenes and incidents. It is a book one believes from first to last. The accessories are described so beautifully; it is true poetry.

I know it is very forlorn to depend for intellectual intercourse on books and absent people. But for you who have so many resources, I hope it is not quite so bad. At any rate, how you must be feeling yourself useful. Still I am sorry for you; you seem somehow (all sensitive people do) to get so much more pain than pleasure out of your feeling. I wonder whether you are ill-balanced, and your bodies ought to be more vigorous to match your organisations; or whether you are, as it were, martyrs, for us to love and look up to, and learn from and delight in; but appointed, for some inscrutable reason, to bear a large share of the pain of

---

[1] A former pupil.

the world—to be purified to a higher point than we, until the last sorrow shall be put under your feet.

Any way and every way, God bless and keep you.

14, Nottingham Place,
November 29th, 1868.

To Miss Baumgartner.

We are all assembled again, and very happy.

We have a *very* large number of pupils, as many as we could take in ; but these are mainly under my sisters' care, who enjoy the work, and thrive in it. I only teach the girls a few things, and rejoice in their bright young life. I give a few drawing lessons, and am managing my dear houses, which are getting into such excellent order as to be a great joy, and but little painful care. I am drawing again at last, too, to my great delight, and am able to see a good deal of my friends, and to bind up all the links of knowledge of the details of their lives, broken by my illness and absence. So it is a quiet, beautiful, thankful, busy, but not oppressed, life.

14, Nottingham Place,
March 7th, 1869.

To Miss Harris.

My dearest Mary,

I have had a most delightful week. The crowning day was last Sunday, when I dined at Ruskin's It was exceedingly interesting. I had been determined to ask him a little about Greek mythology, literature and art ; and how, without knowledge of Greek, one might enter into some comprehension of all these ; for I have lived long enough to remember the passionate revolt of our then young thinkers against

the dead formal worship of all that had its origin in
Greece ; and now I am interested to notice the men,
leading from weight of earnestness, tho' educated in all
the Gothic and Teuton sympathies, turning back to
Greek thought, and even imagery, as if it contained
nobler symbols of abiding truth than our northern
legends.   Yes, even to feel the influence of the Grecian
wave myself.   So we got into interesting talk.   He told
me that there was little translation of Greek which he
knew or cared for ; that he had done a little himself,
which will be published with next Tuesday's lecture ;
that Homer, even translated by Pope, taught one a
good deal ; that some tales by Cox (do you know
them ?) were intensely good ; but (as I was pleased to
know that I had instinctively felt), Morris's Jason was
the most helpful almost of all.   He sketched for me
most beautifully, a kind of plan of Greek mythology,
saying that the deities who governed the elements were
the primary ones ; the earth the sustainer of man ; the
water governing the ebb and flow of his fortunes, the
two fiery deities earthly and heavenly ; and the goddess of
the air the inspirer.   He quoted curious parallel thoughts
from the Bible ; " the wind bloweth where it listeth."
He told me some strange things, too, about Minerva
giving men strength from winged beings, and once,
when enduing Menelaus with courage to fight Paris,
giving it from a mosquito ; whereas most gods give
them strength from quadrupeds that are strong.
Round these central deities are grouped many minor
ones ; Mercury, the cloud-compeller, often represented
as a shepherd, guides the footsteps of men in life and
death.

I asked him how far Virgil was too Roman to be
trusted.   He seemed very much pleased to find that I

could read Virgil, and was fond of him ; it seems that he is very fond. He said moreover that Latin was untranslateable—being so magnificent a language ; whereas Greek, mainly depending for its interest on thought, could be perfectly well translated. I found that he and I agreed in liking the 2nd and 7th books best, he rather inclining to the Infernal Regions and the Fall of Troy. He told me that the exquisite tenderness between fathers and sons delighted him above all things in Virgil, and led one to the root of the main source of Roman greatness in its noblest time.

You will be sorry to hear that Miss Cons can only, at present, give one day and a half weekly to the work ; and that Miss Sterling is so much interested in what she calls "linking my little affairs to whatever has life," that she will not work except near us—nor of course could Miss Cons do more than this in so short a time.

On Wednesday we are to have our play.[1] We are actually to have an audience of 200 poor people. Everyone is very kind about it ; we have a splendid room, and all promises well.

Oh, Mary ! life and its many interests is a great and blessed possession. I love it so much. . . . And yet it seems such a simple, quiet thing to slip out of it presently ; and for other and better people to take up their work, and carry it on for their day too.

May 9th, 1869.

To Miss F. Davenport Hill.

. . . . The trees are of course very small ; but the creepers helped us, and the playground never looked

---

[1] This refers to a performance of the "Merchant of Venice" in Dr Martineau's schoolroom in Portland Street Octavia acted Portia.

so pretty. Our new swings were put up; and three
people were entirely occupied with superintending
them the whole time. Each child had a definite time
allowed; and all others were kept out of the way;
no easy matter with children so eager and so unaccustomed to control. The little band acquitted itself
admirably, considering how young it is yet; it is an
acquisition. We had numbers of games of course.
The see-saw was crowded all the time. Two people
took charge of it; and it seemed about as much as
they could manage. It was very touching to see the
children, when they first saw me open the gate. Our
tenants were to come in first; and I had to pick
them out from the dense mass of eager faces Such
impatience! as if a few minutes were hours! Such a
break of light came over the face as I caught the eye
of a tenant; the " Mary, you may come," or " Dickey,
you next," was entirely unnecessary to the child
addressed, but was the signal for others to make way;
and thro' such tiny avenues, or from under bigger girls'
skirts, the tiny creatures emerged to the wonderful
place of flowers and the many welcoming friends. I
was rather proud to see that I was usually guided
by a neater dress or cleaner face to a tenant. Then
followed the admission of a few children coming to
classes, or members of the band or drill classes, but not
tenants. And then the mass of children from the
neighbourhood. Oh such a troop! The grown up
people crowded on any place from which they could
see. I wished our wall had been moved, and the rails
up, both for the extra space, and that more people
might have seen. All children had flowers, cake, and
an orange on leaving. My conclusion is, the place is
really getting into order.

I had the report from a surveyor on the houses for which we are in treaty. He says very naively, " It seems to me the houses are much out of repair, tho' considered by the landlord in excellent condition for the class of inmates." He says, too, the property in the neighbourhood is in excellent condition, and will let well . . . Will you send me a copy of papers respecting boarding out ? I should much like to send them to Mrs. N. Senior. I believe the chances are better in the country, and the plan more likely to be tried there.

I am glad you think it is best to wait and see the June list for Macmillan. It will be very odd if the thing ever is published. I am looking forward so eagerly to throwing the burden of the playground expenses, at least partially, on our new buildings ; they are such a perpetual worry to me, and for so small a sum it seems a pity to be annoyed. If the surplus profit of the rooms will, as I hope, pay for the superintendence, it will make a great difference to me. We hope to finish the building this week. I feel so ungrateful when I complain of anything, when all has prospered in this wonderful way. Perhaps I am a little tired to-night.

14, Nottingham Place,
April 13th, 1869.

To Mrs. W. Shaen.

I cannot tell you what my people are to me. We are such thorough friends. Sometimes small actions of theirs go straight to one's heart, making me feel how nice our relation to one another is. The other day I went down the court, once so savage and desolate. I saw two or three of the worst boys in the neighbourhood looking very happy and smiling. "Have you seen Mrs. Mayne?" they clamoured eagerly. Mrs Mayne is our superintendent there. "She's got something taking care of for you." I found that the boys had walked twelve miles, doubtless delighted with the expedition, but specially to bring me back a great quantity of "palm." And, as I came out carrying it, "Will you have some more?" "Wait a bit and have some more," they cried. When I remembered that these same boys had been our greatest trouble, defying authority, climbing walls, breaking windows, throwing stones, with their hands against us in all things, I could not but feel that we had got on a little, however the houses may fall short in external perfection of what one longs for them to be. I have hardly any of the teaching at home; dear Andy and Minnie having thrown their strength fully into it; so Flo and I only take special classes; but the bright young life round one is very refreshing; and I grow much attached to some of the girls;—not the old sense of being any longer their head; this, you will understand, I am not sorry to resign, however precious the position was. Meantime, I have my little sanctum here and go out among my ever-increasing circle of real friends. My work now is mainly teaching drawing, which I enjoy much.

June 7th, 1869.

To Miss Florence Davenport Hill.

. . . We are having a large meeting in the parish this week to try to organise the relief given; very opposite creeds will be represented—Archbishop Manning, Mr. Davies, Mr. Fremantle, Eardley-Wilmot,

and others.   I must go myself.   I shall try to get
Rose to go too. . . .

Lady Ducie writes that she is perfectly engrossed in
your book, and tells me she must get it.   She is quite
appalled at the state of things in the workhouse ; it
seems quite to be weighing on her mind.

June 9th, 1869.

To THE SAME.

. . . I daresay one is apt to overrate one's own work ;
but one is the more anxious to have it fairly weighed,
and receive all advice from other people ; and I do
want to have it fairly considered, and get the authorities
to recognise it   Mr. F., the rector of our district, and
the main mover in the matter, is to call on me to-day.
May some power inspire me with intellect and speech !
I have hardly a hope that they will place me on the
Committee.   I shall try boldly ; but I think no ladies
will be admitted   Mr. F. is happily a friend of Lady
Ducie's.

P.S.—Mr. F. has just been, and will propose my
name at the Committee.

Ben Rhydding,
September 10th, 1869.

To EMILY.

. . . Life here has been a great success every
way.   It is odd, in a place like this, to get on so well ;
but energy and enjoyment are such a delight to people,
they forgive much, where they can secure them and
have these.   A large picnic party went to Fountains
yesterday.   They begged me to go.   I could not, and
said, " I will ask all the people, and, when you are
started, you really won't want me."   " Oh," said a

young, buoyant Quaker youth, "but we do want you to talk." . . . In pity also give me some more teaching; it is the only anchor I have, and I shall be destroyed by dissipation if you don't preserve me. Oh dear, I have been writing three hours; and I did so want to do my miniature; for you don't know how much I want to finish it.

6, Clifton Villas,
Bradford,
September 17th, 1869.

To EMILY.

To-night there is to be a dinner party here. Dr. Bridges and several influential people are asked to meet me;—I do feel such a take-in of a person. I wish someone would explode me; it is so difficult to un-humbug oneself. It is all taken for extreme modesty (fancy mine!) and laid to one's account as so much excellence. A Mr. and Mrs. R. K., who are looked upon as great guns, are giving a dinner party in my honour. Really it's very ridiculous; what I *am* glad of is that I am going to see Saltaire, a model village near here which has grown up round a manufactory, belonging to a Mr. Titus (now Sir Titus) Salt; no beer shops there, only model cottages, schools, etc. . . . I'm very happy, and as bright as can be; but save me from this again! I'm going to settle down to a steady, quiet old age, if ever the happy time arrives when I reach home.

CHAPTER VI

1870—1875

THE period from 1870—1875, if it contains less of what may be called new departures in Octavia's life than the period which preceded it, or that which followed it, yet can show phases of struggle, constructive work, and the discipline of trial and opposition, as remarkable as at any time of her life, and it also includes an important change in her circumstances, which much affected all her subsequent career.

It may be said, perhaps, that the distinctive characteristic of this period was that it brought her greater publicity than her previous efforts had produced, and so answered her question to Ruskin, " Who will ever hear of what I do ? "

First of all the time was one in which a variety of circumstances had been compelling many, who had not hitherto shown much interest in the poor, to turn their attention in that direction ; while many others, who had been anxious to do their duty to the poor, had begun to realise that the hap-hazard methods of relief hitherto in vogue had broken down.

The failure of large Mansion House Funds, which had been, raised in the 'sixties to meet special distress, had brought home to many workers among the poor the need of substituting closer co-operation for their isolated efforts. Some of those, who had realised this need, also perceived that it was necessary to make enquiry into the conditions of the applicants for relief, before they could discover the best means of assisting them.

The great variety of characters and ideals and experiences

which marked the people, who were thus temporarily drawn together, naturally tended to produce considerable collisions; and, in order to understand Octavia's attitude to the Charity Organisation Society, one must remember the different difficulties with which she had to deal. There were, of course, those who had rushed into the movement, as they would have taken up any other new fashion in dress or mode of life or locomotion, and who wished to do nothing that would unduly offend fashionable feeling. These were backed in many cases by people of a higher stamp,—tender-hearted men and women, who were impressed by the misery of the poor, and who merely looked to the Society as a newer, and more efficient, relief agency. At the other extreme were those who thought that organisation and rules could do everything. Then again the attempts at organisation of charity had led to the discovery that many so-called charitable societies were utterly corrupt in their objects, and that many more were unwise and careless in their methods of relief. This raised a furious desire for radical reform, which at one time threatened to substitute destruction for organisation. Along with this iconoclastic zeal was a violent anti-clerical feeling, founded on the belief that the clergy were the authors and chief abettors of the old irregular system of relief. Into this vortex of controversy Octavia was unavoidably dragged.

It will have been seen (and it will have to be reiterated in various forms) that she believed in personal and sympathetic intercourse with the poor, as far more important than any organisation; and that, where co-operation and organisation were necessary, she preferred small local efforts to great centralised schemes. At the same time, she felt that the giving of money, when dissociated, as it too often is, from real sympathy, does infinite harm, and should be checked by reformers of charity.

Both points were emphasised by Octavia in the paper which she read before the Social Science Association in 1869 on the "Importance of aiding the poor without alms-giving."

"Alleviation of distress," she says, "may be systematically arranged by a society; but I am satisfied that, without strong personal influence, no radical cure of those who have fallen low can be effected. Gifts may be pretty fairly distributed by a

S

Committee, though they lose half their graciousness ; but, if we are to place our people in permanently self-supporting positions, it will depend on the various courses of action suitable to various people and circumstances, the ground of which can be perceived only by sweet subtle human sympathy, and power of human love."

And again —

" By knowledge of character more is meant than whether a man is a drunkard or a woman is dishonest ; it means knowledge of the passions, hopes, and history of people; where the temptation will touch them, what is the little scheme they have made of their own lives, or would make, if they had encouragement; what training long past phases of their lives may have afforded, how to move, touch, teach them. Our memories and our hopes are more truly factors of our lives than we often remember."

With regard to her relations to the clergy, I may mention that, while the Charity Organisation Society was still in its infancy, she began an experiment in a Marylebone district which was entirely under the guidance of Rev W. Fremantle, the Vicar of the parish, now Dean of Ripon. So much was Mr Fremantle impressed by the usefulness of this work, that he persuaded Octavia to send in an account of it to the Local Government Board.

It was also through this work that she became acquainted with Rev Samuel Barnett, then curate to Mr. Fremantle, and since so widely known as the promoter of various good works, and especially as the Founder of Toynbee Hall. It was in connection with this Committee that Octavia insisted most on the desirability of substituting employment for relief whenever possible , and out of this plan also arose the scheme of Charity Organisation pensions, which has since formed so important a part of the work of the Society

It may seem strange that, with her preference for individual effort, and for small local organisations, she should have consented to become a member of the Central Council of the Charity Organisation Society. But there was much in that position which chimed in with her aspirations. The Society was, after all, a federation of local Committees, acting in sympathy with each other, but quite independent of each other in many of their arrangements. Then, in theory at least, the Committees acted on the principle that every case was to be dealt with on its own merits; a principle which, if fully carried out, would have been a great protection against mere officialism. The Central Council too was a debating Society, for the exchange of ideas on specially pressing difficulties, rather than a regular governing body. And, in spite of what I have said of the mixed elements in the Council, it must be remembered that the membership of that body brought Octavia into touch with many eminent workers in the reform of charity, amongst whom I would specially mention the courteous and tactful Secretary, Mr. C. P. B. Bosanquet, whose services in the stormy birth time of the Society are too often forgotten.

Nevertheless there were some reforms in the spirit and methods of the Society to which Octavia found it necessary to give attention; and, as I often went with her to the Council meetings, I may claim to know the points which interested her. Thus she soon began to be alarmed at that iconoclastic zeal of which I have spoken; particularly as in some who then influenced the Society's action this zeal had produced a positive delight in attacking for attack's sake. A long struggle, in which Octavia took part, ended in changes which at least modified this unfortunate state of mind.

Another and marked defect in the organisation of the Council led Octavia to abandon, for a time, one of her special beliefs in order to enforce another, which seemed to her of more importance. The Committees of the Society, through which direct relief work has always been carried on, were divided according to the chief London districts; and thus some Committees of the richer parishes were much more able to raise funds in their own neighbourhood than could the Eastern and Southern Committees. The consequence was that the Central Society was obliged to supply funds to supplement the needs of the poorer districts; and, in return, claimed to exercise a control over the distribution of those funds, which could not be claimed over the richer Committees.

s 2

Thus the poorer Committees were deprived of the independence secured by the richer ones

In order to equalise these arrangements, it was proposed to centralise all the funds of the Society in Buckingham Street. Octavia advocated the change, but the majority of the Council felt that such a change would destroy that local interest in the work, on which the strength of the Society depended, and subsequent modifications in the arrangements of the Committees, aided, perhaps, by a considerable change in the *personnel* of the Council, did, to some extent, reform the defect which I have referred to   It may be said generally that, as the aims of the Society became more coherent and definite, and the chief workers grew more alike in their fundamental principles, Octavia's sympathies with the Society increased, and when Mr Loch succeeded Mr Bosanquet as secretary of the Council, her friendship for the new secretary still further strengthened her approval of the action of the Society.

Her sympathies with the enquiry traditions of the Society, and with the restrictions on reckless relief, often startled and repelled some of the more impulsive philanthropists; but one of the most earnest of them wrote, " I remember taking to her a typical case for advice, and she gave me what I thought stern advice, and I demurred.   But she was right, and I often thought of it afterwards."

During this very period, her attention was painfully drawn to the difficulties of her local and more individual work, and to the dangers of that purely official view of charitable movements, against which she was always on her guard.

She had published in a magazine an account of the courts which had been placed under her care, and of course, in explaining the object of her undertaking, she was obliged to describe the condition of the houses when first she undertook the management of them   Unfortunately, some fussy person took the article to the medical officer, with the question, " If these things were so, what were you doing ? "   The medical officer was at once seized with a panic, and ordered the destruction of all the houses in that court   Octavia thereupon went to remonstrate with him, and, after hearing her explanations, he withdrew the order. But he had to report to the Vestry, so the matter could not end with that withdrawal. The majority of the Vestry took the side of their officer ; and one zealous vestryman exclaimed that he hoped they would hear no more of Miss Hill and her houses. The bitterness was so keen that Octavia feared that the tenants of the court would be affected by the local opinion. Mr. Bond, however, who took an active interest in the workmen's club, which had been formed in the court, explained the circumstances to the men , and the general feeling of the tenants was drawn to Octavia's side. Mr. Ernest Hart undertook to discuss the matter with the medical officer ; and gradually the official feeling changed, or at least was greatly modified. But three incidents bearing on the affair should be mentioned.

During the controversy, Octavia's attention was called to the dangers which would come to the court from a public house built close to it. Her first idea was to secure some kind of disinterested management which should prevent the evils of the ordinary public house ; but, finding that, for the time, this was impracticable, she addressed herself to the work of defeating the licence. This she succeeded in doing, but one of the J.P.'s, who had specially championed the publican, was so furious that he addressed insulting remarks to her in reference to her management of the houses.

On the other hand she was much cheered by a letter from Ruskin, received during this crisis Not long after the first houses were bought he had begun a little to cool towards the work, partly from not understanding Octavia's attitude towards alms-giving; and partly from that horror of London ugliness which led him to think that any London scheme must fail. But his personal regard for Octavia remained untouched; and, visiting Carlyle during the crisis, he spoke of Octavia's work, and received such a warm expression of admiration from the "Sage of Chelsea," that he noted down the words and promptly sent them to Octavia, greatly to her delight.

The third incident refers to the attitude of her friends on the Charity Organisation Council. Some of them thought that her management of the courts should be considered as affecting their movement, and that a friendly enquiry into her methods would strengthen their hands She disliked the thought of greater publicity, but reluctantly consented to submit her books and papers to the Special Committee appointed for this enquiry. Though they were friendly in tone, Octavia greatly disliked the visits of these gentlemen, and, when they wished to examine the tenants of the courts to find out the moral effects produced on them by the changes, Octavia put her foot down, and declined to allow this interference between herself and her " friends"

I have given what some may think an undue prominence to this attack on her by the Marylebone officials ; but I have two grounds for that course One is that it was the first important exhibition of that officialism which increased in Octavia her strong dislike of State or Municipal management. The other is that the intensity of her feeling on the matter brings out a point in her character of which many were unaware. I remember well that when Mrs. Nassau Senior was smarting under the attacks on her report on Workhouse Reform, two men remarked that " Miss Octavia Hill would not have felt such attacks, as Mrs. Senior did." Both were intelligent men, and both had some personal acquaintance with Octavia. But both were mistaken.

It was in the middle of these difficulties and struggles that her attention was partly diverted from her own work by her interest in the affairs of a friend ; and, for what I believe to have been the only time in her life, she took an active share in an attempt to return a Member to Parliament. This was in 1874 when Mr Thomas Hughes came forward as a candidate for Marylebone. Her personal admiration for him, dating from the old Christian Socialist days, and strengthened by her experiences as teacher to his children, decided her to abandon her general indifference to Parliamentary work ; and she declared with her usual vehemence that they *would* return him. Canvassers went out from 14 Nottingham Place with electioneering circulars, and all friends whom Octavia could influence were pressed into the service. Unfortunately, for reasons which do not concern this biography, the effort failed, and, by a curious combination of circumstances, several people were led to attribute Octavia's zeal to an interest in the cause of Female Suffrage.

This mistaken idea seems to make this a proper place for a short word of explanation of her attitude on this question. The fact is that Octavia never felt the keen interest in the public questions of the day which animated Miranda; and, since she had discovered that she could do a definite piece of work for the good of the poor, she had begun to feel a positive dislike for Parliamentary life, and party politics, as tending to draw people away from "cultivating their own garden," into taking part in wider, but less immediately useful, work This opinion she felt it specially necessary to emphasise in reference to women.

First; it was with women that she specially co-operated in her work among the poor; and her discovery of a new outlet for their energies, and her warm appreciation of their possible capacity, led her to look on the Female Suffrage movement as a sort of red herring drawn across the path of her fellow workers, which hindered them from taking an adequate interest in those subjects with which she considered them specially fitted to deal. Secondly, even in that pacific phase of the Female Suffrage movement, there were champions of this cause who thought it more important to call attention to what women could accomplish than to undertake regular work. Thus they seemed to promote that intense love of advertising which Octavia abhorred. Lastly, there were always people who assumed that one, who had done so much efficient work, must be in favour of a change, which would enable so many other women less well provided with powers of work to accomplish more than they could now succeed in doing. And this mistake was strengthened by the constant confusion between Octavia and her friend Miss Davenport Hill.

Although she acknowledged in a letter (written from Tortworth and published in this book) that this indifference to these larger issues deprived her of some valuable information, and put her at a disadvantage, she always continued, to the end of her life, to act in these matters rather (as in the Marylebone election) from motives of personal sympathy with some special adviser than from those carefully considered reasons which guided her in the work identified with her name

Of course in the biography of any original thinker or actor one must record apparent contradictions, and it is rather curious that this same period, which contains her one interference in a Parliamentary election, is marked also by her one active attempt to assist in the framing of an Act of Parliament, the Artizans' Dwellings Bill, which brought her into some opposition to more extreme individualists than herself. The main part of her action in this matter will be best brought out by the letters which follow; but there is one point which may be over-looked, and on which I should specially like to insist. In the very period when she was enduring such harsh treatment from the medical officer and the Vestry, she helped in promoting a measure which increased the power both of medical officers and of local councils, in dealing with houses like those under her charge Thus she made it clear that she could see the general advantage of machinery, which had been, and might be, turned against herself.

It must be remembered that all this trying work was carried on while she was still engaged in teaching the pupils at the Nottingham Place School, and many of her friends had felt, for some time, that the effort, needed for the two kinds of work, was too great a strain on her strength An offer of pecuniary assistance by a friend a few years before this time had been gently, but firmly, refused, but, under Mr. William Shaen's guidance, a number of wealthy friends succeeded, without her knowledge, in organising a fund which should make her free for the further development of the housing-reform schemes As this plan had been brought into a definite form before Octavia was aware of it, and as she remembered that one break down in her health had recently occurred, she felt bound to accept the offer, under the limitations mentioned in the letter to Mr. Shaen given in this chapter And thus she was placed for the rest of her life in a position which raised her out of the struggles, which had hampered her early years.

In 1875 Miss Louisa Schuyler, President of the State Charity Aid Association, collected five of Octavia's Magazine articles, and brought them out in America under the title of " Homes of the London Poor." This book was afterwards published in England, and later on translated into German by H.R.H. Princess Alice.

About 1870.

OCTAVIA TO MR. COCKERELL.

I am sending to the East my new assistant, Miss G. By her quiet, gentle manner and familiarity with the poor and their ways, and from being firm, kindly and chatty, she has been more help to me than any assistant has been for many a long day. She has all the powers I have not, and has filled in my deficiencies in B. Court in a way that had made me look forward to working with her very much. Difficulties vanished at her touch ; she had always time to chat with the people, knew all the little news which throws so much light on character, noticed small excellence or neglect about the workman's doings, and kept much of the detail right, leaving me free for the deeper personal intercourse with the people that I happen to get to know best, and to meet the greater difficulties of some of their lives. I shall miss her sorely there ; while I am there, I could have worked well with her ; she would have done all the essential work I do, if not all, at great cost. I am glad to give her to the East ; she lives there, the need there is far greater, and it is all right she should go, we must train the new workers here. It is right she goes, and that is enough.

About 1870.

MR. BARNETT TO OCTAVIA.

I am just back from an evening with the men. I can't help writing to tell you of their talk. They were all of one mind in approving of your system. "It is charity, and it is not charity," said one man. "It is charity because it is human kindness; and it is not charity because it does not make people cringing." Another said, "We had heard that none but your supporters spoke; for every complaint brought out more clearly what you had done." A third thought that they ought to get up a testimonial to you.

November 23rd, 1870.

To Miss F. Davenport Hill.

I send a list of my appointments as they stand at present; of course I can't bind myself to them all; but they show the probabilities.

> *Thursday* —9 till dark, at Hampstead, drawing.
>   7 o'clock Tenants' children's party (I could leave them for an hour or so)
> *Friday.*—9-1 at home drawing.
>   1-1½ at Walmer St. receiving applicants.
>   ¼ to 2 to ¼ to 3 drawing class at home.
>   ¼ to 3 to 4 Walmer St. (if possible) visiting
>   4 to 6 ladies come to see me about work at home.
>   Evening—Half-year's accounts for Drury Lane.
>   Invited to dine out—don't expect to go
> *Saturday.*—9½ to 11 Latin class at home.
>   11 to 1 Committee at 151, Marylebone Rd.
>   Afternoon Walmer St and week's accounts.
>   7 to 10½ Collecting savings at —— Court

Saturday evening, December 3rd, is our party for our old tenants here Oh! do come, if you possibly can; I shall so specially want you. I cannot tell you how I want to talk to you.

January 3rd, 1871.

To MIRANDA.

Your humble servant, the writer, is in good health and spirits, but is growing so deeply devoted to the delights of her own sweet society, that she is somewhat alarmed, and fears that on your return she may be found to have lost the power of speech.

To such tremendous reactions does Nature at times lead us !!! The circle of interest grows also narrower daily, (barring Walmer Street). She cares for nothing and nobody beyond her reach, while she sits in her beloved arm-chair.[1]

Entre nous, however, I think there is still somewhere some little tenderness in her heart for her respected and absent relatives.

I don't know how to sign myself, my persons being hopelessly now in a jumble ; so beg you with your ordinary penetration to discover

THE WRITER.

14, Nottingham Place, W.,
April 24th, 1871.

To MATTHEW DAVENPORT HILL.

I was so much touched and delighted with your letter. Words, such as those from such as you, do so much to help on our way those of us who are struggling, somewhat alone, to meet and master the difficulties that beset us. What I am trying to do is simply in my eyes a bit of adult education or reformatory work, among a few people corrupted by

---

[1] A present to her from the tenants on her return after illness.

gifts. It seems to me that, if we will give them a little sympathy and counsel, we do something for them; but that, if, in addition, we let the grand old laws of the world have their natural fulfilment, we do still more. For a long time the feeling of the people was very awful in its bitterness; but now we are such friends; in fact all the time of difficulty seems quite past in every way. The hissing is all over; and smiles and kind greetings come to me, as in my own houses; and the people come to me for sympathy and advice.

Speaking of a scheme of the Church Council of St. Mary's, Marylebone, as an extension of her scheme, she says

I rather fear their going too fast and far, and letting the practice of supplying work take the place of training and test by means of it.

You will be glad to hear that all the houses are prospering. Our new ones are just built;—the new tenants are to enter them next week. The rooms have been eagerly sought for, as they are in the midst of a densely populated part of Marylebone.

B—— Court, the last purchased property, is still in a dreadful state; oh! so dirty and dilapidated; but the people are so charming; we have such a wonderful hold over them, and can therefore do so much with and for them.

I brought up from the country ninety bunches of flowers. There was one for each family, in three sets of houses. I had such a work distributing them; those in B—— Court had to be given at night, when we went to collect savings. I got such a delightful greeting as I went from room to room. I could not help thinking of the old days, and how changed all was.

September 5th, 1871.

FROM MR. COCKERELL TO ——.

I am very glad to think that you are going to
Ben Rhydding. As we have just come back, it may be
a little amusement to you to have sort of an introduction to some of the people among whom you are about
to spend the next three weeks First and foremost of
all the guests at Ben Rhydding, in my opinion, comes
Miss Octavia Hill; an unobtrusive, plainly dressed little
lady, everlastingly knitting an extraordinarily fine piece
of work, whose face attracts you at first, and charms
you, as you become acquainted with the power of mind
and sweetness of character, to which it gives expression;
a lady of great force and energy, with a wide, open and
well-stored brain, but, withal, as gently and womanly as
a woman can be; and possessed of a wonderful tact,
which makes her the most instructive and the pleasantest
companion in the establishment. Miss Hill has done
great things among the poor, in her own district of
Marylebone; and has written on the subject of homes
for the poor in the " Fortnightly " and " Macmillan."

Undated.

To MISS MAYO.

I hear continual news of all my tenants. To-day
they are to have a tea at our house. It always gives
me satisfaction to think of any amusements provided
for them. I wish we could get them more into the
country. Does it not always seem to you that the
quiet influence of nature is more restful to Londoners
than anything else ? But picnic parties got up among
the London poor, even tho' they are attended only by
the better class, carry London noise and vulgarity out

into the woods and fields, and give no sense of hush or rest. What I should like better than being able to organise large parties (those might be most valuable, and a great deal could be done to give a sense of order and peace to them) would be to be able to take eight or ten people, either children or grown up people, or two families, into some quiet place. If one could afford to give Saturday afternoons to it, for a few months in the year, one might do a great deal. I am sure that the power of enjoying things that are lovely and quiet is one of which the poor stand in need, that it wants cultivation, which means in this case sympathy with the germs of it which are innate, and a little food to nourish it, and occasional quiet to let it assert itself.

Church Hill House, Barnet,
September 26th, 1871.

To Miss Mayo.

It is no joke to get £3,000, to ascertain precisely the value of the property, and to negotiate with all the people concerned, in exactly the right order and way. I have not had a spare five minutes I think till now; and I have thought of you so much, and so very lovingly.

There is something ludicrous in attempting to foresee events. On the *principles* we may build, for they do not change; but the outward things and their teachings we cannot foresee.

Somehow personal poverty is a help to me. It keeps me more simple and energetic, and somehow low and humble and hardy, in the midst of a somewhat intoxicating power. It pleases me, too, to have considerable difficulty and effort in my own life, when what I do seems hard to the people—even though they never know it. I could not tell you all the many ways it helps me. All the same, I know very well that, if in any way that I call natural and right, I found myself set above the necessity for effort and denial for myself, I should bless God, and feel it a relief and help. Only, I should like it to come *only* if it came naturally.

I suppose I told you of dear Minnie's engagement to Mr. Edmund Maurice.

I am thinking of writing on the subject of women's work from their own homes. You know how strongly I believe in its practicability and power. How I should like a talk with you on the question. I am under a promise to write some paper; and I am sure that this would be the most useful, though another about the houses would be most popular. Of course, if I write, it would be with the view of bringing the definite scheme for making volunteers' work more efficient and available before people. My only doubt is how far it is wise to write now, or to wait till we have worked at the question this winter, and can speak of the plan as in more vigorous action. I daresay the question of my having time or not time to write will decide the matter.

12, Victoria Square, Clifton,
December 30th, 1871.

To Miranda.

How I have thought of you, not for your sake, but for my own! I wonder whether it will always be so with you, that people want you always for themselves. No one ever comes to you without being sure of your sympathy and tenderness. But I'm past even your teasing now. Still I am very happy. Ruskin was right in saying I was sure to be.

Undated.

I dined at the Barnetts' last night, met Dr. Bridges, Dr. Abbott, Mr. and Mrs. Courtney, etc. Mr. Barnett is trying to get four acres of land, which is full of lodging-houses. . . . I see he does not think it would be well for me to join the County Council.

The donations come streaming in with such *beautiful* letters.

I am to speak at Fulham Palace on Friday for the Charity Organisation.

12, Victoria Square, Clifton,
January 1st, 1872.

To Miss Harris.

Everyone is very kind, and you know that I have a knack of being happy nearly everywhere; but I grant it is harder to one in holidays than at any other time.

As to public work, Oh Mary! how it is growing and prospering. This is the first day of the year; and looking back on the past one, and forward to the promises of this year, how infinitely much I have to be thankful for! I do not know whether you know that Walmer Street and Walmer Place are actually bought by Miss Sterling; and that we have been able to purify them in a wonderful degree.

Have you heard of the death of old Mrs. Ruskin? It has been strange how, lately, Ruskin has turned back to me I have had such letters from him, asking for my opinions on the triumph of good, and the life after death. I do not think that words, still less letters, are of very much use; still one is glad to say what little one can.

. . . I wonder if you have read either of Browning's

last books;—Balaustion is beautiful. I have the greatest delight in Hercules; and the growth in Admetus is very wonderful; especially the approximation of his nature to that of Alcestis,—as gradually the impression of what she is, and has done, sinks into him. He was beginning to be like his wife. I think that the contrast is marvellously drawn between the extreme joy of a being like Hercules, utterly ready to die at any moment,—prepared therefore for all things,—and the selfish cowardice of Admetus. The dawning in Alcestis of the perception of his defects is very terrible, but very true to nature. The conclusion is beautiful; but I think that I cannot fully have understood it. Browning would never have made such a mistake as to represent people, meaning to do right, and yet being allowed by God to have the fulfilment of their prayer, if it was not really the best for them, and for the world—especially as they never seem to see it; so it has taught them nothing. They realise the holy and happy individual life of love; but miss for ever the power of blessing their country. So I read it. Tell me if I am wrong when you have read it.

Oh, we are getting on so beautifully at St. Mary's! I cannot tell you of half our successes, or the vistas of hope that open out before me. May I only have a long life and many fellow workers!

Crockham Hill Farm, Edenbridge, Kent,
January 3rd, 1872.

To Mrs. Nassau Senior.

DEAREST JANEY,

Stansfeld wrote to tell me that he had written to you. Oh! I do long to hear the result. If you

T

cannot do it, no one can ; and it wants doing, so I hope you will try.

I am so thankful and so touched about your help about the Public-house. You are the only person except myself who has as yet found a soul to help. I can't tell you what a sharing of burdens it feels. I am nearly sick of writing about it, or rather of the thought that by any post now the matter may have to be decided ; and I may not know of enough money to say, "Let the arrangement be made." I dare not promise a farthing more than I have been promised. I never trust to the future for help ; it would seem to me wrong, as I have not of my own what would enable me to meet the engagement ; and, tho' one must get something more, one never knows how much. . . .

I do not know when I have felt such joy as on receipt of Stansfeld's letter; oh! Janey, do try the work if you have a chance.

I am your ever loving friend,
OCTAVIA HILL.

Crockham Hill Farm, Edenbridge, Kent,
January 5th, 1872.

To MRS. NASSAU SENIOR.

Thank you most heartily ; your offer of help did me more good than anything ; somehow such a spirit puts new heart into one. I had a very nice letter from Stansfeld, telling me result of interview ; he appears to have been highly satisfied. God bless and help you in the work. I am a little sorry in one way that it does not take you more away from home. I hoped that you might have had a few hours to rebound from the weight, and might have been stronger for home work for the daily absence. But, in some ways, it will make the work easier ; and I suppose the sense of progress and of public work do one good any way, and carry one thro' a great many small and some most heavy trials with a sustaining sense that there are larger and deeper interests than are contained in our own circle, which is so small, tho' so dear. So the work may help you thus after all, as I'm sure you will help it.

You don't fancy for a moment that I would be so mean as to take your money. No, Janey dear, I could not. Spend it nobly and well as you are sure to do, but don't think of giving it to me. We will try yet, in trust that there are richer people enough forthcoming to do the thing. I shall tell Mr. Hughes this, if he writes. But you can hardly tell how much your offer cheered me. One gets a little impatient and bitter, quite wrongly I am sure, waiting for the slow rich people to make up their leisurely minds, when one's keenly cherished plans hang upon their decision. We, who have gathered our impressions down among the people in long past years, on whom the swift sight of the possibility of good to be done bursts like a clear ray into darkness, who hold our few possessions in money somewhat lightly, ready to risk them, and counting them a small gift to offer for any chance of good, we who are to hold the reins of power, and know just how far we may hope to win, must use a little imaginative patience with those whose training has been so different.

It makes one feel a little lonely sometimes, but in the beginning of things one must be *that*.

April 28th, 1872.

To Mary Harris.

We had our playground festival yesterday, with all its wonderful memories, and the blessed sense of progress. . . Out of the utter loneliness of those first days of work, on that little beloved spot, what a wealth of love and help has gathered, even for me personally. And oh, Mary! what a progress in the people, and the dear old place! The cottages looked so neat and clean, the whole place so fresh and substantially good. I looked at my lamp that stood as a guard throwing light, before which dark deeds quail, night after night where darkness had reigned before,—a type of much of the character of the way we have to work. Neither punishment, nor rewards, nor rule is what we hope most from, but *supervision*, a glance, a look, a bringing things to light. I looked at my cottage with its heightened rooms, —a definite bit of tangible good, strange type too of our work—taking off the weight from above that presses down, in order that the human being may have room to breathe, to expand, to rise. Then how the children have improved! What a number of games they know! And as to my singing class it was quite delightful. They sang with all their hearts, and seemed never weary, song after song I had a troup of them round and about marching and singing "Trelawney." So many of them knew the same songs and games. It was capital! Such days are worth living for.

Tortworth Court,
September 3rd, 1872.

To Mrs Shaen.

Pray tell Mr. Shaen I should lose some very great advantages if he made any alteration as to the "disputing." I hope he never will. It is only that I was amused at Miss Shaen's confirming my impression. I don't at all wish for any change ; it certainly is never unfriendly disputing, and always interesting.

The marriage was very bright and quiet; all was solemn and glad. The tenants gave the Bible, as Minnie and Edmund stepped out of the vestry ; and one of their children gave the loveliest bouquet. I like to think that the blessing of the poor rested on them.

14, Nottingham Place, W.,
November 18th, 1872.

To MRS. NASSAU SENIOR.

I had written to Stansfeld[1] before your letter arrived, but have only just received his reply. I want you to meet him before we enter upon the question of your fitness in any detail. I have therefore told him nothing but that I think I know someone who will do. He is coming to the party on the 28th, as he has long wanted to come to one ; and I shall introduce you to one another there, if all be well. I am sure that you are the very person ; and if he has any sense, he will feel this. We shall see. . . .

Thank you all the same for the offer to take the responsibility. I have really very little to do at this set of parties: my only duty is to bring the entertainers and keep them happy and harmonious. It is not as when my own dear poor are the guests. If you are there, and keeping all going, I shall just rest happily in seeing all go well.

I had a triumphant interview with Longley[2] and the

---

[1] This refers to the appointment of Mrs. Nassau Senior, as the first woman inspector of workhouses, by Mr. Stansfeld, President of the Poor Law Board.

[2] Secretary of the Local Government Board.

guardians this morning, obtained all, more than all I had hoped.

I somehow believe, dear, that we shall get this appointment under Stansfeld managed. It seems so entirely the right thing. I am sure it would be the greatest interest to you to have such a work, and it might even tell as a rest. I am sure that you would do it splendidly.

Nottingham Place, W.,
November 19th, 1872.

MRS. HILL TO MRS. EDMUND MAURICE.

Octavia's mumps at present are nothing but a subject of joy to her; for she stays at home and gets thro' quantities of work with the most gladsome spirit. She gave me a delightful impression of her visit to you; but of course her fatigue, which had been rapidly accumulating for a week reached its climax in that 7 mile walk in the cold and dark. She said the petting she received made up for everything.

November 28th, 1872.

MRS. HILL TO MRS. E. MAURICE.

It seems the tenants have so completely taken it for granted they are to come here on O.'s birthday on December 3rd, that Miss Cons thinks they would arrive on that evening even without invitation. Octa clings very much to you and Edmund being here. . . . . .

Undated.

SAME TO THE SAME

Octa is so interested in the Sanitary Committee of the C.O.S. . . All the men who have worked from the beginning are there and many others besides.   It is not wonderful that Octa should be among them, and able continually to say a word in season.   Dear child, the mantle has fallen on her.[1]

14, Nottingham Place, W.,
December 15th, 1872.

To Mrs. Nassau Senior.

As to the points on which you and I equally differ from so many clergymen and churchmen, if we think Maurice's interpretation of the creeds the true and simple one, is it not doubly incumbent upon us to uphold it *in* the Church?   Leaving it would be like saying we could not honestly stay in it.   Then does not all the best, most thorough, most convincing, most peaceful reform of any body come from within?   in family, in business, in nation, in Church?   Does not all growth and reform come from those who remain with the company in which they find themselves?   Is there not almost always a right at the root of the relationship, which may be asserted and vindicated, and on the recognition of which reform depends?   *That* body must be corrupt indeed, which must be left by earnest members of it.   Surely there are abundant signs of growing healthy life and reform in the Church; all the vigorous and new things nearly are signs of good.   Why should you set up the decidedly old-fashioned interpretation of doctrine, and *that* held by a certainly decreasing number in the Church, and feel hardly honest in differing from it and remaining in the Church?

Don't think I am special-pleading.   Except for the

---

[1] An allusion to her grandfather, Dr. Southwood Smith.

sake of the Church, I don't care where you are. While you are what you are, you are safe everywhere; for you will find grace and goodness in all things; and God's Church certainly comprehends those not in the Church of England. If you are sure that the services do not speak to and with you in words that help; if there is a lurking sense of want of courage or candour in remaining, which is real, not fancied; if you have a sense of antagonism and alienation, not support and fellowship, why not leave the Church? Those who love and know you would never feel you further from them; and, if you found support and peace greater from other teaching and other services, why not go where you would have it? To me, of course, the old services, which first opened to me the sight of how things are, and how they should be, come home to me with a gathered force almost weekly. To me there open continually new visions of how our Church will expand and adapt itself to the large comprehensiveness and new needs of the time. I believe the men who are now in her will cling on, with passionate affection, to the creeds and services; but that they will link themselves more with the outer world, and see with clearer eyes; and that the Church will insensibly grow with and by their growth.

I see in such movements as Mr. Fremantle's Church Council, open to people of all creeds by election, a sign of much deeper and wider faith than churchmen have hitherto recognised as possible in the Church. I see in it, also, much ground of hope in the added responsibility and interest possessed by laymen. The new permission to use churches for lectures on secular subjects seems to me another sign of the breaking down of formal distinctions, and recognition of life as holy.

14, Nottingham Place, W.,
January 22nd, 1873.

To Mrs. Nassau Senior.

You slipped out so that I did not see when you went ; and I do not seem one-half to have thanked you for all your help ; it was of a kind I never can forget. Neither do I seem to have told you how very happy the news of the arrangement with Stansfeld made me.

I hope you were not damped by the hitch about the " Public." I am so accustomed to this kind of thing, and to its coming all right, that I seem to see beyond the difficulty. Will you, when you are seeing or writing to your friends, tell them of the delay in the immediate starting of the plan ? It *shall* be done soon somehow, and might come to an issue any day ; but I feel a little anxious lest any contributor should begin to think we did not intend to try the plan, if they hear nothing for some little time. You will know best to whom this temporary pause had better be explained.

February 8th, 1873.

Miranda to Mrs. Durrant.

Did I tell you that Mr. Barnett, the curate who has worked with Octavia so admirably in St. Mary's, has just married Miss Henrietta Rowland, one of Octavia's best workers ; and now they are going to live and work in the East End ? Octavia thinks it such a splendid thing to have such a man at work down there —she thinks it quite a nucleus of fresh life ; and Mrs. Barnett, of whom Octavia is very fond, is admirably fitted for the work too. The wedding was very touching—the church was crowded with poor people ; even the galleries were filled with them. He

was so much beloved—one of those men with strong
individual sympathies and an intimate personal knowledge of the people in their homes—a strong Radical
too, with a horror of class distinctions, and practical
disregard of them, which you don't find in all Radicals.

14, Nottingham Place,
March 6th, 1873.

To a friend who had been calumniated.

No rumours nor published statements, or chattering remarks would ever confuse me, or weigh for a
moment against the quiet assurance of anyone whom I
trusted.   The *facts* which really concern one about
one's friends are not those of their business or circumstances, but of themselves ; and I think one knows a
little when and how one may trust.   When one does
feel confidence, much more confusing circumstances
than these have ever been do not touch one's trust.
I think one often has to hold two truths apparently
utterly inconsistent, side by side in one's mind, knowing that, both being proved true, there must be some
possibility of reconciling them by some unknown third
truth, which time may reveal.   And I am sure that
trust in anyone, known to be good, could not be
shaken by merely outward appearances.   One likes
to know how things are.   One objects to be puzzled,
and to have no word of explanation about how things
are ; but trust in human beings is no more to be
determined by want of sight, than the trust in God
Himself is by the impossibility of seeing why He leads
us by certain ways we cannot understand for the
moment.   For the human trust is based on that which
is part of His nature, and as such is quite firmly
planted. . . . We read half a controversy, and largely

resolve that the truth lies somewhere between the two correspondents. We do not long for judgment, but " hush matters up," or let them " blow over"; and do not bring them out to the light, and choose between them.

March 9th, 1873.

To Mr. COCKERELL.

I am in a frantic state of excitement (which I fear will be dashed very completely) as to the public-house. Mr. Fremantle handed me a slip of paper at a meeting yesterday to say that the licence of the " Walmer Castle " had been refused, and asking if he should see Sir J. Hamilton (who is chairman, I think he said, of the Bench), about granting one to us. . . . Since which, tho' I have written and sent messengers, I cannot get any answer. . . . To-morrow I purpose going myself and waiting till I can see him. . . .

I wonder why you enjoy Jason " immensely." It is marvellously real, and so old-world as to be a refreshment to those mixed up with nineteenth-century things. The images are lovely, and the music of the verse soft ; but the sustained melancholy of the whole poem is very terrible, I have always thought, a certain measure being put on all joy by the belief that it has no outcome, no fulfiment anywhere beyond itself. You have not, I daresay, finished the book to see how, with all his fortitude, just because he misses the highest joy of all, he chooses so low a one as to reject all that had made the majesty of life, the companion at once of pain and of his greatness too. I have always longed to see how Morris would treat a distinctly Christian story, and was full of regret that he withdrew—or never wrote—his promised " St. Dorothea."

March 16th, 1873.

To MARY HARRIS.

How strangely people do come to me, Mary! I cannot make it out. There is something in the work which strongly attracts them. Mr. —— seemed perfectly engrossed, and could hardly tear himself away. What it is, I cannot tell; but either pity, or some other feeling, is gathering round me a company of allies so kind and so zealous that I ought to achieve a great deal. It is well for me that I am served so willingly, for I would rather do anything at any cost than have it done for me unreadily.

March 23rd, 1873.

To MARY HARRIS.

We have heard to-day a sermon of Kingsley's for the Girls' Home. It was almost wholly about Mr. Maurice, and gave him fully the place one believes he has. It was a sermon full of Kingsley's own peculiar power; and there was not a word in it that was not true and beautiful. It was to us a sight of deepest solemnity. The church,—*that* where we were baptised, and confirmed and where Minnie was married—was crammed with people, and one knew every second face. It was filled with the old Lincoln's Inn and Vere St. people, and with their spiritual inheritors of all that teaching. Mr. Davies, grave and intense, was the moving spirit there. . . .

We had a very good meeting on Wednesday at Willis's Rooms. I was the only lady on the platform, and in the ante-room had such interesting talk with all the people. Lord Shaftesbury and Lord Westminster and Lord Lichfield and Mr. Hughes, Mr. Andrew Johnston, Mr. Longley, and hosts of people were there.

Mr. Hughes stayed by me all the time and was so kind. Did I tell thee about dining at the Cowper Temples and meeting Kingsley and Lord and Lady Ducie ? It is all very interesting ; but thou knows how often the loveliest and best things one meets are not among the celebrities at all, but by piercing below the surface of those who are supposed to be commonplace. I cannot tell thee how often this happens to me.

Brantwood, Coniston,
April 27th, 1873.

To MARY HARRIS.

I have stores of lovely memories, to last for many a day. . . . We drove to the foot of a steep ascent, and then climbed the steep slope,—such a road. It was by smooth slopes set with fir and larch and sycamore, by mountain walls covered with ivy, till at length we got to where the lake lay far beneath us. Then we left the road and went on to a central point, where the peaks stood round us like a great company of spirits ; and one ridge beyond another showed their great blue flanks ; past a mountain tarn, and wild stream, which flowed to the valley, by cascades and dark deep brown pools, and banks set with primrose, anemone, and wood sorrel. . . . It ended very brightly and sweetly after all, quite to my heart's content.

14, Nottingham Place, W.,
May 11th, 1873.

To MARY HARRIS.

The cupboard [1] is come and is fairly established in my room. You cannot tell what a rest and delight it is to me. For, first, it looks quite at home and gives a

[1] A cupboard sent specially from Cumberland, dated 1605

solemn old-world feeling to the room which is in itself a
rest. But, secondly, the carved frieze on which are date
and initials, is thrown forward and its projection throws
a great quiet space of shade which the eye cannot
penetrate. It is like some of those old Byzantine
palaces, or the shadow below the Palazzo Vecchio at
Florence. The recess panels, old knobs, even the key-
holes, give sharp shadows much smaller, but full of
beauty. I did not the least anticipate the beauty of
this while the cupboard stood in the hall. The double
light was very unbecoming, while the height of this
window and the nearness of the cupboard to it makes
the shadows beautifully steep. The shade it throws on
the door is very nice   As to the Doge, he looks quieter
than ever up above the dark oak. The room looks perfectly beautiful to my mind. I need hardly say the
cupboard stands behind the door, the sofa with its end
towards door. I sit in my green chair and gaze at the
cupboard with greatest delight.

May 18th, 1873.

To Miss Harris.

I have bought a house in ——, certainly the
worst Court left untouched by us on this side of the
parish.

Mr. Longley writes to me from the Local Government
Board, to say they are really thinking of appointing
Mr. Barnett a Guardian   I am just going to St. Jude's
(Whitechapel) to spend the evening.

We are deeply interested about the rebuilding in
B. Court. I wish we could pause a very little, and
reinforce ourselves in our old positions, before extending
further. I almost tremble when I see how little power
of growth any of our schemes have, where I withdraw

myself.   However, I say to myself, "Courage! it will
the more bring out the character and power of your
fellow-workers." I often and often pray heart and soul
as I go in and out, that someone with wisdom and zeal
would arise, and take my place or part of it. The Store
is doing very badly, and I wish you would send me a
prospectus of the Manchester Store. Dearest Lady
Ducie is more and more in —— Court. It is a great
blessing.

14, Nottingham Place, W.,
May 25, 1873.

To Mrs. Nassau Senior.

I shall be delighted to see Dr. Mouat as well as
the others, on Wednesday. I only ought to point out to
you that in going through the courts, especially if we
go into any rooms, we must divide. Five of us could
not well invade a small room unexpectedly; also that
in areas, yards, and courts, one can't talk so well to a
large party, to point out what has been done, or tell
what was. It might be well managed in this way.
You might all come here; and we might sit and have a
nice talk before we start. We might appoint that
Miss Cons should meet us in the Court; and two might
go with her, and three with me, to see what is to be
seen. She can and does tell and show as well or
better than I. Wednesday is by no means a hard day,
thank you, for me; especially as they have determined
that the Dwellings Committee at the Council should not
sit this week. I shall enjoy dining with you very much;
it would do me all the good in the world; as to meeting
Mr. Bosanquet, it would be a great pleasure. He is a
man who lives up to his Christianity, moment by
moment, and in silence teaches it more powerfully than

almost anyone I know. He is just a touch conventional, and alarms me in proportion ; but I like him thoroughly. I wonder how you are. You say nothing of that. It will be so nice to see you again.

June 15th, 1873.

I have had a great delight this week. Browning has been reading his last volume at Lady D——'s. The intense fervour of the man dominated the company into a hush of awe.

The MacDonalds are home and so kind. Mr. James Cropper of Kendal has asked me to go and stay with him.

14, Nottingham Place, W.,
June 22nd, 1873.

To Mrs N Senior.

I never realised till this moment that I had not written to tell you how very glad we shall all be to have Miss C. here. I think it may help us all to get on better together I wish I were gentler, and better able to let people see what I feel. In one way I can conceal nothing. Everyone knows what I think, right or wrong, which passes ; but few know how much I care for them Sometimes people almost make me wonder whether I love in some other, poorer way than most people after all ; one cannot measure one's own love by that of others ; but I feel as if I loved very deeply, rejoiced in natures, would serve people thankfully, never forsake them ; but it seems to be very difficult for any but a few to know this I daresay little thoughtfulnesses and gentle gracious acts are worth a great deal more ; and these I miss doing very disgracefully. Well, I do try to amend ; and where I fail, people must forgive me, and take what they can get from me, hoping to find what they need most from others.

It will be very delightful to see you to-morrow night. There is a kind of piano at the Club; we shall want plenty of songs. Probably you know the kind; simple ones, that will do them real good, and especially "Angels ever bright and fair." The room is tiny, and very close; but we will do our best to air it; you said you perferred meeting us there. The hour is 8 o'clock.

Cullen,[1] Banffshire,
September 6th, 1873.

To Mrs. Edmund Maurice.

As to me I am as well as it is possible to be, and very happy. We had magnificent weather for our journey; and here the weather is very nice, tho' we have hardly a day without some rain. We don't pay any attention to it, but manage to be out seven or eight hours daily. The sea is so grand just now; there have been storms out at sea; and the swell sends the waves rolling in, and breaking in masses of foam about the rocks. There was a revival here among the fishermen twelve years ago; the effects of it seem really to have lasted; and everyone dates all the reforms from *that*. The fishermen are a splendid race here; vigorous and simple. Mr. MacDonald seems so at home with them; and we often get into nice talks with them on the beach. The sea-town, as they call it, and another tiny village called Port Nochie contain nothing but fisher-men; they hardly intermarry at all with the land popu-lation; but are a distinct race, tho' within a few yards

[1] She was on a tour in Scotland with George MacDonald and his family.

of us here.   They have only about six surnames in the
place ; every man is known by a nick-name.   We spent
the day on Wednesday at an old castle on a promontory
of rock, washed on three sides by the sea itself.   The
position and plan remind me forcibly of Tintagel.   It is
called Finlater Castle, and is now nothing but a ruin.
The family is merged in that of the present Lord
Seafield, who is the head of the clan Grant ; and bears
for his motto, " Stand fast Craig Ellachie ! "   Do you
remember Ruskin's allusion to it in " The Two Paths"?
Lord Seafield's house is close to here.   They are away ;
but have lent Mr. MacDonald keys to the garden
and house. . . .   I am delighted that you got the girl
that situation. . . .   How very nice about the Work
Class tea.   I do so much like to hear of things like that
when I am away.

> 14, Nottingham Place, W.,
> September 28th, 1873.

To Miss Harris.

> . . . . The number of people whom I saw who
were interested in the work was very great.   Among
others, Mr. F. Myers, the poet, offered me £500
for houses.   Mr. Crowder did the same.   Did I tell thee
that his father is dead ?   He comes into a large fortune,
and is full of schemes of his future work.   He has two
friends, clergymen, with them he hopes to work ; but
they seem to me set on the country, and he on London
work.   If he comes alone to London he says that
it would be to me , but I should try to transfer him to
Mr. Barnett.

They all got up at five o'clock, drove some miles, and
came by train to Rugby to talk over matters with me.
They are such a splendid trio.

1873 (?).

To Mrs. Fitch.

Can you interest anyone in the plan described in the enclosed ?   And will Mr. Fitch give his name to the North Marylebone Committee ?

I shall never forget Mr. Haweis's action in this matter, and shall respect him all my life.   He saw the magnitude of the undertaking, but never paused, for fear he should be leading a forlorn hope ; he resolutely and earnestly took the matter up.   He has got us a worker as Honorary Secretary, at once, and thinks we are certain " to succeed if we do the thing well," as we only want money.

Hope is the one article which is deficient ; but, though I have always the smallest imaginable supply of it myself, I feel as if, for the sake of securing air and light and beauty for the hundreds I see up in those fields, when I take my own people there, I had resolution enough to nerve every one else in London for the effort.   We have nearly £4,000 promised, and have only been at work a few days ; but the provoking thing is that so many people say they will help, if the scheme is carried out, instead of seeing that it depends on them, and such as they, to say what they will give, before we can tell whether it will be carried out.

Perhaps I am impatient ; but I wish small people would build like the ants, and believe the heap will grow bigger, if they persevere ; and that big people would take pattern from Mr. Haweis, and be a little more courageous, even if it should turn out that they lead a forlorn hope ; and that they would not hang back, till they see if others of their kind come in a flock.

These fields are within the four miles radius,—are

within a stone's throw of a station of the Metropolitan ; their view can't be built out because they are on a hill ; the houses are rapidly creeping round their fourth side ; they are within an easy walk of Lisson Grove and its crowded courts, to say nothing of our people here. Of course they are not central, yet no one can make a park, when a place has become central. Let them try in St. Giles or Clerkenwell ; we must a little precede the builders, if we are to have central places. I have one idea at this moment,—" the fields." Laugh at me as much as ever you feel inclined ; but get Mr. Fitch to help us.

14, Nottingham Place,
October 5th, 1873.

A special extra letter to fellow-workers about a proposed inscription on Freshwater Place

．　　．　　．　　．　　．　　．　　．　　．

I should have liked to have written to each, because I should like to have recalled the special thanks, which makes me anxious you should each consent to help me in a piece of work that I have in hand Some of you have worked side by side with me in the court which it will benefit ; some of you have helped me with money and with sympathy never to be forgotten, in difficult undertakings, before the world smiled on them, or success crowned them ; some of you stood by me when my work was unpopular, and seemed to many cruel ; some of you have knelt with us in daily prayer, lived among us, learnt things from us, cheered us with your glad young lives, and are now gone back to other homes. Perhaps you were interested in our work, when you were among us ; perhaps you understood and cared little for it then ; but it may look more important and

useful as you look back to it. Some of you have never
lived or worked with us at all, but have entered into
the deeper fellowship of sympathy, have hoped for
the same bright things, prayed for them, and feel
(though separated by space) "one of us," in a deeper
sense than *that* in which some of you have used the
phrase.

I cannot write to each of you; but, if, on any of
these grounds, you would care to help in a plan that I
have much at heart, I earnestly wish you would.

You all know Freshwater Place, our first freehold,
Mr. Ruskin's court, where we have our playground,—
which is mixed up with May festival memories for
many of you.

You know something of how hard I worked for it
long ago; my difficulties in building the wall, and in
contending with the dirt of the people; how gradually
we reduced it to comparative order, have paved it,
lighted it, supplied water cisterns, raised the height
of rooms, built a staircase, balcony, and additional
storey; how Mr. Ruskin had five trees planted for us,
and creepers, and by his beautiful presents of flowers,
helped to teach our people to love flowers. You know,
or can imagine, how dear the place is to me.

For some six years now, I have thought that, if ever
I could afford it, I should like to put up along the
whole length of the four houses which face the playground on the east side, some words, which have been
very present to me many a time, when my plans for
improving the place for the tenants were either very
unsuccessful for the moment, or very promising or
very triumphant, or very bright, but far away in the
future.

The words are these :—" Every house is builded by

some man ; but He that built all things is God."   They have been present to me when I have been at work in putting to rights visible, tangible things there ; they have been no less present to me, when I have been trying to build up anything good in the people. They have reproached any presumption in me ; but they have revealed to me the sure ground for the very brightest hope that I have ever cherished for the worst of them ; for it is indeed but a very limited sense in which we build anything ; we only work as His ministers ; but all that is built, or shall be built and established, He doeth it Himself.

How much of all this meaning the passers by may see one does not know, nor very much care.   The words would assuredly be a blessing to some people when they come suddenly upon them, in a city full of places, that almost make one think that God did not build them,—has forgotten them,—and does not mean to rebuild them in the years to come, when we listen to His voice more

Now will you help me to place the words there ?   I am not likely ever to be able to afford to do it myself ; but I was talking one day lately to a friend about my six years' wish to do it ; and he suggested that many people might like to help.   There are fifty-six letters ; if each letter is a foot square, the inscription will occupy the full length of the four houses ; each letter will cost nearly 8/-.   If any of you will give a letter, you may like to feel that you have helped to write a sentence that will speak when you are far away, and after you are dead.

I want to make the sentence very lovely in colour, that the mere brightness of it may be a joy to every one that sees it.   It will be done in tiles, so that every

shower of rain may keep them clean and bright. I
want them to be done in blues, purples and greens, and
very bright ; for, though the loveliest effect comes from
a subdued glow with sparks of brilliant colour gleaming
out, our inscription, costly as it will be, and though it
will run the length of four houses, will be a little space
compared with the dingy spaces of wall in the court,
and but a spot compared to the still dingier spaces of
all London ; so we must treat it as the spark, and let
it glow with bright colours.

She ends by two long quotations from Ruskin, of
which she says :—" They, no doubt, taught me to care
for permanent decoration, which should endear houses
to men, for external decoration which should be a
common joy."

October 26th, 1873.

To Mr. Cockerell.

Thank you very much for the nice rent book.
It is such a pleasure to me to see things nice ; and I
am sure it has a good influence on everyone concerned.
Just because I do so little to put them right myself, it
gives me quite a thrill of gratitude and pleasure when
anyone else does. . . . Miss —— is sure to consider it
quite thrown away labour. Why is this in her, I often
wonder ? She would do a thing of the kind any day
to spoil me, but she would think me quite mad to care,
all the time. I went to Mr. De Morgan's studio. *I*
think the things lovely ; and I think I mean to decide
the matter according to my desire, partly because I
care very much, partly because the thing will last ;
and I think the world is coming round towards such
colour and design almost every year ; so I shall feel

only a little in advance of it, not out of harmony. But I am quite sure that the dim subdued solemn colour, and blurred uncertain suggestive outline, will not seem to people in general half so pretty, or so *good*, as the clearly defined edge and crude but gay colour of some other tiles. There is an artistic loveliness about the one, which one must watch to care for ; while the vulgar completeness of the other commends itself to modern taste. So far, I know you personally will agree with me ; and we must prepare other people to be disappointed. But, in my next decision, I don't know that I shall carry even you with me. The more I thought out the question, and the more I saw of the tiles, the more I felt as if blue, and blue only, would look best. I can't see how we can get a look of unity in the inscription, if we introduce other colour. I dislike a distinction between capitals and other letters in colour, when one has no difference in height. I dislike the idea of a line round the inscription ; besides, it would decrease the size. I therefore strongly urged blue only, but gradated blue, such as I saw there. I know in his heart Mr. De Morgan agreed with me He has, however, a lovely copper lustre, which gleams like a fish's back, and tells now as light, now as dark, like gold, according to how the rays fall on it ; and he sorely wants to see this ; also he has a deep crimsony red which he is fond of. I never wavered, however, in my adherence to the blue, except in sight of one plate, —green blue and purple shot like a peacock's tail, but in a lighter key. I really decided nothing ; first, because I had not the money, but I might have decided provisionally, and let a postcard finish the business with the one word "now," when all the tiles are promised ; but Mr. De Morgan, like a true artist, pressed so hard for leave to try different colours and designs, on his own responsibility, and for his own pleasure, that I agreed at last that he should do a few letters in the next kiln. Of course it is all gain to us; and I was most decided that none of the money subscribed should go in experiments.

E . .Miss Harrison
V . .Mr. Smalo
E ...Mrs. Godwin
R .. Miss Smith
Y ...Mr. Downs (Ruskin's Gardener), who planted the trees in the playground.
} Old fellow workers specially connected with the court itself.

H...Mary Harris
O . .Mr Young
U...Lady Ducie
S Mr. Shaen
E ...Mrs. Shaen
} Very great personal friends of old standing, except Mr. Young, who has been a very true helper.

I ...Mr. & Mrs. Hughes
S ...Mrs. N. Senior
} a word a family.

B ...Mrs. Hill
U ...Margaret
I ...Miranda
L ...Mr. & Mrs. Lewes
D ...Myself
E ...Mr. & Mrs. Maurice
D ...Florence
} a word a family.

B ...Mr Barnett
Y ...Mrs. Barnett
} word for family, initial letters too.

S ...Mr Harrison
O ...Mrs. Harrison
M...Mr. Macdonell
E ...Mrs Macdonell
} a word a family now solemnised by death

B ...Mrs Johnston
U ...Miss Trevelyan
T ...Miss J. Trevelyan
} a word a family.

H...Ruskin
E . .Mr & Mrs MacDonald.

T ...Mr. Mayo
H...Miss Mayo
A ...Miss A. Mayo
T ...Miss C Mayo
} a word a family.

B ...Miss Baumgartner
U .Mr S. Beaumont
I Miss Dittrich
L ...Mr. Matheson
T ...Mr. Barrington
} Somewhat miscellaneous, but a beautiful word, and all worthy of it

A ...
L ...
L ...
} Our pupils, including Miss S Burgess.

T .Mrs. Whately
H...Emma Clover.
I ...Mr Boyle.
N ...Col. Gardiner.
G ...Stansfeld.
S ...Miss Sterling.

I ...Alice Meredith
S ...Miss Humphreys
} a word for two great friends.

G ...Ruskin.
O ...Mr. Watson
D ... ,, ,,

Blank Tiles

Mr Bond.
Mr Kincaid.
Miss Ridley.
Miss J. Trevelyan.
Miss Bain and her friend.

November 11th, 1873.

DEAREST MRS. SHAEN,

Mr. Shaen's repeated help, again and again, has alone carried us through difficult crises in the work. It is not only his power and thoroughness nor only the amount of heart with which he has entered into its objects, but the blessed sense of quiet and assurance it gives to feel how completely one can trust him, that makes me know that we owe more to him than to almost anyone else who has helped us. I shall never forget his help at times of difficulty, and uniform kindness always.

14, Nottingham Place,
October 12th, 1873.

To MRS. N. SENIOR.

I have not felt at all like a friend in not answering you before, as I often do when people do or write loving things, and I never utter a word. But I did not feel so—for I knew that you knew quite well much that it was in my heart to say. Only now I do delightedly seize the time for writing.

I do see very distinctly indeed how ladies might be enrolled in the service of the Poor Law, just as we do it here. I think that the plan has immense advantages, so long as we have out-door relief; and that it might help to break down the system very much. If I were doing the thing, I would enrol not ladies, but volunteer men and women. They must have a definite head and centre. That centre might be either paid or unpaid. I think our relieving officers and guardians would report well of the scheme, even as it works now; though, after it has been longer on foot, of course we could prove more results. We could be used to any extent for an extension of the scheme, if it were decided on, and if the time had arrived for extending it. It is very different from the larger questions which Stansfeld asked you to grapple with, and comes down to the individual work, and would fit on therefore with ours here. I will delightedly see you about it, at any time or place that you arrange. This, of course, touches nothing but the question of *out-door* relief I don't think that I have anything practical to suggest about the in-door poor, among whom, no doubt, women's work is much needed. One sees a great many principles, which ought to be brought to bear in the workhouse, if only one went there in power; but I have neither experience nor time to help in this direction.

I see certain definite lines of work, in which I shall be particularly glad of help; but of course it would never do to break in upon a definite course of reading.

Miss Peters,[1] my new assistant, has not come yet unfortunately. I almost pray that she may stay, as she seems so exactly all that I have so long wanted.

Mr. Barrington is so good that I grow much interested in him, and am very grateful to him.

The following letter refers to a testimonial presented to Mr. Cockerell by the members of a Workmen's Club.

December 21st, 1873.

To Mr. Cockerell.

Surely the recognition of and approval of good work depends on the degree of the perfection of the perceiving and measuring power of onlookers. There is much glittering meretricious work which everyone sees and applauds; there is much of the noblest work which

---

[1] Afterwards Mrs. Loch.

few, if any, see; but surely, while we have spirits and hearts, we must sometimes catch a glimpse of the good things done among us, and of their value. You must indeed have a low opinion of your poor club friends, if you think that, because they see it, and respect it, and delight in your work, it must be bad. There was no oppressive sense of obligation among them; there was no flattery, expectant of returned compliments; there was no thought of your expecting word or token of thanks; but so far as I could see, a happy over-brimming sense of help, joyfully given and joyfully received. Nothing delighted me more than the earnest, intense way in which when the speaker poured out his epithets of "liberal," "gracious," "generous," the noun that had to come was (rather, I thought, to his own surprise) "advice." It seemed to me quite beautiful that, with the wide class gulf between you, the relation was so manly, so happy, so independent; and that the adjectives were so evidently hearty and sincere and the gift so pure from all taint When you read the end of Brook Lambert's letter, or Lowell's Sir Launfal, you will know why the relationship between you seemed to me so real, even tho' their sense that the only thing they could give you was not a *thing* at all, but a few words to tell you what they felt Did you feel so "dumb"? Well! it did not strike me so I believe I anticipated *that*; I do not think people can do otherwise than as their nature prompts them, especially when suddenly tried. But do not be uneasy; your life has not been "dumb" to them, and will not be; perhaps will speak none the less deeply for that very dumbness . . .

Yes! I suppose you too would have shut yourself out from the inscription, if I had been foolish enough to mean, and you had known me so little as to think

I meant, that you should measure the amount and form of your faith, before helping us. I never meant it. It is good to be wholly honest, and to say the difficult and unpopular thing, when one has to answer a question, and to be cautious not to confuse a feeling with an opinion, nor a hope with a logically proved conviction. But I should be the last person to ask the question, especially in that way, or to desire to shut out anyone in the cold, who had not clearly thought out their belief, or to whom gigantic problems loomed terrible between themselves and the desired belief. . . .

I didn't want the gift made unwillingly, nor, certainly, insincerely ; but the latter I never suspected. To me the real man is the man when his hope is brightest, and the vision of what *may be* almost trembles into certainty, that that best thing *is*. This is the man I see and know, see as I myself believe that he will be when the veils are rent asunder, and he sees, after having learnt what it is to be alone and blind. To me too there is much the same kind of distinction between a man's distinctly grasped and well defined opinions, and his gleams of what may be beyond them, as Browning shows, between his achieved work and visions of better things, when he says :—

Then she quotes the three verses beginning " Not on the vulgar mass," from Rabbi Ben Ezra.

Hastings (George MacDonald's).
December 27th, 1873.

To Mr. Cockerell.

I am not a little amused that the idea that the best man is the real man should seem to you in any way new. I am sure you must always have felt it and acted on it, with children, with wrong-doers, when they, whom you have watched and cared for, have wandered from what is right; whenever you have tried to reconcile a quarrel, whenever you have tried to forgive anyone who has done you a wrong. It can only be the definite way of putting the thought into words that can be new. I think all the sense of peace one is able to have in this world comes from this conviction; certainly all who have tried to reform themselves owe their strength to this faith. It seems to me the only ground for preaching freedom, and the only right foundation for hope for any of us. . . . Miss Cons came out with such a great proffer of help that it made me feel how real her friendship was, whatever little clouds or freaks might obscure it; how it was something that might be depended on in need, and was real and true all the time. It did me such good. I came down here quite encouraged.

Tortworth Court,
January 3rd, 1874.

To Mr. Cockerell.

I wonder what you would think of life here. I often feel how much most people would learn and gather from men actually engaged in the political world's work; and how much I lose it all, for need of knowledge enough to learn. I come in, like some queer new being, from another region; but I think it enlarges one even to see and listen to those whose interests are so different. Lady Ducie I know you would like heartily and deeply. I feel it a great privilege to see her so thoroughly. What a strange thing it is to glide so wholly into a sense of ease and perfect harmony with such a variety of people as I know, and to meet them on such simple human grounds of sympathy !

March 26th, 1874.

MRS. HILL TO MRS. EDMUND MAURICE.

Octavia had her party of 300 costermongers from Drury Lane last night. She did not sit down once from 3 o'clock till past eleven, nor did she eat in the interval. It was a grand success. The people thoroughly enjoyed themselves. Of course they did ample justice to the tea, and liked the music so much,— poor people. Miss Antoinette Sterling sang beautiful, rather solemn, music, in her rich alto voice. When she and her friend came in in opera cloaks, the people cheered ; " it was all the opera cloaks," she said to Octa. . . . The clergyman was enthusiastically delighted, and told O. she should have a great hall in his parish whenever she wanted it. . . .

Undated.   Probably April, 1874.

MRS. HILL TO MRS. EDMUND MAURICE.

. . . Mr Barnett's illness *is* sad. . . . Octa went there on Sunday evening, and had a very interesting talk with him. She asked him what would be the end of the East End. Would it disperse, or what ? He said he thought it would change ; that there is a great deal of building going on countrywards—houses that implied an income of £500 a year or so ;—these were taken by people who had got their money in the East End, and who would continue their connection with it, and help to raise it. He thinks it more airy than the West End. His house is better built than Mr. Hart's in Queen Anne Street. Mr. and Mrs. Hughes sent Octa a pressing invitation for Sunday evening ;—but the Barnetts won. . . . O. is going to dine this evening at the Seeleys'. She keeps wonderfully well, and is as busy as a bee—in and out—in and out—very *like* a bee— and like it too in her happy murmurings whilst at work, and evident pleasure in the work. . . .

> Derwent Bank, Broughton,
> April 12th, 1874.

OCTAVIA TO MRS. EDMUND MAURICE.

Thank you very much indeed for the letter of introduction to Professor Caird. . . . I hope I may have time to see him ; but I shall only be there two nights, and have my time pretty well promised. . . . M. will tell you that the C.O.S., St Mary's, the Council, and a private lesson prevent us from taking any other day for the excursions, except Wednesday.

> June 16th, 1874.

OCTAVIA TO WM SHAEN.

I did not manage to say to you to-day what I was wanting much to say, which was that, in spite of the extreme kindness and beautiful feeling shown by whoever has given all this help, I must request you not to receive for me one farthing more. The thing is done, beautifully, efficiently, abundantly ; *there* really it must rest. I have more than enough for holidays and every-thing I can possibly want, as much as ever I wish to have. And it is one thing to accept once for all a great gift like this ; and quite another to take help for special objects in this way. I do assure you I would rather not ; in fact I simply can't do it. I don't know that I could logically defend my position, but I feel the distinction very deeply ; and I do assure you I mean what I say.

. . . I can never want or have to earn again, and I feel richer than I ever did, and able to do things I never dreamed of doing. But once more and most emphatically I decline more. I have enough.

1874.

To Miss Harris.

It is very nice being again right down among the tenants; and, oh! dear me! how things do get on when one does them oneself! It has all caused a great change in my life; for I have now *four* nights weekly engaged among the people,—often *five*; so I have to refuse nearly every invitation that comes, and, except for my near fellow-workers, I see little of anyone, except the poor. However, the fellow-workers are now very numerous, and care to take trouble to see one.

Andy and the girls are entering most heartily into one or two plans for the poor. Agnes Yarnall's [1] great interest is such a help among the girls. The girls are to issue invitations, devise entertainments, and order things for the tenants' children's party. And Miranda and they are to practise sacred music for one of the St. Jude's Soirées (*i.e.* for Mr. Barnett's church in White-chapel). I am so glad, for the old interest appeared to have cooled so of late years; but now they are full of it. I went a long walk with the Barnetts at Wimble-don; it was so lovely, and I brought back fresh green moss, and a few gorse flowers.

June 18th, 1874.

Mrs. Hill to Mrs. Edmund Maurice.

. . . Octavia's affairs *do* grow. This morning she received offers of four other properties. I don't

---

[1] Daughter of Ellis Yarnall.

know that she will accept them. Miss Cons and Octa
have gone to dine at Mrs. Backhouse's. . . . O. was
tempted by the attraction of meeting her dear Mr.
Cropper; else it was a struggle to her to give up the
Charity Organisation Committee. . . . O. proposes to
take me to Normandy for a fortnight.

14, Nottingham Place, W.
July 19th, 1874.

Miranda to Edmund Maurice.

. . . I think all went very well; and the deep
purpose of Octavia's statesmanship—for which the
party was given, that of uniting St. Mary's people
somewhat—seemed to have succeeded. I feel frightened,
when I discover what deep reasons of state Octavia has
for her actions. I am afraid of spoiling some political
combination (parochial rather than political) by some
awkwardness of mine, from being wholly incapable
of telling what it all means. I feel as if Octavia were
a kind of Cecil in her sphere. . . .

We were much amused, because we heard there was
to be a children's service, after which a collection was
to be made for some benevolent institution for school-
masters and schoolmistresses. I thought the children
would not be willing to give. Octavia thought they
might, if they looked on it as a propitiatory sacrifice;
or if they hoped to pension off the teachers quickly,
as infirm and unable to teach. Then Miss S. told us
that Lord Shaftesbury had once asked a boy why the
Eunuch "went on his way rejoicing," and the boy
replied, "Because Philip had done the teaching of him,
Sir"

The Mill, Limpsfield.
September 20th, 1874.

To Mrs. N. Senior.

. . . I was longing for news of you when the rumour reaches me that your Report is really out. What that will really mean to you of suspense, anxiety, of doubt of what it will be right under given circumstances to do or not to do, I can only imagine. But this I know, and should care for you to know,—that one, at least (one who is probably the sample of many), will be thinking of you with love and perfect trust. Whatever the newspaper critics, the interested officials, the angry partisans, may say, there are those who know that your work has been done with conscience, patience, singleness of eye and heart. There are those, too, who know that out of such work God will in His own time bring results valuable to the world ; that it is like good seed sown in good ground ; and, though it may seem to die for a time, it will bear fruit. No momentary ebullition of feeling, no apparent failure, can ever confuse us as to this, we shall not be puzzled by having to wait for results ;—nor will any minor points draw our attention from the fact that the work is thoroughly sound and good, governed by a right spirit ; and it will vindicate itself as such, in the best of all possible ways, by achieving success, in the deepest sense of that much abused word " success."

You and I know that it matters little if we have to be the out-of-sight piers driven deep into the marsh, on which the visible ones are carried, that support the bridge. We do not mind if, hereafter, people forget that there *are* any low down at all ; if some have to be used up in trying experiments, before the best way of building the bridge is discovered. We are quite willing to be among these. The bridge is what we care for, and not our place in it ; and we believe that, to the end, it may be kept in remembrance that this is alone to be our object. But as we are human piers, conscious of our own flaws, we are apt to fear that, so far from forming strong supports, we may, through our own defects, be weak foundations for the bridge. We must remember always that God has been always pleased to build His best bridges with human piers, not angels, nor working by miracles ; but that He has always let us help Him, if we will, never letting our faults impede His purposes, when we struggled that they should not . . .

. . . I shall be home on the 28th, when I shall hear of any important article. I fancy your part is done ; and that you will now have the easier duty of passive silence, leaving whatever has to be said to others. . . . Edmund wants much to have a copy of your Report, and would like, too, to write an article for the "Contemporary," [1] if you know of no one doing it. Charles (Lewes) is sure to know how to get the information that he needs.

This rest has been such a blessed thing for me. I got such a break from responsibilities of work as I never remember since I was a child.

Limpsfield, Red Hill,
September 20th, 1874.

To Mrs. Shaen.

My great fear was Miss P.'s leaving, as she is independent of salary. Her greatest friend tells me that at first she thought it all almost overpoweringly

---

[1] This article came out in *British Quarterly Review.*

sad.   I remember that she wanted to help people more, and do repairs faster, than I thought wise.   I told her to do exactly what she thought right as to helping them with money.   But I told her strongly what I believed, and urged her to watch the result closely.   I told her the amount to be spent for repairs, and that she must *not* exceed that; but that she might spend it exactly as she chose in the house under her care.   It has ended in her feeling great loving confidence in my greater experience, appealing to it most willingly, and yet exercising and enjoying power, which has made her very much attached to the tenants and the house that I gave her to manage.   I look for great help from her in the future, and I am very fond of her indeed.

October 18th, 1874.

To Miss Harris.

I think the division of the work is going really very well.   It makes a great difference certainly to my work; it is quite curious how it simplifies matters; of course it remains to be seen whether the things are well done; but if not, we must improve or change our workers.   At least now we and they know their duties; and they have a chance of proving if they are, or can grow to be, up to them.   If we succeed at all, we shall succeed much better than ever.   Dear Miss Cons is more good and sweet than words can express; but the pain to her is still very great, and thro' her is costing me a great deal.   I, however, have the consolation of clearly seeing the better end.   The other workers are most happy in their freedom and distinct responsibility, and in coming nearer to me; and I shall know better what is in them.

November 1st, 1874.

To Mary Harris.

We had a teetotal meeting at B. Crt. on Thursday. Mr. Smale is going to take the lead there in the teetotal cause. It was very touching and very beautiful to see him take the pledge. He looked so young and so good, and took it wholly for the sake of the people. The speeches of the men from an old established teetotal club, " The Dauntless," were very beautiful. I never heard anything straighter from the heart, nor saw more living fire burning in men's eyes. We have begun a series of *paid* entertainments in B. Crt on successive Saturdays. Last night the season opened with a capital play by the MacDonalds. The room was crowded to overflowing. The next performance is to be an operetta by Mrs. Baylis and her friends. . . . Mary! I do so often tremble lest I should spoil all by growing despotic or narrow-minded, or over-bearing, or selfish; such power as I have is a quite terrible responsibility , and so few people tell me where I am wrong.

This letter refers to the attacks of the medical officer on the B—— houses

November 17th, 1874.

To Mr. Cockerell.

I enclose copy of attack, and will send one of my answer as soon as I can. I am afraid the meeting *may* be much more troublesome in consequence ; but I am glad that it is fixed independently of all this. My fear is that the meeting may appear to them extorted by fear; but we can but do our best. Of course it *must* deal with the same questions. Much will depend on the result of Thursday's Vestry, on which occasion

I have asked to have my letter read, when Dr. ——'s report comes up.

Everyone has been kinder than I can well say; but the sort of thing is troublesome and tiring very.

14, Nottingham Place,
November 23rd, 1874.

To MRS. EDMUND MAURICE FROM MIRANDA.

. . . Mr. Bosanquet says the Vestry *cannot* condemn the houses. Octavia has called a meeting of B. Court tenants to consult as to how *they* can keep things in better order, keep front doors shut, &c. . . . She is very sorry it should happen now; but she had fixed the meeting before this Vestry row occurred. She fears the tenants will be in a very bad state, because of this affair; and I fear she will come back very dispirited. It almost feels like that old Walmer Street meeting. She wants to get co-operation; and the people think she is only to hear complaints.

14, Nottingham Place,
November 27th, 1874.

FROM SAME TO SAME

The result seems satisfactory on the whole. The Vestry *did* adopt Dr. W.'s report; but the question of the measures to be taken was referred to Dr. W. and Octavia together. She was asked if she would be satisfied with *that*, and said she would. She said this on the strength of Mr. E. Hart's co-operation, —who had seen Dr. W. the evening before the Vestry meeting, and had shown him how utterly untenable his position was. Mr. Hart looked into the matter thoroughly with O., and said he thought she had a *very* good case; and that, if Dr. W. persisted, he

would only get into difficulties So, Dr. W. was most
anxious to retreat, and agreed to have a meeting with
O. and Mr. Hart to settle measures of reform after the
Vestry meeting. . . . Several strangers in the Vestry
were very nice about O., and the feeling very much in
her favour at last.

December 8th, 1874.

OCTAVIA TO MR. COCKERELL.

I don't like the idea of simply repaying the
balance after repairs are paid for. These repairs are so
vaguely enormous that we should never know where we
are. Besides, I fancy all successful management of
finance depends on walking open-eyed forward, having
weighed possibilities and results. . . .

I have just returned to-day from Leeds, after such a
happy visit, in which I do hope I have been really
successful. The conference was most interesting, and
composed of very influential people. They collected
£3,000 at once, which is ample to buy and improve the
court they want to begin on ; and they will wisely
begin on a small scale. Evidently more help would be
forthcoming directly if wanted. I don't think the
Corporation will move yet. Everyone was kind, tho'
they were all strangers. Somehow it was all very
bright and seemed to contrast strangely with Dr. ——'s
memories.

The following letter requires a word of explanation Ruskin
had written to Octavia quoting the words which Carlyle
used about her —" Of a most faithful disposition, with clear
sagacity to guide it You can't get faithful people, they're
quite exceptional. I never heard of another like this one."
(A pause) "The clear mind and perfect attention, meaning
nothing but good to the people, and taking infinite care to tell
them no lies."

December 20th, 1874.

To Mr. Ruskin.

I am more touched than I can well tell you, at your thinking of sending me Carlyle's words in the midst of all your trouble. It was very kind and showed me,—what I cared for most about it—that you had not given a bad account of me to Carlyle; for, as he does not know me, he must have judged me from your account, I like to presume. But, besides the comfort of finding an old friend speaking kindly of me, I must say the words, coming from Carlyle, came to me like the blessing of a prophet; something as if they partly bound me to live up to them, partly crowned me with honour for having suggested them, and partly soothed me for present troubles, and helped me to see how ephemeral they were. . . .

I am avoiding all newspapers, meetings and committees, and just going on my own way, with silence and sound work and patience. How my friends have come round me no words will describe; and I do believe, and must believe that I shall win in the deep sense of the word " win," in the long run. But somehow Carlyle's words came, as I say, like a fresh message, teaching me to see all he has taught so magnificently, that the true thing is the strong thing, and that the perfect act will prevail against the wordy clamour.

The words shall be a standard for me to live up to.

December 26th, 1874.

From Ruskin.

I have been prevented from telling you in answer to your lovely letter, that what Carlyle said was absolutely his own gathering and conclusion from what

he had seen and read of you, or heard, in various
general channels, and had no reference whatever to any
report or praise of mine.   I am very glad I had it to
send you just when you are beginning to feel the
Adversary at last rousing himself ; and that you respect
Carlyle so much as to be rejoiced by his thoughts of
you.

The next letter refers to the housing scheme at Leeds

FROM REV. ESTLIN CARPENTER TO MRS. EDMUND MAURICE.

On the practical side, Miss Octavia Hill had
extraordinary mastery of detail.   She was kind enough,
when I was living in Leeds, to accept an invitation to
come and describe her methods to a company, chiefly of
business men.   We arranged a meeting in the theatre of
the Philosophical Hall, and some of the leading citizens
were there.   I well remember the surprise of some of
them at the clearness—not only of her opening exposi-
tion—but of her spontaneous replies to questions con-
cerning all sorts of matters affecting the treatment of
house property, sanitation, repairs, bad debts.

CHAPTER VII

1875—1878

THE OPEN SPACE MOVEMENT

THE period recorded in the following letters marks the inauguration of a movement, which Octavia considered almost as important as that housing work with which her name is especially connected—the movement for the preservation of open spaces. It will be remembered that, in her first efforts to deal with tenement houses, she had been particularly anxious to secure a house with a garden, and, failing *that*, she had devoted a large part of her energies to laying out a play-ground, and brightening it by May Festivals, in which efforts she had the hearty co-operation of Mr. Ruskin, who sent his own gardener to plant the trees.

It was natural, therefore, that she should desire to keep open all outlets for her poor friends in Marylebone, which would enable them to enjoy the fresh air and open country.

Hence she became considerably alarmed, when she heard, in 1873, that some difficulties, which had hindered the destruction of the fields near the Swiss Cottage, had been removed, and that building plans were in preparation. The fields were dear to her, not only as the nearest country outlet for the Marylebone poor; but also as recalling her childhood, when they formed part of a wide stretch of open country where she and her sisters had played. She at once threw herself into the promotion of a scheme for saving these fields from the builder, and securing them as a recreation ground for the public. She enlisted the sympathy of Dean Stanley, Mr. Haweis and other well known Londoners in the movement, while Mr. Edward Bond and Mr. C. L. Lewes and other Hampstead residents tried to stave off the encroachments of the builders from Hampstead But the agent, who had the building scheme in hand, when he found that the purchase money was likely to be raised, succeeded in throwing such difficulties in the way, that the scheme was defeated , and Fitzjohn's Avenue rose upon the ruins of the memories and hopes, which I have described

About the same time Octavia's attention was called to the attempt of some members of the Society of Friends to build over the Bunhill Fields burial ground ; an attempt obviously dangerous to health, and shocking to the feelings of many whose friends and relations were buried in the ground. Again, after a struggle Octavia was defeated in her attempt to save the whole of the ground.

These defeats convinced her of the desirability of rousing public opinion to the need of open space and fresh air for the poor , and it was while she was considering this matter that her sister Miranda read, to the pupils at Nottingham Place, a paper on the need of bringing beauty home to the people. This was a scheme, first, for decorating clubs and hospitals and other institutions used by the poor ; secondly, for bringing first-class music within their reach , and, lastly, for preserving disused burial grounds and other open spaces. Octavia was so much impressed with her sister's suggestions that she persuaded Miranda to read her paper again before a meeting of the National Health Society How much the movement was in advance of the public opinion of that time was shown by more than one incident.

Even on the very occasion when Miranda read her paper to the National Health Society a pause followed the reading ; and then a lady started up, and tried to turn away discussion from the subject of the paper by introducing a reference to some new invention, which she considered much more important to health than the securing of open spaces could be. Octavia at once rose, and recalled the audience to the subject of the paper , and some sympathy was roused in the audience.

But, outside that circle, a chorus of scorn came from comic and Society papers , and, if mockery could have stifled a movement, this one would have been nipped in the bud But cold water sometimes makes such things grow Several notable and helpful people came to its support; and I well remember that one gentleman was stirred, by the attacks of *Punch*, to send a subscription to the new Society.

The name of the Man of Ross was chosen as the most fitting, badge of the new movement, and Her Royal Highness Princess Louise consented to become the President. Thus the Society which began with a small knot of friends, meeting at Nottingham Place, became widely useful, and Kyrle Societies were formed in other parts of the country, while the London Decorative branch was assisted by such artists as Leighton and William Morris, and the Musical branch was helped for many years by Malcolm Lawson.

When a sub-committee was formed for dealing with open spaces, a very zealous and energetic lady was chosen as Honorary Secretary. She was full of the wrongs suffered by the poor, in the destruction of their rights over commons. Octavia was no less impressed with these grievances, and she took an active share in the work of the Commons Preservation Society; but she felt that the Kyrle Society had a different function from that of the larger and more combative body; and that to secure open spaces, and lay out disused burial grounds, was a work which could not be joined on to the struggles for legal rights undertaken by the Commons Preservation Society. As the Honorary Secretary of the Open Spaces Committee was unable to recognise the desirability of the separation between these two kinds of work, she resigned, and 1 took her place for a time. Like all good work, this movement led to unexpected consequences; and while much of the preservation of Metropolitan Open Spaces was afterwards undertaken by the Metropolitan Boulevards Association, Octavia, as will be shown later on, took an active part in still wider developments of this and similar undertakings.

Thus it will be seen that the Open Spaces movement had a great many branches ... and its growth was well summarised by Octavia in a remark to her sister Miranda.

" When I first began the work, people would say, "I will give money for necessaries for the poor , but I do not see what they want with recreation." Then after a few years, they said, "I can understand poor people needing amusement; but what good will open spaces do them? And now everybody recognises the importance of open spaces."

This change of public opinion was, no doubt, produced by the joint action of many people, and amongst Octavia's fellow-workers in this matter none was more sympathetic and efficient than Mr. (now Sir Robert) Hunter. He had taken an active part in the formation of the Open Spaces Committee of the Kyrle Society; as Solicitor of the Commons Preservation Society, he had been able to further, by timely advice, many of the movements for securing the legal rights of the public over various commons and greens, and, while residing in Lincoln's Inn Fields, he had been the soul of an attempt (then indeed a failure, but the prelude to a more successful effort) to persuade the municipal authorities to throw open the garden of Lincoln's Inn Fields to the general public. Indeed, with the possible exception of Lord Eversley, the open spaces movement owes more to him than to any other man

But it will be easily understood that this important movement, even if it had been always successful, must have added a considerable strain to that sense of growing responsibility which was produced by the supervision of the tenants; and when accompanied with the kind of failures which I have mentioned, it often brought much vexation. And this period was also marked by the deaths of two of Octavia's most valued fellow-workers, Mrs Nassau Senior (that most lovable and charming sister of Mr Hughes) and Mr Cockerell, a most able and sympathetic member of the Committee of the Workmen's Club, in which Octavia took so deep an interest.

While these and other troubles were already breaking down her strength, there came the additional trial of that misunderstanding with Ruskin, to which so much attention has unfortunately been called. As the correspondence has been published, I do not propose to refer at length to that painful incident But I feel bound a little to anticipate events by saying that we have ample evidence that Ruskin regretted his hasty words, that he showed his renewed confidence in Octavia by the manner in which he finally made over to her the possession of his houses; and that, on the other hand, her old affection and admiration for him never wavered in spite of that passing cloud.   I may bring the allusion to this episode to an end by quoting the words which she used in her Letter to her Fellow Workers in 1899 on Ruskin's death :

" The earth seems indeed sadder and poorer that such a man lives on it no more.

" That penetrating sympathy, that marvellous imagination, that wonderful power of expression, that high ideal of life have not only blessed his friends, but have left their mark on England.

" To me personally the loss is irreparable.   I have cared to think of the master and friend of my youth, in his lovely home, and to feel that he was among us still.

" He has passed to the great beyond.   All his noblest aspirations are opening before him, the incompletenesses passed away, the companionship of the mighty dead around him, the work accomplished, the love fulfilled, the peace complete, the blessings of thousands upon him."

But I have only introduced the subject in this place in order to emphasise the circumstances of the break-down in Octavia's health, and the interruption to her work, which, as will be seen in the next chapter, produced so remarkable a change in her life.

February 14th, 1875.

To Mary Harris.

. . . . Hast thou seen that Mr. Cross has brought in his Bill ?   Thou mayest think how intensely eager we are over it.   I dined at Mr. Kay Shuttleworth's on Wednesday to discuss its clauses with him and a few experienced people, that he might know what to press on the House; and on Friday Mr. K. S. called together another small company at the Ch. Org. Soc. to rediscuss matters.   They think the bill may be made to work. They say the omissions are from ignorance, and will be willingly corrected when pointed out, as everyone wants to work it I dare hardly hope ; it seems so very near the realisation of much one has wanted so long Stansfeld was there, and was so kind, and Mr Shaw Lefevre. I am a great deal in B. Court just now, and right down among the people there, which is very nice I am sensible how much I lack swiftly turning perception, and unfailing gentleness, and a certain cautious reservation of speech. My only chance among the people is trying to be all right, so that it mayn't matter their seeing right thro' me. I have no powers of diplomacy ; these I don't regret, but the power of non-expression might be an advantage. However, I don't get into great messes somehow ; and I suppose one was made like *this*, to do some particular work in the world. The people are delightful down there, so responsive, so trustful. . . . Dost thou know if ever I write again I shall make a point of dwelling on Ruskin's beginning the work ? I fancy he feels sadly his schemes have not succeeded ; and they only want the admixture of humdrum elements to make them into bodies , the soul is all there. His share is the soul, and this ought to come prominently out.

I enclose the report of Stanley's sermon, and of Mr. Kay Shuttleworth's speech. . . .

I daresay I may feel more courageous after to-morrow, when the public-house trial comes on. We quite expect to be defeated here, but hope to win on the appeal It will be very horrid to-morrow ; there is such strong personal feeling . .

Miss Martin, the lady from Leeds who is staying here, is so very nice. She has great power, and will do the work admirably She has great perception of character, and is so much interested in all our people, poor and rich. It is a real pleasure to see her with the people. . . .

Mr. Cross has accepted nearly all we submitted to him. So far all is very satisfactory; but on the other hand there is likely to be considerable delay; also Mr. Fawcett, representing extreme political economy, and a Mr. Cawley representing vestrydom, are hatching a great opposition. We are much afraid of clogging amendments being carried; and no one knows what the Lords will do. I have secured an able and earnest young supporter for the Bill, in the person of Lord Monteagle, who will really master the details, and may secure more powerful allies in the world's opinion; though I believe in the careful whole-hearted work of young men really in earnest, much more than in the chance of a few words from a man of influence. Dost not thou?

I have been much engrossed about Mr. Cross's Bill this week. I was in the House on Monday when it was read a second time. Mr. Kay Shuttleworth and Mr. Lefevre came up and had a long talk with me, and it was very interesting. I did not learn very much; and tho' they and Mr. Stansfeld and Mr. Plunkett and Mr. Rathbone are talking over amendments with me, I feel as if, now that the matter was well before the House, they and others were far better judges of what amendments would work, what there was a hope of carrying, than I am. It was very solemn, tho'; and a thing I never shall forget. I was sitting quite alone in the gallery belonging to the Speaker's wife; it was very late, and she and her friends had all gone home. The gallery is high up above the House, but one sees and hears beautifully. I had been listening intently, but, when Mr Kay Shuttleworth began to speak, I thought I knew all that he was going to say, and was leaning back thinking, when suddenly my own name caught my ear.   Mr. S. was speaking of the Macmillan article ; and, instead of quoting dry facts and figures, he read aloud from it the description of the wonderful delight it gave me to see the courts laid open to the light and air.   And then he read the bit about the Chairman of the Trust going over the old plans and photographs, and remarking on the changes, and the longing that arose that someone, someday, in London might be able to note similar purification.   The words recalled vividly the intensity of the longing, and the wonderfully swift realisation of the prayer ; and a great gush of joy rushed over me.   But, besides *that*, somehow it seemed a blessed thing to have half suggested, and wholly anticipated the feeling on the part of that bright, promising young man, and thro' him to the whole House.   One felt so small, so alone and out of sight ; and there were thoughts bearing fruit in ways of which one had never dreamed.   I can't tell how tiny it made me feel.   Mr. Kay Shuttleworth happened to have told me that he had been spending Sunday in the country, and could not get the subject out of his head, and that he had re-read the article.   I did not hear Mr. Rathbone's mention of my work, as I had gone to get some tea ; my head was so very bad.

A Miss Martin, a friend of Mr. Estlin Carpenter's, is coming to stay with us till Easter, to learn our work, that she may help in the houses that they are purchasing in Leeds.

In am heartily enjoying my work in B. Court.

FROM LORD SHUTTLEWORTH TO MR. EDMUND
MAURICE.

On the Artisans' Dwellings Act of 1875.

I was closely associated with Miss Octavia Hill
in 1873, during the inquiry by a committee of the
C.O S. into the whole question of the dwellings of the
working classes in London. It was a remarkable committee, over which the late Lord Napier and Ettrick
presided, and to which nearly everyone then prominent
in the work of improved dwellings belonged, including
such men as Lord Shaftesbury, Sir Sidney Waterlow,
Mr. Hughes (Tom Brown), etc., etc. Mr. Bosanquet
was then Secretary of the C.O.S., and took an active
part.

In 1874, with encouragement from Miss Octavia Hill
and others, I brought the subject before the House
of Commons, basing my speech a good deal on the
excellent and very practical report of the C.O.S. Committee. In the debate on my motion, Mr. (now Lord)
Cross, who was then Home Secretary, promised a Bill,
which he introduced and passed on the part of Mr.
Disraeli's Government in 1875—the Artisans' Dwellings
Act. In the consideration of that Bill Miss Octavia Hill
again gave valuable advice ; and when, a few years afterwards (about the year 1880), a committee of the C.O.S.
was appointed to consider the working of the Act, and
how far it should be amended, she and I again worked
together upon that committee, and I remember gratefully
the signal help which she then gave.

Miss Octavia Hill was pre-eminently fitted for con-
tributing an exceptional amount of practical knowledge,
experience, and wisdom at the meetings of such committees and conferences on a subject which she had

Y 2

made her own. She would quietly listen to a discussion of some point, and at last say a few weighty words in her calm, impressive, tactful way, which would carry with her the general assent of all, or nearly all, who heard her, and would thus promptly bring the debate to a sound conclusion.

I think it was in the 'eighties that, in a certain London parish, a progressive clergyman and his Church Council rather impulsively took up a housing improvement scheme Before launching it, they were persuaded by one of their members to ask Miss Hill's advice. I was present at the meeting of the Council which she kindly consented to attend. According to what, I think, was her habit, she sat quite silent for perhaps an hour or more, while various members propounded their ideas and sketched out the scheme. When they had quite finished, she very quietly and gently, but convincingly, said a few words of common sense which showed that the scheme, though admirably intended, was unpractical; and from that moment it ceased to exist This was an instance of the weight which she carried, by her tact and wisdom and experience, even in a meeting of people who, with one or two exceptions, were, I believe, complete strangers.

Derwent Bank, Boughton, Carlisle,
March 28th, 1875.

To MRS. N. SENIOR.

The boarding-out here is really heart-cheering to see.

What do you think that the Barnetts' great news was ? That they had had a legacy, and wanted to spend it in rebuilding their worst court irrespective of

making it pay, or waiting for the Bill. Of course I
said by all means; and now, if they can but purchase,
I think that it will give new life to their future there,
to see some tangible and radical reform actually
achieved.

14, Nottingham Place,
April 19th, 1875.

To Miss Harris.

On Tuesday a batch of orders was issued by Dr.
—— which (or rather all that grow out of that fact)
gives me a good deal of trouble,—more I believe, a great
deal, than it ought. I believe that, if I could make up
my mind that I see the right thing pretty distinctly,
and can do it and leave the result, it would be far
better; but I am apt to go over and over the subject,
hoping to think out better measures, brooding over it.
I know that the way to succeed is to think perpetually
of things, till one suddenly sees the straight way
through the difficulties; but it becomes, sometimes,
very wearing; and it is useless, whenever the only
straight way is that of waiting till the right has time to
win the day by its own innate force. I fancy *that* is
the case here; our action has to be next to nothing;
time, extreme silence, and great patience will secure the
final accomplishment of whatever may be best with
regard to the poor houses. I need not mind if little
plans of mine fail wholly; still less need I tremble if
dangers threaten them. There may be fifty reasons
why it may be best for them all to sink to nothing.
But it is not they and their outward forms that I have
lived for, but all they are meant to help to achieve;
and this, well thou knows, must succeed if I and they
are annihilated.

Mary, I think the thing I most failed to convey to thee of all I had wanted thee to know, was the intense blessing that Mama is to us all. I think I understand her so very much more than I have done all my life ; her sympathy is so delightful ; and, now that I am sharing her room, I have time to tell her the events of the day. I think the sense of life is a joy to her ; while often she puts before me principles bearing on questions under consideration quite beautifully.

14, Nottingham Place, W.,
April 25th, 1875.

To Miss Harris.

The public-house trial is over ; and we won triumphantly and conclusively, and are very thankful for it. But the spirit of the people was very dreadful ; and it doesn't augur well for the future work. Fifty vestrymen and 150 ratepayers signed in favour of the license. Several vestrymen attended and gave evidence.

Mr. Fremantle was very brave and true-hearted. Sir J. H. was in a towering rage, and tried to annoy me with things that didn't touch me. But it all points to future difficulty. However, I cannot say I am discouraged. As long as there was hope of peace from explanation and care, I was full of anxiety ; but *now* we must go straight on ; and, if storm comes, the law is over us all, and what it decrees, we will all readily do.

Miss Cons, as always when need is great, is very good just now.

April 28th, 1875.

To Mr. Cockerell

I see by Saturday's *Mercury* the doctor promises another report on B. Court soon. But I,—well I read

CAROLINE SOUTHWOOD HILL.
Octavia's Mother.

From a Photograph by Andrew Whelpdale

Cromwell, and listen to Mr. Bond's advice about taking things coolly, and go on steadily with my work, and don't trouble much about things. I got a bit of encouragement yesterday, which *ought* to keep me up for many a long day. I am paying periodical visits to all the courts; and I came upon one yesterday, beginning to go quite after my own heart, like Mrs. Fitch's in other hands than mine, and not a very brilliant success yet; but sure to grow; for the volunteer there was on the most perfect terms of quiet gentle power, and happy intercourse with the people, noticing, and managing cleaning, repairs, rents, everything. I am so thankful.

May 6th, 1875.

To Mr. Cockerell.

I wonder whether the news has reached you of Mitchell's death. We can hardly realise the thought. He died the next day. The loss to us all will be heavy, and the pain great. If one had dared to single out the life which seemed of most value to the corporate life of the court, it would have been his. We must try to make his death draw us all together; and we must try to take care of his widow and children in the way which will be lasting gain to them. I don't see how yet. Everyone's heart is brimming over with sympathy, and they will have enough, and more than enough perhaps done for them just now. At any rate now money help would be of little value; and we must leave place too for the friends near him to do their part, and make the little sacrifices (often so much greater than ours); and we will come in with strong, quiet, lasting aid to help her to earn, or something of that kind.

14, Nottingham Place, W.,
May 16th, 1875.

TO MARY HARRIS.

I do not know that I have much that is beautiful
or helpful to tell you, except the natures of people;
those are the loveliest things that I see; and they *are*
lovely—some of them. Janey's, for instance. I saw
her for a short time yesterday, as I had to be in
Battersea to meet Mr. Erskine Clarke's district visitors.
She is looking better, and spoke with grateful joy of
your letter about the boarding out

I was much delighted with G. Place, which I went
over on Tuesday. Miss Cons *has* got it well in hand.
I mean I was pleased with her dealing with the place.

About 1875.

OCTAVIA TO REV. S. BARNETT.

I have no suggestions for the Com. or Admin.
Com.[1] which would be capable of being embodied in a
report. My engrossing and continuous thought about
them is the hope that they will manage to secure the
right men. But there is no receipt for the selection;
and probably the Com. has not to nominate for election, but will have to recommend methods of election,
numbers, division of work, about all which I am not a
specially good judge. The one thing I should have
been saying, had it pleased you to leave me at my old
post, would have been that the important point was to
get the right men, and that they would be found
among those who have worked among the poor, and

---

[1] This refers to the formation of an Administrative Committee of the
Charity Organisation Society to be elected by the local committees.

who have power of grasping facts. I should have been urging them earnestly to consider quite solemnly the importance of the duty they have to discharge, and to put *no* one on out of politeness, or because they "must," or because they have this or that influence, or have given time, or will "feel"; to let no minor considerations come in; but to concentrate their full force on the thought "how *is* this organising of charity, this great work of caring for our poor to be achieved?" And I should have been adding that, in my opinion, experience among, or care for, the poor was a *more* essential qualification for a seat on the Admin. than the other one power to grasp principles; and for this reason that the knowledge of the poor will *not* be gained afterwards at Buckingham St.; but the principles may be learnt by the mere fact of dealing with large numbers of bare facts, probably will be learnt there by any men who have it in them ever to learn them at all. This and a few words about the actual men to be selected would have been my contribution to the work, had I been there. But now I feel it is all out of my power to touch, and I rejoice more than words would say to see how triumphantly it and much else goes without me. A few words would influence so many things if I wrote them; but I may not; and so instead I have the privilege of looking, as if I were dead, to see how they go when I do not speak a word, and learning first how magnificently they go in the main in the way I have hoped for so long; and secondly how little it matters that much goes otherwise than it would, if I wrote ever so small a sentence.

About June 12th, 1875.

OCTAVIA TO MR. LUDLOW.

I have not seen anything of you for many years,
nor heard anything of you lately; but, when I was
thinking over the names of people resident at Wimble-
don, who might possibly care to help with a party of
four hundred of my tenants whom I am going to bring
down there on Wednesday, yours naturally suggested
itself, as I have some impression that you are still
living there. I do not know that I should have
ventured to write, having no special claim for these
my people on you; but, your name having once
occurred to me in relation to the question, I could
not help feeling a wish to ask you just to walk over
and see us, if you could without trouble, some time in
the afternoon or evening at or near Cæsar's Camp,
where we expect to be. I have vivid memories of
tailors' "bean-feasts" long ago, with which those with
whom you were working were associated; perhaps
there I then first learned both the great good
which grew out of such association with the people
in their joys, and also how much was needed to
make such gatherings more refined in tone, and gentler
and quieter. If, as a child, I learned all this from
what I saw, it was years before it became possible to
me to realise what I saw to be needed. Though the
thought of these my present excursions and winter
parties was untraced by me to its germ so long ago,
though now my people are quite unconnected with the
Associations and founders of Associations, it yet remains true that it was the early connection with that
body of "Christian Socialists," to which much of my
present work must owe its spirit. It had to find its
own form, according to the needs and possibilities of

circumstances; but its spirit must have been influenced deeply by the deeds and words of all that group of men, among whom it pleased God to lead me, when life was just first presenting its puzzles to me. The form of much of your work has changed, died down, and withered, as forms often must; but the principles you were all teaching do not change; and now that many of them are understood by the younger generations, now that they who belong to those younger generations are coming forward so earnestly to work, grateful as I am for their help, and glad of their sympathy, there always remains to my mind a peculiar silent, more solemn, link with all who are associated with the earlier more difficult and lonely efforts of the past. It has pleased God to alter much since then. The voices that taught us are silent; but His voice still speaks; and, if He has made of the child who learned so much of the people (just from being one among them) now the leader of 3,000 tenants, He doesn't forbid that she should still be a child again, in thinking over the old days, and better still, in listening to His teaching.

re Swiss Cottage Fields?
July 19th, 1875.

To Mr. Cockerell.

Thank you very much for your letter about the city. I saw Mr. Bond yesterday, and again had a long talk with him about the best way of proceeding; and we decided that, for the moment, we would let the big-monied people alone, till we are better worth their notice, and work among those who cannot give more at the utmost than £25 and £50. I believe (thank God!) more in nobodies than in " somebodies."

Tortworth Court, Tatfield, R.S.O.,
Gloucester.
August 3rd, 1875.

To MRS. SENIOR.

I feel as if you ought to know what we are doing and deeply thinking of; yet I have been afraid to write to you for fear you should tire yourself by helping us   Now, however, that " Macmillan " is out, I fancy you are sure to hear of our work; and also I have increasing longing for the sense of your sympathy. Do you not know how one turns with longing for such sympathy, when vistas of effortful work look interminable, and when so many people "begin to make excuse." I send you then the papers with my love; and I hope you will see " Macmillan " , but do not help, except with loving sympathy, this time, please.

I came down here last night. It is infinitely peaceful, and Lady Ducie is very sweet and loving; and all is so very quiet. But I feel leaving my fields so that I could almost cry.[1]

We have got on very well, better than anyone could have expected. We have collected £9,500 in little more than three weeks; but the vacation has come upon us with its inevitable pause; and it becomes a question whether the owners will give us time to try, after it.

How strange it seems to me (does it not to you?) that the momentary difficulty is to persuade the owners that there is a chance of anyone (any body of people in London or England), being in the least likely to be inclined to give the money for a place which must

---

[1] This refers to the movement for purchasing the Swiss Cottage Fields for the public.

be a blessing to hundreds now, and hundreds yet to come—a great free gift to their city, and the chief city of their country. Fields reminding men and women long lost in the whirl of London, of child days and places near where they were born; fields where little children can see the wild flowers grow, as they are beginning to do once more on Hampstead Heath, but nearer their homes. Let other people look, if they know where, for the millionaire to do it all at once. Happy for him, if he be honoured to do such a thing! say I; he will find his buttercups more abidingly powerful and blessed than his sovereigns; but, as to me, I believe in the hearts of our poorer people, professional men, ladies with limited incomes, who know what homes, and families, and the poor are; and who will make for once an effort and sacrifice, to give £25 or £50 to save a bit of green hilly ground near a city, where fresh winds may blow, and where wild flowers still are found, and where happy people can still walk within reach of their homes These have come forward, are coming forward; but I begin to realise how many of them it takes to contribute £1,000.

Please God, when October comes, if time is given us, we will begin in full force. Meantime I must write many letters.

Tortworth Court,
August 9th, 1875.

To Mrs. N. Senior.

Many and most loving thanks for your letter, and all your sweet help.

I think of little else but my Fields[1] day and night.

---

[1] The Swiss Cottage Fields.

We have now £8,150. The collection goes on slowly, but quite steadily, day by day ; very well I think for the time of year ; but we are in great fear that the owners will not wait

I wonder owners are not a little awed by possession of so important a treasure, and do not pause a little, before they use it wholly without reference to the people.

> 25, Church Row, Hampstead,
> August 19th, 1875.

To Mrs. N. Senior

You will have heard from Charles of the sudden collapse of all our schemes for the purchase of the fields. The owners withdrew their offer after five days' notice. We were led to hope that this notice might be reconsidered, when the owner returned ; but he confirms it, tells us we must consider the offer absolutely withdrawn, and refused even to receive a guarantee within a week for the full amount. I think the loss very great. The spirit of many of the people who helped us was so beautiful. I shall never forget *that*.

> 25, Church Row, Hampstead.
> August 21st, 1875.

To Mrs. N. Senior.

We could almost have cried over your letter, dear, dear, Janey , how delightful is your joy in doing what is blessed and helpful. I will think over the generous offer ; but I believe now we had better pause, for sufficient time to learn really which are now the best places available, and which those most needing space. These fields, which we knew, being gone, there is no such immediate hurry; and I thought of seeing a member of the Commons Preservation Society, with whom I have been in communication, learning what they are doing, and what they see before them of definite work. Also whether they would care to enlarge their work, so far as to appoint some one to examine into the provisions for every part of London, district by district,—the possible central small open spaces, the nearest available larger ones. If they won't do it, I will, or will get it done, and then bend my energies to whatever direction help is most needed. Isn't this best? Then, please God, we shall get that silly clause repealed, which prohibits the proceeds of the grain dues set aside for open spaces from being applied in the district of the Metropolitan Board of Works. And, if that is done, we shall have a fund yearly coming in, and may buy and buy as opportunity serves. Last year it came to £10,000, and was spent in a Park at Stratford; but, on most sides, except the east, the Metrop. Bd. of Works has jurisdiction for fifteen miles round London. Fancy debarring the City money for open spaces being spent in that area! In short, Janey dearest, I will assuredly go and see your farm. But I must, I think, review the whole area, and see where and how space will tell most. And I ought now at once to go and finish my holiday in Ireland. I go with a tenfold lighter heart for the love and generosity and sympathy of your letter; and you need not fear that nothing will be done, because we don't act at once. For the moment I am a little broken by the loss; and it would be difficult to begin just at once to work again; but, please God, if I live, I will see something efficient done, if power of mine, first or second hand, will do it; I promise you that.

14, Nottingham Place,
September 22nd, 1875.

To Mrs. Edmund Maurice.

Thanks for the *Hampstead Express*. I think it very important you should know what to say about the Traitors' Hill [1] question for me if anyone asks you. I do not purpose pledging myself to any one spot, until I have carefully prepared a general map, to see where space is most needed. My impression is that I shall care most (now that the Swiss Cottage Fields are gone) for small central spaces; but this may not prove to be the case. I shall work first to secure that £10,000, and the grave-yards, and shall obtain co-operation from the Com Pres. Society, or else some new body appointed *ad hoc*, before I do anything for any one place, as, in all probability, I shall not, myself, work in so much detail for any. Those which remain to be secured are, so far as I know them, so much more on a level in importance, that I can work for them gradually, quietly and less personally. But I can pledge myself to nothing of any sort or kind till I have met Mr. Hunter, Mr Redford, and a few others, and have explored the subject in its general bearings.

October 3rd, 1875.

To Miss Harris.

What have we to tell thee of brightest and best? First I was most delighted with what I learnt of the B——'s Court Women's and Girls' Institute at a little Committee at Mrs. Hart's on Tuesday. I knew the influence was strong and beautiful there; but I had not realised how very much corporate life there

---

[1] Now better known as Parliament Hill.

was among the women themselves; *how* much they felt the Institute their own; how they cared for and worked for it. I am to help the singing class there myself, this year, to try to introduce better songs and thoughts in the court. I hope for much help from musical people; but we want all so very simple. I shall keep the conduct of all myself.

Did I tell thee that Miss Peters is engaged to be married? I am very glad; and yet I am, perhaps, selfish enough not to be able quite to forget my own loss. However, she stays with us for a year, and is very sweet.

It is very nice being so much in B——'s Court now. I do like the people there. B., who was so utterly drunken—has been steady now for many months; he has such a nice house, and is a leader among the teetotalers. Quite a large group of girls were gathered round the notice board announcing the re-opening of the Institute. We used to say that no notice was of any use; but they were eagerly reading, and asked me to read to them the new teachers' names and explain other points;—and this though there was a counter attraction in the shape of a quarrel.

Good progress is being made in Leeds. They have bought two more blocks of buildings; Miss Martin and Miss Bakewell are to manage them.

October 3rd, 1875.

To Mr. Cockerell.

You will be glad to hear that Dr. —— has reported to the Board of Works as to districts requiring to be dealt with under the Art. Dwell. Bill, and has *not* included B——'s Court. I think he has chosen the right spots, and am glad, tho' I was prepared for the

z

other course being adopted. How glad one is if anyone one has suspected does better than one has hoped!

The next letter refers to the Bunhill Fields burial ground.

14, Nottingham Place,
November 21st, 1875.

To MISS HARRIS.

Thanks for letter to Mr. Harrison. I hope to make way in the matter ; but it is a little difficult to know how to begin. However Mr. Bond and I are to see the ground on Wednesday; and, on Saturday, Mr Lefevre, now Chairman of the Commons Preservation Society, the Secretary and the Solicitor are to meet Mr. Bond and me ; and then I presume we shall make a formal application to the " Six Weeks' " Meeting. I long to get the ground ; but though the Local Board will surrender immediately their seventeen years' lease, so far as I at present see, there is no chance of the Quakers doing anything, except selling at full value. We may manage the cost ; but it points to securing churchyards if possible, which would only entail the cost, very heavy I imagine, of making them beautiful, not the purchase also   However we shall see : at any rate, it is a definite bit of ground in a popular poor neighbourhood to be sold ; and the thing is to learn the price, to see whether we can raise it ; and if so, whether it is the best expenditure for the money. Perhaps, if the Six Weeks' Meeting can do nothing in the way of generosity, the application may interest individual members to give. At any rate we must see. I am full of thought about it all. I wonder if you see the Charity Organisation Reporter, and noticed the appointment of Mr. Loch as secretary. Did I tell you that he is engaged to Miss Peters, and so good? I daresay

Miranda has told you of Miss Potter,[1] who has been staying here. She wants to stay on for, possibly, two or three years. She is very bright and happy here ; extremely capable, and has been through a good deal in her life, though she is young. She seems to fit in among us very well.

By the way, dost thou know I have found a motto in George Herbert which I intend to appropriate, as expressive of the way that I get on now, by means of my friends ? "A dwarf, on a giant's shoulder, sees further of the two."

We have chosen a pretty one for the Girls' Institute in B. Court—"God hath oft a great share in a little house."

14, Nottingham Place,
December 12th, 1875.

To Miss F. Davenport Hill.

    . . . I do love life and all it brings very deeply, and should like to live long too, to see the progress of so many things that I care for ; I think a past is as great a help to a life as to an institution. It seems as if one were bound to live up to it. What I always fear about my own life is the tendency to excuse myself from small daily duties ; yet I am certain they are the real test of life. I don't mean that great claims ought to be sacrificed to small ones, nor that the duties remain the same for a woman as for a girl. Many small manual duties pass wholly away ; but it is by the small graciousnesses, by the thoroughness of the out-of-sight detail, that God will judge our spirit and our work. My difficulty is always to secure this exquisite thoroughness, which alone seems to make the work *true*, and yet to delegate

---

[1] Now Lady Courtney.

it. However, I learn gradually how to overlook and test it better and better; and I gather round me an ever larger, more capable, and more sweetly attached body of fellow-workers.

As to the gracious thoughtfulness for others, and silent self-control and sweet temper, I never had much gift for them; and I do fear that, deeply as I honour them, and hard as I strive to live up to my ideal, I still fail very decidedly,—which is wrong. I used to think that time would soften passionate engrossment, and leave me leisure to perceive the little wants of others; but I think I pant with almost increasing passionate longing for the great things that I see before me.

We are getting on about the open spaces gradually, and, I think, surely; but there is no need to trouble anyone yet, till those we have in view are more definitely arranged about. It is a great joy to me that something will be done. Will you be interested I wonder, in the enclosed letter? My sister [1] wrote it for our pupils, past and present; but I was so delighted with it, that I took possession of it, and printed it for private circulation. Though it is only a week old, it is meeting with the warmest response, so that I fancy we shall have to let it become something larger and more public. I want our Clubs, Institutes, school-rooms, when we have our parties there, and the outsides of our churches and houses, to be brighter.

May 22nd, 1876.

FROM RUSKIN.

What time, I wonder, will it take, before we fairly encounter the opposite tide, wave to wave—you with your steady gain—the Enemy with his steadier and

---

[1] This is the letter by which Miranda inaugurated the Kyrle Society.

MIRANDA HILL.

From a Photograph by Maull and Fox.

swifter ruin ? When is the limit to be put to the destruction of fields ? [1]

June 8th, 1876.

FROM RUSKIN.

My question, a very vital one, is, whether it really never enters your mind at all that all measures of amelioration in great cities, such as your sister's paper pleads for, and as you rejoice in having effected, may in reality be only encouragements to the great Evil Doers in their daily accumulating Sin ?

Venice, shortest day, 1876.

FROM RUSKIN.

I have received to-day your letter, with its beautifully felt and written statement. It comes to me on my birthday to the Nuova Vita ; this day last year being the one on which I got signs sufficient for me that there was hope of that life ; and I am very thankful to know that I have been thus of use to you, and that you feel that I have ; a much mistaken sense of a separation between us in essential principles having been for two or three years growing upon me, to my great puzzlement and pain ; so that this paper is a very moving and precious revelation to me.

June 24th, 1876.

FROM RUSKIN.

I was greatly delighted by your long kind letter ; *and* it is much more than a delight to me, *and* it is a most weighty assistance in my purposes, that you can take this house [2] and put it to use. . . .

---

[1] A reference to Octavia's past attempt to save the Swiss Cottage Fields.

[2] A house in Paddington Street which Octavia undertook to manage.

I wanted to say something more about your and Miranda's work.[1] I cannot say more, however, than that, whether in the best direction or not, it cannot but be exemplary and fruitful.

14, Nottingham Place,
May 28th, 1876.

To MARY HARRIS.

Miss Cons has taken supervision of the Drury Lane district from her own house, Mr. Westroper being wholly, and her sister partly, told off to her, and several volunteers; if it works well, it will be grand. The Bishop's meeting doesn't bear fruit in the distinct way that I had hoped; the visitors won't organise before they come, but come singly, which means that much more indirect work will have to be done before we get our organisation However all the result is good, as far as it goes.

Miranda's paper[2] was so very beautiful. I do wish it had been heard by a larger audience. The room was quite full, however; and the hearers were just those in whom the thoughts would be likely to bear abundant fruit.

June 2nd, 1876.

To WM. SHAEN.

I am writing to ask you whether you will do me a service, which will really be a considerable one. It is to take the chair for me at a meeting of the Liberal Social Union on the 29th of this month, when I am going to read a paper on the subject of Charity. The people are all strangers to me; and I gather that their

[1] The Kyrle Society.　　[2] Re Kyrle Society.

spirit is not one with which I shall feel very heartily in tune. It is a large gathering, and may be difficult to keep to the consideration of what we *can* do, instead of what we *can not* do. I am extremely anxious about this latter point. It is so easy to denounce what has been done, so difficult patiently to consider what can be done ; and I don't want the opportunity to be lost of doing this. It will depend more on the tone of the meeting than anything. Personally, too, it would be a comfort to feel in sympathy with the chairman, and full confidence in him, which I certainly should do very completely if you would kindly fill the office. The chairmen suggested by no means seemed to me satisfactory ; and I was delighted that the letters, which named them, contained also the proposal that I should select one. I looked all down the list of members ; and there is not a single one whom I know, except yourself, whom I should like for the post. I feel the moment an important one. Unless we get volunteers in greater abundance, and *that* very rapidly, the Charity Organisation Society must suffer very considerably from the necessarily hard routine of official work compared to spontaneous work ; and I am trying to do what in me lies to secure the help of as many people as possible. Among the members of the L.S.U. I believe we should find the wisdom, and freedom from parochial work ; and, if we could but stir up their living sympathy with the poor, we might do much.

14, Nottingham Place, W.,
July 17th, 1876.

To Miss OLIVE COCKERELL.

I sent you a little brooch, which I want you to wear in remembrance of the day you were baptised, and

of the words which we then heard together. Ask
Mama for a piece of her hair to put in the brooch;
and, when you wear it, think of her love. It is a funny
little old-fashioned brooch, but I thought it was very
pretty; and I liked it, because it looked as if it had
a history. I thought you might like it for this reason
too But I am afraid it will not begin to speak to you,
like those delightful things in Andersen's stories. If
only it could, what a quantity it might tell you! I
wonder whom it belonged to; and whether it has been
given, with words of loving hope, ever before, to any
one; and whether the hope was realised or not. Does
it not look as if its pearls might once have been tears,
but had lost their passionateness, and had become quiet,
like old people's tears, that are slow and still and deep,
and much sadder, often, than young people's, though
more beautiful in power of reflecting? What do the
old people's tears reflect when they have lived good
lives? Oh, Ollie dear, they reflect all the things
which are round them, or have happened to them; and
each looks lovelier than the other; some rose-coloured,
some gold, some blue like the heaven, some white like
snow. We may all be glad to have tears like these,
set like jewels in a crown, to make our lives look
royal.

This old-fashioned brooch, too, seemed to me like a
good christening present, because those words that we
heard have a history, like it;—those words, I mean,
about your being signed with the sign of the Cross, in
token that hereafter you should not be ashamed to be
Christ's soldier and to fight under His banner against
the world, the flesh, and the devil. Many a mother,
Ollie, like yours, has heard them prayed over her little
girl, and has wondered whether, when she grew to be a

woman, she would remember them.   Many a father has
listened to them, asking for strength to bring up his
child, so that she shall live as she ought.   Many loving
friends have stood by and prayed for the child, for her
own sake, for the sake of the parents who love her, and
for the sake of the great God who loves her even more.
And the little girl has grown up, and lived her life, and
had her history.   And the same beautiful old words
have been prayed for others; and, whether they have
remembered them, and lived as if they were true, or
whether they have fallen away, still the memory of the
words has always borne witness to those who loved the
children, that they really did belong to God, and that
they had no business to be mean or cowardly or un-
truthful or anything bad.   If the children forgot all
this, and did wrong, still there was hope that they
would return and be good some day; for that they
were under God's own care, and that He wanted to
gather them under His wings.

We, who were all together that day, asked for
you, my child, that you might have courage to do
right.   We know God means *that* courage for you,
that He will give it to you.   Remember this all your
life long; and remember too, the love which gathered
round you as a child.

I send you a few words, more precious than any
pearls; for they contain the wish of a great and good
man for his little girl.   They are very much like what
we might have said to you; only that they are set in a
sweet, solemn, and lovely way, which will make you
remember them better.

Take them, dear, as the expression of what all
who love you would say; and let them ring in
your ears in the coming years.   I, your loving god-

mother, Octavia Hill, write them on the next page for you.

The lines appended are Kingsley's poem beginning —

"My fairest child, I have no song to give you."

14, Nottingham Place,
July 23rd, 1876.

To Miss Harris

Our failure this year has been on the open space question.   Dora will tell thee about the Friends.   Not that they stand alone ; the matter is one on which much preliminary work has to be done   People don't know about the importance yet.   It is so sad ; for the places are going for ever so rapidly.   I have written, by Mr. Lefevre's request, to *The Times.*

January 28th, 1877.

To Mrs. Hill

Bunhill Fields contract for sale has fallen through, and the Quakers are again considering the matter.   I hear hopeful news about Lincoln's Inn.[1]

B——'s Court is going so beautifully ; every room and shop let ; the people so happy and good ; the clubs full of life ; the finances so satisfactory.

14, Nottingham Place,
February 7th, 1877.

To Mrs. Gillum.

. . . . . The fact is my time is so utterly engrossed that it is absolutely true that I have not time to see even old friends quietly, unless under special

---

[1] A premature attempt to get the gardens of Lincoln's Inn Fields open to the public

circumstances warranting an exception. It is strange, but the strain of responsible schemes under my continuous charge, the thought necessary for dealing with all the new large plans before me, and starting them wisely and well, the ever-flowing stream of persons with whom I have to make appointments on business, and the incessant buzz around me of my assistants and immediate fellow-workers, leave me in a state of utter exhaustion on a Saturday night, which makes perfect stillness the only possibility for Sundays. Even the walks are often taken up by the companionship of persons who want to talk over with me this plan or that ; or to submit to me some difficulty. I cannot tell you how difficult it is to see anything even of Mama and Miranda, and as to Gertrude and Minnie I rarely see them, even if they come here. It is well for me that in the course of work I do naturally see many of my friends ; and that I do love and care very deeply for many of my fellow workers. Else I don't quite know what would have happened to me by now.

I know you will begin to tell me I ought to give something up. And I could only answer my whole life is giving up of work. I part with bit after bit often of that I care for most, and *that* week after week ; but it is the nearest of all duties, added to the large new questions, in which a little of my time goes a very long way, which thus engross me. Such, for instance, as those I have now in hand—the purchase for Lord Pembroke of £6,000 worth of houses for the poor. He gives money, pays worker ; one of my fellow workers trains her. Mr. Barnett sends me names of courts ; but the seeing the spot, its capabilities, value, the best scheme to improve it, getting surveyors' and lawyers' reports, I must do. I have six such schemes in hand now, small and large together at this moment. Then I had to see Sir James Hogg, the chairman of the Metrop. Bd. of Works, on Tuesday about the Holborn rebuilding under the Art. Dwell. Bill. I have obtained leave from Sir E. Colbroke to plant the Mile End Road with trees. I have all the negotiations with the vestry to make. The C O S. takes much of my time, tho' I have left all our local works to others Then all the time I have 3,500 tenants and £30,000 or £40,000 worth of money under my continuous charge, and, though I only see my people in one court face to face as of old, and the ordinary work goes on smoothly, yet even the *extraordinary* on so large a scale takes time. Questions of rebuilding, of construction, of changes of collectors, of introduction of workers to one another,—I assure you the exceptional things I can hardly refuse to do (so large is the result from half an hour's work), use up my half hours nearly every one I do read, I must, in holidays, when I go right away out of reach of frequent posts daily on those blessed Sundays, sometimes the last thing at night, that I may sleep better. I now and again catch (as if for breath) at a picture gallery ; but *so* rarely, and only suddenly, when I see I can.

Venice,
February 18th, 1877.

FROM RUSKIN.

MY DEAR OCTAVIA,

I have your beautiful letter with account of donations in print, and am greatly delighted with it. You will find yourself, without working for it, taking a position in the literary, no less than in the philanthropic, world. It seems to me not improbable that the great powers and interests you are now exciting in so many minds, will indeed go on from the remedial to the radical cure of social evils : and that you have been taking the right method of attack all along. . . .

Ever affectionately and gratefully yours,

J. Ruskin.

Derwent Bank, Great Broughton, Carlisle,
March 21st, 1877.

To Mr. Cockerell.

Did you know Mrs. Nassau Senior ? . . . I sit waiting for the telegram that shall tell me that she is gone from among us. I feel stunned ; for I had large hope from her vigorous constitution ; and now this relapse is strange. She was, among my many friends, one of the noblest, purest-hearted, bravest to accept, for herself and all she loved, pain, if pain meant choice of highest good ; with an ardent longing to serve, a burning generosity, which put us all to shame. Moreover she loved me, as few do ; and I her ; and, when I think that I can go to her no more, I dare not think of what the loss will be. But neither dare I grieve ; she seems too high, too near, too great, to grieve for or about ; the silence will be terrible, but if one keeps one's spirit true and quiet, and in tune with the noblest part of the absent loved ones, strange voices come across the silence, convictions of how they feel, and what they would say, if they could, to our listening hearts ; only I know this and all things come straight to us from One Who cares for us ; that His truth, somehow, the fact He has allowed to be, *is* best ; and it is a help so to have loved Truth thro' all one's life, that, when she veils herself in darkest guise, we dare not turn from her. . . .

I am busy about Quaker's Burial Ground, and Archbishop's meeting and other things.

Derwent Bank,
March 27th, 1877.

To Mrs Edmund Maurice.

I have replied to Mr. L. and Fawcett pretty much in full . . . and reiterate my own strong conviction that the railway is not needed, that it will spoil the Heath's beauty and need not increase accessibility ; compare the erection of a station to any which might be erected in Kensington Gardens on the same plea ; state my own opinions strongly, and "let it work." You will judge whether to do more. I am doing my little best—which means many fruitless letters about Bunhill Fields, the Archbishop's meeting, . . . and my poor Lambeth. It is unfruitful work so far ; but all things must have a season of sowing, and the reaping must come some day. Numbers of people, too, are doing their best to help, which is beautiful. . . . I have, you see, so very much of many kinds in my life.

A letter on the opening of B. Court Club on Sunday.

April 13th, 1877.

To Mr. Cockerell.

I think, as I live so very near, and as my life is so much in my own hands to plan, so that I can (and I *will*) rest on other days, that I will, if I am better and return, take up some small bit of work on a Sunday, afternoon, down there, or perhaps get the girls to come to me in the evening. My life seems meant for this, if for anything ; only the worst is that I seem not to have that glad bright sympathy with young things, which makes some of my friends able to make such classes a real joy to the girls. However, I will try—or try to try.

14, Nottingham Place,
July 7th, 1877.

To Mr. Cockerell.

. . . I rather thought of "St. Christopher's Buildings" if the name must be changed. I'm very fond of St. Christopher. His early history, less known than the later parts, is to me very beautiful; and, associated in my mind with B. Crt., the way he learnt that the good thing was the strong thing, seems to me very grand. And he learnt it by service and bearing too. The world would fancy it was named after some old church; and I should hear the grand old legend in the name. Is it too fantastic a name? Do you know the early part of St. Christopher's life, I wonder? I think in B. Crt. we want all to be reminded that the devil is himself afraid when he really sees the good thing. Also I like St. Christopher's respect for his own physical strength. . . . Everyone is so kind. I think I have a magnificent set of friends. As to Mrs. Shaen and Lady Ducie they really are like angels. I hardly knew Mrs. Shaen's height of nature till now, and her expressiveness makes her a great delight; while Lady Ducie's magnificent silent sympathy, and that exquisite depth of tenderness of hers, are so very beautiful. The servants too, and the children, and the people who come in and out to help, and are not very near,—their silent little acts of thoughtful kindness touch me often very much. I ought to be so very full of thankfulness and joy.

No date.   Probably 1877.

To MARY HARRIS.

I cannot tell you what important work we have in hand. We are restoring and re-establishing a provident dispensary here. It implies an immense deal of thought, judgment, money. Mr. Crowder is quite the leader in it all. I am quite proud of him . . . Then we were laying deep foundations for Mr. Hughes' future success.[1] This week we have our blind concert at which 660 tenants also will be present.

I went over the new buildings in B. Court on Wednesday. They really are beautiful. It does one's heart good to see them. I think Lord Ducie must be delighted.

August 22nd.

To MRS. SHAEN.

Everyone falls in with my plan for the little orphans,[2] and I am trying to place them in the village where Miss Harris lives   Boarding out is most successfully carried on there. Dear Janey came and stayed there and saw the houses. My former pupils would watch the children for me, and, if I go there, I should see them myself.

.   .   .   .

Not dated.

MRS. HILL TO MRS. EDMUND MAURICE.

Octa arrived safely yesterday in perfect enthusiasm about her visit and certainly better for it. She dined in the evening at Lord Monteagle's, and

---

[1] This refers to a petition circulated among the electors of Marylebone asking Mr. Hughes to come forward again at the next election.

[2] She boarded out one of these orphans in memory of Mrs N. Senior.

found Fawcett quite opposed to the Bill. She talked with him at dinner and afterwards, and I believe quite altered his views. In wishing her good-bye he said he owed to her a most interesting and delightful evening, and he was glad to have met her. He apologised to Lady Monteagle for having engrossed the conversation, and kept it on this topic ; he hoped to meet her again, and not be so absorbed.

Saturday (1877).

MRS. HILL TO MRS. EDMUND MAURICE.

A change has come o'er the spirit of our dream. Octa has seen Dr. Hughlings Jackson three times ; and Lady Ducie has seen him once ; and he insists, in a way we cannot gainsay, that Octa shall *at once* cease work. She is going abroad, but we don't yet know where—and is organising work in the houses to go on without her ;— all the other work must of course take its chance in other hands,—those in which it now is.

Dr. H. Jackson thinks she will ultimately quite recover, and says she must have immense strength to have gone on all these months.

December 7th, 1877.

OCTAVIA TO MISS LEE, NOW MRS. HUDDY.

Believe me the work you have done for me in B. Court during the past year has been the greatest consolation to me. It often sits heavily on my heart to think how much real deep personal work goes undone in the courts, while I am called away, or which I am not fitted to do ; and, when I see that you and such as you are taking it up, I feel so thankful. I know that *that* is the work which is of deep and true value.

A A

CHAPTER VIII

1878—1881

FOREIGN TRAVELS—MANAGEMENT OF HER WORK AT HOME

I MENTIONED, in an earlier chapter, the way in which Octavia's difficulties had, on more than one occasion, called out the help and sympathy of new friends. This good fortune was remarkably exemplified, when she broke down in 1877. Miss Yorke, who now came forward to give her sympathy and help, became one of the most important figures in the remaining years of Octavia's life, and, by her persistent devotion to her comfort and active help in her work, did much to encourage her to new efforts. But, for the moment, her help took the form of accompanying her in a foreign tour, which turned Octavia's attention away from the troubles which were weighing on her mind, and gave her new sources of interest

In the letters chosen to illustrate the tour, I have, as a rule, preferred those which show her sympathy with the people and modes of life with which she came in contact, rather than those descriptions of scenery, which often strike readers as familiar. But her strong artistic sense gave her so great a power of realising and describing natural beauty, that I have occasionally made exceptions to this rule

As the final decision to go abroad was only accepted after considerable hesitation and delay, Octavia had to make all her provision for her time of absence in the course of a week. Under these circumstances, her sister, Mrs. Lewes, consented to undertake the guidance of the fellow workers in this emergency. As, however, Mrs. Lewes could not assume all the responsibility which had fallen on her sister, a certain amount of decentralisation was effected, and greater power entrusted to the fellow workers

The capacity and disposition possessed by each thus became more manifest, and, while some showed administrative power, but with little real sympathy, others, who had felt more of Octavia's personal influence, threw themselves, with hearty delight, into the life of the poor people. I have chosen letters from two of these sympathetic workers, as best illustrating Octavia's purpose. One was a lady whose name I do not venture to quote, because I have not been able to find out where she is now, or obtain her consent to the use of her name ; but I am sure that she cannot be offended that her cheery, and rather unique influence should be remembered. The other is Miss Emily Harrison, to whom I have already alluded in an earlier chapter; whose little painting room near the playground was the scene of much friendly intercourse, and much more useful guidance than a more conventional teacher could give. At the same time Octavia's personal influence on the tenants was shown by such experiences as Mrs Lewes relates   One tenant said to her, " We shall be all right now you've come. We do understand Miss Hill and Miss Cons " And again Mrs. Lewes writes, " At the D.'s I began with a locked door, a barking dog, and a notice to quit, and ended with a gentle interview, a promise to pay up largely, as soon as ever he is in work, and a withdrawn notice."

It will be seen that one victory, though of a temporary kind, marked this period. The public-house, which had been so bitter a bone of contention at an earlier stage of its existence, was turned into a coffee-house ; and, under Miss Cons' energetic guidance, succeeded in holding its own for some time.

Still more cheering news came to Octavia during her absence. Her example had been producing effect in other towns; movements for housing reform had begun in Liverpool, Manchester, and Dublin, and a very efficient worker, who had come to Octavia for advice and training, was carrying on a satisfactory scheme in Leeds.

January 10th, 1878.

MIRANDA TO MARY HARRIS

As to Octavia's work, she means to get Gertrude
to be the centre, as far as she can, but each of the
volunteers to be put in direct communication with the
owners, and to be answerable immediately to them ;
and she will ask the owners to understand that she
expects them to look into the balance sheets, each
quarter, and to see how things are going for themselves ;
not to hold her responsible any more just now.　Meanwhile she leaves all the work *in train;* and Gertrude
will advise and help the volunteers, and direct the
assistants as far as she can, but will not take Octavia's
responsibility to the owners.　Of course she *could* not,
as the work cannot be her first duty ; and she might
have to break off any time.　O. thinks the plan will
make the volunteers splendidly independent, and will
answer very well wherever there is a good worker ; also
that the worst can do little else than not make any
great improvements in their properties.　The management of the Donation Fund she leaves with Minnie,
whose judgment she trusts very much.

Hôtel D'Holland, Cannes,
January 24th, 1878.

OCTAVIA TO HER MOTHER.

We reached here last night.　Miss Yorke is
kinder, brighter, and with subtler sympathy than I had
imagined　She is an excellent manager, and prevents
one's feeling forlorn in travelling　It is an immense
comfort that all my work is so well started, and that I
am anxious about nothing. . . . I hope dear Gertrude
found all as easy as could be ; but one feels how

OCTAVIA HILL.

From a Drawing by Edward Clifford, 1877.

puzzling things might be, from there being omissions of form, when once the living voice was gone.

Villa Cattaneo, Nervi Riviera de Levante,
February 4th, 1878.

The MacDonalds are very kind, but I rest much more on Miss Yorke's quiet, strong, wise help. There is something so sterling in her. She says little, and does so much. I am deeply interested about the war, and long for news. We get no newspapers here! And, for the first time in my life, I do miss them sadly.

52, Wigmore Street,
January 24th, 1878.

EDWARD CLIFFORD [1] TO OCTAVIA.

DEAR MISS HILL,

I write just a little greeting to you, as one of the many friends who are thinking pretty often of you, and longing for the time when you may come back, revived, to all the folks who need you here.

I wished so much for you to go, that I can't be sorry, for a moment, that you are gone. What I hope now is, that you may have a delicious sky above you, and hills and green plains on each side, and a few unexpected roses, and the promise of anemones and violets before long; and that you are already feeling, as it were, in a new planet, and as if everything had happened about forty years ago. Distance and time are more like each other than might be supposed.

Don't, of course, think of answering any note of mine. I shall hear of you, I hope, from Miss Miranda.

Yours sincerely,
EDWARD CLIFFORD.

[1] The artist who painted Octavia, and who, afterwards, went out to Father Damien, to help the lepers.

14, Nottingham Place,
January 27th, 1878.

Mrs. Hill to Octavia.

My own dearest Child,

I feel it a great blessing that you have no anxiety about your work. I am glad, both for its sake, and for yours; for I am sure you could not recover, as we wish you to do, if you felt things were likely to go ill. I hope this change will prove an improvement in its organisation, and the beginning of an easier life for you. You have climbed the hill far enough to look back, and survey the road passed over; and reflection will suggest to you by what future paths the goal you set before yourself is most likely to be reached. Accept this interval, as a precious time lent you for retrospect and prospect, and for renewing the bodily health that you have expended so unsparingly.

Your loving Mother.

c/o George MacDonald, Esq.,
Villa Cattaneo,
February 9th, 1878.

Octavia to Emily.

I should greatly prefer, if you have time, that you should train a lady on each Committee[1] to wise relief with the fund,[2] rather than spend it on entertainments. You see I want to distribute power, not to accumulate it, and to bring it *near* the workers, who are face to face with the poor.

We know *no* news except what we learn in private letters; not a creature here sees a paper. I don't know, if the six million is voted, nor whether the Pope is dead.

---

[1] The Charity Organisation Committees.   [2] Her Donation Fund.

Villa Cattaneo, Nervi,
February 12th, 1878.

To EMILY AND EDMUND MAURICE.

.... We found Vaccari, a young shopman
in a jeweller's shop, in a little back street in Genoa.
He was greatly delighted, and told us it was the
first donation they had had from England, he thought.
He was so sorry not to show us the house himself, (he
could not leave his master's shop on a week day) so that
we fixed to go in to Genoa, on purpose, on Sunday, and
to see the house and the tomb.

We drove first to the cemetery. On a little plateau
there were four tombs. One of Mazzini's mother,
buried in 1852. It seems he chose the spot himself.
He came unknown to Genoa, made his way into the
cemetery, mingled with the crowd, wandered over the
place, and chose this spot for her burial. He then
returned to Geneva, and wrote to a friend of his in
Genoa, asking him to arrange the burial. He planned
the stone himself. There is a profile bas-relief of her;
and the stone simply records that it is that of Maria
Mazzini, the mother of the exile, Joseph Mazzini
(escile is, I suppose, exile). Six very beautiful cypresses
stand round the tomb, three on each side. The feeling
is one of space, air, freedom, simplicity, and tenderness.
Next to her tomb is that of Savi, much less simple, but
beautiful. The third grave is that of a stranger. Behind
the three is a kind of cavern, in the side of the steep
rocky slope which rises high above. This cavern has a
very simple massive Egyptian-looking entrance over
which alone stand the words "Giuseppe Mazzini."
Within is the tomb. The whole was designed by a
young workman not twenty years old, but a disciple of
Mazzini's.

We went then to the house. High but very humble ;
a dark staircase leads to a dark back room looking out
upon one of the narrow viciola with which Genoa is
traversed ; here an old man, looking very poor, but
(V. told us) who had known M. well, was carving
little wooden frames by the faint light which came
in just by the window. V. led us very solemnly into a
small room leading out of this, where he told us Mazzini
was born. This contained a book-case with their club-
library—not in all more than double the size of mine—
and several more portraits and relics of their heroes.
It was evident the club used this as a little reading
or committee room. There were besides numerous casts,
engravings, photographs, and little busts of Mazzini,
Mamelli, M.'s mother, and others ; a little glass case
with the quill pen with which M. wrote one of his books,
the cockade he wore at Rome, two pairs of his spectacles,
a tiny little letter from him, and a lock of his hair ;
another autograph framed, nearly undecipherable, had
been written the day before his death.

The whole morning was to me very interesting and
instructive, of course I judge from very slight data, but
it appeared to me that we had come upon a man of
deep and strong conviction, of much education, much
thought, one of a company of poor men, bound together
in closest fellowship by a common reverence, a common
hope, and memory of a time of real danger and
adversity. Their efforts were very touching. We
asked what hope there was of collecting the remainder
of the money. V answered that they meant to do it.
" Mais, madame, pour les ouvriers ça demande du temps."
We asked about the chance of securing the books.
" Some of us," he replied, " have the works of Signor
Mazzini ; it is our intention to present them to the

library. We have ourselves read them, and made notes, that we may be able to spare them the better." Something like a library *that*, written first indelibly in men's minds. Their small contributions, too, for purchasing the house were touching.

I could not help thinking it strange that a man of such thought, dwelling on the far future with quiet hope, speaking of education as *the* thing to desire, and having come face to face with great men, at great epochs, should tell us, with such impressiveness, that one man in Genoa had Mazzini's purse, his sword and other things. No body of workmen in England would speak so of any dead man's possessions. Has the worship of saints' relics thus coloured the forms of reverence ? Was it that the times in England have needed and produced no such heroism, as that of the man who held his life in his hands for years, and chose exile for his fellow citizens ? Was it that definite creeds of Catholicism had been cast aside by these men ? no other profession of faith except reverence for country and heroes adopted ? Is it southern adoration ? Or what made the difference ? I ask myself and know too little to reply. But of one thing I am sure ; it is *not* that the *spirit* is less important than the accident of form. Except in that question of the autograph, I was struck again and again at the way in which Vaccari went right thro' the non-essential to the essential.

All thro' the interview I felt painfully that I knew too little to learn a tenth part from him of what I might. He gave me credit again and again for knowledge, and was disappointed by my ignorance. I stopped him to tell me about an inscription on a house I had noticed. It was to Mamelli saying that he gave his blood to his country, and his poems to posterity, and that in that house he had his cradle and his dwelling. He thought I knew that Mamelli had died young, wounded at the siege of Rome in 1849; and his face lighted with joy and he broke from French into his native Italian as he said it was he who sent Mazzini the message, "Rome is a republic! Come!" He told me that the mother of Mamelli still lived in a garret there, and his sister I admired the stone and inscription, and he said with pleased smile, "It is we" (that was I think his circolo or club) "which drew out and planned it there."

I suppose it will live rent free, if these three little rooms, of to them holy memory, are purchased.

I wish Edmund would write to him, if ever occasion offers. He seemed so delighted with sympathy, and must have felt me very stupid—of course I am ignorant, and the difficulty of language was great. I could understand, but not talk. I could have done nothing but for Miss Yorke, who was so kind; she knew less than I did, much! But she took such pains, and asked everything I asked her. They look upon England as very rich, and cared for sympathy. He did not want us to think they were not really in earnest because the matter took time here, said it was so different in England; and, when Miss Yorke said there were rich men in Genoa, he said, "Oh, yes, but not so many, and it is not they who listened to Mazzini."

OCTAVIA.

Rome,
March 14th, 1878.

OCTAVIA TO HER MOTHER.

I write to-day, to be sure to send a letter in time for your birthday; time and strength are so uncertain

now, one has to be beforehand with things. I think of
you so, and shall think of you on the day. My
thoughts of you all make me realise how you are all
doing, and have done so much, and how little I am
doing to combat the difficulties that every day brings.
I do hope you all know that I am better; *that* will
make one anxiety less. How I think of you all, of
dear Andy bearing the burden of all management; of
dear Florence keeping to work with her frail health; of
dear Gertrude so marvellously carrying on my work;
and of dear Minnie doing all so perfectly, and thinking
of everyone. Among them all, however, you seem to
me to have the heaviest weight, who have to care for
us all and think for and of us, and be our centre and
head.

> Hotel Vittoria, Rome,
> April 3rd, 1878.

To HER MOTHER.

I have been thinking that it would be a very
good thing if, at the end of May, you were to come out
to me for a month. By that time I shall be in Switzerland. I am not a very bright companion, and we
should not be able to travel about; still, I think you
might enjoy the beauty and the quiet; and, if you
were to bring a few books, we might sit out of doors
and read together. . . . We went to Albano and La
Riccia, which Ruskin knew; and I began to look a
little more; the flowers were lovely, and I liked seeing
the site of Long Alba, and Monte Cavo, sacred to
Jupiter Latiaris. I drew a great tomb there. Yesterday we went to Ostia. I drew the castle, and also
drew, in a great fir wood near the sea at Castel Fusano.
We have been sixteen long drives to places since we

came here—many of them full of beauty and interest
Ruskin and Virgil made me feel more at home at
Albano and Ostia. I fancy, too, I am really better the
last two days.

Hotel Vittoria, Rome,
April 4th (1878).

To HER MOTHER

. . . We drive to-day to Tivoli, to-morrow to
Subiaco (St Bernard's Monastery); on Saturday to
Olevano; on Sunday we drive thro' Palestrina to
Frascati. On Monday we shall see Tusculum, and then
drive to Albano, where we shall probably stay some
days. Miss Y. has gone to tell the carriage not to
come before post-time, because I want news of you all
before starting. We drove yesterday to Veei; it
was a lovely drive. I am certainly better. I am much
stronger. but I must not try yet even a little walking:
it hurts my head. How interested you would have
been with all these beautiful places and historical
associations! It is a splendid way of seeing them to
drive out, as we have been doing for the last three
weeks. Of course one loses much by not being able to
walk, even a little, when one gets there; especially in a
country where the existence of a road to a place seems
an exception to be noted

Perugia,
April 14th, 1878.

To MIRANDA.

You would have been interested in Assisi. It is
quite unspoiled. There is not a new or unsightly
building there. It is marvellous to see how one man
has stamped his mark upon it for 550 years. Where

he has marked it, and where he could not make his
mark, is equally notable.   It was interesting too to see
the place now, when the institutions he founded, and
which necessarily have preserved many outward rules
of his, are on the eve of passing away : and to pause
and wonder what effect their disappearance will have on
the influence he exercises.   The little town stands on
the sunny side of a very bare hill.   It is full of towers,
and balconies and loggie, and old arches ; it seems well-
to-do, but old-world, living only by its memory—St.
Francis a kind of living soul preserving and pervading
its body.

Inside the town stands the tiny little church of San
Damiano, the one he wanted to rebuild at first, and for
which he took the money.   Sta. Chiara and her nuns
were first there.   All has been preserved as it was then.
The tiny church, the rough choir seats, the simple
nameless burial place, the vaulted refectory with its
rugged seats, the small rude infirmary, Sta. Chiara's
little room, are all there, and have received, as herself
did, his own stamp of humility, simplicity, and poverty,
more truly, more abidingly than any others.   They say
she kept the Saracen from touching them by looking
from a window ; but, when she died, the nuns were
frightened ; and the citizens built for them a church and
nunnery in the town.   This, a large church, has now
no marks of either simplicity or special beauty that I
cared for, except four frescoes by Giotto, on the vaults of
so high a roof that I could see little except the exquisite
glow of resplendent colour, and enough of angel form
to fall in with the general impression Assisi gives, that
these glad and bright visitants were by the holy and
humble men of heart, who dwelt and painted there, felt
to be all around them, whether they kneel on earth

during a crucifixion, or support the head of a dying saint, or guide a mortal on his dark path, or in bright companies fill the visible heaven, or, with stately splendour, stand in myriads before the rapt eyes of the man who conquers temptation. One feels no surprise; the sight of their high holy and cloudless faces seems quite familiar; it is as if earth and heaven must be filled with them; one feels one might hear the rush of their great wings any moment, or hear their swift strong tread either; and they are companionable too, not far from men, " not too bright and good for human nature's daily food "; or, at least, the barrier is so slight a one, that it gives us no surprise when they step down among men, or when a weary man is lifted suddenly by and among them.

The monk who showed us over the church gave us a very graphic account of the discovery and opening of St. F.'s coffin fifty years ago. It reminded one of " Past and Present." No one knew exactly where the coffin would be; they only knew the church had been built for the body to be brought there, just after his death. The Pope declared the coffin would be certainly under the altar. They would not disturb this, and so tunnelled sideways. They worked at night only, not to disturb the minds of the townspeople. They worked fifty-two nights, then they found the coffin. The head lay pillowed on a stone, the arms crossed; the figure was perfect for a moment, but crumbled as the air reached it. Medals proved its authenticity. It was sent to Rome to be certified by the Pope; then carried in procession through the town which was "full! full!" the monk said, "for everyone came, for he was not only a saint, but he did much good to all people; so everyone came to it." Then they replaced the coffin on the solid rock, where for 500 years it had been, hollowed a chapel round it, and there it is. And he so humble a man, who wanted to be out of sight ! Strangely sweet did the tiny little church of Portiuncula seem; and the little hut by it where he died, which now are enclosed by the great dome of St. Maria degli Angeli in the plain just below Assisi. They seemed to bring back the simple, child-like heart of the man; they and the home of Sta. Chiara seemed to me almost more to recall him than even the solemn glory of the frescoes on the twilight richness of San Francesco. And now the order he established will pass away.

May 11th, 1878 or 9 ?

MIRANDA TO OCTAVIA.

Miss Cons has spent Mr. Crewdson's £10 on the Walmer Castle library, which has now 300 volumes and sixty members, many of them lads from sixteen to twenty. Miss Cons goes to the Walmer Castle herself from three to eleven every alternate Sunday afternoon; to set the managers free to go out. She said half-apologetically, " I don't serve unless there is a great press ; but I see that things go right."

July 21st, 1878.

GERTRUDE TO OCTAVIA.

When I was in B. Court I took round some of the notices about the Club, as Mr. Brock had spoken so warmly of its efforts to right itself; and I had a very nice talk with Hobbs. He promised to go and talk to Mr. Brock that evening, and spoke with pleasure of the old days, when those who were teetotalers and those who were not worked side by side, and its own funds made it self-supporting. Bristow, too, spoke to Miss

Garton most heartily He brought out a chair that they might talk more comfortably; and he said he would sacrifice "I don't know what time and money" rather than see the Club broken up. This week, too, Miss Kennedy sends good news from Dublin. She says she has been afloat three weeks with her father's property in Dublin, which was neglected. She has adopted all your plans and books, and writes up for printed forms; and she seemed so interested. But just as keen as ever about B Court. She says, "I had a delightful interview with Mrs. Fitch, just before leaving London, and we talked out all or most of our new ideas and wishes. So I hope the 'alliance' will be most satisfactory. I will do all I know to make it so."

Hôtel Bellevue, Thun,
August 5th, 1878

To Miranda

We go on so freely just from place to place as each day seems best, quite out of the beat of tourists, and off the regular tracks, really near the lives and heart of the people. We see them in their chalets and gardens, and in the upland fields bringing back their harvests. To-day we have crossed sunny plains and uplands, and come along the ravines beside lovely rivers, and stopped to lunch at queer old-fashioned inns I don't expect to like it so much when we get to the grander scenery. I expect the roads are fewer, and the tracks more beaten; we shall meet more tourists and tourists' inns. But still, as we take carriages and stop where we like, we can avoid the worst places. We have all our luggage with us; and, when the horses are fed, we take out our books and cloaks, and sit in fields and woods. At the inns and hotels Miss Y. is perfectly at her ease, and makes every place at once like home. She is, too, up to all emergencies, like Mr. Barnett or Miss Cons; so, if we have an adventure on the way, she knows what to do and all that is safe and right. She knows at a glance which carriages are large enough, what hotels are suitable, which drags are strong enough, at which places we may leave luggage unwatched, what men would fulfil engagements without supervision, etc., etc.

How you would rejoice to see the simple happy homes of the people, and all the wild woods, streams, and rocks, and pretty fields!

Bernina Hospice,
September 14th, 1878.

OCTAVIA TO HER MOTHER.

We are here at the queerest, nicest, out of the way place. It is a capital hotel, the people kindly, simple, and capable. We are the only people staying here, tho' travellers call continually. To our great delight last night heavy snow began to fall, and has continued all day. The sky is evidently full of snow, and we cannot see far, but, between the swiftly falling flakes, we dimly see the great slopes of the near mountains, and a white ghost-like lake fed by the glacier opposite. Beyond it we see a narrow little barrier of rocks (which was black when we arrived, but now is quite white) which separates us from another little lake called Lago Nero, fed not by glaciers but by springs, and which therefore is dark and clear, not thick and white like Lago Bianco. The narrow little barrier marks the watershed, from which streams descend on one side to the Black Sea, and on the other to the Adriatic.

B B

Zernetz,
October 1st, 1878.

To HER MOTHER.

The drive to-day was magnificent, the weather beautiful (this was our fifteenth pass, this is the only one we have been over twice). It is much more beautiful, now the snow is so much more abundant. The larches are the brightest pale gold. The cloud shadows were lovely to-day. We get the warmest welcome from all the people we have seen before. Miss Y. sees, recognises, and remembers all about them all. It is quite funny when we drive thro' a town or village ; she sees the driver who took us to one place, or the girl from whom we bought something ; it is marvellous how she remembers them after such slight acquaintance, or under such different appearances It makes all the people so pleased. It is very strange ; the season is over, and the hotels are closed, or not expecting visitors ; and the masters of some of them are hard at work, in rough clothes, doing field labour—some of course have other hotels at Cannes or Nice—but others, who looked so spick and span in the summer, you meet now with a long whip in the lanes, following an ox-cart with hay.

We had such a pathetic, interesting driver to-day, a brown, weather-beaten, much-enduring man. He drove us in the summer, and won Miss Y's heart by taking so much care of his horse, and so little of himself. He looked worn and shabby then, when everyone looked spruce His little flaxen-haired girl of three years old ran out to see him, and he took her up on the box for a few yards. To-day we engaged him again, and he was so pleased ; he's so hard working looking. I think he is rarely employed as a driver. The 40 francs seemed a *very* large sum to him ; and he put on such a gigantic, very clean collar in honour of the day. He walked a large part of the forty miles to save his horse; and Miss Y. noticed what a small dinner he ordered, and that he never lighted a cigar all day (so different from most of the drivers) till just as we were coming here, when, with a solemn and pleased air, as if it were the right thing, he lighted one to drive up smoking. He doesn't look wretched, only long-suffering, as to weather and work, and very careful. We have engaged him to take us on thirty-eight miles to-morrow; and I daresay he will carry home his 80 francs and spend or save it very providently.

Tyrol,
October 4th, 1878.

To MIRANDA.

Will Minnie look into the question of the Commons Preservation appeal, with a view to considering whether or not to give £20 of the Ruskin donation money? On the one hand they must be careful *very* about litigation; on the other, their hands ought to be strengthened to carry on that which is wise.

Bruneck,
October 13th, 1878.

To HER MOTHER.

I think you would be much interested by the old-world life here, and the customs handed down for generations. Maggie is very kind in explaining the things we see. Yesterday troops of cattle were returning from the mountain pastures to their winter homes near the farms. Each troop had its best cow decorated with a cow-crown, a high and bright erection of which the creature was very proud. She wore also a bright,

broad, embroidered collar, and a gigantic sweet-toned
bell, *much* larger than I ever saw in Switzerland. Cows,
goats, oxen, sheep, and men all came together, most of
them more or less adorned with flowers, ribbons, bells,
and embroidery. But the principal cow, quite conscious
of her honour, walked in a stately way in front. The
people came out in force, in every village, to see them
pass; and the greatest excitement prevailed to see in what
condition they returned. To-day, after mass, they are
all turned into the largest field on each farm, and the
neighbours go round to pay visits to see how each herd
has prospered. The senner or dairyman, who has been
in charge, brings down in triumph all his butter and
cheeses ; and they go quite far out of their way, to pass
in triumphal procession with the flocks through Bruneck
itself. I suppose as a kind of type of the plenty he
brings, it is the custom for him to store his pockets
with cakes which he gives to the villagers on his
way down. Maggie told us last year their queen cow
broke her horn just before they should return ; and she
had to be deposed, and was very depressed ; another cow
had to be trained to wear a crown ; they practised with
a milking stool, and had to teach her to walk first. I
thought Blanche would like to hear all this. We drove
yesterday to Tauffers, a village twelve miles from here. It
lies at the head of a valley, and six weeks ago was a lovely
village full of gardens and surrounded by meadows
But, one Saturday, the river ceased to flow ; and they
were alarmed. It seemed a mass from an avalanche had
fallen into it and blocked it , and, after the body of
water had accumulated behind it, it suddenly broke
thro' the dam and tore in headlong force along, carrying
great rocky sand and trees in its course. For six hours
it tore along ; and then the men could get out to see to

the cattle. Every bridge between them and Bruneck and the outer world was torn away. There were some Austrian tourists there; and two of them volunteered to scramble over the waste of ruin, and climb along the edge of the mountain down to Bruneck with some of the villagers; and they came to the burgomaster here, and bore witness to the desolation. The burgomaster sent a great drum thro' the town announcing the catastrophe; and all the peasants round brought food and carts and horses, and worked with a will.

The Tyrol,
October 27th, 1878.

To MIRANDA.

Did I tell you how here the elder brother has all and the younger has nothing but the right to support, and labourers' wages in return for labourers' work, on the ancestral estate? Some go away to make a place for themselves elsewhere; but many don't. They can never marry, and they grow old in a life of humble service on their brother's land.

Mr. Howitt has been much touched by the life and character of the brother of the old man who owns this farm, and wrote these lines which he would like you to see. He told us of the old man's silent life, strict attention to the cattle, reverent raising of his hat, and letting his grey hair be caught by the wind, as he prayed in the field when the vesper bell rang in the distant town, and of his unnoticed place among the other labourers; and how when his nephew was married, he thought he must make him a present; so he asked leave to go into the bedroom let to the Howitts, where the chest of drawers containing his own earthly possessions stood; how he took out a green little old jug made in the form of an animal, of no value, but all that he could find to give. Take care of the lines, for I like them.

Lienz,
November 2nd, 1878.

To MIRANDA.

I should be frantic if you didn't so beautifully report all you send, so that I know what there ought to be.

I was so delighted with Miss Martineau's letters ; it seems to me to show how much things have taken root, and how much heart there is in things, and how people are helping one another. I wonder if Mrs Wilson is sure to be fully occupied. It is delightful when the volunteers themselves do so much ; but I hope they will use the assistants in other fields.

It is no use frittering time and strength in many places.

St. Michael, November 9th, 1878.

To HER MOTHER.

I really ought to tell you of our travels, they are so full of interesting things. At Heiligenblut, on Wednesday, we hadn't very fine weather ; the sky was dark as when snow is coming ; but we went a scramble up to a high point (where there was a ruined chapel with a fine view of the Gross Glockner) and all the snowy valley and peaks, and all up, by an icy stream, which reminded me very much of Lowell's Sir Launfal. On Thursday the weather was really magnificent, clear, bright, and so sunny. We saw the Gross Glockner to perfection, and then drove three hours to Winklern We had a dreadful char-a-banc with such gaps in the

boards of the floor; it was very draughty for our feet,
but we had such views! At Winklern we changed
carriages, and started for another four hour drive to
Ober Vellach; but the fates seemed against us; first
the axle of the carriage broke and quietly deposited us
on the ground to our infinite amusement. The driver
went off with the horse to try to borrow another; and
I sat in the sun trying to draw a chalet, with *such*
Indian corn outside it, and above, the golden larches,
and beyond them the slope of snow; but I hadn't time
to do *any*thing. The man returned with a kind of
cart, but very comfortable. We drove some way in it,
when the man looked and saw the cord, which had tied
our luggage, loose, and all the luggage gone. We made
him drive back some miles; and there quite quietly in
the middle of the road stood the luggage, neither
walker nor driver having passed. It began to get late;
the sun set, in wonderful splendour; and then the
moon rose. We were driving thro' a long defile in
which a torrent joins the Möll. It is a wildly de-
structive one, and has strewn the whole valley with
stupendous stones, and dug channels among them, and
tossed them here and there over all the waste. The
road threads its way, now down into channels of half
frozen water, now up great banks of stones; here and
there the Moll expands into small lakes, in which the
opposite slopes of snow-covered fir trees and the moon
and snow peaks were exquisitely reflected; and for miles
we went without seeing a house. It was very lovely.
On Friday we drove only 20 miles to Spital; the
weather was quite lovely, every blade of grass sparkled
in the sunlight, and the frosty air made everything
bright. We had two fine grey horses, which greatly
delighted Miss Y. They trotted along the frozen snow

at a fine pace. To-day we have driven 29 miles, from Spital, by Gmund and Rennwig, here. It was not clear when we started; a snow cloud seemed to darken the sky. We climbed a long steep bleak hill, and then saw the folds of the hills north, south, east, and west, and the river, by which we were to travel so long, deep in its channel, far below us; still the light was not beautiful. Gmund is a funny old-world place, with an arched gateway to enter by, and another under a château to go out by, and a fine old statue on a bridge,—nothing pretty in it, only it looks so asleep. The road led on for nine miles more by the river, till we came to Rennwig. There we were to change our carriage for one with two horses, as the Katschburg over which we had to pass is steep. We went into the inn to have some coffee. There were the maids spinning and the mistress working, and our driver came in for his food; all in the same large warm sitting-room where we were. To our intense delight, when we came out, we found we were to have a sledge and two large horses, strong as cart-horses, to draw it. It was very comfortable; we had no end of wraps; and Miss Y. bought us each some great warm over-boots this morning. There we sat, as warm as could be, with our luggage packed round us. We saw at once that the day, the middle of which had cleared and been splendid, had changed its mind, and more snow was coming, as a heavy cloud hung over the mountain in front. Slowly, lightly, thickly it began to fall; the great fir-covered slopes were seen through the mist of it; the landscape was little changed by it, for there was much before; the road was thick with it, the drifts white and deep; the mountains loomed large and white; then the moon rose, and the snow ceased. Such a silence, such a scene I never saw ; for nine miles we drove without passing a house or a person. Our driver had a great horn, which he blew before a bend in the road, to warn any sledge that might be coming ; and the unfamiliar sound seemed to make the silence more marked. We are on a post road, and employing postal vehicles, and all is safe and familiar, and easy to the people evidently, but very impressive to us. We are, as you say, seeing the country as it is, and not in gala dress for tourists. We like the people much. We seem a great marvel to them ; they see few tourists here, and few English anywhere. We are in a very comfortable inn, but surrounded by deep snow. We are much amused with the people in the room where we had supper. A perfectly sober, orderly, well-behaved set of men and women came in to supper. One great dish was placed in the middle of the table ; they all helped themselves to it with spoons, which they took out of their pockets. When they had finished, they sucked their spoons and pocketed them. The master and mistress of the hotel, their servants and children, came next. They had a plate each allowed them, but only one glass amongst them. They give us many things which they think the right thing ; but they evidently regard them as great luxuries, and to be taken *great* care of. The little bits of carpet beside our beds they carefully fold up every morning and put away all day, and get them out for us each night. Their little charges are somewhat touching. They ask us how much bread we have eaten, and charge accordingly. We go on to Radstadt to-morrow. Don't be anxious about us, we are very cautious , and I never saw anything like Miss Y.'s knowledge and observation. She knows the strength and power and time and chances of all things.

St. Johann in Pongau,
November 11th.

We had such a day yesterday ! We came sleighing fifty miles. We came by Unter Tauern down to Radstadt, and then it being only 3.30 o'clock, and as we had only driven forty miles, we thought, after dining and asking for a chance post card, we would go nine and a half miles to Wagram, as we wanted to see the winter sunset over the snow, and it would give us more time at Gastein. We drove off, still all in sledges; and a splendid sunset it was. It was quite dark when we drove into Wagram, which appears in large letters on the map ; but, as Baedeker mentions no inn, we had enquired at Radstadt which was the best. It was a rough place indeed, but the woman took us upstairs, promising a room, when suddenly, whether it was that in the light she saw we were quite unlike the country people, or what, I can't say, but she turned resolutely downstairs, took us into a kind of top room to parley ; and nothing could induce her to give us a room Moreover, she declared that there was no horse in the village which would take us on. The master, our coachman, and all the men in the room supported her. Miss Y really believed them, she is so *very* disinclined to suspicion , they seemed to send and see, but became more positive. " Oh," I said, " get a room ; they'll send us on to-morrow." " There was no room," they said. I thought they looked simple people frightened at us, so I said, " Ask her what she advises us to do." Go back to Radstadt, two hours' drive in the utter dark. However, there was nothing for it, and laughing we agreed. We still stood talking " Tell her we're English," I suggested, " and have many railways in England, and no sledges " ; for I saw one of the great

causes of suspicion was that we hadn't gone round by
railway. Miss Y. told them; and they became interested.
She was very gentle, and, I think, touched them; for
suddenly the men made a sign to her to accompany
them. I followed their flaring tallow candle thro' great
barns, out into the stable yard, where in solemn circle
they showed her a sledge, such as peasants use, just a
platform of boards on runners. " Would that do ? "
" Certainly, perfectly." So persistently truthful was
she that she thought they meant a man would drag
it, and said pleasantly, " Oh, it didn't matter about a
horse at all." Horse ! they'd a beautiful horse, she must
really see it; so she was conducted thro' great barns
to the stable. She admired duly the great animals, but
still clinging to her belief in their truth, said, " But
they can't go in the snow." " Oh, beautifully ! " they
exclaimed. So all was settled. The good woman,
touched by her gentleness, couldn't do enough for her,
and fetched her own great slippers lest her feet
should be wet, and they all took us under their
wings. They would make us go into the hot tap-
room, and there kept us for two hours, while they
prepared our room. We were made to draw up to
the common table, and saw the moderate drink and
food, the strong young women walkers who came in for
their dry bread and beer, laid down their bundles, and
set off again to walk all night. We saw the men drinking, and they looked with much interest at our maps.
Meantime we saw them wash our sheets and bring them
in to dry ; and we felt the preparations the women were
making above, while the men did the honours below.
We hinted our fatigue; but it was all of no use. At
last we got the man to take us up to our room. The
woman was giving it a final sweeping, and wasn't very

pleased; but we admired the room and won her heart. A long low room with beams showing fine tiny latticed windows, a great massive wooden door with such a carved pediment, a long shelf running all round the room under the ceiling, set all round with shining pewter plates, two feet in diameter, against which hung numerous glass tankards. The beds were very small, but quite comfortable. The man asked the woman if she had given us water, " Oh yes, sehr viel "—very much —she replied. We found it a decanter full, and we had one towel between us; but evidently her very best, all embroidered at the end. They did their utmost for us. They seemed a little relieved, and very much pleased when Miss Y. paid them this morning. The man showed it to the woman, as much as to say, " I told you they would pay all right"; and she nodded a self-controlled, satisfied little nod. We all shook hands; and we drove off, sitting back to back on the sledge, our feet down at each side; they could be put into a ring like a stirrup when we chose; our luggage tied on near us, and we came merrily on here thro' the snow. Now we are going on to Lind.

November 26th, 1878.

OCTAVIA TO HER MOTHER.

I hope you will receive safely a letter I posted from Innsbruck to tell you that I am coming home for a very short time, and that I expect to arrive on Saturday evening, November 30th, but may be as late as Monday 2nd (evening).

We drove here from Imst to-day, forty-one miles thro' the Ober-Inn-Thal, and passed all along the defile of the Finstermunster. It has been the worst day we have had for seeing the scenery; still I thought it very grand, and was glad to see what threatening snow looks like. The great swirls of wild white cloud, breaking and clinging against the mountain sides, and lying level in narrow ravines, were very grand. The Finster-munster is very impressive, the Inn threads its way 500 feet below the road; and the craggy cliffs above the road were stupendous. We hope the snow may fall heavily to-night, and leave it clear for the Engadine to-morrow. Yesterday, when we drove thirty-seven miles from Innsbruck to Imst, it was quite fine nearly all day. Here we are in our old quarters at Nauders, at the old-fashioned inn we liked; but we have had to come to the other side of the house to secure a room with a stove, very necessary with snow deep round every-where.

I shall turn up in a very forlorn condition, as to dress fit for London. . . . I try not to think of coming back; I daren't.

Salzburg,
November 17th, 1878.

To HER NIECE, BLANCHE LEWES (aged 6).

I was so pleased by your sending me the little bunch of roses in Mama's letter. I was glad to hear of your moving to Elm Cottage. I fancy it is very pretty. I hope you and Maud like being there.

I suppose you very often go to see Aunt Margaret. You would be interested to see the way we travel here. There is thick snow on the ground; and we go on sledges,—that is carriages that have no wheels, but go easily in the snow. They go very fast.

The other day we started before it was light. The moon was shining brightly; there was a little light in the sky where the sun would rise. Miss Yorke and I sat in a sledge, which is so low that one feels almost on the ground.

The driver had on a great fur coat, a fur cap, and great fur gloves. He looked like a picture of a Laplander; but we had a horse, not a reindeer, to draw us. There was another sledge behind us with our luggage. I couldn't think why the white horse that was drawing it kept coming and rubbing his nose against my shoulder; and I thought, too, that it was a little frisky sometimes. When it got excited, it seemed to prance about a good deal; and I wondered why the driver let it.

But soon we saw that the good little creature was being trusted to follow without any driver at all.

He followed for twelve miles, till we changed horses, over the mountain and over the wide tracts of snow, where the road was only marked by posts which stood up from the snow; and through the quiet little mountain villages, where the people were just waking and coming out to cut a way through the snow to their cow-houses or wood-sheds.

Every now and then the driver of our sledge turned back and called, "Cieco, Cieco" to the horse; and he trotted up, and rubbed his nose against my shoulder. We met the peasants walking. It was hard work in the snow; even where our horse had been, it was over their knees. One boy had a little dog with him; he wanted to keep it out of the snow, and had buttoned it into his coat in front; its little head looked so funny, wagging in front of his chest. We went up over the mountains where there were no more houses, and hardly any peasants to be seen, only just snow-covered mountains, and fir-trees loaded with snow, and all the streams were covered or edged with icicles, some of them as tall as a cottage.

There used to be wolves there ; but I suppose there are none now. It was strangely solitary ; so much so that we saw two pretty chamois going over the snow together into a fir wood. They left pretty footprints in the snow. There wasn't another road going in the same direction for a hundred miles ; so, though it was so high and cold and snowy, the people have to go over it all the winter. It was very beautiful to see the sun rise, and the snow on them looked quite rose-coloured in the light. We drove fifty miles in sledges that day. The people here all have a little ground, and they plant what they want to eat and to wear too : and they hardly ever buy anything in shops. Their cows and goats and fowls give them milk and eggs and cheese and milk ; and their sheep provide them with wool ; and they have flax and hemp, and the women spin and weave it ; and they make it in the winter ; and they make even the leather for their shoes at home from the skins of animals. Very little corn ripens here ; it is not warm enough ; but they make great racks, like gigantic towel rails, with numbers of rails twice as high as the houses ; and there the little corn that they have and their hay are placed, that they may get sun and wind and ripen and dry.

They are very fond of their country, and have fought for it several times.

I mustn't write you more of a letter to-day. With love and kisses to Maud and baby and Papa and Mama.

About 1878.

To Mr. Ruskin.

Thank you very much for your letter.

Please don't think about me. If in anything you

ever did or thought there is anything you would wish otherwise, forget it, as if it had never been. Never mind telling me, or even telling yourself, whether there was anything, or nothing, or if anything how much, or what it was; just, if it occurs to you, put it from you like an unreal thing; never let it trouble you. You know this is what I wish always.

Be sure not to trouble, so far as I am concerned, about any painful thoughts of me, which remain to you, if such there be. They are either true and will abide, or false and will vanish—it can but be for a little time.

Bagnieres de Bigorre,
February 5th, 1879.

To MRS. EDMUND MAURICE.

There's a thing I am anxious about; and that is I fear I've led you into what may be troublesome, as it turns out, and that is the Kyrle Open Spaces Committee. . . . You never said or felt or implied that you'd time for a great new work, which this kindling would be; and I write to say to you that I quite realise this, and shall not be surprised or disappointed that the K. S. C. becomes a very different thing from what we three talked of that morning, or even what I wrote of from Paris. I daresay you and E. will manage to make it a most useful opening up of the Open Space Kyrle work in London; and this will indirectly help the wilder commons slowly; in fact there need be no difference in programme; but I think you ought at once to know that I see a wide difference in expectation. It is clear there is no large or zealous body to gather together; you can't even get an Hon Sec., but the effort will be good as far as it goes. . . . It is the want of general interest, without a fire in the midst, that is telling. But never mind ; only don't think I expect much, nor strain yourself to do anything you don't see your way to. Take it very quietly ; go on till it grows into more life, if it may be, before all the commons are gone. . . .

> Hôtel de France, Bagnières de Luchon,
> Haute Garonne,
> February 8th, 1879.

To BLANCHE LEWES.

I hear you were interested by my other letter. Now I am in quite another country. I am in France, and very near Spain. We meant to have ridden to-day a little way up the mountain and looked down into Spain ; but there is still a little too much snow. They have no sledges here, as they had in Tyrol. The snow soon melts here. All the carts are drawn by great oxen. They draw them with their heads, not with collars as horses do. They have their heads harnessed, because their necks are so very strong. They have great sheepskins fastened on their horns, partly to look pretty, and partly, I think, to prevent the harness rubbing them. On Wednesday, we were driving in a carriage with two fine horses. We began to go up a hill, and we passed a cart with a heavy block of granite, and twelve strong oxen to draw it. We went on a very little way, and then our naughty horses didn't like going up-hill ; and, instead of going on, they went back ; and they wouldn't press against the collar ; and, the more the coachman tried to drive them on, the more they went back. This is called " jibbing " ; and it is very dangerous, because they can't see where they are pushing the carriage ; and they might send it off the road, down a precipice. Miss Yorke and I got out, as

c c

well as we could. The coachman, who had been very proud of his horses, and who had driven past the twelve oxen very dashingly (the oxen go very slowly), now said very meekly, " I must get two cows." So he called the driver of the oxen to lend him two ; and they fastened these in front of the horses. It looked so funny to see how the patient things pulled slowly and steadily up the hill ; and the naughty horses couldn't help coming, though once, when the rope broke which fastened the oxen, the horses again tried to go backwards. The man talked to the oxen all the way ; they seemed to know all he meant them to do when he shouted. We couldn't tell what he said, for the people here don't talk French among themselves, but an old language that their neighbours can understand. They wear bright handkerchiefs tied round their heads, instead of hats or bonnets, and their boots are not made of leather, but all of wood ; they are turned up at the toes, and oh ! they make such a noise on the floor ! Besides the oxen they use a great many mules ; and they carry the milk to market in bottles slung on each side of the mules. It is much warmer here than in England, and many flowers are out already. The snowdrops grow wild in the woods.

March, 1879.

MRS. HILL TO OCTAVIA.

Miranda gave your message to Mrs. Hollyer[1] whilst she was doing my grate. When she had left Mrs. Hollyer said, " Paradise Place is so quiet now ; there are such nice respectable people. We are all so comfortable there " ; then she looked up in my face

[1] A tenant

with such a nice expression, and added, "Will you tell Miss Octavia so?" I did think it such a delicate way of returning your sympathy in her illness.

Rome,
March 27th, 1879.

To Mrs. Shaen.

Did you see dear Mr. Howitt's death? We found him dying, when we came here. He was one of my oldest friends. I remember their house as one of the happiest and best I knew as a child. He used to take me for walks, when I was six years old. Mrs. Howitt looks so clearly thro' to the meeting in the future, and has none but holy and happy recollections and the human grief is so natural, and yet the peace of trust so great. It is beautiful and helpful to me. I was almost a daughter to her, and her son who died in Australia one of my earliest companions; so she lets me slip in there, and there seems more life in the house of death than in all the sunlighted hills, for God seems so near her, and she feels *that* so.

Verona,
May 9th, 1879.

To Mrs. Edmund Maurice

I am very sorry you are having so much trouble about the name; perhaps now that the real work is so abundant, and must be so engrossing, this question may die down. I *do* feel that the name, be it what it may, ought to mark the much larger work you propose to yourselves than the C.P.S. does; else you may here-after have difficulty in getting all the work recognised as yours; and also people will be puzzled continuously

and practically by your not being a branch of the
C P.S Remind Mr. Haweis that you have to encourage
gift and purchase and beautifying as well as " preservation"; that you have to do with *private* land as well
as *commons*, and that you have to do with Metropolitan
as well as rural open spaces. A name never includes
all objects ; but a narrower one belonging to a somewhat analogous society would be very confusing. So I
feel . . . . Mr. Barnett you have probably seen.[1] His
letter strikes me as depressed, and I am sorry. I realise
what he says about throwing stones, but such practices
often die down, after a little ; and tar paving is such
uninteresting London stuff; you can't plant, or even
have a may-pole in it; nor feel as if it were the earth.
I hope they won't put it, and certainly wouldn't give a
farthing to help; but I'm so sorry the burden of that
and the Pensions is on him. . . . How splendid all the
life of the movement you describe is I have no fear if
the people now interested can only be kept working with
some result, enough to keep up their hope ; if so, the
things must grow.

Freshwater Place,
1879 or '80.

MISS EMILY HARRISON TO OCTAVIA.

I got two nice little letters from children, when I
was away. I heard they took my answers, and read
them to the other children in the Playground. Wasn't
it nice of them ? I send you my little neighbour's
artistic efforts ; he is only a little chap. They had
trained my scarlet runners, and left everything just as
it was in my room, and welcomed me back so tenderly,

---

[1] About a playground in Whitechapel

saying the place had felt *empty* and dull without me. A girl, who has a lot of sisters to mother, came to tell me she had found the motto she liked best, " Love is the greatest force," evidently learnt from experience ; for they are all so fond of her. She and four sisters, and other little and big neighbours, came yesterday to work for an industrial exhibition we are going to have ; and whilst they did needlework and pasting, etc., we read the " Fairy Spinner." [1] I think M. H. was really the only one who could listen to it, as she has been ill and didn't feel the excitement of the novelty so much as the others. Some of the dear little tots kept running past crying to the swallows and butterflies painted on the wall, " I'll catch you bird," " I'll catch you butterfly," almost as happy, dear, as if they were real ones, I think. . . . We came home to that dear Haven named Miranda, looking so sweet and rested and full of delightful sayings and doings of other people. Can't you see her upturned face telling them, and a twinkle in her eyes at something funny ?

No date. (Probably 1879.)

FROM MISS EMILY HARRISON.

DEAREST OCTAVIA,

Oh if one could but have a penny botanical garden in the Marylebone Road for the hot little children and weakly old people !

" Now I hope you'll enjoy yourself," with a hearty grasp of the hand, as much as to say, " You *must* now," was the last word I heard at Freshwater Place.

I didn't at all like leaving it. The children enjoyed

[1] Miranda's Fairy Story.

their *field* day very much, I think, and kept asking, " Wasn't it nice on Saturday ? " with such a little hug of your hand ! I was so pleased with one child, who, I *knew*, in the midst of amusing herself, simply to give me pleasure, came away to me with, " Won't Miss like to have a game of six acres of land ? " and the girl with the dreadful face behaved splendidly, and carried poor little Shannon all the way home to Swiss Cottage ; for we nearly killed the poor little fellow. The cab-door burst open, and he was shot out, and I expected him to be killed on the spot. But on Sunday he was on his legs again—quite a hero ; and instead of pitching into me, his parents were so kind ; only too anxious to reassure me, and show how well he could walk. In fact, Johnny has come into notice ever since. I had a nice talk with grave Mrs. Wilson, who is going to lend books, and to honour me by getting me a cup of tea there ; and I went to say, " How d'ye do ? " and " Good-bye ! " to B. Court Club, and found Mrs. Lewes there.

She was so pleased to get her rents all right ; but also disappointed at many things. It seems that it is when everything looks like failure that courage comes from some bright spot, or something to start you afresh.

FROM A LADY HELPING IN B. COURT.

The cobbling class that I have superintended since the 2nd of December has kept up, as well as I could expect, in some respects, and very much better in others ; for, though it has not increased in numbers, some boys have *never* missed coming They have really learnt to mend well, and have improved so

wonderfully in their manners to each other and to
me, that, in three or four cases, we have got really
fond of each other, and that is my hope for the future.
Good, I like to think, may result. Nine boys attended
the last evening, and seemed very sorry that it was the
last, asking if, next winter, the class would be again;
and, as they have once or twice hinted their hope of
my taking them for something else in an evening, I
am going to try; and we shall read English History to
begin with, and talk, and so on; for we are really so
comfortable with each other that just to be together
is a pleasure to us now. They are only young. But
I found that they and older boys did not do well
together. . . . The boy beyond all the others whom I
care for is James ——; and as I fear you may have
heard anything but good of him—for I am the only
one of your ladies who has any liking for him, except,
I think, Miss Leighton,—perhaps it may be a mistake
to like James as much as I do, and to hope that he will
do so well. But I am quite sure that if *you*, dear Miss
Hill, had the same cause as I have to admire all his
ways and work that I can see, you would also care
little for what is said about his mother and father.
The first evening that he came he did nothing but
watch me, and stand, rather rudely, with his cap
on all the time. Also he had brought no halfpenny;
and I told him that just for that evening he might
stay, but that another time he could not without
paying.

His large head and the powerful expression of his
face made me think how bad, or how good, he might
be, according to the way he turns. I heard that
evening that he was one of the worst (English
" troublesome ") boys in the Court. To my surprise

he came the next time with his halfpenny ; and, when I said that Lush the cobbler was late, he offered very civilly to go for him. I thanked him, and *made much* of him. During the evening he worked more steadily than any of them ; and ever since he has been my best boy, both as regards working, and coming even when he has nothing to mend, just because he seems so happy to be there and to do any little thing that he possibly can for me. Mrs. Jales says that he is now much better in the Court too. To say I like him says little, for I do a great deal more than that. A woman would be strangely made who did not get to feel him as somewhat her own property, and, even if he goes wrong afterwards, not to lose her affection for him easily.

Braemar,
September 16th, 1879.

To Mrs. Shaen.

In an age when doubt assails so many young spirits with its light destruction of belief in the eternal and intangible, will not the possession of such a brother be perhaps to the elder ones something no other possession could be ? Those who have never loved and lost may think of the dead as buried and done with; those whose lost ones had nothing noble or specially characteristic which was good about them, may think of them as *having* lived ; but whoever has seen and loved a being with peculiar beauty and nobleness, will have moments, and those the best and deepest in life, when the certainty that *that* being still lives, will be quite quietly triumphant over all clever talk or brilliant flippancy. I think to you all Frank will be always a blessing—in spite of pain.

On the attempt to save the site of Horsemonger Lane Gaol
as an Open Space.

Braemar,
September 24th, 1879.

To Mrs. Edmund Maurice.

I think we could get the Archbishop to hold a
meeting.   In fact *I have no fear about getting money*, if
dear E. can only get it into a working shape where that
only is needed.   After all, even if Government *did* give
it, that only means all being taxed ; and surely, so long
as riches exist, there is need to call upon those who have
them to give of their abundance freely and heartily
to such places as Southwark ; even without *asking* them,
to make it possible for those of them who *want* to give
to give helpfully, and, so long as there are even quite
poor people with any surplus, it is a pity they should
not have the joy of giving freely.   Is it to be all compulsory taxes, and no free-will offering ?

B. Court Club,
October 18th, 1878 or 1879 (?).

Gertrude to Octavia.

Mr. Blyth asked to come to see me on purpose
to know what I thought about things.   He is very
hopeful, much pleased at the quiet dignified way in
which the (Temperance) Lodges men behaved.   They
asked the *old men* (who are chiefly boys) what they
meant to do about the debt, and their reply was that,
if they could not meet it otherwise, they must sell the
furniture, billiard tables, etc. !   So, finally, the teetotalers have formally taken the debts (now said to be £5)
upon themselves, and have also taken the tables, etc., as
part of the club belongings.

There were, last week, forty-five new teetotal members, and there are twenty-four non-total abstainers— sixty-nine in all. Seventeen and threepence was paid in entrance fees, the whole room cleaned and put in order; and Grimmins's first act was to fasten up with his own hands, in the renewed room, the tablet to Mr. Cockerell's memory. They want it to be just as it all was at first, and to have a penny subscription and no ballot at election.

Eland House,
November 3rd, 1879 or '80.

FROM MRS. EDMUND MAURICE to OCTAVIA.

We went to the opening of Walmer Castle, which was a great success. There were large crowds both of rich and poor. Among others Mr. Hughes, Mr. Hart, Mr. Davies, Mr. Diggle, General Gardiner, Charles and Gertrude. After the "public" had been admitted to the tap-room, and before they began making their purchases, speeches were made by one or two people. Mr. Hughes made a very nice speech, and so did Mr. Diggle, who was much applauded He came up and asked very warmly after you, and said you would be glad to hear that all the work in St. Mary's was going on well, and some of it was being carried on with more vigour than ever. Miss Cons looked very happy, and was busy talking to everybody. The whole place looked very clean and comfortable, and all the food very nice; there were decorations of flowers, and bright flags flying outside. We went over the house, and saw the beautiful dining-room upstairs and the smoking-room, and some very comfortable furnished little bed-rooms for respectable men. General Gardiner turned to a friend and said, " We should some of us have been very glad of as good a bedroom as this at the University." My fear about the bedrooms is that they are too dear. A shilling a night is not much to pay for so nice a little *furnished* room; but, if a working man has to pay seven shillings a week for his room, I fear he will think it too much. Downstairs there is a nice large room to be used for the Boys' Club. It is to be decorated by the Kyrle Society.

14, Nottingham Place,
October 17th, 1879.

FROM MIRANDA.

I don't know whether Minnie will write and give you any account of the Kyrle Committee Meeting yesterday; but, in case she does not, I think you will be glad to know that all went, I think, very satisfactorily. Your letter was received with pleasure, and your offer of transferring the St. Christopher work to the Kyrle was received with warm thanks. Somebody is to be found to undertake the drawing. . . . Can you tell me where your large St. Christopher is? I was asked to show it yesterday, that the Committee might see how much needed completing.

The money was voted for the choir without any difficulty. We have two applications to decorate rooms for working girls.

Minnie asked, on behalf of the O.S. Committee, whether they were at liberty to appeal to the public for funds without consulting the General Committee on the subject. It was decided that they could not. Mr. N. said that he thought they never ought to take any public action without consulting the General Committee. We explained how impossible it would be to work at all, if *no* public action could be taken without reference to the General Committee; for all the work is dealing with public bodies, vestries, etc., and, when Minnie pointed out that in any doubtful case like Burnham Beeches, the O.S. Committee always had, and always would, consult the General Committee, Mr N. was satisfied.

14, Nottingham Place, W.,
December 15th, 1879.

OCTAVIA TO A VOLUNTEER WORKER.

In order to bind the work in the Court (not the collecting, to which this letter does not refer at all) and to make the arrangements simpler and more organised, it is proposed to unite the teachers of the evening classes into a little Committee.

I hope you will be able to join this Committee. I do not think that it will involve you in any labour which will not be very easy, even to so busy a person as you; while it would, in many ways, save you trouble in making arrangements a little more organised and easy to deal with. I think you would all enjoy the little reason for meeting from time to time.

Unless any unforeseen business presents itself, I should think two meetings in the year would be ample; one to settle summer and one winter arrangements, for it is proposed to leave everyone utterly free to do on their evening precisely what seems good to them, so that the only questions that the Committee would have to deal with would be those which might clash with or influence other workers, or in which they would wish to have a voice. My sister, Mrs. Edmund Maurice, will be Secretary of the little Committee. There would be five members, including yourself; but if large questions of general interest were coming before the Committee, it would be well to invite the other workers in the Court

to attend and vote, as the landlord is anxious for the
room to be as generally useful as possible, especially as
Lady Ducie has given up hers to the general use of the
Court so entirely by giving the use of it to the Club. I
am not without hope that I may have the great pleasure of
seeing the Committee meet just once here, after Xmas,
before I go. I hope rather great things from it, do you
know? I feel how much the life of the Court has
developed since I left. All of you seem to me stronger
and quite knowing your own strength, which is an
immense help. The work is more individual, more
living, more firmly rooted ; but I don't like to think
that you should lose anything by my absence ; and I
sometimes dare to hope that this little Committee might,
while leaving to each of you full, free scope, give you each
the *little* connecting link you seem as if you might lose
in losing me. I mean the power of all meeting for
common work, of gathering strength each from the other,
of adding power and life each to the other's work, of
knowing and meeting one another, of understanding
each what the other means, of pausing for a moment to
see if there is anything to learn, to accept, to use in the
other's work, the sense of a common cause and of being
one body to interpret that common cause in the noblest
way in which it can be conceived, and to sink all little
narrow views in the broadest and deepest ones.

Rome,
February 18th, 1880.

To MIRANDA.

What an interesting account you give of Mr.
Clifford's discussions ! I believe few people *will* grasp
what he meant the main point of the discussion to be ;
but I do believe they will be *very* useful, if they show

people who are doing tangible good, or good less spiritual, that distinct teaching about God Himself may be needed I think the reaction from doing *that* only has been too great, and that I and many people need to be reminded of that deepest way of work; tho' I think we always take it up when we have the power, but we hardly look out for, or abundantly use, the people who have the power, nor cultivate it in ourselves. I think it is the next thing we have to aim at. In fear of undue pressure, we hardly appeal bravely enough to the indwelling power of response there must be in every one.

Brindisi,
February 20th, 1880.

To her Mother.

. . . I am glad you like the Diary of an Old Soul. I think MacDonald singularly excels in that quaint, simple, deeply religious poetry. Somehow he has naturally the habit of making those queer comparisons, and sudden leaps from great to small things which one finds in the old poets; and, in the same way, his deep faith atones for the strangeness. There is even something captivating in it I think the book very beautiful. I went to see Mrs. Grey in Rome. She was so *very* kind and nice, and so interesting too. We talked of old times, and of the Public Day Schools, and the Kindergarten work We also saw the Marshes. . . . Yesterday we came from Beneventum here. The day was wild, and there was even rain; but it was very interesting, first to cross the watershed between the Adriatic and Tyrrhenian Seas, then to traverse the great plain lying round Foggia, where four and a half million sheep used to graze, returning in winter by three great roads called the Strade dei Pecore. The merino sheep

used to be there, *now* the plain is gradually being cultivated ; but there are still half a million sheep, and one
sees herds of great grey cattle, and droves of 40 or 60
horses, looking almost wild, grazing among the glades
of oak trees, or on the open ground.

February 21st, 1880.

MIRANDA TO OCTAVIA.

One of the lady workers was talking of giving
food to one of the B. Crt. men, who has been ill ; but
I found he had just got into work, so I suggested he
could get on for himself now.   I then explained to her
that your plan was to let St. Thomas's Relief Committee do any absolute relief, and then to strengthen
them with gifts, if you can make any.   She was so
much interested, and very glad to know it.   She said
that she had no idea you worked with the Church
authorities to that extent.   She knew you were a member of the Church, but had no idea you co-operated
with the clergy to that extent.   So many people
thought you chose to be independent.   I explained how
anxious you were that the clergy should be willing to
be co-operated with, and told her that your desire was
to work with them and so was that of the C.O.S. if
they would but be worked with. . . . Mr. E. writes :
" Will Mr. M. contribute to the Thirlmere Defence Fund ?
He may be induced to do so when he remembers Miss
Octavia Hill's words " (evidently some words you spoke
some time ago).

Hotel St. George, Corfu,
Tuesday, February 24th, 1880.

TO HER MOTHER.

We reached here on Saturday.   We found no
post left here for England till to-day ; I hope you will

not have thought it very long before you heard. We
had a splendid passage here . . . I lay on the deck
nearly all day, and saw the wild, blue, beautiful Albanian
shore, such a land of bare wild mountain-land. The
name of the people means "Highlander." Then we
floated past the islands and into the narrow sea between
Corfu and Albania, where the Venetians and Turks had
their last sea fight, and the Turks tried no more to
advance into Europe. It was a glorious light as we
floated into Corfu about half past. When we had passed
thro' 13 miles of this forest country with the mountains in view, and here and there, but *very* far between,
a village or two, we came out on a cliff over the sea,
along which we drove three miles. The road had been
made by the English soldiers, but it is now all going
gradually to pieces ; the arches which support the
bridges over the little streams (which, by the way, are
now *quite* dry) are all cracking, their keystones pro-
truding ; the well-built walls supporting the road on the
slope of the hills are crumbling gradually down, taking
the road with them. Great hollows are appearing in
the road, and large stones in thousands rolling down
upon it. The driver said, "Il governo non fa niente
per la strada." And there it is crumbling to decay. It
does seem a pity.

We are going on board the Greek boat to-day en
route for Athens. We hear the "roughness" only consists in the want of good food ; that the *boat* and
arrangements are good. There is at any rate much less
open sea, and the scenery is finer. An English lady
who sat by me last night said she had been both ways
and much preferred ours, but the gentlemen here make
a great talking about the food. I daresay it will do for
us. I am doing very little drawing and no good with

it ; but it is possible I may later, and this sea could not be attempted without emerald green.

Athens,
February 28th, 1880.

To MIRANDA.

Patras, their new commercial city, is nearly as pathetic and nearly as interesting as modern Athens ; and one feels that from there actual *safety*, as well as education, and even the possibility of seeing the beauty, must spread gradually. The difficulties of travel are quite extraordinary, quite independently of the question of safety. There are no hotels, no lodgings, no beds, hardly any food, no relays of horses, no posts, no accurate guide-books, no trustworthy people to give information. And somehow one feels it will all come gradually from this little town, springing up, as it were, yesterday, with its little throb of life, which must permeate the whole before it can be healthy or alive. Even from a tourist's point of view, mountains and woods and defiles and rivers are no use because you can't get at them ; and what of the life of the people, their education, their power of using the good things that the earth brings forth ?

Hôtel des Étrangers, Athens,
March 3rd, 1880.

To HER MOTHER,

Mrs. Coupland's introductions have been *most* useful . . . Dr. Milschaefer came himself to give us a lesson in modern Greek, and brought such an interesting young Greek to teach us the pronunciation. It is very interesting to see how the young national life is flowing instinctively in the old grooves. The great thing they have progressed in, since their independence, has been education. Their University is evidently becoming remarkable, and people are coming from Asia Minor and Turkey to study. Their girls' schools and boys' schools are evidently what they feel they are succeeding in. They regret, however, that everyone tries to be a lawyer or something of that kind; and that agriculture and manufacture are neglected. Evidently agriculture has a great future here. The country is much less fertile than in olden times, partly from the bad systems of cultivation, partly, I should guess, from the neglect of trees. They excuse themselves by saying that the ancient Greeks had slaves; but one feels free men ought to work as well as slaves! and one can see they know they ought to do better. One great want is population. They can and do live by the rudest systems of culture. I daresay the utter insecurity of country life, which for years (I suppose ages) has prevailed, will have prevented anyone seeing to, or caring for, farming. The Greeks look as if they had *much* more stamina than the Italians. I fancy their sea life has kept it up; and perhaps their mountain fastnesses, and the fiercer oppression have really been better for them than the enervated life of Italian cities under Austrian, or despotic, cultivated home rule, where the richer and nobler classes must have had the ease of civilisation without the responsibility or duty of self-government. But this is all theory to account for the greater energy one sees. Certainly the Greeks seem to me to have dealt really well with brigandage, in contrast with the Italians. After that dreadful affair in 1870,[1] the House of Deputies enacted a law for four years, punishing the

[1] This evidently refers to the seizure of several Englishmen and their subsequent massacre.

relations of those who were with the brigands, and the villages near which it occurred, which law the English minister here tells us, really extirpated it in a few months, so that the English consuls were able officially to report that, except on the borders and in Thessaly, it no longer existed. Brigandage broke out some time ago in Acarnania, and they instantly re-enacted the law, and it disappeared. It seems to me wise and right in cases where, as here, the crime could only exist by reason of the collusion of the surrounding people. And it must be much kinder than dallying on, as the Italians keep doing in Sicily, first sending and then withdrawing troops. Mr. Corbett was so kind. Gen. Gardiner got me a letter of introduction thro' Mr. Eric Barrington, who is Secretary to Lord Salisbury; the letter was evidently a very kind one. Mr. Corbett called at once, and gave us full and kind assurances and directions as to our movements. The border land is evidently, as *every* one has said thro'out, quite unsafe; but everywhere else confidence has been quite restored for some years. We have the very *best* advice, and shall strictly follow it, so you need not have *any* fear. By the way, do you know those four poor gentlemen were given a large escort, and they insisted on galloping on, and leaving them two miles behind!! So Mr. Corbett told us. It really makes a *great* difference as to the blame attached to the Greek authorities.

We went up Mt. Pentelicus on Monday. The day was not fine, it was wet and cold, and we had no view from the top; but I did enjoy it so very much. The colours of all the wild landscape near were so exquisite . . . I never saw such lights, even in Italy. (Here follows an account of flowers found, and the difficulty of identifying them without botany books.)

I never shall forget the sunset light coming back last
night, as we saw it on Pentelicus, Parnes and Hymettus,
and on the Acropolis of Athens.   There was the grey-
green foreground of stone and dead thyme ; the red
ground here and there ploughed up, the grey-green
olive, or full dark pine, set far and far between; then there
were the blue shadowed sides and bases of the mountains
and their snow-covered tops, now in blue shadow, now
in rose-coloured light, and then all the sun-lighted sides
of the mountains were rose and gold ; and the blue-green
sea, turned in places into one silver sheet of ripple,
broke on the shores with sweet musical voice.   It was
like a dream of perfect beauty . . . Mrs. Corbett turns
out to be a cousin of Lady Ducie's, and writes most
warmly about seeing me.

About difficulties in the school.

> Athens,
> March, 1880.

OCTAVIA TO MIRANDA.

Something has set the girls out of tune.   I
know how trying it is, and how the sense of it shuts
one up, and makes it impossible to be oneself, or to
trust to them.   But I believe, if one could remember at
such times what depths of better things there are in
every human heart, and how they only need to be
believed in and appealed to (especially in these young
things), to spring up and grow and thrive, one would more
quickly get past these trying times   There is usually
either some stupid misconception, or false standard of
what is desirable, confusing the young mind, some
phantom, which seems good to it, and is not good ;
or else some real evil, which the child herself knows to

be evil, and against which she—the better self—will side
with you the teacher, if you can but assume that she is
ready to do so. One may beat about the bush for any
length of time, by dealing with manifestations of wrong;
but if one can get *near* people, and get their spirits into
harmony with God's will and purpose, and make them
feel that one only wants *that* done, one strikes at the
root of the evil, and loses at once the sense of jar,
because it is lost in the sense of harmony with the good
in people.

Hôtel des Étrangers, Athens,
March 10th, 1880.

To HER MOTHER.

. . . . I suppose this will reach you a little
before your birthday (tho' that seems hardly credible);
let it bring you my loving wishes for all that is
brightest and best. We went on Saturday to Tatoë,
which is a little place on Mt. Parnes, where the king
has built a little place for summer. It is close to the
old pass of Dekelea, which the Spartans fortified, and
held during the Peloponnesian War. It was a glorious
day, and we thoroughly enjoyed it; Mt. Pentelicus
looked quite beautiful. There is a great quantity of
fir-wood near the king's place. They have cleared away
trees here and there; I fancy, to let one see the giants
of the native forest, which stand magnificently, throwing their arms up in the sunshine, a foreground to the
blue mountains. The ground was covered with wild
golden crocuses, blue anemones; and, here and there, if
a little bit of land was sown with corn, there were great
crimson anemones growing among it. The utter solitude
of the country is so strange here. One drives for miles,
and hardly sees a creature. We drove on Monday to

the Bay of Phalerum, and spent the afternoon at
the Acropolis, and saw the sunset from there.
Yesterday a wild, tearing wind arose. We were to
to have gone to Phyle, and the mules had been
sent on ; but the storm of wind raged, so we did
not attempt it ; in fact we could hardly stand
on the hill of Areopagus, or beat our way back
along the streets, when we returned from seeing the
theatre of Dionysius, and the Stadium. We spent
Sunday evening at Mrs. Corbett's, and last evening at
Mrs. Finlay's, and met Mr. and Mrs. F. Noel. They go
to Euboea soon, and we shall follow soon. . . . As I
sit, I see the snow heavily falling between me and the
cypress trees. It does look so out of place. . . . Every
one agrees in one united testimony as to the extinction
of brigandage. . . . Here it is pretty to watch the
restored confidence, and the life that is able to grow
up under it. They seem to be very cautious still, and
send mounted gendarmes out over all these solitary
roads ; but it is nice to hear the pride with which the
gendarme tells you you can go anywhere. . . . People
are beginning to build little houses in the country, and
there are other marks of confidence. How interesting
it is to hear, on all sides, of the love of education ! It
seems quite innate ; the children clamour to be taught,
and especially do they delight in politics. They had *no*
toys till lately. Old Mrs. Hill, who first established
schools here for girls, forty years ago, says she never
sees the toy-shops without remembering how she brought
the first dolls to Athens, and tried to teach the children
to play. She says they all sit down to read ; boys and
girls stand at the corners to discuss politics. Children
used to walk from Eleusis and back to attend school
here.

Athens,
March 18th, 1880.

To HER MOTHER.

We saw, some few hundred yards from the
hamlet, an old, broken marble pillar placed there to
mark from the surrounding hilly open common a tiny
space separated by a rough ridge of earth from the
common; but even the ridges had gaps in them, one of
which led to a stony path. We followed it, and found
ourselves in the churchyard. A few graves, marked
with little crosses, and planted with sweet rosemary,
gathered round one which alone had a stone, a little
railing, and a young date-tree planted at each corner.
To our astonishment, we found the inscription in French.
It was: " Oh you who pass by, pause and know that
here lies an angel who waits for thee beyond there,
Beatrice B. . . . who died in her 15th year, 1877." It
was so simple, and, having no surname, seemed to mark
this more. We wondered whether French people were
the cultivators, and what was the history. The people
were all Greeks at the house doors in the hamlet, and
we don't know enough Greek to ask who has begun the
cultivation. Still, we are getting on fast with our Greek.
We often wish we knew more. There is an exciting
ministerial crisis here—M. Tricoupis, the Liberal candidate, trying to overthrow, on financial questions,
M. Koumondouros, the Conservative. People say M.
Tricoupis is the man of most principle, but that he
has not a strong party. Some of the deputies stay at
this hotel, and every night at dinner they have a hot
argument; but we cannot even follow the main drift—
we only catch a few words here and there. If we knew
more, we should learn much more. We have had a

Greek master every night, and have been learning the grammar, when Miss Y. would let me; but it is slow work till one gets to the point of hearing.

Hôtel des Étrangers, Athens,
March 20th, 1880.

To MIRANDA.

. . . . There seems so much to tell you of what we see here. I feel always as if I ought to dash into a sort of swift summary of journal, instead of writing, as I should like, about all the things you tell me. I am sure you know how my heart and thoughts follow you all in them, and I think you will like to know many things I am seeing.

The weather has been so wild and wintry that we are glad to be settled here, and shall not move till it is assured spring time. Meanwhile, we are seeing things within a drive, learning Greek, and trying to gather what we can about modern Greek life. Yesterday we went to see Mrs. Hill's day school for girls. Dr. and Mrs. Hill came here nearly fifty years ago; their work has been supported by the Americans. This school was the first house built in Athens among the hovels. They used some foundations of an ancient market, and say the steps of the school, which were found when they were digging the foundations, may be those up which St. Paul stepped. Dr. and Mrs. Hill built their own house at the same time; and it stands in quite the poor part of Athens, the palace and all the better houses being later, and forming a new quarter. Dr. Hill is now quite blind, and Mrs. Hill too old to teach; but a vigorous and most sympathetic Scotch lady, Miss Muir, lives with them, and carries on their work. I was delighted with her; she and they seem to have been

animated with the true spirit of trust in the people,
love for them, and desire, not to proselytise, but to work
with all that is good and pure in what the people themselves believe—to strengthen that, instead of dwelling
on differences.   Hence they have never found *any*
difficulty in working with the Greek priests.   The lady
who was with us kept pressing difficulties upon Miss
Muir, and asking her if she was not hampered by this
or that ; and it was very beautiful to hear her answers.
" Have you not great difficulties in not being allowed
to read the Bible ? "   " No," said Miss Muir ; " we read
it from end to end if we wish."   " But how about the
Greek doctrine and the procession of the Holy Ghost ? "
" O, the Filioque ! we haven't to touch upon it any
way !   Do you know there is a little school at the foot
of Mount Parnes, from which the priest wrote, asking if
we could spare any old spelling books, or maps, or school
things, and we gathered together what we could ; since
which, we have always been interested in the school.
And some time ago the priest said they would like some
copies of the Bible.   I wrote to America, and they sent
out twelve copies of the New Testament.   Twelve of
the elder lads and the priest walked all the way to
Athens one day, in pouring rain, to receive these.
Some months after they wrote to say that, in reading
the New Testament, so many questions came up for
which they wanted to refer to the Old Testament.
' Might they have the Pentateuch ? '   So I wrote to
America again.   When the books came, I drove to
Parnes to take them.   The priest was absent for a few
hours ; on his return he rang the great village bell, and
all the peasants assembled, and the great boys came
forward to receive their books, and I wrote their names
in them.   ' Tell me,' I said, ' is it true that you read

these ? So many people say you don't.' 'Every day,'
he answered, ' we have our food of necessities, and something to give it a relish ; so daily we have our lessons,
and something to give them a relish.' Many missionaries tell the people they should not cross themselves.
To me," she said, " it is beautiful to see them do it, when
I remember what centuries they have lived under the
Turks, as a despised and oppressed nation, and think
what it must have cost them to make that cross publicly,
as they do when they pass a church It is the assertion
of their Christianity. I sometimes ask myself how
many of us would have power to make that cross ? "

" But aren't you obliged to have a priest come in and
teach ? " " No," said Miss M. ; " many come in as friends,
and we always invite those we know to the examinations and gatherings , and we have a large number of
priests' children as scholars, but in this school we never
had a priest to teach. In Mrs. Hill's other school she
often had a young deacon as pupil teacher. She used
to prepare her Bible lessons with him. They are very
ignorant, and were delighted to learn and then teach."

All the human sympathy was so quick and so deep.
She showed a tiny orphan boy of 4, left by his mother,
at her death, whom they placed in school, to live with
the teacher. We asked for a Greek teacher, and she
recommended one of two orphan pupil teachers, to whom
they had given rooms in the building. All the education in Greece, of rich and poor, was initiated by
Dr. and Mrs. Hill. They have still this school of 700
boys and girls, and train their own teachers ; but the
larger work they helped the Government to start,
and then gave it up to them. . . . I wonder what will
be done about the unveiling of St. Christopher. They
are not Lady Ducie's houses, you see. I should like a

little ceremony; but it is difficult to imagine a simple natural one, and there seems no place for it.

Athens,
March 25th, 1880.

To HER MOTHER.

I wonder how you are. It seems so strange not to know. We went to see Dr. and Mrs. Hill the other day. Such quiet interesting beautiful old people. They remind me of Quakers. They are beloved and respected by every one, Greek and English, poor and sick, and seem to be the only missionaries who have won the people's hearts, by trying to get them to do better in the way their consciences told them. They are full of stories of all they have seen. They came after the battle of Navarino. The Turks were still here for two years after they came; but the protocols were signed, and the Greeks were preparing to return. They told us lovely loving little stories of the people they had known; of their first teacher, a Greek girl from Crete, who came to them as a child, and became like a daughter to them, and of many of their protegés; but all in the same honouring, affectionate way people speak, who have the power of drawing out what is good in those they meet. There has been the wildest excitement here about the change of ministry. M. Tricoupis has just succeeded M. Koumondouros. Mr. T. seems to be universally respected. The English say he is *the* Greek they trust. The Greeks say he is before the age, too good for the time, &c. He is the son of a much respected Greek who was for years envoy in London; and he and his sister are supposed to owe much of their enlightenment to English influence; they are much attached to England. His main object is to abolish the payment of a tenth part of the agricultural produce to the Government, which is supposed to press heavily on the people.   We hear that it was one *great* cause of the War of Independence; but it has never yet been altered.   He is also understood to be most anxious to alter the practice now in force here, according to which every Government employé, from post office clerks upwards, changes with the ministry.   It seems there are £2,000,000 of uncollected taxes in Greece now, the arrears being largely due to the tax-collectors being unable to employ any compulsion, the debtors simply threatening not to vote for the party which enforces payment   There are 500 doctors and 500 lawyers trained here in the University every year; the doctors, they say, do very well, for they go off into the villages in Asia Minor and Turkey.   They are trying to improve the education of the priests, and train many; but only five out of every one hundred remain priests. But it all sounds to me like the swift cultivation of a large number of educated men, who must help.   It is clear that party feeling runs high, and it is difficult to be sure with what bias statements are made; but, various as are the views, the statement of facts is curiously unanimous; and one listens to the quiet people who sympathise and talk quietly, as well as to the bursts of indignation and scorn; and we seem to learn a good deal.   As I say, the facts that all tell us are much the same.   We were fortunate yesterday, in being taken to Mlle. Tricoupis.   She was very kind; her brother, of course, was too busy to be seen, and she was very tired—she had been receiving till two o'clock the night before, all the Greeks calling to offer congratulations to the new Prime Minister; but she was very kind and talked some little time, tho' not about

any of these burning questions.   We are to go
again. . . .

Athens,
March 26th, 1880.

To Miranda.

I shall be so glad if anything is managed in the
way of a little ceremony in Bts. Crt. for St. Christopher.
I see many difficulties, but I *should* like it.   I am
specially glad if it leads to telling the people the story.
Will the unveiler read one to the people, I wonder?
And where?   It seems a pity there is no space in the
court where the people can gather.   I had been
wondering what could be devised in the way of a
ceremony, and had thought of little medals with date
and motto to be given to eldest and youngest child in
each family resident there a given time, and their
marching in procession thro' St. Christopher's room to
receive them, with music and flowers and flags; but
I think it would mean a great deal of labour.   I think
these common memories good for tenants and workers.
I don't much fear stone throwing; but one never *quite*
knows how people will see things; *one* may throw a
stone where *fifty* look with interest.   I hope and
believe they will like the thing; but if anything *does*
happen I am always ready for failure in preparing the
hearts of people for any new thing; some one must pay
the cost in disappointment.   I am quite willing to
do so.

Athens,
April 1st, 1880.

Octavia to her Mother.

. . . We went up Pentelicus and had a lovely
day.   It is a splendid view from the top.   One sees
Euboea with its long range of snow mountains and its

narrow strait, and Helena and Andros and the mountain ranges of Parnes, Cithæron and Parnassus; and Hymettus, and Athens and its plain; below lies Marathon with its red soil and blue bay—indeed blue bays of the sea seem to be around one almost everywhere. Last evening we spent at the Hills'. Mrs H. was saying that letters, when first they came here, were 7 months coming from America; that they could negotiate no bill of exchange here; when they wanted money Dr. H. used to have to go and fetch it from Smyrna, to which, of course, moreover, there were none but sailing ships. She said they never knew how long it would take, especially because of the quarantine. Plague raged at Constantinople and Jerusalem, so that vessels were often and often kept six weeks with passengers in quarantine. She says the last plague was in 1843. . . . We went to the House of Deputies to hear a debate, in the box of the Diplomatic Corps, and could see well, and could have heard had we known more Greek. It was very curiously interesting to see the House. The gallery is open to the public, and was quite densely packed with a crowd of the very poorest people, with earnest, eager eyes, watching and listening, with an intentness beyond what I ever saw at the play. Crowds outside, too, were standing, talking and waiting; and this goes on day after day Mr. Darcy, the clergyman here, took us; and he knew all the members, and pointed them out to us and told us about them. I have been reading some very interesting statistics about Greece, published seven or eight years ago. Do you know that since the independence her population has doubled, and her revenue has increased 500 per cent. ?—the children in school were between 6,000 and 7,000 and are now 81,000. I forget the increase of acres cultivated, but it is *very* large.

Athens,
April 8th, 1880.

To MIRANDA.

We went yesterday to Phyle, and saw the actual fortified place held by Thrasybulus against the 30 tyrants. The gigantic walls still stand. We went with Miss Muir, who is so friendly and delightful with all the people, it is beautiful to see. It reminds me of going about with Miss Cons. She always finds out all about the people and finds helpful things to do for them ; and it makes one see all the gentle, helpful, friendly, hospitable side. It is *so* different from going about with guides. We had such a glorious day. We drove for 10 miles over a very bad road to a village called Chassia, quite up in a ravine of Parnes. There the road stopped, and I had a mule, and we went for $2\frac{1}{2}$ hours into the folds of the mountain ravines, till we came to the great promontory-like rock. The utter solitude, the exquisite blue of the shadows on the gigantic cliff-like rocks, the clear sun-filled air, the fresh breeze, the far away look of plain or hill or bay alive with noble memories filled me with a strange awed joy. I am much touched with the nation. I am afraid I shall never tell you all that makes me feel towards them as I do. I am getting such a vivid impression of the people, its hopes and admirations, and capacities. It is *clearly* growing. I have been reading a great many official statistics, which show the wonderful growth. I cannot but believe it has a great future. I sometimes think of Matthew Arnold's ideas about Hellenism, and wonder whether in very deed the people may be destined to bring out that side of human nature he speaks of as so wanting in the " Hebrew " ;—the sort of intellectual grasp and reverence for thought and

intangible things. Yet the nation has hard work just
now with its tangible things, and is working to get
them into order. Also it has, in its suffering under the
Turks, clung with tenacity to its Christian faith, which
is more than life to it; and this feeling is intensified by
the faith being connected with the *nation*, the early
martyrs for national freedom being many of them
bishops. We were present in the metropolitan church
at the anniversary of Greek independence. The king
and the children were there. It was strange to see the
tremendous crowd, the solitary Lutheran king, the tiny
children standing between him and the people crossing
themselves, and the gorgeously dressed priests who
seem so human and so near the people compared with
the Catholic clergy. With respect to the national
worship for an idea—THE families who are considered
great here are those who have lost their all at Misso-
longhi, or in supplying ships from Hydra!

Athens,
April 8th, 1880.

To HER MOTHER.

. . How delighted you will be about the
elections ! Is it not really marvellous ; I never expected
it ! It is strange sometimes how silent England is, and
yet how her heart rings true ! I am filled with prayer-
ful, almost tremulous, hope that the new Government
will live up to a high standard. Oh ! do you think it
will ? It is pathetic to see how happy the Greeks are
about it, and how much they hope from England now.
Sometimes I fear the Liberals will not have courage to
tax to meet past expenditure quickly, as they ought ;
or to deal generously with the little struggling
nationalities. Those *I* shall feel the test questions for

them, as to their consciences. I believe they will deal with the question of land, which will be good. The Barnetts are here, and Mr. B very much interested about the elections in England. . . . Mr. B.'s *whole* heart is at home, and in talking of it. . . .

Corinth,
Sunday, April 11th, 1880.

To Her Mother.

We started on our travels again yesterday, and seem to have seen a great deal. We drove from Athens to Megara yesterday—we being Miss Yorke, Miss Muir, a very nice Swiss lady, and myself. We were received and entertained by a hand-loom weaver, who knew Miss Muir. They were so kind ; they gave up to us a large room, their best, and all slept in their second room, which led thro' ours. Our beds were spotlessly clean, but laid on the earthen floor, after we had all had supper together, father, mother, married son and his wife, and half the village looking on. I never saw more affectionate welcome, or more native courtesy than they all showed. The son and his young wife spent the afternoon taking us to call on their friends and relations. It was so touching and beautiful ; the very poorest people receiving us with such a dignified bearing ; and everywhere we had to take something. One old woman, the mother of 12 children, and quite poor, was quite distressed she had nothing but some figs and nuts to give us. She remembered the time of the Turks and the dreadful hardships. Our host had come out of Thessaly to be in " free Greece," after it was known that Thessaly was not to belong to Greece. " Oh " ! he said, " they brought the children away in boxes, or anything, to get them safe into Greece."

E E

Megara is a populous village, almost entirely composed of houses of one room only. The people wear the most lovely costume, and carry themselves magnificently, so that every group forms a picture There was nothing pretty in the old houses, so I am glad to hear they were beginning to build themselves better ones. We saw more of their life than we *could* have seen anyhow else, and heard more of their sayings. I shall just jot down a few, anyhow, to be sure to tell you. They never speak harm of anything, especially in the evening They call the worst bit of a road Kali Scali, Kali meaning good ; and in the evening they respectfully call vinegar "the little sweet thing." Many of their expressions are formed from agricultural work. When Miss Muir's glove was lost they were much distressed, and said someone must have "reaped" it. The bride and bridegroom are married in crowns which are framed and hung up; and when they die they are buried in them. The sons have to marry in regular order of age, and must not do so till their sisters are married off. The boys and girls—mere children—never stand together ; the most eager crowds of lookers-on yesterday sorted themselves, the boys being on one side, and the girls on the other. They speak very freely to those above them in rank, our host kept addressing Miss Muir : " Oh, sister, what sayest thou ? " tho' the you is well distinguished from " thou." There is no water in the village, but a large washing place outside it—great stone troughs by the spring ; every girl, when she marries, has to receive one as part of her dowry The unmarried girls wear a complete skull-cap made of half drachmas, about sixpence each ; they never wear the cap after marriage, and never unthread it for use, unless in dire need. These people gave us food, lodging, and all their time, and turned out of their

room, and would not hear of receiving anything. As
we came along to-day, we met a flock of sheep with
lambs ; and Miss M. heard the muleteers tell the
shepherd to wait till they came back, as they must take
the Paschal lamb back for our host's family. So we
united to send the lamb back as a present. The people
are all rigidly fasting; their Lent is not over. Not a
man will touch any meat we offer him. At Easter
every family buys a lamb, fattens and kills it. We
had a sort of royal reception ; the priest, the demarch,
the schoolmaster, and all the people coming down.
Here we four, utter strangers, rode up dusty and tired,
sent in to the banker here a letter of introduction for
Mr. Dufour, and all four were instantly received, lodged,
and fed as a matter of course.

Patras,
April 12th, 1880.

We came on by the Greek steamer here yesterday.
Mr. Barnett brought me from Athens your delightful
letter and dear Miranda's, and some newspapers. . . .
We have seen the Consul and his wife—delightful
people. They have recommended us a former servant
of their own, who was with them for years, to drive us
to Olympia. The same man lately took Mr. Newton,
the chief man at the British Museum. It is a four
days' drive there and back, and Miss Muir and Mr.
Dufour left us at Corinth, so we are thoroughly glad to
have a trustworthy man. We are in high spirits, the
weather glorious ; and we are looking forward to going
very much. Part of to-day's drive is thro' four hours of
oak forest ! I do not know if we told you about
Olympia. The Germans are excavating there, and have
found all the temples buried under sand brought down

by the Alpheus, and some grand statues, one of Hermes, as fine as any of the world-famous statues. It is very fine of the German Government to take all the expense. They spent 10,000 francs annually on it till this year, when they are too poor; and the Emperor himself has given 5,000 that the work may not cease. Yet they are to have nothing for it except the right of taking casts. Everything they find is to belong to the Greek Government; only they stipulated that the Greeks should make them a road. Scientific Germans are there directing, with 500 Greek workmen. They say they are such splendid workmen, better than Germans—so the director says. We take all our food with us to-day, and sleep at a khan At Olympia the director's cook will take us in. It is all very funny. Here there is a very nice hotel. We find our Greek *most* useful. I am so delighted about the English news of elections.

Pyrgos,
April 14th, 1880.

To HER MOTHER.

I seem to have such a number of things to tell you, I hardly know how to begin. We left Patras at 6 o'clock on Monday morning, and drove on and on for miles, along the bright sea shore, just on the beach; then we turned inland, along the roughest roads; no boundary road in a remote district in England could be worse. We had to go at a foot's pace; but it was all lovely, great masses of asphodel in full bloom, bushes of broom one sheet of gold, crimson carpets of great cranesbill; olive, oak, and terebinth; and between, and over them, we saw the bright sea and the blue mountains. We drove thro' countless streams, large and small, now fording rivers, now plunging down steep banks. Then we came to the oak forest thro' which we drove, incessantly, over the smooth turf, or gravelly soil, for four hours. The oaks stand, not close together, but as in an English park, here and there, thicker or more scattered, on slopes, or spaces of turf. Many of the trees were old and knotted; some had suffered by fire; here and there were parts full of rich underwood; and then we came to smooth sheets of delicate blue with the tiny iris; the mountains were always in sight. There was hardly a trace of cultivation; hardly a house the whole day to be seen; and we drove incessantly till 6 at night. We stayed the night at a khan, they say one of the best in Greece; and the wall and beds were clean; but it is a strange kind of savage accommodation. The dogs barked so, and the wind howled over the great plain we had reached; I could not sleep much. Next day—yesterday—we started at 5 in the morning, having cooked and eaten our breakfast. The clouds, which had gathered over night, broke away before the sun; and we had a magnificent day. We drove on and on, thro' uncultivated wastes rather like our heaths, thro' water courses, and usually *off* the road, it was so bad; but with the most splendid light, and a view of the sea, and Zante in the distance. At mid-day we dined here; and then drove on to Olympia in a sunlight I never shall forget. The road from here to Olympia is very good. It has been made by the Greek Government, that being the one condition the Germans made on undertaking the excavations. We excited the greatest amazement, as no ladies do anything alone here; it is very amusing. The country is much more cultivated near here; and, going to Olympia, we saw several villages; but still it was very strange to drive for $3\frac{1}{2}$ hours up, as it were, into the heart of an untraversed

country, and find the road stopping in the heart of a
remote valley, where a handful of Germans had undertaken this curious great work.   Five hundred Greek
workmen were digging and carting and shovelling.
Our coachman led us to a sort of foreman, who asked us
if we spoke German or Greek.   He spoke no English,
but some Italian.   We asked for a lodging, and he sent
one of his men to take us to the cottage of the director's
cook, who has 3 spare rooms.   We climbed a steep
hill overlooking the excavations, on which stood one
new, well-built house.   We were led to such a cottage
that I felt as if we hardly could sleep there.   However
the bed was clean, and the view something splendid.
We ate our dinner laid on a board on the top of a stool ;
and we sat on the bed.   We had not an atom of blind,
nor a chair !—After that we got a man with a lantern ;
and, armed with one of Mrs. Coupland's introductions,
a visiting card, and the name of a Dr. and Mrs. Irvi,
mentioned to us by the Consul at Patras, we went off to
what the peasants call the "German house."—I had
hardly sent in my card with message of enquiry before
Mrs. Irvi came out with kindest words and hurried us
in to a room where sat, after their dinner, the little
company of Germans, who are directing the work.   She
introduced us to Herr Kurtzius, who speaks English.
Such a man ! but I must tell you of him later.   Mrs. I.
was *so* kind, would make us have coffee and stay, and
would go back with us to see where we were lodged.
She laughed, saying, "Oh yes ! its our *very* best hotel
here, you could not do better."   Three gentlemen
friends of theirs were sleeping there too.   The German
house is quite full.—We breakfasted with the Irvis at
7 o'clock, and then Herr K came with his plan, and for
three hours shewed us over the excavations.   He is

such a man! It has evidently been the dream of his life to do this thing; and now it is nearly done. You can see by the far away look of his great blue eyes, and the way he stumbles over the wood and stones in his path, that his thoughts are of the past and the future, or, at any rate, not of the earth, earthy. It was he who imagined doing this thing, mentioned it to the Crown Prince, who got the German Parliament to pay; and now they have excavated, at a depth of often 20 feet of gravel, the whole space on which the temples and their surrounding buildings stood. The space occupied is that bounded on the south by the Alpheus, just where a smaller river joins it. This triangular space lies at the foot of a small sand hill. But such a valley as it is! And between the mountains that bound it you can see the opening to the defiles leading south to Messina, north to Corinth, east to Sparta; and all round the wooded hills look down upon the sunny plain, and you can almost see the old Greeks trooping in from every quarter. The foundations of all the buildings are found, the bases of walls and pillars in their places, the steps, the entrances, the pedestals of the statues all in their places. Twenty-one statues (or the principal part of them) from the pediments have been found, besides the Hermes and Bacchus of Praxiteles, and numbers of Roman statues, and a lovely Greek figure of the Winged Victory descending. The Hermes is splendid. He carries the infant Bacchus on his arm, such a sweet child; the head was only found last week. The early statues from the pediment are very powerful, massive and expressive, but not so delicate nor so exquisitely true in artistic power. I almost think the whole scene impressed me most. The great temple of Zeus stands in the centre of the ground, its mighty pillars shattered by earthquake. One sees the pedestal of the gold figure of Zeus sixty feet high, which was taken from Byzantium : one sees all round the other temples. The one to Hera is one of the oldest. Pelops has a temple too ; but, being a hero who died, not a god who lives always, its entrance is to the setting sun, not on the East like those of the rest. Then there is the Gymnasium, where the youths practised with the rough stones, that they might not slip in wrestling, and the smooth ones for their masters still lying in their places. Beyond are the eleven treasure houses, built by eleven of the Greek towns, each for their own votive offerings to the gods, which on great feast days were opened and their glories displayed. Then I was interested to see the one that belonged to Megara. There is a great arched passage, leading from the space where the altars were, thro' which, after sacrificing to the gods, the judges and competitors in solemn procession walked, not being visible to the people assembled to see the games, till they came out of the passage Two statues, one of Fortune and one of Nemesis, were found, which watched over this way—the one supposed to remind competitors how Fortune might favour or injure them, the other to warn the judges and competitors alike of the punishment which certainly overtakes any breach of fairness. We saw the stone from which the runners started ; and, exactly 600 feet beyond, where they knew it ought to be, these Germans dug down twenty-one feet thro' the gravel, and found the goal or opposite starting place. We saw the men washing tiny little bronze figures of animals about one and a-half inches long, which they had just found, which are supposed to be votive offerings from the very poor to the god. They are green with age now.

These Germans leave in a month or two; and the 500 men cease working. They will be dreadfully missed; for they have brought work and money, and civilisation and visitors, right up into the heart of the country. The place will be left—the Greek Pompeii— to the Greeks to take care of. They have to build a museum and arrange the treasures. Herr Kurtzius carries away all he has learned. He has sent to Berlin the casts and plans and maps; and there they are making models of the thing as he found it, and as he thinks it was of old. He takes, one may say— nothing; but one sees that to him to have done what enables him to *know* is all. He doesn't look as if he worked for fame, or for others, but to know and to see. As he showed us the things, now and then he flashed up, as if it were all before him, and spoke of the life that had been as if he *saw*, sometimes gently stroked the faces of the statues, pointing out how perfect they were; now and again his eyes looked out as to some further thought he did not tell.

We post this at Patras, where we arrived safely to-night (April 16th); to-morrow we go by steamer to Athens, where I hope to find news of you all.

Achmetaga, Eubœa,
April 24th, 1880.

OCTAVIA TO HER MOTHER.

. . . I must try to tell you something of all we have been seeing. We left Athens on Tuesday at five o'clock in the morning, having engaged a carriage to take us to Thebes. It was an exquisite morning, and we drove by Eleusis thro' a pass of Cithæron, sup-posed to be that of Eleuthera. We saw the ruins of

the fortress of the ancient Greeks guarding the Attic
end of the pass. As we came down on the Bœotian
side, a magnificent view of Parnassus opened on our
left, the site of Platæa was in sight; but nothing
remains to mark it, as seen from a distance; far away
to the East we saw the grand snow-covered range
of mountains in Eubœa, and the beautiful peak of
Delphi (Delphi in Eubœa) rising highest in the chain.
When we got to Thebes, which stands very picturesquely
on a hill, we drove thro' its main street, thro' the
savage barking of fierce dogs, and rather wild-looking
people. Mr. Petousi, the deputy to whose care Mr.
Noel had recommended us, was away; so we drove
on to the house of Mrs. Theagenes, to whom Dr.
Hill had given us an introduction. We were quite
unexpected, but were at once received most kindly,
and arrangements were made for us to stay all night.
Mrs Theagenes is the widow of the Colonel who
tried to help about the freedom of those young
Englishmen near Marathon, and who went to see the
brigands about them. He felt the matter so deeply,
that it is said to have caused his death. . . . He seems
to have been a man of culture, and thought and
principle, and a friend of General Church and the early
Greek patriots. His books and pictures remain; and
his widow and son and daughter were *most* kind. . . .
They took us out to see the town, which was dirty, and
looked neglected. We did not come upon traces of
any progress or life Of course we may be wrong;
and we were most touched by their kindness; but the
town did not inspire one with hope. Next day we had
a splendid drive across to Chalcis; the road, an excellent one, leads down in sight of the Euripus and
Eubœan mountains. The fortifications at Chalcis are

very picturesque.   We slept at Chalcis at the house of a
Mr. Boudouris, whose sister was carried off by brigands
many years ago from there, but very kindly treated, till
ransomed. . . . From Chalcis we started next morning
at daybreak, on mules, under the charge of a sort of
head man of Mr. Noel's, not the steward but another,
and a second servant.   It was a very impressive
journey, and gave one an idea of remoteness.   For
eight hours we went steadily on over hills and along
ravines, beyond all roads, with nothing but rough
bridle paths.   The forests were beautiful, the mountains
grand, the sea fair and smooth as a lake in the distance,
but *not* a house, nor a trace of man did we pass for
hours.   We came along beside a lovely half stream,
half river, in a deep ravine, set with fir and plane, and
oak trees, and with great bushes of white heath.   At
last we came upon a sort of clearance in the forest, like
an English village, only without any road to it, and in
sight, and quite near, of mountains on three sides, one
covered with snow. · Here and there among the wooded
hills there were cleared fields of corn, maize, and vine,
well-built stone houses, very small, but with tiled roofs
clustered at the foot of one wooded hill, on the slope of
which, above the cottages but below the trees which
crown it, stood the house we are now in, with its wide
vine-covered trellised verandah, its walled garden and
great well.   We rode up and alighted in the great yard,
round which the long stone houses for grain, the stables,
and houses for oxen, and the wood-sheds are built.
We were led into the drawing-room, and then into our
bedroom, which looked like that in an English country
house.   We looked out on the park-like scenery and
the busy village below, and felt what a work had been
done.   Here, forty-six years ago, came three young

foreigners quite alone. Mr. Noel was but twenty. The place was all forest. The few people in straw huts had gone to the other side of the estate, fifty miles off, to be away from the road—this little bridle path—to get away from the Turks. They had built their doors low that the Turks mightn't lead their horses in. Hardly could the peasants be persuaded to come back, so frightened were they. Fever seized first the brother-in-law, then Mr Noel, who was lifted on to his horse by Mr. Muller, and taken to Chalcis. The brother-in-law died. Dr. Hill, then in Athens, heard there were two young men ill at Chalcis, took a boat, as there were no steamers, and came and fetched them, took them to his own house, and nursed Mr. Noel for a year. "No doubt he saved Noel's life," says Mr. Muller quietly, quite unconscious of the spiritedness of their own action. They returned, built, planted, encouraged, watched, and have made of this a little sort of oasis in the desert, in its life, like that gathered round an English landlord. And yet, oh how different! The life here reminds me very much of that led by Flora MacIvor and her brother. The same loyalty to Mr. Frank Noel appears to prevail among the people; the same distance from law makes him the judge among them; the same wild habits seem to prevail; the same virtues, and those only. . . . There is no road to this place; and when Mrs. F. Noel was married she wanted a piano. "How did you get it here?" I asked. "We had it brought in a small boat to the sea-shore, about three hours from here; and some fête day, when the men were not working, Mr. Noel went out among them and said that I wanted my piano, and which of them would go and carry it? Thirty-six of them sprang up to go, and they carried it for three hours over the open country in relays of twelve. Mr. Noel and I, of course, went too. In the evening they came in, and we had a good supper, and I played to them. They would have been much hurt if we had offered to pay." Another time Mr. Noel came in from seeing some of the tenants, and said, " —— has been to me to ask me to lend him one of my field guards to help him to carry off by force the girl he was engaged to, who has broken off the affair with her parents' (consent). I told him it wouldn't do, but that they must return the presents." " And double them," added Mr. Muller. " Certainly," said Mr. Noel. " A girl has been waiting here all day to see you," said Mr. Noel, " she has brought a large bottle for you to give her some medicine ; the gendarmes came to take her husband ; and her blood is quite cold ever since." And this sort of thing goes on incessantly. One hears too of one man, who lost his presence of mind when one of the great forest fires surrounded the seventy villagers, and Mr. Noel, who had been three days and three nights trying to stop it. He lay on the ground, and would not stir ; Mr. Noel raised him and dragged him on and on, and, as the man says, saved his life. It is beautiful to see young Mrs. Noel among them all, so gentle and brave and stately. It was such a picture last night, as she stood near the house door in the great yard. The great oxen were feeding or lying about ; about twenty men and women, in the beautiful costume of the country, stood about listening to her, and watching her one little child, a girl of nearly two years old, who was carried about and petted, first by one and then another It was near sunset ; and the long sloping rays fell on the group. Mr. Noel was away for some days ; and she and the tiny child were the only representatives of the race that rules here by education and gentleness. The rest just look, love, and obey.

Constantinople,
May 6th, 1880.

To HER MOTHER.

I don't know if it is my fault, or the strong pre-conceived impression, or the absence of sun; but this place feels to me like a cursed or doomed one, a city of corruption and decay. It doesn't strike me as the least beautiful.

We went on Sunday, which was the Greek Easter Eve, to the midnight service here. We got capital places in the part railed off for the priests, where no ladies are allowed, nor the congregation. At midnight the old tradition says that fire comes down from heaven.

There seems to be no distinct belief in *that*, as a miracle, here; but it was a beautiful service. The priest came out at midnight with the light; and rapidly every single soul there lighted the taper he held, the light spreading from the priests with wonderful rapidity. The church was crowded with earnest, rather rugged looking men. They read the Gospel on Easter Sunday in eight languages. They go out at night to look for Christ, and come back saying, " He is risen." There was a good deal of dress and ceremony, but a good deal of fervour.

We have seen a great deal since I wrote to you,—the large silent mosques with their space and simplicity, the triple walls which surround the town, with ancient Greek inscriptions built into them. The Golden Gate in *them*, thro' which the emperors made triumphal entry; the walled-up gate, so dealt with because the Turks believe the Christians will re-enter by that gate;

wonderful old Christian churches now converted into
mosques, with the crosses and Christian symbols muti-
lated—one, however, very beautiful, where the mosaics
were preserved. Then we have seen the large vault
underground, supported by 1001 columns in old times,
built to supply Byzantium with water; the strange
cemeteries of the Turks, the dismallest of places; the
stones high and narrow are tumbling about in every
direction like ninepins; the graves are in quite untold
numbers by the road sides, on banks, in ditches, anywhere and everywhere, without fence, without protection,
without reverence; even the cypress trees among them
look forlorn, and the stones much more forlorn because
of the vermilion and emerald green and cobalt and gold,
which once made them gay. It was such a contrast to
cross to Skutari, where the British dead, who fell in the
Crimea, lie. The ground is enclosed with a well-built
wall; it is quite bright with flowering trees and shrubs,
and lies on the sunniest slope overlooking the blue sea.
Comparatively few graves have any stone, or name, or
record; but the greenest, brightest, sunniest, best cared-
for turf covers them. The inscriptions suggest such
stories; here the record of two brothers about 20, sur-
viving one another 4 days; several erected by brother
officers, one to a private by his companions, one by a
young sister to her brother, who, she says, "cheerfully
surrendered his life to his country"; nineteen, twenty,
even eighteen once or twice, are frequent ages for the
dead. The hospital, where Miss Nightingale worked,
stands just above and looks so good, and solid, and in
order. We went a ride yesterday round by the Sweet
Waters of Europe, all round the Golden Horn. We came
back thro' the Greek quarter. It was such a comfort to
see the windows clean and bright, and without the dismal

wooden lattice work, which shuts in the Turkish houses, and the women with bright, uncovered faces sitting at the windows sewing.

I think so constantly of you all, tho' I write nothing about it.

On the Danube, off Turn Severin,
May 13th, 1880.

To HER MOTHER.

I am sitting on board one of the Danube steamers in the twilight writing to you. We are lying at Turn Severin for the night, because they want daylight to go thro' the Iron Gates. We had a good passage from Constantinople to Varna; the Bosphorus was very beautiful as we sailed up. Just beyond Therapia the population on its shores seems almost suddenly to cease. It makes one feel how it is only the overflow from Constantinople. Beyond Therapia one sees little but Genoese castles, a light-house or two, and a *very* few tiny villages, cliffs, bare heights and points. It is strange to see the fortified narrowest part, kept by such different nations, and a point where Byzantine and Turk of old looked at one another across the narrow water from their respective fortresses, and measured their respective strength. Varna has no good port; they say it is as far from the steamer as Jaffa, and the passage horrid in rough weather, because no mole is built; but happily it was calm, when we went on shore in a large boat with four rowers I was interested to land in Bulgaria. One wonders what these young nations are going to be, somewhat as one does about children. The country looked strange and very uninhabited; but it was much more beautiful than I expected. We went by railway thro' it to Rustchuk. First we went thro' the flat bottom of a valley, bounded by low wooded hills. A river flowed thro' it, which often spread into what looked like lakes, they might be floods. Further on, we seemed to mount and pass over hills—I suppose low spurs of the Balkans. There we saw miles and miles of the most exquisite spring-green woods, spreading over waves and waves of hill away to the far distance. We came to downs too, great stretches of swelling hills and hollows of green grass that had never been cultivated ; on them here and there we saw herds of buffaloes and horses feeding. At Rustchuk we came upon this boat. We sailed between Roumania and Bulgaria first ; then we came to Servia on the right bank of the river, and soon we shall come to Austria on the left. It has been exquisitely beautiful to watch the great stretches of river, with the sky reflected in them, to walk up and down the deck and watch the sun rise and set, to pass the willowy islands, and note the great tracts of unin- habited land, decreasing, I suppose, as we get higher up the river. Yesterday we passed numbers of wild- looking Servians. I never saw any people look so like savages They were in funny boats just made of a trunk of a tree hollowed out, and cut short off at either end. They looked heavy and clumsy and very primi- tive ; the men had little clumsy wooden paddles, and were dressed so strangely, and looked so poor and crushed down with labour. They were mostly fishing ; those on the shore were dressed in something exactly the colour of the sandy banks. I wondered such people could exist on the shores of a great water highway like this. A gentleman on board told me they were " all robbers and murderers," which made me very angry, for I don't think he knew anything about them. I was glad to remember Miss Irby, and to be able to say a

F F

quiet word about knowing a lady who had worked
among them for years ; and that I did not believe she
had found them such dreadful hardened people as he
seemed to think " Oh," he said, " she probably lives
in one of the towns, and has a dragoman to intervene
between her and the people." " No," I replied, " I
believe not ; I think she has travelled all over the
country, she is working about schools there, and, I fancy,
knows the people "

We pass by little villages with minarets, and red
roofs, and then for miles not a house again, only the
great river going on and on ; sometimes we pass a funny
raft, sometimes a Greek steamer or tug ; always every
change in sky or shore reflects itself in this great river.

Approaching Pesth,
May 16th.

The morning after I wrote this, I was up at 3 o'clock,
because the steamer was said to start before the dawn,
and I wanted to see the Iron Gates. I came up on deck,
and all was very still ; the stars reflected in the water.
The shore of each bank was still quite flat ; but, in
front, one saw the hills. Just as the sun rose with its
round globe out of the water, the boat started. In what
seemed but a few minutes after we had been in the flat
plain, the gates of the hills appeared just in front of us.
The morning sun lighted the great cliffs on one side of
the water-paved ravine, and left the other walls of rock
in deep blue shadow, while just in the place where the
rocks on either side looked as if they met and closed the
passage, a wreath of rose-coloured morning mist lay,
which, gently rising with the sun's heat, spread itself
in faint, thin, lovely streaks along the wooded hills,
rising gradually and losing themselves in the blue sky.

Everything was reflected in the sheet of smooth water. The river is almost at its fullest, I believe. This same large steamer can come from Rustchuk to Pesth. I believe the ice is melted, and had not yet reached the sea, as it were; so we saw less of the rapids than if it had been later in the year; but, here and there, the river was all churned into foam; and, in places, a great line of white breakers showed where a great ridge of rock ran right across the channel. Nothing could exceed the beauty of that sunrise scene; but the scenery is even grander further up, in what is called the Defile of Kasan. It was very interesting to see distinctly the remains of Trajan's road. What a work to make a road thro' such a defile, without gunpowder! One sees the strong hand of the Roman, as one watches the road cut on the buttresses of the great cliffs above the deep, wild water, and traces still the clear-cut holes in which wooden supports were placed; and there is the Latin inscription still on the rocks. After we had passed thro' the wonderful defile we came where the Danube spreads out almost like a lake; and, since then, we have come on and on, up and up it, watching sunrise and sunset, and moonlight and thunderstorm; seeing the fortresses that guard it, the very few villages and towns on its banks, that is to say very few in comparison with the miles of uninhabited shore, lovely woods, of island after island covered with thick woods, of great plains over which the cloud-shadows float. It has been a most interesting and most delightful life. Miss Y. took a private cabin, where we have all our things as comfortably about us as if we were at home, and can make our tea or lie down within view of the river; but mainly we use the higher deck as our sitting-room; there we have two easy chairs, and our work, our books,

our writing by us Or we pace the deck till the stars
come out. We shall be quite sorry when it comes
to an end. The tourists go by train now, the great
bulk of them at least; a few come on board just to see
the Iron Gates, but they leave at Orsova, and don't
even see the Defile of Kasan; nor can they realise
anything of the great history of the river how it
lives till it reaches the Gates; of its course thro' this
great Hungarian plain, past the high sandy cliffs which
protect its tiny villages on the one shore from the great
floods which must break at times violently over its low
left bank. They do not see its free towns, still exempt
from military service, except in time of war; nor note
the mouths of the Drave and the Theiss, and the
thousands of streams that feed and swell the Danube.
They do not see the floods out, and the people in their
flat-bottomed boats sailing about over the meadows,
nor the herds of grey cattle, nor the vineyards on
the slopes, nor the reedy banks, nor the lonely stacks
of wood in the forests, nor mount the paddle-box and
see the country people on the fore part of the ship,
Servians, and Hungarians and Bulgarians, the strange
costumes, the funny German life; nor see the local fête,
the fireworks from the boats on the flooded meadows,
the corn-grinding mills in the middle of the river; they
cannot watch these, with the free cool air blowing all
round them, and the sun shining, and every mist and
wreath and change of cloud visible all round in the
whole space of sky. I wish we did not get to Pesth
to-day. But we shall have some more of the Danube
between Vienna and Linz I do not the least know
what we shall do beyond Dresden. I must write when
we have fixed, with fresh directions about letters. I
think of you so often, dear Mama, and wish you

were here.   I fancy you would enjoy the kind of thing
so much.

We shall post this at Pesth.   I suppose some day
they will prevent the floods here.   It is beautiful to see
how much of the earth has still to be filled with happy
home life; and, near lovely things, this is *not* the
impression one gets in England.

Nuremberg,
May 24th, 1880.

To her Mother.

We saw the Rathhaus where the Imperial Diet
met till 1806. . . . The town looks very comfortable
and flourishing, as if the old things had been taken into
use and would stay ;—not like Italy and Constantinople,
as if every breath of purer or more living thought would
sweep away some of the beauty, and substitute hideous
Paris or London models.   Trees grow among the houses;
and children play round them, and clean industrious
women knit at their doors ; and comfortable little shops
are opened in them ; and you see "Bürger Schule" put
up over their doors; and yet they aren't all torn down
and replaced with rows of houses, like Camden Town,
and shops like Oxford St. ; and still these gardens for
the people everywhere look reproach on me, when I
think of England, and every tree and creeper and space
of green grass in the town reminds me of our un-
consumed smoke, and how it poisons our plants, and
dims the colour of all things for us. . . .

We hope to make a few useful outlines here for
windows, &c., in possible future houses in London.

Harrogate,
August 25th, 1880.

TO MRS. SHAEN.

I have been very much delighted lately with some correspondence with some of my fellow-workers about the Artizans' Dwellings Acts. We had a great blow about the work itself just as I left town,—one likely to create dissension and call up bad feeling ; and somehow the correspondence about it has, instead, shown how nobly men respond, when they manage to find the right way to look at things. I often wonder how men manage to get into such messes, when human hearts ring so true if struck rightly. It has been really quite beautiful to see how men will put temptation and bad feeling (even when almost justified) under their feet, when reminded of the cause for which they should work. I don't even know that it is a question of reminding. The good men see nobly and act accordingly. I am obliged to keep very much out of all (even thought of) work. The home claims are very strong just now, and my own strength not very great. It is very strange to have to put the old things so wholly second. I do not know, however, how to be entirely sad about it. I often think that now people want more to see how noble private life should be, and can be, than to take up public work,—at any rate exclusively.

Harrogate,
September 4th, 1880.

MRS. HILL TO MRS. EDMUND MAURICE.

If you were to spend all your time from now till Christmas in guessing what Octavia was doing last Friday afternoon you would never guess aright, so I

will tell you.   She was acting to a Harrogate audience
the part of Piety in the MacDonald's "Pilgrim's Progress." On Thursday we had spent the day at Harewood,
and on our return found Lily and Bob here waiting to
ask if she would act for poor Grace, then lying seriously
ill of hæmorrhage, at Ilkley. The rooms for the performance were engaged, and it seemed impossible to
postpone it. Octavia agreed and learned her part (eight
pages) that night. I cannot tell you how beautiful she
looked, and how lovely her voice sounded. It was *most*
pathetic to see the MacDonalds so brave and energetic ;
but all so pale and feeling-full. Poor Mr. Jamieson
acted Mr. Brisk. MacDonald was so chivalrous and
beautiful to his poor wife and to us,—forgot no tenderness to her, or politeness to Miss Yorke and to me.

September 20th, 1880.

To Mr. Blyth.

I was grieved to hear of so much wrong in the
court, and to think of you in the lovely autumn, trying
to stem it. But, in one sense, one is never lonely in
one's efforts to stem wrong. So mighty is the Power
that fights with us.

Do you ever think that the want you feel in the
people is due less to the amount than to the kind of
help. Part of it is due to their own selves, there is no
denying it ; but is it not also due, in part, to many of
the present workers acting rather from a supposed
height, than face to face, and heart to heart, from real
human sympathy and friendship? I think so. The
outward gift never wins gratitude, or calls up the
gracious sense of affection. The human sympathy
always does. Do you know, by the way, Lowell's "Sir
Launfal"?

CHAPTER IX

1881—1889

APPOINTMENT BY THE ECCLESIASTICAL COMMISSIONERS

THIS period of return to work was marked by many very welcome successes. The consent of Ruskin to the legal transfer of his houses in Paradise Place to Octavia, and the purchase by Mr Shaen of Freshwater Place were proofs of the stability of her plans

From 1883 to 1889 lasted the great movement for rescuing Parliament Hill and the neighbouring land from the builder, and adding it to Hampstead Heath, and many other victories in the open space struggle were also achieved at this time

But perhaps the most remarkable change in Octavia's position, as a worker, was her appointment by the Ecclesiastical Commissioners to manage a great part of their property in Southwark. She was asked to attend a meeting of that body. They wished to learn if she would buy some old courts belonging to them   This, she said, was impossible. Then they asked if she would take a lease of these same houses, and, when she declined to do so, they asked if she would undertake the management   This she consented to do, and the Commissioners were so much impressed with the capable business-like character of her remarks, and with her subsequent management, that they afterwards extended the territory under her care

It should be noted, in this connection, that this position gave her the first opportunity of planning cottages, while Red Cross Hall and Garden gave further occasion for her development of entertainments and outdoor-life for the poor.   It is in this period also that her links with foreign workers were extended. Some housing work had begun in Paris, at an earlier time, and the translation by H.R.H. Princess Alice of " The Homes of the

London Poor" into German had led to the formation of the
"Octavia Hill Verein" in Berlin. Swedish and Russian ladies
also came to ask advice, and Miss Le'Maire has given an account
in an Italian magazine of the impression left upon her by her
visit to Octavia.

It was during this time that Octavia took over the management of some houses in Deptford, the care of which seemed to
weigh heavily on her mind. If, indeed, one compares her
descriptions of these South London courts with the early letters
about some of the Marylebone tenants, there can be no reason
to suppose that the prospects of improvement were more hopeless in the later effort than in the earlier; but Octavia had now
begun to realise that management from a distance was an almost
insuperable difficulty; and that to delegate or transfer distant
work would become a necessary duty. Although, therefore,
marked improvement was made in the relations between her
and her Deptford tenants, as will be seen from the letter written
in 1885 during the Trafalgar Square riots, she felt it better in the
end to hand the care of these houses over completely to a very
efficient fellow-worker, who succeeded in managing the courts
in a satisfactory way.

A curious incident connected the Deptford work with another
successful effort to save an open space. When visiting one
of the tenants in Queen Street, Deptford, Octavia noticed a glass
filled with flowers, and on enquiry found that they had been
picked in a place known as " Hilly Fields." Octavia was struck
with the name, followed up the clue, and eventually succeeded
in securing the Fields as a public open space. This story rests
on the authority of the American lady, Miss Ellen Chase, who
worked with Octavia in Deptford, and who, on returning to
Massachusetts, carried out the same principles in the management of houses in her own country.

Park Farm, Limpsfield,
April 16th, 1881.

To Mrs. Edmund Maurice.

Now I come to my crowning news. I have had
a most grateful and affectionate note from Mrs. Severn,

with messages from Ruskin. He gladly accepts my offer for Paradise Place, and will be *very* glad if I can find a purchaser for Freshwater Place. I think, the receipts and expenditure shewing so very good a balance, I should have *no* fear of our buying it too ourselves; but there are several things to think of, one being the question of ready money. I must try and take up the things, one after another; they take so much thinking.

This refers to questions of preservation of a common near Sheffield.

Abinger Hatch, Dorking,
April 21st, 1881.

To Mrs. Edmund Maurice.

I must say in spite of what Mr. H. says I cannot help thinking it *would* be better to help them, always supposing one could get a barrister, who really cared, and was in earnest.

You see one great reason Mr. Hunter seems to hesitate is, that he says so rich a place as Sheffield ought to do it itself, and that the people of the place have not done much for themselves. But first, it seems to me hard to punish the poor of Sheffield for the omissions of the rich, second, I think the subject still so new that a town may wake up too late, and bitterly regret what it has lost; third, these commons seem to me national treasures, and less and less to concern only the towns or villages nearest to which they happen to be (I am sure we are feeling this just now in this little driving tour); and there is no reason to punish England for supineness on the part of Sheffield; and fourthly, I am not at all sure that Sheffield *has* been supine Clearly from Mr. B.'s letter a section of the public there are keenly interested, and have been at work.

All Mr. H. says might tell with a society heavily weighted with past efforts, as I daresay the C.P.S. is, or bound to keep power to take initiatory action where local strength may be forthcoming after a time, but not necessarily governing my decision about the money that I really *have* in hand, available for precisely the only opportunity open at this moment, by which I can help forward the preservation of commons. Every year that we can keep them, people care more and do more ; every acre kept is a certain possession for ever. The more serious point of Mr. Hunter's letter seems to me that in which he calls Mr. A.'s "not a strong case." By which I gather that he means not sure to win. But then he goes on to say that it is an important suit, as keeping the common till some plan for regulation can be arranged.

On the whole, therefore, I am strongly inclined to give the money. . . . If it be lost, in the sense of not winning the suit, and yet if the suit is essential to keeping the question open, it is worth while for someone to be the loser. I expect that causes are like stakes which are driven into a marsh and are buried, but carry the roadway ; and who could lose the money better than I, to whom the hope and future are so clear, and to whom people have trusted money, just that I may be able at critical moments to *dare* something for a great and possible good ?

April 25th, 1881.

To Mr. Shaen.

I am indeed delighted to hear that there is a chance of your buying Freshwater Place.

So strongly do I feel about the playground and a garden, so sure am I of the great pressure that would be put upon owners to sell or let, for building a church or a chapel, or a school, or an institution, if not houses, that, quite independently of my old affection and memories of the place and the tenants, I feel as if it must not go into strange hands. I've been thinking it all over, and whether I ought to buy it myself; but, if I were ill, or away, or dead, its management might be a trouble to my sisters. Now would you be afraid to share it with me ? I couldn't throw myself into the personal work down there; I couldn't stand it; but, while I keep at all well, I would look into its affairs, choose and watch its workers, remove or guide them, and have its accounts regularly audited. There would then be an almost certainty of its paying 5 per cent ; and, at the worst, if anything prevents my watching it, you would only have risked half the money.

Abinger Hatch, Dorking,
May 3rd, 1881.

To MRS. SHAEN.

Oh, dear ! I am so thankful about Freshwater Place. I wonder what you will all think of it, and do with it. I hope you do not expect much. It is only when one feels what the *narrow* courts are, and how the people get maddened with the heat of them in summer, and how the children have *no* where to play, and how their noise hurts their mothers' nerves, that one feels what these few square yards of ugly space are.—But, things being as they are in London, *that* air, *that* space are quite riches to the poor.

I quite feel what Mr. Shaen says about joint owner-ship ; one never gets the same love for a place, because never the same sense of responsibility.

Brantwood,
May 5th, 1881.

FROM RUSKIN.

I have had great pleasure in hearing, thro' Mrs. Severn, of the arrangements of Marylebone, etc., and am entirely glad the thing should pass into your hands, and that you are still able to take interest in it, and encourage and advise your helpers. I trust, however, you will not be led back into any anxious or deliberative thought. I find it a very strict law of my present moral being—or being anyway—to be anxious about nothing and to determine on nothing!

Letter to a Mr. Green, who had served on the Battersea C.O.C., but who had afterwards broken down in health, and who had sent some flowers for the children of the tenants —

May 18th, 1881.

TO MR. GREEN.

I do want some common daisy roots, not the double daisy, but the ordinary white daisy. They bloom on and on in London so vigorously, and quite startle one with pleasure, when one comes on these little white flowers, against the dark background of some London court. I think their very simplicity reminds the people of their childhood. As for me, I have quite a longing for them, and have only two here; so I should venture to keep some, if you are good enough to send some. They are things we have never had sent to us; and I do not often get an opportunity of bringing any. But I hope that you will take no real trouble; only we should be glad if it were easy to send them.

June 3rd, 1881.

To Mrs. Shaen.

We had such a *very* interesting afternoon at Morris's. He took us all over the garden and into his study, and such an interesting carpet factory, which reminded me of Megara in its simplicity, silence, beauty and quiet. It was just in his own garden The tapestry he had been making himself in his study was beautiful ! !

Tortworth,
February 27th, 1882.

To her Mother

All the visitors have now departed except Mrs. S. and myself. I had not been very fortunate in seeing much of Lowell till this morning, when we had a long and very interesting talk over poets and poems, specially Browning and Mrs. Browning. I like Lord Aberdare very much, and had a good deal of interesting talk with him. Of Mr. Hughes I have seen much, and had much talk of old times and people ; one felt very heartily and deeply in sympathy with him. . . . Lord Ducie has been asking me to look over some Greek charts, and tell him about what we saw and did ; so I must do it before afternoon tea, to be sure to be ready. Mrs. Lowell is much of an invalid still, having had a terrible fever in Spain, from which she has not recovered I had a long and interesting talk with her to-day.

San Gemignano,
April 18th, 1883.

To her Mother.

The people here look very flourishing. I can't help thinking education is beginning to tell. The young people look so well-behaved and intelligent and clean. They still spin as they walk in the fields, and weave in their dark hollows of houses ; but I hear their voices singing among the olives as they lay out their linen to bleach ; and the contadini, who come up with the sleek, well-fed, strong oxen, look comfortable and well to do. . . . I think I shall join some Latin class when I return, tho' I shall have no advanced pupils. It gives a great freshness to one's teaching, and there are many little things one might hear that would be useful. I have never heard Latin taught. I wish I could hear of a good teacher. I should care more for that than for an advanced class. . . . I would rather join a class than have separate lessons. I want to hear other people taught. Individual teachers, if they find you advanced in certain ways, assume that you know the elements.

14, Nottingham Place, W.,
July 19th, 1883.

To her Mother.

A Tenants' Party at Hillside.

I must snatch a few minutes to tell you what a great success yesterday was. Everything was so beautifully arranged. Gertrude had thought of everything for the people. To see little Blanche, flitting about in an utterly unconscious state of sweet serviceableness, was quite beautiful. The others too were very good and happy, but nothing to dear little Blanche. We walked across the fields some seventy strong, but they seemed nothing in those wide, free meadows. . . . The boys went with Mr. Morley, who brought his dog and sent him into the water. The children ran and sang and made merry ; the women enjoyed the bright air and quiet. We all relieved them of their babies as much as we could, and we rested often. Near the lane we found little Blanche, blushing with joy and shyness. She led us back; Gertrude and the others came out to receive us, and we turned into the field, which was looking lovely. The children ran to the swings, and began games Gertrude had had trusses of straw put in a sort of tier of benches up by the summer house, dry and warm, and soft and comfortable. The children had tea there. . . . The elders had tea at the same time in the garden on the lawn. . . . We were very strong in entertainers. . . . The people were delighted with the garden, the field, the house. The boys played cricket with the gentlemen ; everyone was amused, and happy, and good. The arrangements were perfection. Two waggonettes took *all* the women and babies and toddling children back to the station. . . . Dear little Blanche had her wish about the strawberries. She had an exquisite bunch of flowers, which she gave with her own hands to each grown person before they started . .

I have been this morning to see a stately, dear old clergyman, a certain Prebendary Mackenzie, who wrote to me about some ground that the Haberdashers' Company own. He is a member of the Company, and was to-day to bring before them a plan for using the ground as a garden. It is near Old Street Road. I found such a fine old man, with stately, old-fashioned ways. He was sitting with his wife in a parlour in Woburn Square. I send you some more letters from donors ; sums keep coming in. I feel, like Florence, that I like these small sums much.

I have been to-day to see Spitalfields churchyard. It is *the* one I should like to see laid out. . . .

Mr. Mason had his flower show in the little garden ; 400 people came in each night, paying 3*d.* or 6*d.* He says this is the first garden fête in Bethnal Green.

19, Avenue Hoche, Paris,
23rd April, 1884.

FROM A RUSSIAN LADY.

I take the liberty of enclosing an article on the Homes of the London Poor, which appeared in the *Journal de St. Petersbourg*, in which I have expressed very faintly the admiration I feel for your book, and the deeds of which the book gives us a glimpse.

I have scarce the courage of taking any of the time, on which there are so many calls ; and yet I would be very grateful if you would glance through my poor attempt, and take it as a proof of my sympathy and respect.

For people who pass their life in wishing they might be useful, there is something saddening, and yet in-spiriting, to find that all the time some have been up and doing. That is the mixed feeling with which I read your delightful volume ; but what predominated was the pleasure and pride of seeing what a woman can do.

I shall be in London before long, and, if it is not asking too much, may I hope to see you and tell you what I have vainly tried to write ?

.   .   .   .   .   .

I am afraid, after all, that I have gone too far, and that when, if ever, I have the pleasure of standing before you, all my courage will evaporate, and I will be utterly unable to express the feelings with which I look up to you, much as a raw recruit on the general who has led victory in many a good fight.

G G

So accept my unexpressed sympathy, and excuse me again for troubling you.

Queen's Hotel, Penzance,
April 25th, 1884.

To Mrs. Edmund Maurice.

As to the opening of Wakefield Street,[1] the date must depend on the grass   I fear it will have to be late in June. . . . The more difficult thing, to my mind, is to think of the sort of ceremony that would be interesting, possible, and more than a form.   I think the absence of any square space a difficulty.   There is no space for speaking, or gathering people together.   If we could have had anything like our May festival, and had the poor in, I should have liked it; but I see no space for anything but a procession, which would hardly do.   Perhaps some brilliant idea will be suggested. . . .

What a *very* nice account of the donation fund results!   It is just possible Deptford and Southwark may open up new needs to us.   If not, you and I will have still further to lay our heads together to spend the money well.   It takes a great deal of work to spend *well* so *large* a sum.   I don't know if it would suit you for me to come on Saturday; but don't let a creature know I'm coming, if I do come.

. . . . I have quite a tremendous day on Monday, as I have to take over the Eccles Com. work, *and* to see to Deptford.   Besides the necessary work at home, ... Sir C. Dilke asks me if I can give evidence before the Royal Commission on Tuesday. . . .

What a shame not to tell you of the beauty and the quiet! but it is quite late, and I have written such a number of letters.

[1] A churchyard that had just been laid out by the Kyrle Society.   I was opened by the Princess Louise

14, Nott. Place,
Sunday, August 3rd, 1884.

To HER MOTHER.

. . . . I have read a good deal of Mr. Maurice's life. How very beautiful it is, specially, I think, the letter written in 1871, on " Subscription no Bondage "! I have also been poring over "'Thomas à Kempis," of which I never tire. To day at Hillside I read Ruskin's " Story of Ida." It reminds me, in its perfect simplicity of narrative, with quiet undercurrent of unobtrusive feeling, of the very early painters' work. It goes right to one's heart ; and one utterly forgets everything and everyone but the subject. I have read, too, a little of Bret Harte, and liked him better. There was one poem of his about a lost child, found after prayer, and the speaker's conviction that the angels had taken care of the child, which ends with a quaint, but very natural statement that they were better so employed than " loafing about the throne." It makes one feel how much more one real memory of an actual deliverance goes home to a man than fanciful descriptions. . . .

October 21st, 1884.

To MISS BARTER.

I was much interested by your letter. Thank you for it. I have always made the houses under my charge pay 5 per cent. ; but it would be a great respon- sibility to accept for their purchase the entire capital of anyone, and specially of a young lady probably unaccustomed to business. Such undertakings are necessarily subject to the possible variations in value, hitherto certainly advancing, but not necessarily always so, of house property let to working people.

But thank you all the same for thinking of it. The

spirit in which you do so makes me think that possibly there might be some other way in which you could help us. I wonder whether you would care to come any day and talk this over with me, so that I could realise the facts; but I assure you the responsibility of even considering your generous project, seeing it relates to your whole capital, is one I could not take.

1885.

LETTER TO FELLOW WORKERS.

I have, since I last wrote to you, been successful in establishing my work in South London, according to the long-cherished wish of my heart. In March of 884, I was put in charge, by the owner, of forty-eight houses in Deptford. In May of the same year, I undertook the care of several of the courts in Southwark for the Ecclesiastical Commissioners. In November of the same year, the Commissioners handed over to me an additional group of courts. In January of 1885 I accepted the management of seventy-eight more houses in Deptford. A friend is just arranging to take forty-one houses in Southwark on lease from the Commissioners. But I hope to retain trained workers and a portion of the tenants in a considerate and responsible way, which is quite independent of me or my advice. I ought, however, to repeat here once more that there is much which is technical, and which *must* be thoroughly learnt; and that unless intending workers set aside a time to learn their business thoroughly with us or others who have experience, they will do more harm than good by undertaking to manage houses.

One distinct advance, that is noticeable since I last wrote, is the readiness shown by men of business and companies to place their houses under our care. A deeper sense of responsibility as to the conduct of them,

a perception of how much in their management is
better done by women, and I hope, a confidence that
we try faithfully, and succeed tolerably, in the effort
to make them prosperous, have led to this result. This
method of extending the area over which we have
control has been a great help. It has occurred at a
time when, owing to the altered condition of letting in
London, I could no longer, with confidence, have
recommended to those who are unacquainted with
business, and who depend on receiving a fair return for
their capital, to undertake now the responsibility of
purchasing houses.

When we began in Southwark, we secured an almost
entirely new group of volunteers, who learnt there
under one or two leaders, and who now form a valued
nucleus from which to expand further.

In Deptford, I was obliged at first to take with me
helpers from some distance, as we had none near there ;
but gradually, I am delighted to say, we have found
many living at Blackheath and its neighbourhood who
are co-operating with us ; and we hope they, as the
years roll on, will be quite independent of us.

Of the success of our work ? Well ! I am thankful
and hopeful. Of course it has varied with the nature
and constancy of our workers, and with the response
our tenants give us. The new places always tax our
strength, and we have had our difficulties in them, but
we seem to make steady progress ; I feel all must go
well in proportion as we love our people and aim at
securing their real good, and base our action on wise
and far-sighted principles. There is not a court where
I do not mark distinct advance ; but none know better
than I how much more might have been done in each
of them, and how much lies before us still to do.

LETTER TO FELLOW WORKERS, 1887, ABOUT
RED CROSS GARDEN.

It was, when handed over to me, a waste, desolate place.
There had been a paper factory on one half of it, which
had been burnt down. Four or five feet of unburnt
paper lay in irregular heaps, blackened by fire, saturated
with rain, and smelling most unpleasantly. It had lain
there for five years, and much rubbish had been thrown
in. A warehouse some stories high fronted the street
on the other half of the ground, with no forecourt or
area to remove its dull height further from the rooms in
the model dwellings which faced it. Our first work was
to set bon-fires alight gradually to burn the mass of
paper. This took about six weeks to do, tho' the fires
were kept alight day and night. The ashes were good
for the soil in the garden, and we were saved the whole
cost of carting the paper away. Our next task was to
pull down the warehouse, and let a little sun in on our
garden, and additional light, air and sight of sky to
numerous tenants in the blocks in Red Cross Street.

The next work was to have a low wall and substantial
iron railings placed on the side bounded by the street,
so that the garden could be seen and the light and air
be unimpeded.

Then came the erection of a covered playground for
the children; it runs the whole length of a huge warehouse which bounds the garden on one side. It is
roofed with timber from the warehouse we pulled down,
and the roof is supported by massive pillars. The
space is paved with red bricks set diagonally, so as to
make a pretty pattern. At one end of this arcade is a
drinking fountain.

The roof of this covered playground is flat, and forms
a long terrace, which is approached by a flight of stairs.

Hotel Bellevue, Wäggis,
May 24th, 1885.

To HER MOTHER.

I am much interested in the *Spectator* cutting,
tho' I believe myself that the strain of living *in* the
worst places would be too trying *yet* to educated people;
it would diminish their strength, and so their usefulness;
The reform must be, I believe, more gradual. The
newspapers go in for such extremes, from utter separation to *living* in a court! I should urge the spending of
many hours weekly there, as achieving *most* just now,
because it is less suicidal than the other course, and
more natural.

Hotel Lukmanner, Ilanz, Grisons,
June 7th, 1885.

To HER MOTHER.

Dissentis seems to me a very old-world place. A
dear old lady keeps the inn, which is *very* comfortable;
but one seems nearer the life of the people here than
where modern hotels have invaded. . . . How
striking to me is the character of every separate house
in these valleys. Something, of course, is due to the
varieties of the ground, but much, too, I cannot help
seeing, to the fact that the houses belong to the
inhabitants. I wonder if we shall live to see a larger
number of English owners? I doubt it. It seems to
me that the impediments come by no means mainly
from the landlords. Of course they would cling,
especially in towns, to possession where value is rising,
but I doubt the tenants caring to buy *much* for occupation. They, like the landlords, like to buy houses
rising in value, with an idea of letting or selling; but
few, I fancy, desire to bind themselves to one spot and

way of life. They like the freedom and the change of hiring Even young married people, who, as a class, settle in with most sense of attachment to place and things, expect to move to another neighbourhood if work changes, or to a larger house if it prospers. Perhaps it is partly the great cost of living, and the fact that rent has to be paid. But one rarely sees in English towns a house lived in by a family for generations, the large families filling from cellar to attic, and the small ones using the best rooms mainly. One fancies a small family should like a small house. Whereas clearly houses in the country in old times must have been handed down to very various occupants. Some little sense of individuality would be quickly stamped, even on London houses, if they were owned by occupiers But the attachment to things seems giving place to a desire for their perfection, and we seem inclined rather to hire furniture or appliances for special occasions than to accept, even our houses, as in any way permanent. If they don't suit us for the moment, we change them. Well there is a noble independence of things as well as a noble attachment to them ; and " the old order changeth, giving place to new, And God fulfils Himself in many ways." There will have to come back, however, in one form or another, that element of rest in which alone certain human virtues can live ; but it may come in ways we do not know.

Deptford,
September, 1885 ?

To Mrs. Edmund Maurice.

All is very bright and well with us here, except poor Queen Street, which is a constant anxiety. My great fear is that Mr. T. will sell it, and take the management out of my hands. I am sure we should get on in time. However, all that is out of my hands. I don't know that I could have done differently at any juncture; and so I must just abide the result, and accept it as purposed, and look to see what next opens out; meantime, till it is decided, I am clinging on to the hope of it rather passionately. The MacDonalds came to town yesterday. I am to dine there on Tuesday. . . . I've been preparing my corn for a green refreshment to us a little later, and putting in my hyacinths It is a great delight to me to come back to such things from Dept-ford.

October 15th, 1885.

Miranda to Mr. Edmund Maurice.

We hear that the Metropolitan Board received the subject of Parliament Hill favourably. . . . There came in a petition from representative working men. . . . There were trade societies, co-operative societies, benefit societies represented. Mr. B said the co-operative signatures represented 2,000 working men. The petition from East End Clergy had fifty names of clergy and dissenting ministers, and the list was headed by the Bishop of Bedford. . . .

Octavia goes down to Lady Ducie for three days. I shall be glad of the change of thought for her. She is so worn with Deptford. Things are still *very* discouraging there; they seem unable to get respectable tenants, the new ones they hoped were good, turning out unsatisfactory. Still helpers are rallying round her. . . . It is nice to find old pupils coming to the front.

November 11th, 1885.

Octavia will have told you the result of the meeting of the Hampstead Heath Committee *re* Parliament Hill extension. Everyone seems to say " Go on agitating thro' the Press, and get the matter well before the public, there is yet hope." But I think Octavia has little hope.

Did I tell you about the old woman at Deptford who said to Octavia in a voice of reassurance and yet wonder, " You *have* feelings! When you first came you did not know us, and we did not know you ; but you *have* feelings!" As if O. would be as surprised as *she* was at the discovery !

1884 or 5.

Miss Ellen Chase to Octavia.

King (a Deptford tenant) had torn his garden all to pieces and broken pale of fence and windows here and there, and did not show himself at all. We were non-plussed First I hoped to slip notice under door, but the weather-board was too close ; that is a reason against putting them on. Then we debated how legal a service pinning to the back door would be, but Mr. P. thought it would be awkward if I was summoned for breaking into his premises ; and to post it we thought would not be customary ; so we were balked and Mrs. Lynch smiled sweetly all the time at her door. Mrs. T. had the cheek to offer nothing, so I took her a notice. I gave out several jobs of cleaning to even off the £7. Mrs. Sandal's cistern was leaking worst sort. Matthews and Arter both said floor too old to pay for removal. My unlets have come down 10*s.*

14 Not. Place,
November 7th, 1885.

OCTAVIA TO MRS. EDMUND MAURICE.

I am so much interested to hear of all you have
been seeing ; but I think I'd better write of things here.
I've just come back from a Hampstead Heath Committee,
—a large, strong, determined one. They decided to bring
a Bill into Parliament. Mr. S. Lefevre and Mr. Hunter
went off to see Lord Mansfield's agent. . . .

I think Deptford is in a very thriving state in many
ways; we are getting in such a quantity of local
strength.

Miranda seems to me *very* happy, and, I hope, tolerably
well. Her sweetness with everyone is beyond description, and also her merry fun over all that takes place.
She is quite delightful as a coadjutor, bringing all the
people so sweetly together, and never making difficulties
in anything ; and all her spirits and power come out. . . .

The Bishop of Manchester's death is greatly felt.
They say Jews, Catholics, the Greek Patriarch and
people of all kinds went to the memorial service, and
that they call him the " Bishop of all denominations."

Sarsden, Chipping Norton,
October 17th, 1885.

TO MRS. EDMUND MAURICE.

. . . . It is very delightful to escape to sunlight and
colour here from Deptford and London. All, however,
is, I think, going towards good with us in the work.
Mr. T. is prepared to spend a good deal on the houses,
with a view of raising the property ; and I hope it may
be a help to us in raising the people. I hope and
believe too that I and my workers are all better for

a certain amount of difficulty, and unpopularity ; and that it tests them, and draws them together. In these days when benevolence is popular, I think we may be thankful to have difficulty to surmount. All my workers have stood to their guns splendidly, and have been so helpful too.

14 Not. Pl., W.,
November 23rd, 1885.

To Mrs. Edmund Maurice.

We have been having much busy and interesting work of various kinds. No. 8 B. Ct. has been handed over to us in an awful state of dirt and dilapidation, and we are busy with estimates and workmen. Miss J.'s new houses in Southwark will be ready at Xmas ; and the company which owns the new blocks there have made repeated application to us to manage for them. Miss J. seems inclined to get a group of workers round her, and do this. . . .

The Hampstead Heath meeting was in some respects satisfactory. . . . Still the money needed is so large, and only the Met. Bd. can do it, and there isn't a sign they will ; so I have next to no hope, or rather expect something to turn up, if success *is* to come . . . I have been more successful than I at one time feared about the dilapidation money at Pn. Street ; but it is still bad enough. . . . I am just back from Deptford. I really do think it is getting on. . . . The houses are filling slowly. We are getting much more local co-operation. . . .

Interrupted. (Undated) probably November, 1885.

I dined at Lord Hobhouse's on Friday. Mr. Ghose, an Indian gentleman, and his wife were there.

Mr. Ghose's brother is standing for Deptford.   Lord H.
says he would not have a chance with a middle-class or
rich constituency; but that there is a strong feeling
among the working men that he ought to get in. . . .
We have a group of co-operators, who have taken Miss
Y.'s hall for a monthly gathering.   The tenants' plays,
one for grown up people and two for children, are in
full swing.

Casa Coraggio, Bordighera,
December 10th, 1885.

To HER MOTHER.

Thank you for your sweet birthday letter. . . .
To-night we are having some charades in honour of
Mr. MacDonald's birthday.   The house is large and full
and happy, and I think very good for Edmund.   To-day
we have rain.

It is strange they prophesied rain yesterday, in
consequence of a practice, or rather sham fight, of
the French men-of-war.   We heard a violent noise at
dinner yesterday; and, going up to the loggia to discover
the cause, we saw seven large men-of-war.   They said
they were 5 miles off, and that they often went out
from some bay near Cannes, where they spend the
winter, to practise firing.   We could see them all
confused in the smoke, and the great heaving mass
of water somehow caused by the firing,

The MacDonalds are getting up all manner of
Christmas things, among others a series of sacred
tableaux; they say the peasants come from far and
near to see them.

The little Octavia is a sweet child.   It is very
touching to see Mrs. MacDonald with her, and also to
see young Mr. Jamieson's widowed house, with all the

things Grace made and did. . . . I try not to think too much of you all, and of all the things at home, but you will realise how much my heart turns to England. However, I mean to have a really good holiday. It is very restful here, at once very home-like, and yet with no duties. MacDonald's bright faith and sweet sympathy are beautiful; and I must say Mrs. MacDonald's way of gathering people in is delightful to me.

Casa Coraggio,
December 16th, 1885.

To her Mother

I have been longing to write to you. I have been away to Mentone and Nice. I had a delightful visit to Lady Ducie, she was so sweet, looks much better, and seemed so very glad to see me She has a little basket carriage and two little ponies, and she took me the most beautiful drive all along by those lovely bays of the blue, clear Mediterranean, with their olive and cypress set slopes of cliff and promontory, and beautiful waves breaking against the rocks. . . .

All is very peaceful and good here, and the spirit of the house quite beautiful. Last night MacDonald read aloud to us one of Hawthorne's stories; it was so very beautiful. I think it might do to read at Christmas. He has given me the book. But it would lose a good deal in losing his reading; and perhaps some of you will have thought of something better. Oh! to think of the delight of finding you at home, when I come back, and the blessed Christmas time. I shall be *much* happier about Minnie for having seen her, and I like to think of her here . . . I often think of Florence and how she would rejoice in the beauty.

14, Nott. Place, W.,
December 27th, 1885.

To MRS. EDMUND MAURICE.

I have been thinking over your plans. . . . The city (Siena) is quite the loveliest and most interesting I ever saw. As to Assisi, it is just a vision of angels; it is like having looked thro' the gates of heaven for a season. If there's any chance of your going to Assisi, be sure you read, before you go, the little popular Italian book called " Fiorettini di San Francesco " used by the peasants. You can buy it for a few centesimi, Flo says. I should be glad if you'd buy it, and bring it back to me. I'm so fond of it, and it would be good Italian reading for you, it's so easy. Don't be cavilling, but read it and love it as I do. . . .

My love to the MacDonalds ;[1] tell them how entirely happy and refreshed I was by my visit to them, and how glad I am to have seen them in their new home. . . .

I got thro' the bulk of the accounts on Thursday. I had a fine staff, and they are getting capable. Mr. Shaen hasn't finished the deeds, and we can't take over Zoar Street to-morrow ! . . . I have an offer of £2,000 for houses. As a gift or investment, I think I shall risk it, and the Bishop of Rochester's £1,000 to buy houses in Southwark to keep our workers together. I had a comfortable journey, changed carriages at Marseilles, couldn't lie down till Dijon ; but had a reassuring crowded company of 6 ladies !

---

[1] She had just returned from a short visit to the George MacDonalds' at Bordighera where M was staying

January, 1886.

To Mrs. Edmund Maurice.

I knew you would hear some report of the riots, and would be anxious for news. . . . You need not be anxious about Deptford. Of course, after such a breakdown of police administration, one feels as if one *might* meet violence *any* where; but I think of all places I should feel, if it came, safest in Deptford. That this is so marks progress that I had hardly realised till your post-card recalled the old state of things. The people are gentle, responsive, and tractable there, if sometimes a little ill-tempered—that is the worst. At least I know they would stand by us. *No* one thinks the outbreak came from workmen; *no* one thinks it was excited by Socialists. It was just thieves and vagabonds, and the amount of excitement from the Socialists is also clear. I was interested to hear from Sir U. Shuttleworth that it has been the custom of late years to enter into communication with the promoters of working men's gatherings; and, if they themselves considered they could keep order, to leave it to them; and you would notice the workmen mentioned having told off 500 marshals, as if they felt themselves in charge; and from the very first they warned Hyndman and Co. off the ground. Of course Sir U. is retained for the Government; and I hear from others that a force of police *is* always ready, or I conclude ought to be; but it is nice to feel in what way the working men themselves are trusted. I wonder what Edmund would say as to prosecuting Hyndman. My impulse would be for doing so. All seems very quiet now, and people say it is as safe as it is after a railway accident. It has seemed a very strange week in London. We had a very successful Berthon St. party. Ld. and Lady Wolmer came, and he was such a help at the door. I rarely saw such courtesy, firmness, tact, sympathy, and care shown among strangers. . . . We had a C.O.S. meeting at the Davenport Hills' yesterday. Mr. Pell was in the chair, and I spoke ; it seemed so strange, being there without Edmund and you. One felt as if it were unnatural and almost wrong. Dear Mrs. Godwin was there. . . . The meeting was very full. . . . You will have seen about the huge relief fund formed at the Mansion House; it has reached £20,000. No one seems to me really to believe in the exceptional distress. It is a dreadful calamity, this fund being formed. . . .

I dined at the John Hollands' on Wednesday, and met Sir U. Shuttleworth, Bryce, and Mr. O'Connor Power. The former told me the impression was that Gladstone would prepare his scheme, bring it in, be beaten, and then go to the country.

FROM MIRANDA.

Octavia has left her letter unfinished for me to add something. . . . She read such a, very beautiful paper on Saturday. . . . I think people felt her paper very much. She spoke with such feeling.

> 14 Nottingham Place,
> January 17th, 1886.

To MRS. EDMUND MAURICE.

My affairs are going really well. We had a beautiful Hereford party; Mrs. Macdonell's children

H H

have got up a Christmas tree for poor children, and they have let me send six children with Mrs. Read. I am so glad. Miranda's play of " Beauty and the Beast " is to be acted at St. Christopher's. Col. Maurice's lecture at Southwark is on Friday, and our dance at Bts. Court. There was a meeting at the Mansion House yesterday about Home Arts and industries, and the use of the Board Schools for classes for them, for singing and recreation . . . many working men have offered their help as teachers. To-morrow is the C.O.S. annual meeting. I mean to go ; there may be unpopularity and difficulty and one ought to be there, tho' it is a Monday.[1] Deptford is slow, and silence is perhaps best ; I can't help thinking the sound work we are putting into it must be telling. The snow was a *great* difficulty last week, it melted and then froze, leaving three inches of ice in the gutters, which blocked them ; the houses were partly flooded, and much of our expenditure on internal repairs will have to be done again. The tenants were very hopeless and listless ; but, strange to say, *not* angry or ill-tempered. I do get very fond of them, when I am among them. Bts. Court is *most* flourishing. . . . There has been a trial about Cross Bones,[2] and it is decided that they may NOT build. I had a funny interesting visit from Mr. T. who represents the lady who offers the £1,000 for houses ; it is absolutely at my disposal ; now I have to find houses to replace those the Commissioners will pull down. I met the Bishop of London, the other day, at an exhibition of the people's own work Mr Tanner[3] is brimful of energy, and the assistant secretary very capable.

---

[1] The rent collecting day
[2] An open space near the Southwark cottages.
[3] Hon Sec. of the Kyrle Society

14 Nottingham Place, W.
February 7th, 1886.

To Mrs. Edmund Maurice.

We had a most triumphantly successful party at Southwark. It was a huge number, tho' it was only half our tenants. Mrs. J. Marshall came and her band, and they did play so beautifully, and we had musical chairs, and Sir Roger. The hall had been decorated by the Kyrle and looked very pretty. Miss Johnson and Miss Tait brought the loveliest flowers in pots, tulips, red, white and yellow, cyclamen, etc. Miss Barter had sent a hamper of oranges. . . . Lord S. came looking *very* clean and prim. I set him soon to bring some very dusty chairs and so broke the formality ; and he was soon waltzing away with one of the tenants to the merry tune the band was playing. He said most decidedly, in going away, that no one had enjoyed it more than he, and that he hoped I should ask him to the second. The Bishop wrote very warmly, but couldn't come. He is thinking of selling London House, and going to live in Clerkenwell to be near the poor. Miss J. and Miss I. were delightful among their people, and W. was helping heartily. I invited the Ashmores, our new superintendents at Berthon Street . . . On Wednesday we have a party at Berthon Street, and I want Ashmore to take the lead. Miss H. is a great success. A. and I decide that no one was ever so happy here. She seems to pick up like a flower you put in water. She can do everything, and is strong on the human, artistic, and gardening sides . . .

14 Nottingham Place,
February 21st, 1886.

To Mrs. Edmund Maurice.

. . . Even if there is distress, this miserable huge fund, which can be used for nothing radical, won't help. . . . We had a very successful dance at St. Christopher's. Dr. Longstaff came and was the life and soul of the party. We had a very poor man, named Pearce, who lives in our houses in Bell Street, and belongs to Mrs. J. Marshall's band He plays the violin and reads beautifully, and is very glad to earn a small sum by playing, and we feel the violin a great help. Mrs. Martin,[1] from Burley, is living at 3 Adspar Street. . . . She sent me a most affectionate message. Miranda is succeeding delightfully in Horace Street, her gentleness is winning all hearts. . . .

14, Nottingham Place, W.
February 28th, 1886.

To Mrs. Edmund Maurice.

The Mansion House Fund, its terrible mistakes and failures, have occupied us a great deal. Mr. Alford has taken up the matter strongly, and, tho' *deeply* deploring the fund, has undertaken to administer it in his parish and St Mark's. He has a very good Committee. Miranda and I attended the first meeting. I hear that the working-men on the Committees, especially those who represent the Oddfellows and Foresters, are the greatest help in the only four parishes where any order is attempted. As a rule, the most utter confusion prevails; and the crowd of regular roughs awes some

---

[1] A poor woman whose family O had sent to the north, thereby raising them from extreme poverty to comfortable independence

into giving soup tickets! So low have we got with a fund, the only excuse for which is that the distress has reached a higher class than ever would apply! Men in work are getting the relief unknown. Vestrymen and publicans initial papers, which are treated like cheques which must be honoured. People who ought to have £5 have 3s. tickets, and tickets are sold for drink. Five Committees meet in one room to decide cases, the only data being statements written by clerks from applicant's dictation. The City Missionary at Deptford says that, if the money had been thrown into the sea, it would have been better. Perhaps you saw Shipton's magnificent answer refusing to co-operate, and that of the Engineers' Trade Society. The Mansion House refused £2,000 to the Beaumont Trustees for laying out gardens, etc. ; and the £1,000 they did give was not enough, and has had to be returned. Lord Brabazon's money seems the only portion of the fund which is doing good. Everyone is praying for the fund to be exhausted. I am *therefore*, and therefore only, thinking of getting the Kyrle to accept money for labour for Sayes Court and St. George's, if they can be now put in hand. Miranda is delightful among the poor people. She remembers all their wants ˙and knows their characters. It is quite delightful having her as a link with Paradise Place and Horace Street. . . . Miss Hogg is charming, and so valuable among the people. One gets quite human links with the tenants now in her part. We are all much occupied with a family named C——, man in full work at £1 a week, rent 5s. 6d., seven children, the eldest still at school, and the wife able to do nothing but see to them. . . . I hope you will have some real Italian spring before you come back.

August 8th, 1886.

To Miranda about a Tenant in B—— Court.

Mrs. P. had been out in the yard with her baby just before, well and cheerful, and she suddenly burst out crying that it was dead; and, indeed, its eyes were glazing over, and it looked half dead   I said a warm bath at once; but someone cried, "The doctor," on which she tore down the street with it in her arms, quite mad. I sent Sam Moore after her, the only person I could find; and was left alone with two almost babies and the house. I filled and put on kettles, borrowed tub and extemporised sponge and blanket. When they came back they said the doctor had ordered a warm bath. Mrs. C. and Mrs. R. helped nicely, and we left little Albert happily asleep and better.

Loch Maree,
September 18th, 1886.

To her Mother,

I received Miranda's telegram with grand news of the passing of the Heath Bill. I do really think that makes it nearly sure that we shall have 50 acres saved, and every acre saved makes the saving of others more likely. Did you hear of Charles's[1] enormous energy when he saw the Bill was coming on? He *ran* from Crockham Hill to Westerham in twenty-seven minutes to catch the train. I wonder if a letter I wrote was sent to *The Times.*

February 12th, 1887.

From Miranda to Miss Harris

I went with Octavia yesterday to see the piece of ground that the Ecclesiastical Commissioners have given for the garden. It is a larger piece than I had

---

[1] Charles Lewes, husband of Octavia's sister Gertrude.

expected, and is in the midst of poor people's houses. It will be a boon. At present it is in a deplorable state—covered with rubbish, and with an empty warehouse on it, and high back walls on each side. Lord Ducie told his wife he thought it " the most unpromising piece of ground that he had ever seen." But all the more delightful will it be to get trees, grass, and water there. Thou knows that Lady Ducie has promised all the money for the laying out, and O is now busy planning a large hall near the garden, to be available for parties, classes, etc. She thinks that she can arrange it so as to keep several cottages still standing (always her great wish in this time of huge blocks), if the Commissioners will let her lease the site that she wishes for. She has thoroughly interested their surveyor in her plan.

14, Nottingham Place,
March 4th, 1887.

To Mrs. Edmund Maurice.

I gather that you have not seen the terribly sad news which reached me yesterday about dear Mr. Shaen. He is gone from us, and in a moment. I think of the girls and Mrs. Shaen, but I cannot help feeling, too, how irreparable is such a loss of a friend of nearly thirty years' standing, who never failed in noble and wise counsel, and to whose judgment nearly all the work I ever did has owed so much. And one was so sure, not only of his wisdom and generosity, but of his kindness. It is a heavy blow.

14, Nottingham Place, W.,
March 15th, 1887.

To Miss Shaen.

Dearest Maggie,
Looking back on Mr. Shaen's life as I remember it, and his character, as I saw it, nothing is to me so

wonderful as the tenderness and the silence of it. The pity and the chivalry were quite infinite ; and the expression of them was absolutely in deeds only. Then, I should think, there never was a more entire truth of nature than his ; no shadow of lie or equivocation could sully it. Hence, I think, the purity of his nature. Amid the noisy and shallow philanthropy we see around us, how the silent service of a life stands out ! The memory of it is a possession for ever ; and there is a rebuke to our faithlessness in the memory of his faith that the only thing was the right thing. How poor all these words seem ! but, believe me, they come with a love that will last on, and on which you may count.— I am

Your affte. old friend,
OCTAVIA HILL.

The laying out as a garden of the Quaker Burial Ground.

14, Not. Pl., W.
Sunday, March 15th.

To MRS. EDMUND MAURICE.

Miss Y. and I went down to Quaker St. yesterday. The ground seems nicely finished. . . . Mrs W. was very full of joy about it—said she thought it would save the children from accidents ; the streets were so crowded with drays, and children could play in the garden till parents or elders fetched them. She said it had been crowded with children when the man was painting there. Mr W. came in while we were there. He said he had hoped for some little opening (ceremony), but added, " it is a small thing," in a voice that showed it was anything but that to them. He said quite cheerfully he should just have their teachers, and march the children in, and have a little chat about not throwing stones.

April 2nd, 1887.

To SYDNEY COCKERELL.

I think your own instincts will guide you better than any words of mine, when you come face to face with Ruskin, as to what to talk of with him. It will be an event in your life, and I hope you may talk only of what is bright as well as good. If you felt as if any mention of me, or the work you help me in, comes under this head, I should be greatly delighted ; but, if it does not, then I am quite ready to leave all in silence, till the time when the understanding of all we have all meant here shall be perfect. Don't risk clouds in your visit, *whatever you do*. . . .

January 18th, 1888.

I beg you in all advice and in all speech to think *only* of what is best for Mr. Ruskin; that is *really* all that matters now.

June 8th, 1887.

To MR. SYDNEY COCKERELL.

It is the greatest joy to me to think that you and Olive will be able to be such a comfort to Mr. Ruskin, and that you will have the marvellous joy of the intercourse with him. You will gather memories which life will never take away. . . . It is a high honour and great blessing which has come to you both. I believe you will walk worthily of it in the time to come, with, as it were, your shoes put off your feet ; for indeed the spirit which will be near you will make the place holy ground.

April 24th, 1888.

It is very nice to have some news now and again from out of the death-like silence into which the friendship of nearly a lifetime has fallen. As you know, I believe the silence is the best for Mr. Ruskin; and so, if you take my advice, you will not break it on that side.

Switzerland,
(July 2nd ?) 1887.

To her Mother.

. . . I suppose Miranda will have told you of the offer of the ticket for the Abbey [1] to me. I do not know whether it is the news coming here, so far away; but it has impressed me rather. I cannot think why I, who have done so simply, and at no great cost, just what lay before me, should be singled out in this kind of way. I always feel as if I ought to do, or be, something more, in order to deserve it. What a wonderful state London seems to have been in about the Jubilee! What recollections the Queen must have had crowding on her at the service!

.   March, 1887.

? To the Secretary of the Ecclesiastical Commissioners

Dear Sir,

You were interested about the plan of my taking charge of the houses occupied by the poor on the Southwark Estate of the Ecclesiastical Commissioners; and I am anxious you should know how matters stand, as I feel as if the future of the people might be

---

[1] For the Jubilee services

influenced by it. May I therefore tell you the state of affairs ?

I was ready to have taken over all the weekly property in Southwark in the hands of the Commissioners. I was very willing to accept the decision that I should begin with a third or so of it, which I took over on May 5th. I was *most* anxious to have leased to me the portion of the ground allotted to the permanent housing of the poor, which was then unlet to builders. It would have rendered the personal work that we are doing among the tenants tenfold more useful, because we could have continued our work among them, and kept them together, with some sense of a corporate body, when the time came for the destruction of the present houses, instead of their being either scattered or handed over to the government of an ordinary builder.

The portion of the property handed over to our charge appears to be that most directly doomed to destruction, either by rebuilding by others, or by railways, or owing to its condition or situation. A large part of it, we are told, may be wanted this month. The whole of the land for rebuilding for the poor is now let.

The past cannot be helped. But I wonder if there is anything that you can do, to render our work more permanent, or to let it lead up to anything. I have written to Lord Stanhope and to Mr. Clutton to ask, in another form, the same question. They are both most kind ; but I am anxious that you too should know the facts. Their past action makes me a little fear that either they hardly grasp the importance of the point, in their interest and pleasure in the new buildings, or, for some other reason, they may not decide to hand over more to our care. . . .

It is always difficult to take away paid work from those who have done it in the old way well, in order to introduce another plan. Whether it is right to do so, must depend on the excellence of the new plan, which must be a matter of opinion.

In my estimation, of course, such personal work as my friends and I can give is the only way to raise these people. We are quite willing to go on, and do what little we can, till our tenants must leave us ; but what we do can never have the effect that it would have, if, in any way, we could retain them longer near us.

What is still feasible is, first, to give over to our care some of the weekly tenements which are in a more solid state of repair, and which may therefore stand longer as cottages ; and to give us these in addition to what we have. So you would extend our work. So you would give us the interest of more permanent work. So you would enable us, perhaps, to keep near us some of the tenants to whom we feel it most important, when our present houses are pulled down. Second, you might give me, or some of my friends, a lease of some of your houses   As you (as Commissioners) do not see your way to keep them under your own direct control, you might lease them to us, though leases are hateful things.

I fancy the latter plan is the one to which Mr. Clutton sees his way ; but I hope that it will not be all that you will do   Several courts, substantial in themselves, and not, as I understand, doomed to come down, unless they interfere with larger schemes, remain in your hands.

If there is no valid reason, unknown to me, I hope these may be confided to us

July ?, 1887.

FROM MIRANDA TO MRS. EDMUND MAURICE.

Our life is a very busy one, as usual. Octavia's Sunday afternoons in Red Cross Hall have been a wonderful success; the people have come in increasing numbers, and seem to enjoy the music and the books and illustrated papers greatly. . . . We are now very busy and interested about another Open Space—a garden for Vauxhall. Fawcett's house stands there; and the large grounds of that and the adjoining house are offered for sale for a public park. . . . Out of £44,000, all has been promised except £7,000, and Octavia is working with all her might to get this together. There is to be a meeting at Lambeth Palace at which Mrs. Fawcett and Octavia are to speak. It is to us so strange that there is such readiness to give large sums to technical schools, which could be built at any time, and such backwardness about giving to Open Spaces, which, if lost now, can never be recovered. Individuals are generous about it, and certainly public interest in the question has grown; but corporate bodies, with money to give at their discretion, seem slow to see the advantages as yet.

July 17th, 1887.

MIRANDA TO MARY HARRIS.

Octavia and I were at such an interesting open air meeting at South Lambeth yesterday, to consider the advisability of buying The Lawn (Fawcett's old house and grounds), and the adjoining grounds, which are large and beautifully wooded, to form a park for Lambeth. The speakers were in waggons, the audience chiefly working men. The appreciation of the Open

Spaces was very striking.   Octavia said how public
opinion on the subject has grown.   The working men's
comments that we—being in the crowd—heard, were
very interesting.   I must say I thought their spirit
very good.   The only thing was they would not listen
to any speakers on the other side, tho' asked to do so
by their chairman—evidently a popular man ; and tho'
several of the nicest of the audience said, " Give the
man a hearing," " Let's hear the other side."   But the
desire to gain the park, even at the increase of rates,
was *very* strong, quite unmistakable ; also the warm
way in which they responded to a speaker who described
the temptation to drink, of people who had been sleeping and working in impure air, and who said that drink
really took more strength out than it put in.   " What is
the best tonic after labour ? " asked he—and many
voices shouted " Fresh air, fresh air."   In fact I thought
the Temperance view of the question excited more
enthusiasm than any other, except the good the park
would do to the children.   " If we can't enjoy it often,
the little uns will," I heard one man say to another
aside

We are so delighted that the Hampstead Vestry has
at last voted £20,000 for the purchase of Parliament
Hill, by forty-five votes to ten.   There was a majority
of twenty-one against it on the last occasion.

The Countess of Ducie's, Tortworth Court,
August 21st, 1887.

OCTAVIA TO MISS ELLEN CHASE.

I hope that you and Miss Terry reached home
safely. . . . You would find some troublesome little
scraps of paper about roofs.   They were all I could
manage before I left.   I write now to say that I must

ask you to use your own discretion on arriving at Queen Street. My own strong impression is that the downpour probably arose from causes which operated in all sorts of houses, poor and rich ; that is, that the arrangements were not calculated to meet such a storm as Wednesday's. I know the gutters, which run from back to front of houses in Queen Street, are narrow. They are formed of flat pieces of zinc which are turned up at the edges under the tiles—thus.

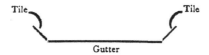

If the bit which runs up is not wide, the water gets over the edge, if the gutter becomes too full, and enters the house under the tile. For this there is no remedy but a wider gutter. This I do not think it worth while to put for exceptional storms. If this seems to you likely, or if you can elicit from Moore that this is the cause, just say nothing ; order the plaster of ceilings, or other urgent internal work to be reinstated. We can take our time as to further radical improvement. If, however, the gutter is itself defective, or Moore distinctly asserts that it is, and that he can patch it up for a few shillings, let him do that ; and the sooner the better. . . . If the E.'s are gone, get on swiftly with repairs required for letting there. Tell French polisher at 33 that we shall have a house when it is done up ; but try not to show it, till it looks pretty nice. . . .

November 14th, 1887.

To Mr. Sydney Cockerell.

You will remember well Mr. Cooper's great gift to us, and will have seen his death in Saturday's paper.

I propose to put up to him a slab in the wall at Southwark, with these words :—

" To the Honble Henry Frederick Cooper, whom we never saw, whom we hoped to see, but God took him to Himself before we could rejoice him by our joy here, or thank him with audible words. November, 1887."

If you think that any of the members of the club, poor or rich, would *like* to join in the memorial by giving a few pence, will you, when occasion offers, ask them ? The money I shall myself provide gladly; so no one need help who doesn't wish to. I write to you because you know all about the gift, and how it helped us. Don't say a word if you think it better not ; I leave it entirely to you.

I send you a copy of our Parliament Hill papers, . . . but we have a huge sum still to raise, upwards of £20,000; it comes in daily, and we mean to carry it through ; but we shall have to strain every nerve

> 14, Nottingham Place, W.,
> March 2nd, 1888.

To Mr. Sydney Cockerell.

After an elaborate discussion of a difference between the members of the club and the trustees, and suggestions for removing that difference, she says they (the club members) are much the best judges of their own business, and if they don't think it does we must see if we can think of a plan that they approve.

I am sorry that they didn't approve of the scheme of our appointing a representative. I didn't mean it for want of confidence in them ; but a club is a changing body ; who is to say which of its members will be there and powerful for the whole time of the lease ?

May 17th, 1888.

MIRANDA TO MRS. DURRANT.

We are very much interested just now in the defence of foot-paths in Lake District. Some land-owners are shutting up old rights of way, and preventing people from ascending the mountains. A very brave clergyman,[1] a friend of Octavia's, who has a parish at Keswick, has taken up the defence of these rights, and is threatened with a very expensive law-suit. He and the other "defenders" are appealing to the public of the large towns to help with a guarantee fund. A meeting was organised at Hampstead which turned out very successfully.

14, Nottingham Place,
July 14th, 1888.

TO MR. SYDNEY COCKERELL.

I hope you have had a very happy time away. What a wonderful thing it seems your meeting Mr. Ruskin! and what an added interest it must have been to all things, translating them into vivid and permanent life! A memory that will be a possession for ever.

You will be interested to see the great Latrigg[2] success! I fancy you may like to have a copy of the speech that I made at the perilous juncture, now happily no more needed for distribution.

Larksfield,
September 2nd, 1888.

TO HER MOTHER.

I think of you, dearest Mama, a great deal, and long for the time when you will be nearer us; meantime

---

[1] Canon Rawnsley.
[2] This is the pass over Skiddaw mentioned in previous letter.

I never feel far away at all, I am so sure of your
sympathy about all I am thinking of and working for.
I do not think you know MacDonald's "Diary of an
Old Soul," do you? There is a very beautiful part of
the August portion of it, about forgetfulness of God,
and His memory of us, and the nearness to Him, which
I think you would like. The last verse always naturally
makes me think of you ; but I think there never could
have been any mother, of whom it was so true that she
desired no personal nearness, so that she was entirely
one with what her children did. Your love seems
entirely free from a touch of self in it ; and I always
feel as near you away as when I am by you.

14, Nottingham Place, W.,
September 23rd, 1888.

To her Mother.

We had the first evening performance at Red
Cross Hall yesterday of "The Pilgrim's Progress." The
hall looked beautiful, lighted up. It was a moonlight
night, and the cottages and gardens looked lovely. I
found the Committeemen very busy and happy and
important. Everything was ready, and the curtain up
and looking very pretty. The hall was full   Many of
the workers were there and very happy. One of the
Committeemen said to me, "Considering the neighbourhood, you couldn't have a more respectable audience!"
The MacDonalds seemed happy and busy. When the
play began it was most beautiful. It is wonderful they
can act it as they do, with the blanks in their company
death has made ; but it only seems to have made it to
them truer and more solemn. Some of the scenes—
notably that in the Valley of Humiliation—seem to me
more beautiful than ever ; so is the grouping. Also, in

the dark valley, when the little boy asks Great Heart to draw his sword against the shadow, and he tells him that no weapon avails there but All Prayer, and they fall into a short procession, Great Heart first, alone, then the two couples of little boys in their red and black little dresses, then Christiana and Mercy, the one in a lovely old black dress, and the other in the fairest blue and white, and they troop off chanting, all their hands raised.   It is *most* beautiful.   The working men, I hear, felt the play most.   I fancy they followed the sense best.

> 14, Nottingham Place,
> October 8th, 1888.

To HER MOTHER.

As you say, the teachings of history show us the reason of our hope.   There is no subject so curious to me as this of the influence of circumstances.   In some cases their power, in others their powerlessness.   But that we must *all* try to make them better with might and main, there is no doubt.   Then we may leave all trustfully in God's hands.   .   .   .

I see no chance of even a day at my beloved thistles[1] as yet—am very busy.

> December 16th, 1888.

MIRANDA HILL TO ELLEN CHASE.

The Lawn Meeting went off very well yesterday at Lambeth Palace.   The speeches were capital, the Dean of Windsor's (Miss Tait's brother-in-law), and Mrs. Fawcett's, Mr. Edwards's (the clergyman of the district, who gave an interesting sketch of the

[1] When she went to Larksfield she spent much time in clearing thistles in the garden ground, which had been a neglected field.

movement) and finally Mr. Lester's. He is a working man, such an enthusiast for the garden, and his was a delightful speech. He told us he was an engine-driver, and was at work from 4 a.m. to 7 p.m. often. He said, I earn my bread by the sweat of my brow and am quite agreeable to do so; but, when I come down from that beastly stokehole, I do wish to breathe some of that pure air that the Almighty has made for all men. I think his speech interested people more than anybody else's. Miss Octavia's, of course, was beautiful, and was valued, I think. Such a beautiful letter from Florence Nightingale was read to the meeting. Miss O. says that of all the people who have spoken or written on Open Spaces, F. Nightingale has got most to the heart of the matter.

January 7th, 1889.

To MIRANDA.

I thought you ought to know before the world that the meeting went beautifully to-day. The men's spirit was really beautiful, so child-like, trustful and dignified. The Prince's face is refined and intellectual and full of power. His speech was beautiful, very simple and very human, very fluently graceful. Mrs. Benson came, and she and the Prince and the Archbishop were charmed with the men's spirit, and the naturalness of the whole little ceremony. They said they wished all meetings were like that. . . . The great certainty as to the thoroughness of the work they had themselves done, mingled with their interest in the Royal visit, was delightful. They were most keen to have a card framed in record of the day, and apologised for not thinking my scrubby little thing quite good enough! I brought them up to the Archbishop telling them he, not I, should sign it, whereupon they explained it was for their "offspring," that if, L. added "I should live, and he should live to be King, I might tell them I've shaken hands with the Crown." Also they were very emphatic about the hearty good shake of the hand the Prince had given each. "None of your shaking with one little finger. We working men know a right good shake of the hand. We haven't all been dragged up," said one man.

January 13th, 1889.

To a Friend who is giving up Art for Business.

I cannot but feel how hard the sacrifice is to you just now; but do you know I really believe that the partnership will be the best. I remember so well a somewhat similar trial in my own early life, and how I seemed to have to turn away from my ideal; and, by unexpected ways, I found, years afterwards, that just the sacrifice I had to make brought me, by ways that I did not know, to that ideal. Anyway, I think that the steady work, combined with the love of all high things, will be so good. Anyway, I pray that all may be ordered for you in your Father's own way for the very best.

South Lodge,
January 21st, 1889.

Mrs. Hill to Miranda.

Octavia told us a great deal about Charles's election,[1] all very pleasant. He seems to have won golden opinions by his directness, and has been much touched by the extreme kindness he has received. The election has been conducted on most honourable and

---

[1] To the first L C.C.

courteous terms. Charles says he never should have
won but for Gertrude. Her wonderful organising power
told on the day. Octa. spoke at the evening meeting
(she seems no longer to dread speaking). Charles's
working men were enthusiastic, waited till two o'clock
in the morning to hear the result.

February 24th, 1889.

MIRANDA TO MISS ELLEN CHASE.

The other week Octavia made such a beautiful
speech for the C.O.S. at Fulham Palace (the Bishop of
London's). I went with her and Miss Yorke to the
meeting there. The old palace is so fine, stands in a
park with a moat, and looks as if it were far in the
country—not near town at all. There is an old hall,
built in Henry VII.'s time (though altered in the last
century), with carved wooden screen and ancient full-
length portraits. . . . In *that* hall the meeting was. . . .
The Bishop—Temple (former headmaster of Rugby), and
his wife were very friendly. He gave a most amusing
account in his speech of how Miss O. had convinced him
and the other Ecclesiastical Commissioners that they
were wrong, and she was right, about certain points.
He said . " When she had talked to us for half an hour
we were quite refuted. I never had such a beating in
my life ! Consequently I feel great respect for her. So
fully did she convince us, that we not only did what she
asked us on that estate, but proceeded to carry out
similar plans on other estates." Miss O. supposes he
refers to the gift of land for Open Spaces, and is very
pleased, not having known before that those gifts were
the result of her representations to the Coms. about
Red X Garden.

14, Nottingham Place,
February 18th, 1886.

To MIRANDA.

I left Mama at South Lodge this morning.   She read me yesterday some of Miss Wedgwood's book,[1] Xl. —the chapter about the Romans and Law.   It reminded me a little of things that Mr. Maurice has said, but was very different, too.   I was much interested by what she says about the influence of women, as shown in Homer and Virgil, and on to the Middle Ages.

March, 1889.

This letter requires a few words of explanation. The long negotiation for securing the addition of Parliament Hill and the adjoining lands to Hampstead Heath, begun in 1884, had just been concluded.   They had involved negotiations with the old Metropolitan Board of Works (which expired just at the close of our negotiations), and with two ground landlords, besides appeals to three vestries and to a large number of private persons.   The meeting, referred to in the following letter, was held at Grosvenor House to decide on the question of the application of the surplus of the funds raised by the Committee.   Octavia and the majority of the Committee were in favour of using the money for the general movement for preserving open spaces ; the proposal of the amendment was to apply it to securing access from Kentish Town to the Parliament Hill Fields.

To MIRANDA.

The meeting was a great success, and very animated.   It was very full.   There were fourteen reporters.

[1] The Moral Ideal

The Duke of Westminster came up on purpose to take the chair, but was ill, and could not.

Rogers Field moved his amendment *re* the balance. Mr. Ewan Christian seconded. There was great excitement, and I thought great sympathy with the amendment. Mr. Baines replied, and then Edmund made a speech. We won by 22 votes. Miss Yorke was very keen, and asked me with great eagerness if she might vote, and did it *con amore*.

Sir Thos. Farrer[1] made a beautiful speech, referring to his memories of Coleridge and Crabbe at Hampstead. Lord Hobhouse made a fine speech, noble in tone, dwelling on London as a whole, and what it might be, if municipal feeling drew together the great Londoners.

Mr. Saml. Hoare referred to the struggle that he remembered his father had had, *nearly alone*, to save the Heath itself, and the growth of public interest in the subject. He also spoke of Mr. Shaw-Lefevre's help in those early difficult days.

Maud[2] was there, and much interested in seeing Mr. Shaw-Lefevre, whose face she much liked

March 30th, 1889.

To MIRANDA.

I had a pleasant Red Cross Committee, very. The gymnasium was in full swing; such a number of great hulking youths, so energetic and happy.

Mr. B. was very much delighted, and said that it did so much good to their physique. He says our sergeant is very good. The appeal for the corps reads so well. Was it you who helped me with it? They propose a meeting, with some military man in the chair, some

[1] He was Alderman of the first L C C
[2] Mrs Lewes' second daughter, afterwards Mrs J Hopwood

afternoon at four o'clock; and the local magnates invited by a card, to be sent out with a printed appeal. The men were delighted with the idea, and seemed so full of sympathy and go.

I thought you would like to see Miss Sewell's nice letter. (Miss Sewell was head of Southwark settlement.) I have, as you will know, replied that we should not dream of any move till winter next year, and must be guided by what we see best then.

I cannot tell whether dear old Marylebone or Southwark will seem the most natural working centre, nor how far such a body as the Settlement would leave you and me enough sense of home.

April 26th, 1889.

To HER MOTHER.

Lady Nicholson has brought the loveliest panels, painted for Red Cross Men's Club. A large set of water lilies and other water plants, with bulrushes and kingfishers for the centre over the mantelpiece. A panel with swallows and wild roses, one with titmice, one with a wren, and one with a robin. She has given me £2 for fixing and mounting. Will it not be nice to have all that colour down in Southwark? Miranda and I were there to-day, and found everything looking very nice. M. was much pleased with Gable Cottages. . . . Miss Cons seems to be doing beautiful work at the L. C. Council, inspiring everyone, and keeping herself in the shade. She amused us much with her account of getting the Lawn resolution passed.

M. and I went to-day to see Mr. Hoole [1] about some more cottages. He was so nice. He is just going to Wells, where you know he is building some cottages for the

---

[1] The architect who for forty-two years helped Octavia.

Bishop. I am so glad to have given him the introduction. He seems to have been delighted with both
Bishop and beauty of town.

We have just received a basket of camellias from
Hillside. I wish you could see their lovely red and
white. *That* is what I am always wishing about all
things. However, the next best thing is the telling
you about them.

Crockham,
May 5th, 1889.

To her Mother.

I went to Waterloo and met Col. Maurice, and
we proceeded to Blackheath. A pleasant little victoria
met us, and drove us to the Ranger's Lodge, a house
which stands facing Blackheath, with a magnificent
view of blue distance ; and on the London side such
a space of blue quite studded with steeples and towers.
The Ranger's Lodge is an old mansion, with great
panelled rooms all painted white, and hung with old
portraits. The house belongs to the Queen, and has
been given to Lord Wolseley for his lifetime. It
belonged to Lord Chesterfield and to Lady Mayo. In
what is now the kitchen garden stood the house where
Queen Caroline lived ; and her mother (the Duchess of
Brunswick ?) lived in the Ranger's Lodge. There are
twenty acres of lovely old garden, with smooth lawns
and great cedar trees ; and all round the grounds
stretch the glades of Greenwich Park ; one magnificent
avenue of chestnuts, in full young green, specially
delighted me. Lady W. is so delighted with the place.
. . . I was charmed with her, and with her simple, tall,
pretty daughter; also I liked Lord W. very much ;
and it was very interesting to hear him talk. He has a

very simple, reverent sort of interest in all sorts of subjects, not his own. . . . They were all very kind and helpful to me. . . .

Mindful of your words, I was out at 5½ this morning gardening in the cool. The cuckoo and lark kept me glad company.

Larksfield,
May 19th, 1889.

To her Mother.

I am specially interested about article by Col. Maurice, because I have been thinking a great deal about the matter lately. Of course I realise all you say about war; but I do not feel any doubts about the Volunteer Cadet Corps; for at least three reasons. First, I do feel defensive war right, if by sad necessity it should ever be called for, which I greatly doubt. Secondly, because the volunteer movement seems to me a helpful form for preparation to take, contrasting strongly with all standing armies. And a peculiarly safe form for military preparation, because (*sic*) men who have homes and professions and very varied sympathies and thoughts do not seem to me the least likely to hurry us on to any war. Thirdly, because I do so clearly see that exercise, discipline, obedience, *esprit-de-corps*, camping out, manly companionship with the gentlemen who will be their officers, will be to our Southwark lads the very best possible education. I see very forcibly all Mr. Brooke says about how it fills a great gap in their education; also I have watched the marvellous growth in the few Queen Street young men who have joined the militia. It has been the saving of them. I dare say a great deal will be said about the movement, on its military side, that I shall in no way agree with; but I a little stand aside, and let the good and true men, who are helping, and whose scheme it really is, carry on, a little by my strength, their own thoughtfully planned scheme; just as I might lend a hall to Salvationists or others, who on the whole were teaching what was right, tho' I could not myself teach or agree with all they say. Only in this case I am more heartily with my fellow workers. I do feel that neither Mr. Barnett nor Mr. Brooke, who believe this movement reaches a sort of boy that nothing else does, and reforms him, are either of them men to desire to strengthen a love of war. In fact I see, what they, who know the lads better than I, say most emphatically, that all the temptations to war are entirely absent from these boys; they are cowardly and wanting in power of endurance, wanting in power of standing together, worshippers of money. All which the volunteer movement will teach them will, I believe, be helpful. So at least they say, and so I believe, and to a great degree have seen. . . .

14 Nottingham Place, W.
May 29th, 1889.

To her Mother.

I am delighted to think of the day being fixed for seeing you. Miss Yorke is not here to-night, but she would, I know, be *delighted* for you to come to Crockham. It is the very thing she has been building on, and caring to try to plan for. I long to have you there in the silent, cheerful little house, which catches every ray of sunlight there is, and where, even tho' we have no real garden, the buttercups, the broom, the forget-me-nots, and the daisies are set like gems among the grass and bright sorrel. Miss Yorke wants you to occupy the room that has access to the balcony, so that we shall have a little out-door sitting room when we want to be absolutely quiet, and there are writing places and things so that we can sit up there, indoors too, whenever we like. I shall bring down needle work ; and I am looking forward to reading and work together ; and it seems to me as if it would be so peaceful and so bright. Miss Yorke has specially planned this little separate place, because she knows how much you care for solitude, and how much I am looking forward to a quiet time with you. . . . I could bring you any or every meal you like. I hope to get the little carriage for some drives ; and I am counting the hours till you come. Still I know what a hermit you sometimes like to be.

. . . No dear Mama, I did not accept the post on the Commission.[1] Even if I could have done the work (and I had no special qualifications), there are others who can and will be pretty sure to do it ; and I could not have done it without losing some of the near inter-course with tenants and workers, and even with you all, which makes work go so very differently. I have so often in my life thought, in deciding about taking work, of Marion Earle's [2] words, when she leaves the work the fashionable people are asking for, and goes to nurse the bed-ridden comrade who is poor and out of sight,

> ".Let others miss me
> Never miss me, God."

I wrote a very careful letter, not a formal one, in reply, and have had the enclosed very nice answer.

---

[1] About Housing.   [2] In "Aurora Leigh."

Larksfield,
June 9th, 1889.

To HER MOTHER.

It is strange how that word "Society" is always used for that which is superficial and selfish, if not worse. I have not read Garibaldi's life, but one gets a vivid idea of it from Mrs. King's "Disciples."

Andy will tell you how busy I have been with references for Ossington. It is refreshing to come in contact with such happy-looking neat little homes. . . . I think a lark has built in our long grass; it returns so often to the same spot; and two wood pigeons frequent the place and perch on the small trees so prettily. The thistles are vigorous; every time I cut them I expect next time they will be weaker, but they are not; however, there are much more various things growing among them, each of which delights me.

14, Nottingham Place, W.
June 17th, 1889.

To HER MOTHER.

I put some heartsease in my dress, a thing I hardly ever do; but there came into my mind that bit from the Pilgrim's Progress when the shepherd hands it to the pilgrims, and says it grows so well in the Valley of Humility, and comes fresh from the king's hand every day, and that it increases by sharing. So, feeling a little low at having left you, I put some in my dress and Margy's brooch on, and sat down to write, a formidable pile of letters being before me. . . . I am glad to have heard the latter part of the beautiful life of Garibaldi.

Larksfield,
June 23rd, 1889.

To HER MOTHER.

Oh it is so lovely here! And it is so delightful
to watch what nature has done, now that she has taken
possession of the ground, what lovely and various
things she has set in it. I have been thinking how
you would rejoice in it all. There are wild roses in the
hedges, and many more foxgloves than last year; then
there are great beds of white clover, and patches of
golden lady's finger, and spaces of buttercup and poten-
tilla, and tall large heads of crimson clover; the pink
mallow is in bud; so is the sweet brier; but all these
and many more are set in great spaces of the loveliest
tall grass and sorrel, every colour from emerald green
thro' gold and silver and grey and orange, to deep
crimson and russet brown, gradating one into another,
and glowing as the wind bends the tufts of grass. . . .
I keep thinking how you would enjoy the wealth of
wild beauty all round; one just steps out of this
window and finds oneself on a sort of fraternal nearness
with tall grass and stately and lovely flower. Every
one that passes away this year I have wished you
could see.

July 6th, 1889.

To MR. SYDNEY COCKERELL.

You have chosen work which is not after your
own heart, rightly, I think; and I believe a great
blessing will be on it. I think it will give continuity
and reality to a life that might else have gone like so
many artists' lives into freaks and fancies, instead
of into practicable, serviceable work, glorified by imaginative thought, high ideals, and artistic joy; but having

chosen it, and the days in the main being not what
call out your full power, I hope you may have many
opportunities of real enjoyment ; and for this you will
need all spare power, seeing that you will, I know,
always be helping those nearest you very abundantly. . .

I quite feel what you say as to the duty of seeing
first to whatever grows naturally out of your own
work. It is certainly a first duty, and I should be very
wrong if, for the sake of retaining your help, I said
a word on the other side. You must discount anything I say with the thought that I may be unconsciously biassed. In fact I hesitate to give advice.
For I think you will probably feel your way to what is
right for you to do, with a true instinct. But as you
ask me, I will tell you one or two things that strike
me about it. I understand your letter to mean that
there are two kinds of work which might lead you to
give up Southwark. One is required for the conduct
and development of the business. On this clearly I
can give no opinion at all. So far as the Southwark
work interferes with due performance of this, clearly it
must be given up, and all one would want you to
remember is the importance of rightly estimating the
" due " ; for, first, it must be generously and liberally
estimated ; secondly it must be estimated with full care
of health ; and thirdly there is a something, small it
may be when one is young, but still a something, which
in every life may and should be given to the help of
the desolate people and districts out of one's beat or
outside one's work, which, rightly estimated, and
deliberately restricted, may be continued for years,
and tell by its continuity, and by the fact that the
donor has gained weight and power in other fields.

Then, secondly, I read your letter to mean that you

think such gift should be to your own employés, and those nearer you. There I am heartily with you; manifestly that is every man's first duty, and all the more so, because the coming in contact with them in business also tests the wisdom and truth of the work and its spirit. So that I should naturally have looked forward to that sphere, when the time comes. . . .

I purposely say nothing of how *very* much I should miss you. I do not like to think of it.

> 14, Nottingham Place.
> July 20th, 1889.

To Mr. Sydney Cockerell.

Miranda and I were delighted with the "Ballad-Monger," and very much interested to think of your pleasure in it. I think Gringoire very wonderful. That artist's nature, *alive* from head to heels; that exquisite appreciation of life full of joy, with the utter readiness to lay it down, which comes from holding things, as it were, loosely, because so much by the heart. It gave me a little the same feeling as St. Francis, against whom everything was powerless, because he was above pain, or loss, or death, or exile, or fear, and yet to whom every bird was a brother. The utter unselfishness and dignity of Gringoire was wonderful.

The King and Loyse were each beautiful in their way; the stillness of Loyse when she is, as it were, drawn to him, was very beautiful. We both have to thank you for a great pleasure.

> July 21st, 1889.

To her Mother.

I am probably going to Oxford on the 31st, to read a paper at the opening meeting of the University

Extension. . . . There will be 1,000 people; but I
understand them to break up into sections. I do not
know what audience I shall have. . . . (Then follows
an account of the " Ballad-Monger ") . . . I went to
Red X Hall yesterday, as the police band were to play.
. . . It was very nice to talk to the men, and see their
great delight in watching the growth of the trees and
creepers and plants. Last night I dined at Lambeth;
the Archbishop telegraphed to ask me. He is to speak
on the clause about children being employed in theatres,
in the House of Lords on Monday, and wanted to talk
it over. I had time to arm myself with a capital letter
from Miss Davenport Hill; and we had a very interesting, and I hope not useless, talk.

July 28th, 1889.

To HER MOTHER.

The great event of the week was the party at
Arthur's,[1] which was beautiful. The grounds and
gardens are lovely. . . . You will have heard of the
torrents of rain as we went to the station, but has anyone told you that the sunlight was quite exquisite all
the afternoon?—also that two waggons and two carriages
took, I should think, quite 100 people? No one is one
bit worse for the rain; they only seem to remember the
kindness and the beauty. . . . We have been making
progress towards securing the " Laundry " long desired
by Miss Yorke. . . . Two ladies interested in the neighbourhood have sent £200 to help the scheme forward.

Larksfield,
August 11th, 1889.

To MIRANDA.

I was *so* delighted to receive your sweet letter
to-day; and quite like a child in my delight at the

---

[1] House of her half-brother, Arthur Hill.

bags. They are pretty, and the letters exactly what I wanted. We pinned some paper ones on on Tuesday; and they all came off, to the great confusion of the money. Also these nice letters give a kind of individuality which I do like in a bag, or a cup, or anything I use.

Larksfield,
August 15th, 1889.

To Mr. S. Cockerell.

I have never thought. the world's regard, or money-success, or worldly surroundings worth anything; and, when they fall away from us, I think that it is often that they may leave us freer to enter into realities.

December 7th, 1889.

To Mr. S. Cockerell.

I return the valuable letter with many thanks to Olive and to you for letting me see it. I had not done so before. I think he is right about the forgiveness; and I think it *is* hard that any of you should expect a man, who had the place in the world that he had when he knew me as a girl of not fifteen years, should ask forgiveness. Not for a moment do I myself wish it, unless in any way it took away from him the sadness of the memory of what he did. I tell you, most distinctly, I do not think there is very much in the whole affair; that is, when the imperfections of earth and speech are taken away, I do not think that there will be very much to clear up between Mr. Ruskin and me. Till that time, touched as I am by your chivalrous kindness about it, I do seriously assure you I think a merciful silence is at once the best and the most dignified course, for him and me. What has the world to do with it, if we both feel silence all that is needed? There are things that nothing will ever put right in this world; and yet they don't really touch what is right for all worlds.

I say this for your sake, that you may feel at peace about it all; else nothing would make me say anything. Be at peace about it. I am. I hope Mr. Ruskin is. He may be. The thing is past, let us bury it; that which the earth will not cover, which is not of it, lives in the Eternal Kingdom; and in the thought of it earthly imperfection or mistakes seem very small things.

14, Nottingham Place,
December 29th, 1889.

To MARY HARRIS.

Thank you so very much for your loving letter. I was so very glad to have news of you. I can imagine what an interest the Home is with all its human work, now that books are more cut off from you than they were; and I like to think, too, that you will have many round you who love you and look to you.

I wonder what you thought of "Asolando." I have hardly read it all yet I fear it does not strike me, that it contains any poems on a level with his finest.

When I heard of Browning's death, in the thought of his rejoining her, I could not help remembering every word of the Epilogue to Fifine, which is very beautiful.

I wish you could hear Mr. Alford's sermons. No one, since Mr. Maurice, seems to me so abundantly well worth hearing.

I have taken charge of nine new blocks of buildings, within a stone's throw of this house. We are buying some of the worst houses that remain in Blank Court.

I am preparing to build in Southwark, besides all the old work. I have a grand band of workers ; but one has much to do for and with them.

14, Nottingham Place, W.
April 28th, 1889.

To HER MOTHER.

Miranda and I concocted a letter to the owners of some dreadful buildings in Southwark, which Miss J. is ready to undertake, asking to have them put under her care. So we have sent that off ; and it *may* bear fruit now or later. Then we finished the accounts of Gable Cottages, and despatched report of same. They are now complete ! Then I settled about the painting of Hereford Buildings. We had an evening's work over Income Tax returns. . . . To-morrow I collect in Deptford ; Miss Hogg is still away ; also Mr. T. is sending his manager to talk over matters with me. Then I have to go right up near Paddington to a Com. of the Women's University Settlement for Southwark. I hope much from the link with them, and the members interest me much. They are all very refined, highly cultivated (all, I fancy, have been at one of the Universities), and *very* young. I feel quite a veteran among them ; and they are so sweet and humble and keen to learn about the things out of their old line of experience. I much delight in thinking one may link their young life with the houses, and hall, and garden in Southwark.

It feels like home now Miranda is back again ; and it is wonderful to see the atmosphere of love and peace and duty she spreads round her. . . .

My horse-chestnut and one oak grow quite tall ; and all my ferns are in little rolls waiting for a little more

warmth and rain and time to uncurl; the children's
voices (but soft and as if far away) are singing hymns
in the school; the birds are chirping, and a quiet sense
of Sunday calm is over things.

December 4th, 1889.

To Miss M. Shaen.

We are busy as usual, and all goes with wonderful success—a sort of thorough, quiet, steady progress
and life that often amazes me. The great stir of strikes
and free dinners and huge gifts, the excitement of those
who feel as if action now alone were beginning, and as
if all had to be rearranged, replanted, as it were, before it
would grow, touches us little; and in the steady friendship of old days, and slow but definite improvement of
tangible things in a few places, work goes quietly
forward as the years roll on. We are helped, no doubt,
by the wave of right hearty sympathy and sincere
sense of duty now pervading the educated classes, and
largely helped; and from my heart I thank God for it.
But for the crude theories, I can only hope that many of
them will be exploded before they do real harm.

October 25th, 1889.

Miranda to Mary Harris.

The *Nineteenth Century* article brought Octavia
several offers of personal help—one which will be very
valuable, I think. Professor Tyndall sent her such a
nice letter, full of sympathy with her article, sending
her £10, and saying if he were younger he would have
offered personal help himself.

Octavia has had so many interviews and so much to
decide—a letter from Chief Commissioner about police,
interview with Ecclesiastical Commissioners' man of

business about land for more cottages near Red Cross, which she *much* hopes to get; interview with Lord Rowton about some housing scheme; besides the Red Cross entertainments beginning next week, which all want arranging for. I am glad to say that she has handed over to me a good deal of the correspondence.

November 12th, 1889.

To HER MOTHER.

I thought you would be glad to know that I had a *most* satisfactory interview with Mr. De Bock Porter, who represents the Ecclesiastical Commissioners. Times are indeed changed! I saw him about what I call White Cross Cottages; and I think they will meet me most kindly about it. It will be very delightful if I can get six cottages there. It will widen the passage, preserve light and sight of sky in the garden, make the approach to the hall by night much better, besides providing six more pleasant homes for people near the garden. I am so very happy about it! I also had a very useful talk about the whole estate.

Larksfield,
September 15th, 1889.

To HER MOTHER.

I am very much interested about my Southwark building, which is progressing well; think of having twenty more such cottages as Red Cross ones! Our working men are so happy about the arrangements for the "Pilgrim's Progress."[1] Each of them will have fifty tickets to give away. They are also very busy and important with the various things with which they can help. It is very pretty and cheering to see them.

[1] Acted by George MacDonald and his family.

14, Nottingham Place, W.,
June 29th, 1889.

TO HER MOTHER.

. . . It is time for closing the books for the half-year ; and I have been, therefore, specially busy this week, but I hope now we are through the worst of it. On Monday I went to poor Deptford. Lady Maud is doing beautifully ; and it is pleasant to follow Miss Hogg's good work, but poor Miss —— seems to have done badly indeed. I hardly knew to what a miserable extent she depended on me. It is very unfortunate. On Tuesday we had our first Ossington collection. In the afternoon I went to the University Settlement meeting. They had borrowed Red Cross Hall. It was a sad meeting . . . but I hope now *that* difficulty is over. Mr. Loch came and spoke beautifully, striking the right note, and pointing out the practical question before the meeting. They *all* responded except Miss ——. It was a splendid body of women, young, thoughtful, refined, and earnest, and looking so pretty. The head of Lady Margaret's Hall, Miss Wordsworth, was there ; and Mrs. H. Sidgwick and FitzJames Stephen's daughter spoke so well. . . . The Lochs had never seen the Hall, Garden and Cottages before, and were so delighted. After the meeting we had tea and talk. Miss Gladstone was there and very friendly. It all kept me so late there that I saw the garden in its evening fullness ; all the people seemed enjoying it.

CHAPTER X

1890—1902

THIS period, while including great developments in the movements in which Octavia was specially interested, was also marked by public discussions, which greatly affected her work. She was much interested in the controversy between General Booth and the Charity Organisation Society, about the General's huge scheme of centralised, and despotically managed, relief; and in this, as in so many other matters, she warmly approved of the efforts of Mr. Loch, Secretary of the C.O.S., to produce wiser views of administration of charity.[1] The same friend also assisted her in discussions with the poorer municipal voters, on the best method of distributing the payment of rates between landlord and tenant, and the most economical method of providing houses for the poor.

This time was also marked by another of the many proofs of Octavia's desire to connect her interest in art with her efforts for moral and physical progress. The fine hall in Red Cross Garden, was used by the neighbourhood for entertainments; and, on Sundays, very good music was performed there by numerous friends, to large gatherings of the people. Among other friends, who helped, was Mrs. Julian Marshall, who

---

[1] Mr. Loch, on his part, was impressed with her way of seizing the point that was "eternally important," and he has, since her death, expressed a wish to use the influence of the C O S in the direction of those more positive reforms in which she was specially engaged in Notting Hill.

trained a band of Southwark boys to play in the Hall. It was now proposed that the walls of the Hall should be decorated with representations of peaceful heroism, and Mrs Russell Barrington enlisted Walter Crane's help in the matter, who most generously designed the pictures The first of these was that of Alice Ayres the servant girl, represented in the act of rescuing children from a fire in Southwark. Her connection with the neighbourhood greatly interested the tenants.

In 1898, Octavia was much encouraged by the growth of appreciation felt for her work, which was shown by the presentation to her of her portrait painted by Sargent.[1] A large number of friends had subscribed for this; and, at the presentation, Mr. Loch was the spokesman. Some of her words in answer will be quoted at the conclusion of this book. She was much touched by this proof of affection ; and the large gathering of friends included those who had known and worked with her for years, and the descendants of others.

But, important as were the developments in her work in the houses, perhaps the most notable of all the events of this period was connected with the Open Space movement. By the efforts of Sir Robert Hunter and other friends, " The National Trust for Preserving Places of Natural Beauty and of Historic Interest," was founded, which undertook to buy or accept from donors places described by the above title, and to care for and manage them for the people. And Canon Rawnsley became Hon. Secretary.

A special outcome of this movement, in which Octavia was much interested, ought to be particularly noticed; the acquisi- on of places in the Lake district, secured partly on account of their beauty, and partly to provide access to the lakes, for the general public.

A different kind of open space, in a very different neighbourhood, was the " Postman's Park "—a recreation ground secured near the General Post Office, where deeds of heroism are recorded by Watts, though without the addition of such pictures of the heroes as were painted in Red Cross Hall. This time saw the band of foreign imitators of Octavia's work

---

[1] This portrait was left by Octavia to the National Portrait Gallery.

OCTAVIA HILL.

From an Oil Painting by Sargent.   Presented to her in 1898.

notably increased, by the visit to England of Dutch ladies, who
formed warm friendships with Octavia, and who have shown in
Holland such excellent results of the training which they
received.

190, Marylebone Road,[1]
1890.

To HER MOTHER.

. . . All goes well with us here.   My room has
been our last household pleasure.   It has turned out so
pretty ; and I am so astonished because it was the room
where all the leavings naturally gravitated.   But you
know it has a pretty bow like the back drawing-room ;
and my one extravagance has been a very nice brass
curtain rod.   On this, with large curtain rings which
draw easily, we have hung the curtains which Minnie
gave,—crimson—and they look so bright in the western
sun, and so snug when drawn at night. ·Then I have
my writing-table in the bow, and my pretty dark book-
case, and the old drawing-room carpet from Nottingham
Place, which looks quite handsome, as good things do.
My photographs group themselves prettily on the walls ;
and altogether it is very nice. . . .

January 19th, 1890.

To HER MOTHER.

One feels that the more intercourse with honest,
truthful people they [2] can have the better ; and that our
work, when least it shows outward progress, has this of
value—that there are, in and out among them, those
who are trying to fulfil at least the ordinary daily
duties of life, as in God's sight.   I am myself a little

---

[1] The house to which they moved after school was given up.
[2] The tenants in the Deptford courts.

cheered about the place just now; and, of course, looking to Miss Chase's return to them with hope. She has so very much human sympathy, and feels, thro' all their faults, so instinctively down to all that is human and good; never palliates their wrong, but loves them in spite of it, and clings to the good in them.

14, Nottingham Place,
February 27th, 1890.

I hope I shall manage to take care of myself, and not give you all trouble again by any stupidity. It is much more easy to be obedient than discreet.

March 18th, 1890.

To HER MOTHER.

Deptford went quite wonderfully yesterday. I do think it begins to improve. Miss Chase's joy in it is refreshing, and also contagious; and she always tells one nice things about the people. Ossington too went well to-day. I had a large group of workers. . . . Each took a staircase, and came back to report to me. I had time to see and help each.

March 23rd, 1890.

To MR. SYDNEY COCKERELL.

I am extremely sorry if any words of mine have tended to intensify any dissatisfaction you may feel with your work in life. . . . When work is good in its object, as merchant's work must be, is it not pretty sure that a good man, whose path has led him straight into the thick of it, seeing its abuses and temptations, has a distinct calling? The difficulties are the foundation of the triumph. The world is all

full of them. We grope about, and seem hardly to
see our way ; but if honestly, moment by moment, we
do as much as we see, somehow the place is better for
our presence ; and in the long years, looking back, we
find we have been led on by paths we did not see,
towards ends we hardly dreamed of reaching. Some
men sit down in their studies, and imagine a world all
different, or speculate as to whether, if they turned it
all upside down, selfishness would not vanish because
comfort had come. We don't know what this world
would be if it were altered ; but we do know how God has
given it to us ; whom He has put near us ; where He
has called us ; what power He has given us. . . . I do
not believe in this God's earth there can be a place
where right is impossible. If it is difficult, the more
glory is there in very humbly, very steadily, leading a
forlorn hope. . . . Remember there is a Truth of
things, as well as of *words*. Our words are indeed
feeble exponents of Truth ; but, whatever fact we meet
in life, *that* is God's own permitted Fact or Truth,
possibly not eternal, but meant for us to accept or to
resist ; but always to deal with, for which effort He
gives strength.

June 4th, 1890.

To Mr. Sydney Cockerell.

Thank you for reminding me about the Brier
Rose. Six of us have been to see it at different times,
all thanks to you. The colour is, indeed, wonderful,
and the vision complete ; and, if there is wanting a
certain strenuous life about it, it is unfair, perhaps, to
look for that in a fairy tale. As allegory, I seem to
miss the energy of life and thought ; but, then, the
beauty of colour !

June 27th, 1890.

To Sydney Cockerell.

I enclose tickets for the opening of the lawn. I send those for Fawcett House for Mrs. Cockerell and Olive. They would there see the general view of things, and the Royal party would pass quite close. . . . I most earnestly hope that you will be able to help us as steward; we shall sorely need reliable ones. I am much distressed that, in spite of almost superhuman efforts, I seem unable to escape being taken up by the necessity of " receiving," and so shall not be free to rush where need may be to see how all goes, and so shall need much to have *really trustworthy* fellow-workers, who will stay where they are asked, and can be trusted really to give signals to those who have to perform any part of the little ceremony.

June 20th, 1890.

To her Mother.

Re the opening of the lawn.

I am to see Sir F. Knowles, who represents the Prince, for final settlement of programme on Monday at 2 30 o'clock; and, after that, we have a committee, and I hope much will get definitely settled and communicable; and *that* I may send to the printers. Next week I have a series of interviews on the ground with the builders, vestry, workmen, police, volunteers, band, and guard, etc. Thursday, a committee to settle distribution of tickets, and after that we shall despatch them. The week following we must get to more detailed decisions as to individuals and their duties, and see the execution of what the corporate bodies plan. . . .

Larksfield,
July 9th, 1890.

MRS. HILL TO MRS. EDMUND MAURICE.

Princess Louise and the Prince and Princess of Wales were *delighted* and thoroughly at one with the people. The Prince of Wales was about to enter his carriage, when he bethought him of returning and making his way through the crowd and seeking out Lester to shake hands with him. . . . Octavia was delighted with the workmen. She says it was entirely due to them that the order was so good. Miss Chase was most sprightly and full of delight with the fun. Miranda in the house . . . was a most happy and useful hostess. Mr. K. and A. were most complimentary to Octavia as to the arrangements. She says they have taken three weeks' " hard work ; " and *her* " hard work " means something. . . . I do rejoice that our Royal family use their great position as they do.

Crockham,
August 14th, 1890.

OCTAVIA TO MRS. EDMUND MAURICE.

We went to see the Poors' Land at Bethnal Green on Tuesday. You know it was left to trustees 200 years ago with an emphatic clause prohibiting all building. It has been let to a lunatic asylum built on adjoining land, which has used it for a huge garden, six-and-a-half acres. The authorities there are *strong* against the proposed building. . . . We went to Oxford House the same day to meet some members of the Poors' Land Committee. They showed us a workmen's club there, numbering 600 members, to which is

attached a co-operative store, doing £10,000 a year
business. It is all under the wing of Mr. and Mrs. B.,
who used to go backwards and forwards from Hampstead
to work, but now have taken a large old house
adjoining the club, and live there entirely. . . .
They have a sacred-looking little chapel, where they
have family prayers, which opens from their house and
from the club, so that any who like can join. They say
few do ; " but they know there is prayer going up for
them in all their troubles, and in what strength and
hope we work." . . . At night we went to Bethnal
Green to be present at a meeting of the local committee.
They met in the first floor room over a cheesemonger's
shop, the cheesemonger being himself one of the
trustees. The committee was all composed of tradesmen of the neighbourhood, except that there was one
very young but very capable lawyer from Oxford House.
Then there was a negro, who, they say, has been most
helpful. He has a wonderful gift of oratory, and has
addressed numbers of open-air meetings. It was a
strange and interesting sight, but oh ! so difficult to get
any business done, tho' they were all very zealous
and touchingly eager to do all which would enable us
to take up the matter. Then yesterday, by way of
contrast, we drove over to a farm . . . to see Mr.
S , who, we heard, would give us information we wanted
to record by way of protection for (a) common. He is
said to have fought in old days for common rights. . . .
He was a very fine, upright, noble-looking man, and
spoke out in a quiet, independent way. The table
cloth was laid, and I saw neatly marked in red marking
cotton on it E . . . S . . . 1822 ; and one felt the
care bestowed, and the dignity, by the continuity, of
the life.

September 1st, 1890.

To Mrs. Edmund Maurice.

. . . Everyone has been so very loving and helpful that indeed I have had a sense of blessing about the time. . . . Nor was I much concerned about the Queen St. matter,[1] except that I could not take it on my own shoulders from dear Miss Chase. I know how little such things mean, and how real a blessing the quiet people feel in our rule; they dare not but pretend sympathy at the moment, but in their hearts they are thankful. We had a *perfectly* calm day to-day; everyone specially bright and friendly to Miss Chase. Mrs. W.[2] got tea ready for her, she says, on Thursday, but dare not offer it in the street; she meant to send it to the station, but thought Charlotte would be tracked. Miss Chase was as bright as a sunbeam; and all seems as past as if it were a century ago. . . . I hear two of the White Cross cottages are let, tho' they are not finished. I am so glad. I was a little nervous, because Miss I. says the street is such a difficulty.

September 10th, 1890.

To Rev. Ingham Brooke.

I cannot defer writing to tell you how entirely and heartily I hope that a very happy and full and noble life may be opening out for you both. I have not the pleasure of knowing Miss Wallick, but I trust she is all you deserve; and, if she be, she must be good indeed. As to sacrifice, I don't know; perhaps there is no great good possible without it; but what one feels is the immensely deeper meaning and joy which comes,

---

[1] The violent behaviour of the tenants at Deptford.

[2] One of the most respectable tenants.

when, as Ruskin says, one gets the equality " not of likeness," but of giving and receiving; the souls that are unlike, and the nations that are unlike, and the natures that are unlike, each receiving something from, and of, the other's gifts and the other's glory. And of such interchange all noble love has much.

That a great new gift has come to you, all your friends will greatly rejoice. You, who have done so abundantly much for the poor, you who have thought so little of self, best of all seem to deserve such graciousness of blessing as a wife will be. I am so very, very glad, and earnestly hope all good things for you both. . . . Whatever change it makes in the work, in which you have been the main stay, indeed which you alone have made possible, I trust you know that I shall feel it all right. Such changes ought to come; you have worked long and hard; and, wherever you are, you will work; but, besides this, all we are working for is to make individual life noble, homes happy, and family life good; and so all foundation of noble married life is a gain to what we are working for, tho' our small schemes of philanthropy may crumble away. . . .

The deep affections which gather round places, and the immense power for good among men which their knowledge and love of us give, make me often feel that the continuity of work in one place *is* a great blessing and duty.

November 12th, 1890.

MIRANDA TO MRS. DURRANT.

You are right in thinking that we want to settle quite near our present house on account of work and nearness to Hampstead too. We have found a house that we very much like in the Marylebone Road. It is smaller than this, and with much smaller rooms; but it is quiet, light, and cheerful (having its chief rooms with a south aspect), and cheap. It is also not a great risk, as we shall take it by the year—at any rate till we know how we like it. It has a garden in front—and a yard behind—to our great delight; a little light space and *quiet* being our chief requirements. The Marylebone Road used to be noisy; but now it has a wooden pavement, a great boon. There will be room for Octavia and me with Miss Yorke and two of the friends now living with us, Miss Pearson and Miss Sim. It would be a great sorrow to part with them; so we are thankful to get a house large enough for us all.

Octavia's work is so wide and many-sided, and she is so large-hearted and wise in giving all her fellow workers leave to work in their own way, that she often hands a little domain over to me to work in my own way. So there is no sense of not carrying out my own ideas.

14, Nottingham Place,
November 22nd, 1890.

Octavia to Mr. S. Cockerell.

I have never really thanked you for sending me Booth's book. They are all reading it with interest. I believe I shall do so, some day, if we may keep it so long; but I prefer "Old's News," like a true disciple of Ruskin's, and would rather read it when the fuss is a little over. I know in my heart of hearts, what I think; and *that* is that it all depends on the spiritual and personal power; and *that* we must measure, if at all, in the courts, rather than in the book. But the book would interpret at least the aim. So, thank you much.

December 30th, 1890.

To THE SAME.

Thank you so very much for sending me " The Dream of John Ball." I began reading it yesterday, but have not had time to get very far in it. Still I hope to do so soon, and send you many heartiest thanks for your kindness in thus sending it to me.

I have to thank you for such thoughtful and powerful help in the past year, I hardly know how to begin. I only hope that the conduct of our business which now falls on you, and so much of the help at the Hall, is not weighing too heavily on you, or curtailing too much your time for refreshing change   You must be sure to tell me if it does. I shall try hard to supplement ; and I think, with all our work in Southwark developing as it is, we ought to reinforce there ; but, in any way, it is the greatest blessing to have such strong, careful help.

Larksfield,
February 1st, 1891.

To THE SAME.

I should certainly think that it would be right to retain statement that the Churn articles appeared in C.O.S Review. It is only courteous and truthful. There is a tendency to accept the help of C.O S., and then to avoid identifying ourselves with it, which I, most of all, should be careful to avoid.

When they give us a lift, we must be most careful to help an heroic and unpopular body, by, at least, having the grace to state the facts.

February 17th, 1891.

To THE SAME.

Miranda was much better on Friday, and ventured to the play. We both enjoyed it greatly.

It is very pretty. Helen's character beautifully imagined, and Maud very natural and cheerful. We thought of you with gratitude.

Larksfield, Crockham Hill, Edenbridge, Kent,
August 21st, 1891.

To Mr. Sydney Cockerell.

Thank you for Morris's pamphlet. I read it all with interest. There are some parts in it that I should like to talk over with you. I felt the *practical* part *very* poor. I also think the miseries of the middle ages slurred over in a marvellous manner! That doesn't much matter practically; but it gives the sense of a crooked way of looking at things. On the other hand I felt heartily one with the author in his longing to better things, and tried hard to see if he threw any fresh light. In fact I thought the *aim* of the book helpful, but nothing else.

Larksfield, Crockham Hill,
Edenbridge, Kent,
April 20th, 1891.

To Mr. Sydney Cockerell.

Miss Sewell, the future head of the (Southwark) Settlement proposes to arrange four lectures on Civic Duty, Socialism, etc., by Mr. Bernard Bosanquet (whose name I daresay you know), in Southwark, to which the Settlement might invite their various associates, workers, and friends. They would have tea and coffee, and a little informal talk afterwards. I think it an excellent plan, and that it would greatly tend to bring the whole body of members and friends together and to work. They asked about the Hall; and it seemed to me that for such an object (which is practically starting good work in Southwark), especially as it is in the afternoon, we ought to lend it freely.

April 26th, 1891.

AS TO CADET CORPS.

The only duty I have is to remind all who can judge that our object is to train good, useful, and healthy men, capable of becoming volunteers ; but that we are pledged, by our own lives and convictions, and by the trust reposed in us by others, not to weigh for a moment military training against good, natural, healthy influences. Having said this, and I say it here in this letter, I have said all I know ; and I am quite happy to leave the decision to the Committees.

June 21st, 1891.

TO MR. SYDNEY COCKERELL.

I am really grieved at what you say. I can imagine the "push" may be very distasteful ; but the decision I should have thought would have been there, and *all* good ; and one hoped such clear power of business as you have, combined with other gifts, would have done instead of "push" even in this age.

I remember a great actress, acting Shakespeare to an untrained audience, being asked how it was they were so silently attentive ; and she said, "When they shout 'louder' from the gallery, I lower my voice." I always remembered that story. I can't help clinging on to the hope of the possible success of useful business, with all its manifold training, bringing one into touch with things, and the high ideals. But we shall see.

July 19th.

Far be it from me to say one word against any decision to stick to business. You know how much I honour it, and feel it worth sacrifices; and, somehow, its regular duties seem to give ballast to characters. . . . We shall miss you at Erleigh.

190, Marylebone Road,
December 29th, 1891.

To Miss Harris.

We have just parted from our Christmas party of dear ones. Mama, Minnie, Edmund, and Florence left yesterday, and Margy [1] on Sunday. Miranda and I are settling in to our usual *most* interesting daily work again, in this new home, which is becoming very dear.

> "As catching up to-day and yesterday
> In a perfect chord of love."

I wish thou had'st ever seen it. Perhaps, when spring time comes again, thou may'st come. Larksfield, too, would interest thee; and thou would'st find it grown, I think.

March 31st, 1892.

To Sydney Cockerell.

I am more and more delighted with the exquisite book. It is indeed lovely. My sister Florence and many others have been rejoicing in its beauty. I have been rejoicing in its beauty. I have only read the preface straight through once. I do not think it strikes me as necessarily very revolutionary, tho' I can

---

[1] Mrs. Whelpdale, Octavia's half-sister

believe some people might think the aim that Morris
sets before us can only be obtained by revolution. I do
not think this, and did not notice that he says so.
What struck me was not that it was revolutionary, but
that I did not feel that it was very true. There are
people to whom Art is a *very* great joy, and to whom
pleasure in making lovely things is great; and one
could believe the number might and should increase,
and the joy increase. But I think there are, and may
rightly be thousands, the main work of whose days may
be some little or even great effort, and their work be
joyful rather in its result than in its doing; and that
this effort is a natural and right discipline. The joy of
many, by far the greatest, is the home joy which
glorifies and gladdens the daily work. And this I may
say without forgetting the blessing of all natural and
created beauty; without wishing to explain away the
undue sadness, and unhealthy conditions of much
modern work. Only I think Morris over-estimates the
sorrow for most men.

Perhaps few but Cambridge men will remember the joke
referred to in the following letter. Doctor Thompson, of
Trinity, said of a young Fellow whose action on a certain
occasion he had resented, that "the time which he could spare
from the adornment of his person he devoted to a conscientious
neglect of his duties"

> Larksfield, Crockham Hill,
> April 11th, 1892.

MY DEAREST MIRANDA.

I fear you must think me very neglectful, but I
really seem to have my time very full. You see, there
is all "the time I spend in the neglect of my duties,"
to say nothing of the rest. You will not suspect me of

devoting much to " the adornment of my person ; " but I *have* ordered a new hat and dress.

Mr. Mocatta came in on Friday, and so did Miss Astley and a friend.   Mr. Mocatta gave a very interesting account of the Jews' expulsion, and what they are doing. . . . He says that they are mainly descendants of the Jews, who were spoiled by the Crusaders ; and that they found themselves obliged to migrate from the whole line of march of the Crusaders, and settled in Poland. . . .   There they lived in peace till the partition of Poland.   Then the Russians restricted them to the " pale," which was large, all towns, no villages or country.   Certain people, university graduates, retired soldiers, etc., might " live out of the pale," and gradually others did so also, by bribing police or escaping notice. . . Then lately the old laws were enforced, and people, who for forty or fifty years have lived elsewhere, were all ordered back to the pale.   He says they all want to get to America, and used to come to England hoping to be helped further.

He spoke, with great approbation, of Baron Hirsch's scheme.   He has a vast tract in the Argentine Republic —lovely climate and fertile soil ; but it must take a year to get ready.

Larksfield,
April 15th, 1892.

(Re HILLY FIELDS ?)

To MIRANDA.

You ask about the House of Commons,   My evidence went all right.   I think I scored ; but I felt from the first it was no use, and they considered that they could not go into the question on what I call its important grounds.   Having passed the second reading,

they could not alter the matter so much in principle. They only really heard me as to access to the
Park for the poor, and a few other things. It was
rather interesting to see the crowded Committee room,
and the row of wigged lawyers, and the small Committee, and to hear the evidence and cross-examination.

April, 1892.

To MIRANDA.

We went to a wonderfully beautiful exhibition
of pictures at Guildhall. There is a very beautiful
Burne Jones, "The Wheel of Fortune." Of course
Fortune is blind, but it is really grand. Also " Love
among the Ruins "; very lovely—the woman's face
really so, and the colour exquisite.

I hope we may get the Bell St. freehold. It would
be a great relief.

Larksfield,
August 12th, 1892.

To MIRANDA.

We had a delightful day yesterday at Lady
Pollock's with a party from Southwark. We had refreshing drives in waggonettes, dinner and tea out of
doors, uninterrupted sunshine, and the greatest kindness. At the station Hallam Tennyson came up and
reintroduced himself; he was so kind and friendly, and
invited me to luncheon there, saying that his father
would be so very glad if I would go. I am to write to
him to fix a day.

Larksfield,
September 4th, 1892.

To HER MOTHER.

. . . . I went to Tennyson's on Monday. Mrs.
Hunter sent me over. It was an exquisite drive over

the spur of Blackdown, among the heather, and with
the loveliest views on each side towards promontory of
hill beyond hill descending to the plain. Then, through
a long quiet lane arched with trees, reminding me somewhat of lanes in the Isle of Wight ; then out again on
to the open heath, and then into Tennyson's grounds.
The house . . . is not interesting ; it stands among
terraces set with great evergreens standing rather like
cypress at the Pitti ; between them the blue distance of
valley and hill. Lady Tennyson was very kind, and
looked as spiritual and full of heart as ever. Lord
Tennyson and I had some talk before luncheon, but
nothing of any real interest ; at lunch some Americans
arrived, and the lady was next to him, and I on
Hallam's right, so I got no talk, and after luncheon
he was tired. So far as he was concerned, it was dis-
appointing. But they were all *most* kind, begged me
to go again ; and I felt as if I had got a real glimpse of
the home. Young Mrs. Tennyson was charming, and I
had a quite delightful afternoon with her. She showed
me a set of large beautiful photographs of the
characters in the " Foresters," which has been acted
in America. She has a large room, with a balcony,
and a lovely view at the top of the house near her
children. . . . Lady Sophia Palmer has asked me to
go to them next Sunday to meet the Bishop of London
and Mrs. Temple, and Jowett, but I am not going.
The Hooles are coming here.

Dear Miranda is so sweet ; we read Dante all three
together, which is very interesting. . . .

I am going to try to avoid going up to town
next week. I seem to long for a little time of quiet ;
and ten days here would be so restful. We shall
see.

December 7th, 1892.

To Miss Harris.

My own dearest Mary,

Thy beautiful letter arrived duly, and was the greatest joy to me. Thanks and blessings on thee for it ! I don't ever feel it easy, of late years, to say anything except about practical things, but thou knowest how incessantly my thoughts fly back to thee, not only now, but as thou ever wert to me in the old, old days.

I have just finished rough draft of *very* dull article for *Nineteenth Century*, also marking map of footpath for Quarter Sessions.

I am sending off Alessandri's lovely Venetian work to the Arundel, after which I hope to send it to Mary Harrison, and I hope thou wilt see it. I am sure thou wilt delight in the beautiful Doge. He lies before me now, so still and grand.

1893.

Letter to Fellow-Workers.

I came down to breakfast one morning and found on my table a letter from Mrs. Russell Gurney, whom I had not seen for many years, saying she had left to me in her will a block of model dwellings, which she and her husband had built years before, but that she would like me to take it now. The gift went right to my heart, and I was delighted But I asked her to make it a trust, and she kindly consented to let it be added to the trust.

This refers to some small freehold houses given by Mrs. Scrase Dickins to be held in trust by Lord Wolmer, Miss Johnson, and Octavia, on the understanding that the interest accruing from the gift should be devoted to some good object.

July 22nd, 1893.

FROM MIRANDA TO MARY HARRIS

We have had a very busy time. Our Southwark Flower Show, the first held at Red Cross Garden, was a great success. We found the plants grown by the poor people much healthier than we had dared to hope in such an atmosphere. Great interest was felt by the poor people; and they seem to feel encouraged; and many more intend to exhibit next year. The scene was very pretty, the garden decorated with flags, and little tables with tea under the balcony where people sat, as in a foreign town. There were two bands, one of them the Southwark Cadets; and the scene was enlivened by their bright coats. The plants were under cover in the hall. Out of doors the people danced Sir Roger de Coverley to the music of the band. Octavia is busy with plans for new cottages. We are so glad that the Ecclesiastical Commissioners are interesting themselves to build such. They have consulted her about plans.

May 17th, 1893.

To MISS OLIVE COCKERELL.

DEAREST OLIVE.

If I don't see you before you start, be sure my love and blessings go with you out into the strange, new world.[1] I hope you will be very happy, and that the lifting of the horizon, which is such a joy to the young, and to those who, as they grow older, still keep the child heart, may be a great refreshment. You leave behind you so much love, and a year so soon slips over,

[1] South America

that I hope the sense in parting will be almost all of gain
and hope.

> I am, dearest Olive,
> Your loving Godmother,
> OCTAVIA HILL.

June 18th, 1893.

MIRANDA TO MRS. DURRANT.

Lord Aberdare is Chairman of the Royal Commission on Pensions for the Aged Poor, before which
Octavia gave evidence last week.   He had been abroad,
and so was not present when she gave evidence ; but he
said playfully he hoped they had treated her properly
in his absence, and said that Chamberlain had " acknowledged himself vanquished."   Octavia had to answer
some rather catchy questions from him ; but her clear,
cool head enabled her to come out with triumph.   One
of the Commissioners afterwards laughed and said to
her privately, " How well you tackled Joe ! " and " You
did stand up to Joe ! " with great wonder and glee.
Octavia said to Lord Aberdare that the Commissioners
had made long statements of *their* views, and had asked
her whether she agreed with these, and that it was
rather difficult to follow and to reply.

November 22nd, 1893.

OCTAVIA TO SYDNEY COCKERELL.

I am returning, with many thanks, " Ruskin's
Life."   It is, even to me, wonderful reading, when one
gets a sort of living impression of the whole, by reading
it thro'.   One or two of the apparent failures brought
tears to my eyes, and the memory of the words,—

" If he strained too wide,
   It was not to take honour, but give help ;
   The gesture was heroic. If his hand
   Accomplishing nothing . . . (well it is proved)
   That empty hand thrown impotently out
   Were sooner caught, I think, by One in heaven,
   Than may a hand that reaped a harvest in,
   And kept the scythe's glow on it."

Then, when one thinks of what the world was in his early days, and what it is now, and what his share in its attainment of higher ideals and simpler life, one realises something of what he has achieved.

The picture of the Brantwood life was, to me, specially charming. Some of the book was, as you will know, exquisitely painful. But I cling on to greater confidence in silence than in words. The chasms and ruins of tempest and earthquake are healed best by the quiet growth of all that is lovely and gentle ; but Time is needed. Time, and to be let alone.

November 22nd, 1893.

To Ellen Chase.

. . . Queen Street goes wonderfully. Miss Gee does wonders there. I have been collecting on your side, and greatly do I enjoy it. I have with me, usually, there a charming young lady, Miss Ter Meulen from Amsterdam, who is spending a few months in England, to prepare for taking up houses in her own country. She is full of power, brightness, and sweet human sympathy. Mrs. C. is clear, never missed a 6d., as she promised you, *very* righteous and grand now ; the home looks very happy and comfortable. Mrs. L. is taking pattern by her, is paying 3d., without fail, but still has £2 7s. 0d. to clear. Poor Mrs. M. met with bad accident, a barrel from a dray fell on her, and she has been in bed for weeks; but M. says with a real loving smile, " I shall have her about again by Xmas." C. is out of work! Maria C. is as responsible and satisfactory as ever. Her influence tells at home; the place is a pattern of neatness. Bridget C. is married; at first I thought the others were going to the dogs without her, and her husband wouldn't let her live in the street; but we had one row with old C., conquered him, and began on sound footing. . . .

Thank you *very* much for report of Public Reservations. It is *most* useful. Mr. Rawnsley has taken up the idea of a similar trust; we are getting it up, and had a first meeting this month Forty-one acres of Hilly Fields are really bought; the four acres of Glebe still hang fire. I am invited to unveiling of Lowell's Memorial at the Abbey on Tuesday; I should like to go, but it is just in the heart of Southwark work. Can I go ?

December 7th, 1893.

To Miss Harris.

How very, very long it is since we met ! but how the memory of all the love of years abides and grows ! . . . It was a very holy and quiet birthday; just at Mr. Alford's church, with Mama and the beloved Hampstead circle. Miranda and Mama wrote me lovely poems with their presents, and flowers poured in; but they were just from the near circle, or very old friends. . . . I had arranged not to go to Red Cross in order to go to Mama. . . .

Hast thou seen Lowell's letters ? They are full of fun, but with a great vein of tenderest pathos too.

190 Marylebone Road,
December 10th, 1893.

MIRANDA TO MRS. DURRANT.

Octavia gave evidence the other day before a
Committee on the subject of the Unemployed. She is
strongly against exceptional measures. She was ex-
amined for an hour and a quarter, and her friends on
the Committee note that her evidence did good. It
took us nearly six hours to correct the proofs of her
evidence.

190 Marylebone Road, N.W.,
February 10th, 1894.

OCTAVIA TO MISS SHAEN.

What you say about work with me makes me
very longing. But, dearest Maggie, I would be the
last to say a word to urge you to strain to do what
would risk your health. It is such a blessing that
you are back among your friends. Only don't forget
me, and let less scrupulous friends press you in, and
make me lose you, if even you can do more, and might
have come to me. What I have always thought that
I should like best of all—what would have seemed to
me to have opened up the maximum of help with the
minimum of exertion,—what would have brought us
together, and would have given us the benefit of your
judgment and sympathy in most useful manner, would
have been to let us elect you on the Women's University
Settlement Committee. It meets only once a month.
Miss Sewell brings up the work in a quite perfect way ;
and, thro' her, one comes into touch with that second
stage of life—the one of helping others—which opens
out to so many Girton, Newnham, and other girls in

M M

this age of service. Your presence among us would be the greatest help.

But, as I say, my most earnest desire is to stand aside, and not by word, look, or deed press you, till you feel able. Indeed, one knows how little one can plan for another. Ways we know little of open for our friends, and lead to better things than our most loving and longing thoughts can imagine.

Viterbo,
April 6th, 1894.

To her Mother.

Here we are, in the quaintest city. It is called the Nuremberg of Italy, and is full of marvellous doorways, fountains, outside staircases, and towers. It is entirely surrounded by walls. The foundations are Etruscan. The people come riding in from the country on mules, with trousers of goat or sheepskin with the hair on, and leather at the back where the saddle would wear it. They have hugely long sticks for whips, and look wild and far-away. . . . Florence would delight in the great cavern-like looking shops, with the people at work in them, and in the streets; and everything goes on out of doors, and the workman makes and sells his own goods at home. We see several hand-looms in the streets. We have been to the Cathedral, and the Council Chamber adjoining, the roof of which fell on its proud builder and killed him, and which has stood roofless for some two or three hundred years. A monk was awakened from a vision in which he saw a black man, who was the devil, striking the wall. First he called the people to help the pope, who had built the chamber; but then he cried out that it was too late—the pope was dead. We go on to-morrow to Narni, and on Monday to Terni. We have here a large vaulted bedroom, about three times the size of the drawing-room at Nottingham Place, with three great doors draped with curtains, a marble floor, and large window looking into the Piazza de Rocca. A great fountain plays therein, and across it pass the soldiers, the monks in procession, the country people coming in by the Fiorentino Gate of the city. It is somewhat like a huge cave at night with two candles; but most Italian by day.

Your affectionate daughter,
OCTAVIA.

Hotel Europa, Terni,
April 10th, 1894.

To HER MOTHER.

. . . We have just come down from Amelia. It is one of the oldest cities in Italy, much older than Rome. There is, however, nothing left of the very old times, except the huge stones of its walls. One can well see how strong it must have been. The river folds round its base almost in a circle; and the deep ravine goes all round, and is set with colossal crags. It is a picturesque place; and, living as we did opposite its gate, we saw all the life which assembled there. Viterbo was much fuller, of course, of artistic and historic treasures; but it was sad to hear of the country being so rough. M. Shaen's friend, a Mr. Fisher, who has travelled about much, and collected such lovely things, was kind enough to make enquiries for us of various people. They say the brigandage is extinct, but the country quite unsafe. One proprietor there pays blackmail to two wild sorts of outlaws, and they keep off others! The professor, who superintends the Etruscan discoveries, has had to give up going;

they all agreed English people were much safer; but all also told us it would be risky to be about the country. So, as we cared little for the towns, and wanted too to drive, we came over at once to this side, which is quite different. We had the funniest arrangement at Viterbo—a palatial bedroom, large, vaulted, and grand, but no food to be had except from a little café. At Amelia it was a small country inn, quite in the country, and with lovely views, but all the arrangements very queer. Here we are back in a regular good hotel with all the comforts of civilised life.

190 Marylebone Road,
October 16th, 1894.

MIRANDA TO HER MOTHER.

Mary Harris *did* enjoy the time! She was delighted to see Octavia; said she felt her "so life giving," and compared her to Herakles in Balaustion. She was struck with the combination of the poetical with the practical, and said, "I *am* glad to have seen that side too!" She enjoyed Octavia's reading of poetry.

190 Marylebone Road,
October 30th, 1894.

OCTAVIA TO MRS. EDMUND MAURICE.

I am very sorry not to get up to see you. . . . I write this in the train en route for Southwark. I have been paddling about all the morning in the courts, with Sir Talbot and Lady Baker, Miss Marriott, Lady B.'s sister, Miss Sim, the surveyor to the estate, a builder and a leaseholder. Such a funny and large company. We were discussing the future of the various cottages and blocks. It was very satisfactory to meet so large-hearted and liberal an owner, and to feel so trusted as to one's opinion. We planned several nice things. I had been dreading an interview, as there were many difficulties, but all went splendidly. We are getting *most* responsive and happy replies about the Browning lectures that we are getting up for the pleasure of our friends. . . . We have nearly finished the alteration in one of the three Settlement houses, and come into full possession of the second on Nov. 14 ; so we are very busy with plans and estimates. I am also busy with plans for two sets of new cottages near Lisson Grove, besides taking over 19 from the Comrs. in Pimlico.

We are in full swing with the Hall, and all is going well there. We had such exquisite flowers last Sunday, sent from Blackmore, and such beautiful singing. The Hall was full.

I wonder how Florence's Dante reading went to-day. It would be a very discouraging day for any but the strong to venture out. I fear, my darling Minnie, it isn't very propitious for your swift recovery. . , .

Mr. Chubb has actually got the deed conveying the Cliff at Barmouth.[1]

Erleigh Court, Reading,
February 9th, 1895.

To MR. SYDNEY COCKERILL.

On Lady Ducie's death.

I can hardly yet realise what the void in my life will be from the loss of the friend of some thirty years, and of such a friend. She was quite unique, the majesty of intellect being only equalled by the depths of her affection, and the greatness of her spirit. The

---

[1] The first bit of land given to the National Trust.

intercourse has been unclouded for all these years ; and there will be a void that nothing can fill.   Still all this is a great possession, and one to be thankful for ; and I feel very near her now, and will try to live better for the sight of what such a spirit can be.

Letter about a book called " Neighbours of Ours," a series of East End scenes.

190 Marylebone Road, N.W.,
March 7th, 1895.

To Mr. Henry Nevinson.

I have received your most kind letter and the book.   I am very much pleased to possess it, but feel rather ashamed at your having the trouble to send it to me.   Thank you for it very much.

It is quite true that I have been deeply interested in it.   It seems to me an absolutely true picture of people in a stratum of society never before described in literature.   It is a picture drawn with real human sympathy, and shows, in a beautiful way, how human affection survives, as the divine spark, in the midst of much degradation.   The dramatic power of the book seems to me remarkable ; the only time that the author reveals himself is in the tenderness of the chosen title, which should go home to us as a rebuke, but to the people as a pledge of deep human sympathy

I fear the book will be little understood.   I can think of but few who will pierce below the low state of civilisation to what is good ; and the absence of the sentimental pictures of virtues our Londoners have *not*, which prevail in current writing, will deceive many. But, for the few who know or who can see how much mess and confusion co-exist in men with sparks of created nobleness, the book will be a record and a treasure. Thank you for it very much.

The fun is most refreshing.

> 190 Marylebone Road, N.W.,
> March 20th, 1895.

To EARL OF DUCIE.

Thank you for the key of the bureau, I shall care much to have the bureau; having been Lady Ducie's, it will come like a message.

I don't think you want me to thank you. You feel, and want me to feel, that the gift comes from her; but you know that I do feel your kindness about it all.[1]

> May 27th, 1895.

To MARGARET SHAEN ON THE PLAYGROUND FESTIVAL.

I write just a few words to congratulate you on the thorough success of the day. I thought it went *beautifully.* Tho' I saw so little of you, I was conscious thro'out of your being there, and of how much all owed to your being owner and head; but most I was thinking that, for you, as for me, the place was alive with memories. There were to us both Presences plain in the place; and, as Browning says, there were both kinds, those who are to be, and to inherit the world we are trying to make fitter for them, as well as the

> " Wonderful dead who have passed
> Thro' the body and gone."

They all seemed so really among us that sometimes I could hardly think of anything tangible to be done. Truly did I think of Ruskin's passage about Association, and how places become enriched by the life that has been passed in them. You will know the passage well.

---

[1] Lady Ducie left to Octavia a valuable freehold which had been managed by Octavia for many years.

The Warren,
June 5th, 1895.

To Mrs Edmund Maurice.

. . . You will be sorry to hear that Miss Plunkett has resigned her Hon. Sec. ship for the Hall. She gives it up after the Flower Show. It will be a *great* loss; in fact it will alter what it is possible to do there. I never find anyone take another's place. Work becomes different with a new worker. I always find help when it is really needed; but I do wonder where this is coming from. However there is time. I had a delightful visit from Miss Tait. She is going to build three cottages on a small bit of freehold ground near Lambeth Palace. She brought me the plans and such a lovely sketch of the outside. The Eccles. Commrs. lent her the plans, etc., of ours, and she said to me, " You *have* fired them with interest about building cottages!" Miss Tait has a lease of the court at the back, so she will have quite a little colony there, and Miss Neilson is helping her. Also Miss Gee has been put in charge of some dreadfully managed blocks close to Mrs. Blyth's which were a great annoyance to them. This is nice in every way. . . . I have done all my work in advance, or farmed it out; I was so frightened of its falling on Miranda; and I have engaged a bright new worker to come three days weekly, Miss Covington now having been transferred to the new cottages at Westminster, and to help on the South side of river.

2 Montacute Gardens, Tunbridge Wells,
June 28th, 1895.

To a Fellow Worker.

It is very important that you should have a good holiday some time, and I know well how difficult it is to arrange holidays.

. . . I am far too deeply impressed with what we owe to volunteers, far too anxious not to spoil the joy they have in going, even to lay any claim to their time. What they give I want them to give with full and willing hearts; and it is only they therefore who can decide what it shall be. . . . It is for each who knows the facts to decide whether she wishes to stay and share the work during the time when the strain is greatest.

I am extremely glad your courts have been going well.

June 10th, 1896.

To MISS HOWITT.

My mother has handed on to me your interesting letter of May 29th, that I may answer the part relating to the Munich schemes. I am delighted to hear of the prospect of extension of such work. Those only who know Munich, its working people, customs, and laws, would know how far our plans would suit; and how far, and in what way, they ought to be modified. But I quite feel with you that some knowledge of them might be most useful to anyone in starting similar work, if only to show a way of proceeding, which would suggest alterations to suit Munich. If anyone came to London with the idea of such preparation, I would gladly show and tell them all I could, but it would have to be some definite time, when I saw my way to give them an opening for real work; and I am afraid that I should have to ask that whoever came should devote a minimum of three months to steady work. *Nothing* could be learnt under that time, and it is a great upsetting of work to arrange it for less.

My little book, " Homes of the London Poor," was

translated by the late Princess Alice, but I am not sure where it was published. The "Octavia Hill" Verein of Berlin might know.

October 26th, 1896.

To SYDNEY COCKERELL.

I suppose you do not happen to know any gentleman likely to do for, and accept, our National Trust secretaryship? I fear we want a great deal, and give next to nothing. Of course, it might grow, but then it might not. The work would be delightful to one who cared for it : all the good results of the Commons and Footpaths work, with little or no fighting. On the contrary, calling on the generous and good people. But then we want interest in the cause, and accurate habits of business. . . . Our want comes about in this way. Our Com. Pres. Sec. has resigned, and we have been able to promote to his post our young secretary,[1] who has done such splendid work for our Kent and Surrey Footpath Committee and the National Trust, giving half his time to each. *Now* he will give all his time to commons, and gather under him our vigorous young committees with a real friendly relation and good grasp. . . . I wonder if you saw my letter about Tintagel in the papers. Last week we needed £84 to save that headland ; to-day we need only £23, so I almost see it ours. Is it not delightful? I must set to work now about Alfreston,[1] a *much* more difficult problem, and hampered by mistakes and delays before we touched the matter. Still, into a safe state it must be got.

[1] Mr Lawrence Chubb
[2] An old Church House in Kent

November 2nd, 1896.

To A FRIEND

(About helping to train a Dutch lady.)

I am most anxious to do all I can to help Miss Maas in learning what she can of work. She has made great sacrifices in coming to England to learn, and I fear it is not easy for her to do so. She is thoroughly in earnest, and it is just in order to help real learners like her, who steadily settle down to some months' training, that I feel it is important not to take round those who can only devote a day or two to the thing.

July 28th, 1897.

MRS. HILL TO MISS G. SCHUYLER.

Octavia's work grows and grows, and according to its wont flourishes. Her heart is chiefly interested just now in saving *beautiful* spots in England, securing them in their beauty for future generations. But more and more and more houses come into her care. For the next six weeks every Wednesday will be devoted to taking tenants into the country. One of the excursions is by steamer to Southend, and will number 500 persons.

Stella d'Ore, Cortina,
October, 1897.

To HER MOTHER.

We crossed the plain of the Piave, and then entered the series of wild gorges which took us up and up by the river, till we reached Pieve di Cadore, Titian's birthplace. There we slept in a large old Italian inn. We visited the little cottage where he was born. It made one feel what great things come from the outwardly small. Such a tiny kitchen, with wood fire made on a great stone in the centre, over which a great canope came down to receive and conduct the smoke. Such quaint old stairs, and such a tiny bedroom, with garret over it. A great bronze statue of him dominates the tiny piazza, and faces the small but beautiful municipio.

October 25th, 1897.

To Ellen Chase

Sir R. Hunter is very anxious to procure the latest reports of the Open Spaces movement in the U.S.A. Both that of Boston Met. Park Commission and also the Trustees of State Reservations. Could you be so very kind as to get them and send them either to him or to me ? I should be so grateful, and I know they would be well used.

190 Marylebone Road,
March 13th, 1898.

To Mrs. Edmund Maurice.

I am just starting for the Hall, where Sir J. Causton's singers will perform. It is just the sort of dreary day on which I think the fire, and light, and flowers will be appreciated by Southwark people. We are greatly enjoying Bryce's book, and grateful to you for telling us of it. . . .

I have just come back from the Hall. We had those nice working people from Sir J. Causton's; such a sweet earnest little girl of nine played the violin ! Her father, one of the overseers, is so very proud of her. The dear little thing looked delicate.

Larksfield,
August 14th, 1898.

To her Mother.

. . . . I am going over to-morrow to Toys Hill, to talk over many things with Miss Sewell. I want to get a general idea of what to aim at about the various pieces of land, which cottages to keep, which to replace, which part to open to the public. Some of the cottages are greatly overcrowded, and with that I must deal. I have also now definitely to settle about the well,[1] and order it. So far as I see, it will be best to throw open the little terrace adjoining the road which commands the farthest view, and which has some oak trees on it. Here, too, will be our well, and, I hope, a seat. The slope from it is so steep that we shall need a little cris-cross wooden fence as a slight protection. It will then be rather like the places one sees abroad—projecting terraces to see a view. Then, also, I think the whole steep bank might be well left open, and the earth that is excavated may be put at the roots of the trees. Two of the cottages I hope may be made both better and prettier. There is some flat ground below, where, perhaps, we may build two. At this moment cottages are so much needed, and the hill is still open ; I think using this land might be best. On my own land I want, this autumn at least, to plant.

February 21st, 1899

Mrs. Hill to her Cousin Miss Price.

Octavia's visit to Alnwick was a remarkably pleasant one. She was much interested in the family,

---

[1] A well given by Octavia to Toys Hill village, the spring being discovered by a " water-finder."

in the castle, in the scenery to which, and through which they drove—and in the object of her visit—the improvement of the sanitary state of the town. It was the first town which adopted the measures recommended by the General Board of Health when my father was on the Board ; so we have memories there. He stayed in Alnwick in 1855 to superintend the sanitary improvements.

Rome,
March 10th, 1899.

To her Mother.

. . . Miss E. took us yesterday to the museum where the various statues, inscriptions, and urns have been placed ; and it was wonderfully living and interesting to hear, in so living a way, what all the things were. It is marvellous to realise how the books explain the sculptures, and the sculptures illustrate the books . . We drove to Hadrian's villa. It was lovely sunlight, I never saw such cypresses ; they and the olive trees looked most beautiful among the stately ruins. Miss E described Hadrian's life and surroundings in the most living way. . . . We drove to an old convent purchased by a Mr. S. It stands on the edge of the gorge of the Arno, and just opposite the waterfall, and his grounds go down to the river. One enters a long old corridor, and the cells, from the bedrooms ; the prior's rooms are the principal rooms ; one looks out on one side to the gorge and fall, on the other to the convent garden, great lemon trees covered with fruit, doves, trellis for vines, a cell where a hermit has lived since the 4th century. Nothing spoiled, only lived in by a noble sweet and sympathetic English family. On a floor below the entrance is the refectory which is their dining room ;

the monks' seats all round were set with lemons in tubs. Below this, but all opening out on level terraces on the steep declivity, Mr. S. has excavated a grand room with a Roman pavement.

August 22nd, 1900.

To the Treasurer,
    Ruskin Memorial Fund.

Sir,
    I am in receipt of the circular letter about the proposed memorial to Mr. Ruskin in Westminster Abbey. I am sorry not to see my way to unite with his friends in a scheme which is meant to do honour to one to whom England owes so much, and from whom I myself received teaching and help, which have greatly influenced my life and work. But Ruskin needs no memorial. His influence is deeply impressed on thousands; his memorial consists in his books, his life, his work.

What it seems to me that we, who knew him, should do, in memory of him, is to carry out more earnestly what he taught us that was good. If, in memory of him, a building were to be preserved in its ancient beauty, or a mountain top, or lake, or river side were to be kept in its loveliness for all to enjoy, I should gladly hail the scheme and care to see the place saved, not so much as a memorial to him—he needs none—as a fulfilment of a hope of his.

The erection in the Abbey appears to me to be at least a questionable good. It is one which he himself might have felt as jarring with the surroundings. He cared so much for untouched buildings handed down to us. I could not join in a scheme for touching them.

                                September 16th, 1900.

To OLIVE COCKERELL.

I like to picture what a meeting it may be of those two in the great beyond, where we dare to hope for so much, and to look to meet those we love ; we, as they, purified and grown, and strengthened. Such thoughts, dear, and not of the grave and death, be yours and Una's, tho' one knows how deep the pain is, and must be.

                                October 20th, 1908.

Do you not believe your Father and Mother see and know ? I do, only we can't hear them speak.

                        6 Montacute Gardens,
                            Tunbridge Wells,
                                December 4th, 1900.

To MRS. HANSON.

. . . You have so much good work of your own on hand that we must be careful not to plan anything which would be a burden, or overtax your strength. To work with full power, to work where one is well known, and where one's character tells, is important.

                        Larksfield, Crockham Hill,
                            May 19th, 1901.

To HER MOTHER.

I did wish I had known how beautiful all would be at Red Cross yesterday, and had suggested your coming. It was really exquisite in spirit and in form. Dear Miss Ironside was there, the inspiring spirit of such a group of helpers, and trembling with anxious desire for me to see all, and to thank the helpers. There were thirty children from each of twelve schools, and one group besides, who this year performed the ribbon dance, led the singing, etc. Teachers both men and women from all the schools were there leading and caring for the children. . . .

The Kyrle flags made a great effect. The garden itself looked lovely ; trees and creepers are growing, and the Good Shepherd gleamed out among them, as if watching over the glad crowd of happy children, who marched and danced and played in bright young unconsciousness. They had almost unlimited pipes for blowing soap bubbles, and a long line of children along the balcony sent bubbles innumerable floating into the sunlighted air. The cottages have lately been painted and looked so pretty. Every window in them, as well as in the blocks of Mowbray and Stanhope, was crowded with onlookers, as was the line of railing separating the garden from Red Cross Street. On the platform in the Hall, tea was served for the teachers and helpers, who went in in detachments. Of course the band made a great feature. At the end it was really most impressive to stand on the balcony and see the great group of children fall into line and march singing to the accompaniment of the band, three times round the garden, making lovely curves over the bridge and by the band stand, the sunlight streaming on them, till they filed into the Hall, where each received a bunch of flowers and a bun, and so home.

1901.

To Fellow Workers.

But by far the largest increase of our work has been in consequence of the Ecclesiastical Commissioners asking us to take charge of some of their property, of which the leases fell in, in Southwark and Lambeth.

In Southwark the area had been leased long ago on

the old-fashioned tenure of "lives." That is, it was
held, not for a specified term of years, but subject to
the life of certain persons. The lease fell in therefore
quite suddenly, and fifty of the houses, which were
occupied by working people, were placed under my
care. I had only four days' notice before I had to begin
collecting. It was well for us that my fellow-workers rose
to the occasion, and at once undertook the added duties;
well, too, that we were just then pretty strong in
workers. It was a curious Monday's work. The houses
having been let and sublet I could be furnished with
few particulars. I had a map, and the numbers of the
houses, which were scattered in various streets over the
five acres which had reverted to the Commissioners; but I
had no tenant's name, nor the rental of any tenement, nor
did the tenants know or recognise the written authority,
having long paid to other landlords. I subdivided the
area geographically between my two principal South
London workers, and I went to every house accompanied
by one or other of them. I learnt the name of the
tenant, explained the circumstances, saw their books
and learnt their rental, and finally succeeded in obtain-
ing every rent. Many of the houses required much
attention, and since then we have been busily employed
in supervising necessary repairs. The late lessees were
liable for dilapidations, and I felt once more how
valuable to us it was to represent owners like the
Commissioners, for all this legal and surveying work was
done ably by responsible and qualified men of business,
while we were free to go in and out among the tenants,
watch details, report grievous defects, decide what
repairs essential to health should be done instantly.
We have not half done all this, but we are steadily
progressing.

The very same day the Commissioners sent to me about this sudden accession of work in Southwark, they asked me whether I could also take over 160 houses in Lambeth. I had known that this lease was falling in to them, and I knew that they proposed rebuilding for working people on some seven acres there, and would consult me about this. But I had no idea that they meant to ask me to take charge of the old cottages pending the rebuilding. However, we were able to undertake this, and it will be a very great advantage to us to get to know the tenants, the locality, the workers in the neighbourhood, before the great decisions about rebuilding are made. In this case I had the advantage of going round with the late lessee, who gave me names, rentals and particulars, and whose relations with his late tenants struck me as very satisfactory and human. On this area our main duties have been to induce tenants to pay who knew that their houses were coming down; (in this we have succeeded), to decide those difficult questions of what to repair in houses soon to be destroyed, to empty one portion of the area where cottages are first to be built, providing accommodation as far as possible for tenants, and to arrange the somewhat complicated minute details as to rates and taxes payable for cottages partly empty, or temporarily empty, on assessments which had all to be ascertained, and where certain rates in certain houses for certain times only were payable by the owners, whom we represent.

CHAPTER XI

SUCCESSFUL as was the period of work mentioned in the last chapter, it was soon followed by an event which produced a deep influence on the remaining years of Octavia's life. Her mother had throughout her life been her most helpful guide and inspirer, and her death at the end of 1902 produced a blank which could not be filled. Yet, in spite of this blow, the last period of Octavia's life was marked by much vigorous work, as will be seen by the quotations from her "Letters to her Fellow Workers" The Ecclesiastical Commissioners had steadily increased her sphere of operations, and at the time of her death she and her fellow workers were managing property for the Commissioners in Southwark, Lambeth, Westminster, and Walworth.

But far more trying were the anxieties connected with the latest acquisition of house property in the West-end, since the houses in this district had been used for evil purposes; and others near them were still misused in the same way This made it doubly difficult to raise the standard of living among the people, and to protect the respectable tenants from annoyance.

Yet even here the vigour and sympathy of her fellow workers gave her much encouragement, especially such utterances as that of the policeman mentioned in the letter dated November 28th, 1911.

In the Open Space movement she was much cheered by the acquisition of land at Gowbarrow overlooking Ullswater Lake; and she threw herself energetically into the plan for purchasing additional land on Mariners' Hill, which had become peculiarly precious to her since the erection of the seat in memory of her mother

But all this progress, in what she considered the proper work of her life, was interrupted, in 1907, by a duty which she was, at the time, rather disposed to look upon as likely to be barren of results. This was her appointment on the Royal Commission for enquiring into the working of the Poor Law. Nevertheless it will be seen from her letters that she heartily devoted herself to the rather exhausting labour of the visits to Institutions in various parts of the country, as well as the attendance at the sittings of the Commissioners. It should be mentioned also that the burden of her labours had been much increased by a recent carriage accident. The letter from Lord George Hamilton, the chairman of the Commission, shows that some, at least, of her colleagues found more value in her services than she was disposed to attach to them, and from other quarters, also, we have heard similar appreciation, from those who had opportunity of observing her work.

As so many words have been wasted on theories about her attitude towards the decisions of the Commissioners, I wish to call special attention to her letter to the Chairman, as showing the exact extent of her difference from, and agreement with, the conclusions of her colleagues.

Her steady dislike to undue Government interference with movements for assisting the poor showed itself also in 1909, in that part of her Letter to her Fellow Workers which refers to the attempts of the War Office to exploit the Cadet Corps.

In the same year she was greatly encouraged by the progress of the housing reform, carried on in Amsterdam and other towns by her Dutch friends, a progress which gave her special satisfaction.

But all these hopes and efforts were marred in 1910 by the loss of her sister Miranda, who from her earliest days had brought so bright and helpful an element into Octavia's life, and who since 1866 had been her right hand in work, and her great support and comfort in times of difficulty.

Though Octavia's health was gradually giving way under various strains, her Letter to her Fellow Workers in 1911 was one of the most hopeful she had ever written, and there was no sign of decay in her interest in the work.   She mentions a scheme which was very near her heart, for preserving land on the banks of the Wandle, as follows—" I have long been anxious to impress on people the importance of connecting larger existing Open Spaces by pleasant walking ways, away from dust and noise : these walks need not necessarily be very broad, but should be set with trees, have near them grass and flowers, if only at the edges, and should be provided with plenty of seats. To women and young children, who cannot get to far-off parks, these pathways would be of inestimable value, and they would save strong walkers, too, from having to tramp through ugly streets, or go by train or tram before reaching the open common or park   Doubly useful would these walking ways be if they could be along the banks of a river.

" I thanked last year those of my sister Miranda's friends and pupils who had given in memory of her seven acres of Grange Fell in the Cumberland she loved so well.   This year I record with deepest thanks that a part of this Wandle land has been given by a large group of her former pupils.   They have sent offerings from far and near."

I may mention here how much she would have appreciated the generous gift, since made by Mr. Richardson Evans, of land which forms part of the banks which she desired to save.

The same note of cheerfulness which marked her last " Letter to her Fellow Workers " appears in the letter written to her youngest sister at the opening of 1912 given at the end of this chapter

Re Saint Didier,
June 10th, 1902.

To her Mother.

. . . Then we came to the lonely Hospice in its waste of snow.   It was not nearly so impressive as the

Great St. Bernard, when you and I went, and of which
I have so vivid a memory. I saw no monks, little of
religious life ; one priest, whom they called the Rector,
seemed the only sign of the religious foundation. And
yet in some ways it was most impressive to realise that,
for nearly a thousand years, travellers, poor and rich,
had been received there by men dedicating themselves
to a lonely and trying life. The peasants told us how
many went over in winter, and how many died from
exposure. There was also in the Hospice a letter from
a man, who was lost in the snow in March, 1901. He
described how a wind came and swept away all traces of
the way ; how he plunged twice up to his neck in snow,
and struggled against despair, and tried to go, in what
proved the wrong direction, when a great black finger,
but shining, twice appeared to him, and pointed in
another direction. He followed, and came upon a
refuge. The shelter saved his life ; and the next day
six men from the Hospice found him and took him
there. Later, on the edge of the pass, we saw the
Roman column to Jupiter, on which a little figure of
St. Bernard stands. It is quite black, and looked so
small in the waste of snow ; but it stands grandly, and,
with outstretched hand and finger, points emphatically
to the Hospice, a sort of type of the things which
out of weakness are made strong ; and one wondered
whether some memory of the guiding hand had returned
to the lost man in the snow.

The old Rector told us he had been there forty years.
He was very apologetic about his dress ; he told us the
snow in winter came up to the roof ; but they always
get light and air at one end, which faced the south, and
from which the wind always swept the snow. The
guide told us the Rector had been made Canon at

Aosta, and, being over seventy, had been urged to go
down there to live ; but he had refused, saying he knew
the pass, and would remain there.   The only living
things we saw were snow buntings.   A few yards from
the Hospice we came in sight of Mont Blanc, its
highest peaks set with its magnificent " aiguilles,"
standing up in a vault of blue air.   Mountain after
mountain stood round it in company, in a magnificent
circle ; and, seen over slopes of glittering snow, looking
back over the upland valley filled with snow, we saw
the little Hospice standing alone, standing out against
the blue lower slopes of the white crested chain of
Savoy, the little figure of St. Bernard, the only dark
thing in the waste of white, throwing its triumphant
small arm out towards the Hospice, which he founded
and must have inspired for so many centuries.   Down
we came into the world of rushing water, of green and
of colour.

190 Marylebone Road,
September 15th, 1902.

To Rev. Ingham Brooke.

You will, of course, have been in correspondence
with Captain Bennett and others about the irreparable
loss which the Cadets have sustained in the death of
Colonel Salmond.   We had all been looking and hoping
for his return.

I feel sure that the movement has much real value,
as distinct from Church Lads' Brigades, etc ; that it
needs a real head with power.   It ought to have grown
much during the past years ; but, as far as I can see,
it has kept its head above water only, while the less
thorough works, like the Boys' Brigades, have advertised
themselves.   Both works, no doubt, are good ; but ours

appeals at once to a lower level, and a more manly kind of lad; and, as a preparation for soldiers and sailors, it is unrivalled.

Derwent Island,
October 16th, 1902.

To Mrs. Edmund Maurice.

The scene [1] was really most beautiful and very funnily primitive. The great tent was blown to atoms; and the little red dais was out under the free sky, with the great lake and splendid mountains, and golden bracken slopes around us; and the nice north country people quite near, and so happy and orderly. The Princess was most kind, and really deeply interested in the National Trust work. I reminded her of the opening of Wakefield Street, and our early days. My heart is very full of the thought of all who helped to get this land. I wished you could have been with us. It really was a wonderful thing to think it was done.

Hilston, Headington Road, Oxford,
November 26th, 1902.

To her Mother.

. . . We had a very wonderful visit to Edinburgh after I wrote to you. We met, I should think, the most interesting Edinburgh people. Dr. and Mrs. Kerr had about twelve guests each of the three nights we were there, and were most kind in telling us, before dinner, who were coming. On Friday morning we had a large meeting of workers, with representatives from Perth, Dundee, and Glasgow, all working in houses, and we discussed practical questions. At four o'clock

---

[1] The description refers to the dedication to the public of the land at Brandlehow, near Derwentwater.

we went to Mr. Haldane's to tea, and met a crowd of people, Provost, town councillors, owners, workmen, donors. Then came the public meeting, when I read my paper. It was crowded and most responsive, and the paper answered the purpose admirably. The chairman, a clergyman, who they say is doing a great work in Edinburgh, spoke of Maurice, Kingsley, and Ruskin as " the giants from whom we have learnt, and drawn inspiration," and referred to my having known them, and the privilege of having heard of them from me, and welcomed me for their sake as well as my own.

That night came a Presbyterian clergyman, who has 1,000 working-men at his Sunday services, and 800 women on Wednesdays. He hardly ever goes out, but came to meet me. Such a fine fellow ! Everyone was most kind, and we had a wonderful departure next day. Thirty or forty of the workers came to see us off, brought the most magnificent bouquet, and large bunches of violets with such words of thanks. It was like a royal departure.

January 25th, 1903.

To Mr. Wm. Blyth.

Your most kind letter telling me of your sympathy, and quoting my mother's own words about Death, and beyond Death, is among the first which I answer. I have wanted to write and thank you so much for it.

And yet how very much we have to be thankful for ! Such memories of a noble and honoured life, prolonged among us in fulness of sympathy for so many blessed years,[1] and now to pass before us into the new life, full of faith and surrounded by all who loved her.

[1] Mrs Hill was nearly ninety-four years of age at her death

The loss to us is very great, but it is so because of the greatness of the blessing we have had. We must try to live not unworthy of our traditions, and to bear well the sorrow sent us to bear. The great kindness of friends is at once a summons and a strength.

February 22nd, 1903.

To Miss Margaret Shaen.

I know you would feel Mr. Litchfield's [1] death. Those who are associated with those we love, and who have gone before us, always catch some of their light; and Mr. Litchfield's true sympathy with all that was good, and his faithful and conscientious help, always made him feel " one of us," as our tenants say, tho' of late years I saw little of him.

My dear mother kept her full sympathy in all things to the last; her marvellous vitality never flagged; we were all with her. She just lived to see her eldest grandchild, Blanche, engaged. Life was full, bright, and crowned with love and hope to the end. Now Elinor, too, our youngest niece, is engaged; and it seems like a trumpet call to come back to life, and even to their joy; and one feels one must not lose heart or hope, tho' all life seems so changed.

April 29th, 1903.

To Mr. Wm. Blyth.

Thank you for the words about dear Elinor. The wedding was very beautiful, and I believe there is every hope of her having a very happy future.

---

[1] Mr. R B Litchfield, one of the founders of the Working Men' College in Great Ormond Street (now in Crowndale Road).

To us the memories of my dear mother were very present I felt as if she must know, and be among us ; a sympathy so deep as hers, a love so great, cannot be bound by earthly death ; only the silence is a pain while it lasts.

Larksfield,
May 17th, 1903.

To MIRANDA.

We had a most interesting afternoon yesterday with Mr. Chubb, going both to Mariners and Ide Hill. We all agreed in favour of the former , partly because of the magnificent view, partly because it is now or never for it. The Ide Hill bit, you remember, faces Toys Hill, and isn't so pretty as to view ; it is more important as to access, and a small bit would give *that ;* also, a year or two hence, the land *may* not be dearer. Anyway, at this moment we can ask for precisely the parts we care for at " Mariners," just as we did at " Ide " long ago It is all vacant ; a little later there might be impediments or curtailment. Mr. Chubb and Mr. Fleming paced it, and I was cheered to see how much three acres would take. Mr. Chubb is now to measure it precisely on map, submit it to us, and then see owners with offer, and see how good an access or accesses we can get.

Larksfield, Crockham Hill,
August 23rd, 1903.

OCTAVIA TO MIRANDA.

Miss Gladstone is here. . . . She is full of wit, animation, stories, and appreciation of the beauty.

The following letter refers to the taking over the management of property belonging to the Ecclesiastical Commissioners.

1903.

LETTER TO FELLOW WORKERS.

It was a huge undertaking, and needed much care and labour to start it well, and naturally we were all keen to help. It was a great day when we took over the place. Our seconds in command took charge manfully for a fortnight of all our old courts; and fourteen of us, including all my own responsible workers, and one lady who had gained experience in Edinburgh. We met on Monday, October 5th, to take over the estate, and collect from 500 or 600 tenants wholly unknown to us. We organised it all thoughtfully; we had fifteen collecting books, and all the tenants' books prepared; had opened a bank account, had found a room as office, and divided the area among our workers. Our first duty was to get the tenants to recognise our authority and pay us. I think we were very successful; we got every tenant on the estate to pay us without any legal process, except one, who was a regular scamp. We collected some £250, most of it in silver, and got it safely to the bank. Then came the question of repairs; there were written in the first few weeks 1,000 orders for these, altho', as the whole area is to be rebuilt, we were only doing really urgent repairs and no substantial ones. All these had to be overlooked and reported on and paid for. Next came pouring in the claims for borough and water rates. We had ascertained the assessment of every house, the facts as to whether landlord or tenant was responsible, whether the rates were compounded for or not, what allowance was to be claimed for empty rooms. There were two water companies supplying the area, and we had to learn which supplied each house.

The whole place was to be rebuilt, and even the streets rearranged and widened ; and I had promised the Commissioners I would advise them as to the future plans. These had to be prepared at the earliest date possible ; the more so as the sanitary authorities were pressing, and sent 100 orders in the first few days we were there. It is needless to say with what speed, capacity and zeal the representatives of the Commissioners carried on their part of these preparations ; and they rapidly decided on the streets which should be first rebuilt, and what should be erected there. But this only implied more to be done, for we had to empty the streets swiftly, and that meant doing up all possible empty houses in other streets and getting the tenants into them. Fortunately, there were several houses empty, the falling in of the lease having scared away tenants The Commissioners had decided to close all the public-houses on the estate, and we let one to a girls' club, and had to put repairs in hand to fit it for its changed destination.

Meantime, my skilled workers had to be withdrawn, tho' Miss Lumsden's staff was new to the work ; and I do not know how the business could have been done but for her immense power, devotion and zeal, and the extreme kindness of friends in offering special help.

The matter now stands thus We have got thro' the first quarter ; have collected £2,672—mostly in silver. Plans have been prepared for rebuilding and rearrangement of the whole estate. and these are now before the Commissioners for consideration. They provide a site for rebuilding the parish school ; an area of about an acre as a public recreation ground ; they substitute four wide for three narrow streets, and afford accommodation for 700 families in four-roomed and six-roomed cottages, cottage flats, and flats of three and two-roomed tenements in houses in no case higher than three storeys.

190, Marylebone Road,
October 19th, 1904.

To a Friend Offering Help.

Thank you for your able and most interesting letter *re* the scheme for the neighbourhood of the Wandle. It is the very thing one would desire to have done. The best advice I can give is that you should approach the able and helpful secretary of the Kent and Surrey Committee of the C.P.S. at 25, Victoria Street, Westminster, and see if they can in any way help. As a rule they work most in the country; but Mr. L. Chubb, their Sec., has more knowledge of how to work such a scheme as you sketch than anyone I know; and I hope he may at least see his way to seeing and advising. I am writing to him and forwarding your letter.

I fancy he will agree with me that your best course would be to form a strong local committee, to get some one or two people to select the exact area as silently as possible, to approach the owners and get an option of purchase, and *then only* to make the scheme public and approach the various bodies and individuals who should help.

I am a member of the Kent and Surrey Committee, and on that body might be able to help; and I should always hear from Mr. Chubb of the progress of the scheme, so as to help at any juncture if possible, tho', individually, I fear at this moment I cannot undertake anything. I have, as you will see from the enclosed, in addition to my regular London work, a large country one on hand.

1904.

LETTER TO FELLOW-WORKERS.

In one way, this Notting Hill area is the most satisfactory to me of any we have. It is so steadily improving, and the people with it. It is meeting so much the needs of those who find it hardest to get on. The group of ladies who manage it are eminently fitted to help on any who can be helped there, whether it be by introducing the young people to better work, by recommending widows for charing, by giving the labourer an odd job of rough work, by immediately calling attention to cases of illness or extreme want, by bringing a little healthy amusement into somewhat monotonous hard-working lives, and in many other ways. The work is much more like that which I was able to do in earlier years than any which is possible in most new buildings.

We have had a great alarm about the work in South London. When I wrote to you last it was still doubtful whether the Ecclesiastical Commissioners would decide to undertake the responsibility of rebuilding, and retaining in their own hands, the whole of the area which was to be devoted to dwellings for the working classes. It was still undecided whether they would not lease a part to builders or companies. They have resolved to retain the whole in their own hands, and to manage it by their own agents, of whom Miss Lumsden is the first. The advantages of this plan are obvious. The Commissioners will be directly responsible for good arrangements and government, instead of being powerless to interfere for eighty or ninety years ; they will be freer than any

lessees can be to modify, should change be needed, owing
to development of science, or alteration of requirements
as time goes on ; they can determine conditions of life
in a large area occupied by working people, which may
have as deep an influence as the churches and schools,
which, up to now, they have felt it their duty to supply.
All this they have felt it possible to do, because they
realise that there is growing up a certain number of
ladies capable of representing them, and possessing
special knowledge. So that in the years to come, as
they will have lawyers to do legal business, surveyors
and architects to see to the fabric of their houses, so
they will have managers to supervise in detail the
comfort and health of their tenants, so far as these
depend on proper conditions in the houses in which they
live ; managers who will be interested in the people, and
will have time to see thoroughly to the numerous details
involved in management of such areas.

> 190, Marylebone Road,
> April 12th, 1905.

About Tolstoi's " Resurrection."

To Mr. S. Cockerell.

At last I have finished your book. Thank you
very much for lending it to me. Of course, one feels
the nobility of the author's aim, and some of the chapters
are interesting as opening a view into life so utterly
different from ours. A great advantage in a book I feel
this to be. But, take it as a whole, I can't say I feel the
book either refreshing or helpful ; and I am a little disappointed even with the art of it. There is growth in
one or two characters, but all the rest are like a series
of very minute photographs without clearness, or

o o

interest, or growth, no connection with the rest of the book, and no beauty. Also the theories seem to me not true nor practical. Wherefore I know I prove myself unworthy and dense ; but I cannot help it. The short stories are some of them perfect, as works of art ; and some have both meaning and beauty. Anyway, thank you for lending them. It is interesting to realise what men like Tolstoi are thinking, and to try to realise why many in England look up to him.

Larksfield,
July 16th, 1905.

To Mrs. Edmund Maurice.

I write to say how *very* glad I shall be if you decide to go with us on Wednesday.[1] Miss Yorke says we are to have a carriage reserved for us, and to be driven to the cottages, of which there are 120 ! So, in some ways, it won't be so tiring as on an ordinary day, and we shall certainly see and hear more. How nice it would be to have the day with you !

I had a wonderful day yesterday. The L C C. opened the garden given by the Ecclesiastical Commissioners at Walworth. The whole place gay ; a platform at one end was enclosed, but in front of us was the whole space crowded with people, the garden being open to all. In front and around were all new houses, with large bow-windows overlooking the garden, wider streets, The whole 22 acres either rebuilt or rebuilding.

The Ecclesiastical Commissioners were represented by Sir Lewis Dibdin and Sir A. De Bock Porter. The former made a most satisfactory speech, showing that he grasped the main points of the work.

---

[1] This letter alludes to a proposed visit to Letchworth where she had been asked to assist in judging the merits of certain model cottages which were to be exhibited there.

I went to dear Red Cross to the Flower Show. There the personal work was more marked, and the people had done much for themselves.

Hotel Metropole, Leeds,
February 6th, 1907.

To MRS. EDMUND MAURICE.

How very sweet of you to write to me, and such an interesting letter! I was indeed glad to receive it. The extracts about tree-planting are delightful. Curiously enough, two of our Commissioners had been at the Distress Committee here yesterday, and had heard of some afforestation being done by the un-employed; the planting near a moorland reservoir belonging to the Corporation. They got £1,000 from the Local Government Board, and were prepared to employ fifty men fencing and planting, but can't get more than thirty-three! . . .

I am looking forward with joy to returning home to-morrow. I believe I shall spend the day at Bradford, and return straight from there. To-day we have been all day at Hull. To give my mind a little change I read Emerson in the train. It was very refreshing. I wonder if Edmund will have seen Bryce. What a wonderful new work his will be!

Edinburgh,
June 13th, 1907.

To MRS. EDMUND MAURICE

I could not finish this yesterday, and now complete it while the evidence goes on. We had a long day yesterday. We saw a large orphan school—1,300 children in separate houses on a large estate, with river running thro' it, church, and school. It was built by a

poor lad, very forlorn in Glasgow, who resolved to help
children if he could. He is dead; but his daughter
showed us over. It is one of those institutions where
they make a point of having no capital invested, or
funded income; they say all depends on prayer. There
is a sanatorium for phthisis, and a farm for sane
epileptics close by. We hear that trade in Paisley is
very brisk, and the demand for girls in the factories
is practically unlimited; the wages often £1 or £2 a
week, and some manufacturers have a very high standard
of duty. The Coatses have built beautiful lodging houses
and clubs for the girls who work there. They would
teach girls work, which is readily learnt. We went over
a large poor-house and lunatic asylum, and attended a
parish relief committee. I am longing to be home.

September, 1907.

To MIRANDA.

I had an interesting interview with Mr. Mackay
on Saturday about giving evidence before Poor Law
Royal Commission. It seems he is a fellow worker of
Mr. Crowder's, hence his wisdom. I liked him much.
By the way, at Islington there was in the chair a
Mr. Robarts, a member of the L.C.C., an ally of Mr.
Murphy's there, and a large builder. He told us such
interesting things about the Labour Leaders there.
Also he put very clearly the present difficulty of employing old or slightly disqualified men at any wages,
owing to the Trade Union rules now; but he added that
the working men were aware of the difficulty, and that
the Amalgamated Engineers were considering the possibility of dividing the men themselves into 1st, 2nd,
3rd class, and fixing different rates. I had a long
interview with Mr. Hoole on Saturday to look over the

Oxford plans. Also the University itself wants to build cottages on a farm of theirs, and wants me to send his address.

Red Cross Hall,
December 14th.

To MIRANDA.

Burns is quite keen about the Wandle scheme; is sanctioning unemployed money for clearing the area on its banks, used for dust. It will then be made into a garden. He will not, after seeing our photographs, have the river straightened.

1907.

LETTER TO MY FELLOW WORKERS.

The Poor Law Commission has necessarily occupied much of my time, and bids fair to continue to do so. It is naturally very interesting. We have visited Lancashire, Yorkshire, the Midlands, South Wales, the Eastern Counties, the Western Counties, and Scotland. My colleagues went also to the neighbourhood of Shrewsbury and to Northumberland; but I could not go. Next year we purpose visiting Ireland. The time has not arrived for making any remarks on the vast field which has opened before us; it is deeply interesting, partly by the great and important questions it suggests, partly by the large number of individuals of whose life-work we get some idea. These latter have often and often recalled to me Miss Alexander's beautiful legend of the Hidden Servants; and, as I 'have got a glimpse of the righteous manufacturer, the devoted leader of the Friendly Society, the generous founder of some out-of-sight charity, the faithful nurse, the energetic matron or teacher, the self-sacrificing wise guardian, the humble and gentle pauper, I have heard echo in my ear the thankful words: "How many Thy hidden servants are."

Of course there is the other side, and the problem appears to me the more puzzling, the more the solution of it depends, not on machinery which Commissions may recommend and Parliaments set up, but on the number of faithful men and women whom England can secure and inspire as faithful servants in their manifold duties.

We have placed on one such bit of land, given to the National Trust in memory of my mother, a stone seat designed by Mr Hoole. Near it her eldest great grand-child has planted an oak; we hope he will remember it in years to come, and connect the future with the past, where it had its root. The seat bears words from Lowell's Commemoration Ode, from the passage —

> " Blow, trumpets, all your exultations blow,
> For never shall their aureoled presence lack ;
> I see them muster in a gleaming row,
> With ever-youthful brows that nobler show
> We find in our dull road their shining track
> In every nobler mood,
> We feel the orient of their spirit glow,
> Part of our life's unalterable good
> Of all our saintlier aspiration
> They come transfigured back,
> Secure from change in their high-hearted ways,
> Beautiful evermore, and with the rays
> Of morn on their white shields of expectation "

In memory has it been given, but in glad memory, and with such thoughts as should be present to him who shall there watch the spring growth, and look out on the beauty of the England he loves, and which is the inheritance of her sons.

190 Marylebone Road, N.W.
April 14th, 1908.

To a Friend Offering Help.

I am glad your houses in South London are doing well. We are having a depressing time as to workmen's houses in London ; one wonders how things will go in the future. I do hope, better.

You ask about our longed-for bit of ground. It is on the range of hills on which Sevenoaks is, but further west ; the hills are a range between the North Downs and the Ashdown Forest range. The exact hill is called Mariners' Hill, and is about equidistant from Eden Bridge, Oxted and Westerham. I was there on Sunday, and the view was quite magnificent. The ground was a mass of primroses in full flower ; and all the wild hyacinth leaves were coming up. There is a great deal of brushwood, through which we shall cut paths ; but there are a few good oak-trees ; and, if all be well, I shall plant some more, and some beeches, where they will not hide the view ; and the upland meadow we shall keep quite clear.

We still want £336 to complete the purchase ; but we have achieved getting the land into friendly hands ; so that we secure time to try to raise the balance. This is a great mercy, especially as I am so very busy that it is difficult to take steps for making the need more known. Till we got the land into safe hands, I dared not mention where it was, lest the vendors should raise the price.

190 Marylebone Road,
November, 1908.

To Lord George Hamilton.

I feel it so important that as many of us as possible should be able to sign the report without reservations, that I trouble you with a letter.

I have always desired an " ad hoc " body ; but I am too ignorant about these statutory committees, absolutely to object to them. But it seems to me that, as at present drafted, the report provides no safeguards against two dangers, namely, the overtaxing of the strength of the county councillors; and the possibility of the nominations (on the Minor authority) being in untrustworthy hands.

If the scheme of nomination be much more carefully thought out, and provided for, it would meet my great difficulty about the authority. Is this possible ?

I hear all round of the impossibility of County Councillors doing the work entrusted to them ; of the duties devolving necessarily on officials ; and of their being put on committees, other than those for which they have aptitude and experience.

The *Minor* Committees are those that really do the work, face to face with the poor ; and I see no provision that they shall be composed of the right people.

I have not seen what Dr. Downes is drafting, yet ; and I do not know how far I may agree with it, but I would willingly come into line with you all if I could ; and, so far as the Authority is concerned, this of the nomination is my difficulty.

I can't see my way about the " Abnormal " scheme of National Work ; nor to accept what seems to me an extension of out-relief. I am ready not to vote for its abolition. I am glad that the out-relief given should be far more wisely supervised ; that we should have country work-houses with space for real work (called Labour Colonies if the world likes) ; but, when it comes to money grants for the able-bodied men outside any institution, and without disfranchisement, because they are thought respectable, we seem to be extending out-relief so as to trench on what can only be done by Charity. But these are points which will come up soon on Part VI.

The other point arises only on Part IX.; and something will, I conclude, go to the Government before it is before us; and I feel, with Dr. Downes, that any dissent, that any of us are compelled to express, must be expressed by them.

This letter, written after Octavia's death to her sister by the Chairman of the Poor Law Commission, is inserted here as bearing on that Commission.

1912.

To Miss F. Hill from Lord George Hamilton.

. . . . I was associated with Miss Octavia Hill for five years on the Poor Law Commission; and, during that time, I acquired for her a feeling of deep reverence and regard. She was a great woman, and in no way did she more show her greatness than in her absolute disregard of the frivolities and fancies of the moment. The work she has done, and the school she has founded, will live and perpetuate her memory.

To me she was a pillar of strength, and, at critical moments of discussion and controversy, she would intervene, and, with a few words of undeniable common sense and insight, solve the problem we were considering.

May 29th, 1909.

To a Friend.

Your sweet letter with all its loving thought, followed me to Italy; and, now that we have just re-returned, I want to write to you and thank you. We have had a wonderful time on Lakes Garda and Iseo, and in Tyrol, and in Switzerland. Miranda and I have returned much refreshed, ready for a spell of work.

I am sure that you do all that is possible, with your health ; and *being* is so much more important than *doing*.

About Notting Hill I am thankful to say that there is much religious and temperance work going on among the people ; and we are in closest touch with those who are doing it, clergy, parish workers, heroic workers in clubs. I trust that it may be telling on individuals ; but those who are doing it are at least as convinced as we are, that, in ordering the homes, in employing and teaching the workers, in purifying the houses, we have a special work to do, which is essential in supplementing the spiritual teaching.

The Vicar is a splendid worker. Miranda's goddaughter Miss Macdonell [1] is wonderful in her work among the girls—but the power, which we have, of preventing certain gross evils is, they feel, the greatest help, in the rescue of these feeble folk.

September ?, 1909.

To MIRANDA.

Dear Mr. Booth has resigned his place on the Commission. There was great sympathy and warmth of feeling shown, and we all signed a letter to him. . . . It was a little breezy ; but L. did not make much way. Mr. Crooks was interesting. It was a very long day. I thought I must stay till Mr. Brookbank had finished. I told the Comn. I did not think I could manage Ireland. I believe I ought to take some Labour Colony visiting. It would be far easier, and much more to the point.

[1] Daughter of Sir John Macdonell and of Octavia's old friend, the niece of Mary Howitt.

1909.

LETTER TO MY FELLOW-WORKERS.

We are, many of us, much exercised now as to
the future of the Cadet Corps. The First London
Battalion, founded in 1887, has always been linked
closely with our work in Southwark, two companies
drilling in the Hall, and the headquarters of the battalion being quite near. The health, the physique, and
the moral training of our lads have owed much to it.
More than eight thousand boys have passed through its
ranks; and many have done honourable service for
their country both by sea and land. The day has now
come when the War Office are about to link on the
Cadets to the general organisation for military service.
They have issued suggested regulations, which appear
to me, and to all the devoted group of gentlemen who
have acted as officers to these lads for now so many
years, to be full of peril to the whole movement.

It is proposed to make the severance of the Cadet
from his officers, comrades, and club, compulsory at the
age of seventeen. This regulation is not proposed for
higher-class boys; and it would seem hard indeed to
make it for such lads as ours. We have always felt the
club life, the camping out together and with their
officers, part of the most valuable influences possible.
If it is to cease at seventeen, when the Cadet is not a
man, when he is open to all the temptations of the
streets, and to the undisciplined life there, most of the
good gained from fourteen to seventeen would be lost.
Moreover, no workman's club is open to him till he is
eighteen.

Setting aside the moral and physical training, it
appears to us a great mistake from the point of view of
those who desire to link such lads on to the organisa-

tion for the defence of our country. It is true that, if they desire to do so, they can join the Territorials. But these boys are not in a strong position to arrange with their employers to be given time ; nor can they afford to sacrifice time or wages. Some do and would join the Territorials at seventeen ; and we should not propose their being barred from doing so ; but we think their severance from the Cadet Corps at seventeen should be optional. If they are inclined for a military career, they are far more likely to enlist in the regular army, where they would be provided for. This they cannot do till they are eighteen. For the sake of that unique and wonderful reforming power, which we have found the Cadet Corps to be for our London lads, we very earnestly deprecate the adoption by the War Office of the suggested rule of breaking its influence off at the early age of seventeen.

June 7th, 1910.

OCTAVIA TO MISS ALICE COCKERILL.

It is a lovely thought of yours to *give* [1] something, and like the sort of inspiration which she gave. I am glad you were at the service. It was indeed a gathering of those who loved her.

The blank here is terrible, but I have so many blessings ; and among the greatest is the memory of life with her.

190 Marylebone Road,
June 18th, 1910.

ON THE DEATH OF MISS WALLICK AND OF MIRANDA.

DEAR MRS BROOKE,

In very deed there is a fellowship of suffering. Our modern way of looking upon suffering as a thing

---

[1] In memory of Miranda.

which, by good arrangements, we can get rid of, misses often that solemn sense of its holiness, which those, who live in constant memory of our Lord's suffering, enter into.

Yours was a far harder loss,—in seeing the young bright spirit pass from among you, with all the promise of life before her.

My sister went, though full of eager and loving sympathy, and rich in openings for useful work, yet after a long and very full and happy life; and she lay, surrounded by flowers, with the love and devotion of the many, high and low, young and old, who had loved her. She had no pain; and she lived all her life so near to God, so vividly conscious of all the spiritual world, that it hardly seemed a step to the heavenly one. And yet the great void remains. I know that it is all right, and that my sorrow is as nothing to that of many; there is no jar to forget, no memories but of blessing and peace; but yet the loss is very great. I had lived on her love for seventy years, and had had the blessing of it daily; and the loss of its daily influence is very great.

Larksfield,
August 28th, 1910.

Octavia to Mrs. Edmund Maurice.

We saw Elinor and Carrington [1] and the children yesterday; all well. Baby Anna was asleep on the lawn. We had a most interesting morning at Mariner's Hill. Capell met us, and we arranged about various short dwarfstone walls, curved, and with ivy in the interstices, here and there, to keep up the bank near the lane and preserve trees thereon. Also for stumps lying

---

[1] Mr. and Mrs. Ouvry.

about to be arranged as seats. It was so nice to see his
interest in the place and joy in the beauty. We did
some cutting to open out view from Mama's seat. In
the afternoon we drove to Toy's Hill, and walked to
Ide Hill to inspect possible future purchase [1] It was
so lovely; the path by the stream promises well, and
on the upper field the heather has really taken hold,
and was in flower; and the trees we planted begin to
be a feature. The stony field is now covered with
vegetation.

We hope to start on Thursday and visit Cheddar.

> On the Mendip Hills above Cheddar,
> September 4th, 1910.

To MRS. EDMUND MAURICE.

Below lies a wide stretch of country; away to
the right are Clevedon and the Severn; in front, the
grand-looking group of the Quantocks; and to our
left, Glastonbury Tor and Wells. We walked up the
gorge where are the Cheddar cliffs, and rejoiced in seeing
what the National Trust has done in stopping the
quarrying.

The cliffs are really grand. From the top of the
ravine we came up thro' a wood and out on to this
delicious ground, where we are spending the day. . . .

Mrs. Lowe has left the National Trust £200! They
are nearing the goal about Borrowdale Fell!

> Dunster,
> September 14th, 1910.

To MRS. EDMUND MAURICE

We are having very beautiful walks. We drove
to Minehead and then walked along a wonderful cliff

---

[1] A proposed addition to the Ide Hill land

with splendid views.   When the road came to an end,
we passed a little footpath thro' fern and heather and
dwarf gorse.   .   .   .   At last we came to a rounded
hill, which formed the end of the high ground ; and, far
below us, we saw Porlock.   We went quite down the
hillside by a lovely path cut on the slope by Sir Thos.
Acland, who also has made innumerable lovely paths
all thro' his woods, all open to the public.   We took a
carriage from the little village of Bossington, and the
driver said : " If ever anything good is done, you always
find the Aclands are at the bottom of it."   This man
had been five years up in London as a grocer's assistant ;
but finding his father overdone with his farm, came
back to help him, and says he and his brothers are
making a thorough success of it.

July 25, 1911.

Speaking of the National Trust she says :

We are a body with many members, and, besides
ourselves, there are the various local correspondents of
all sorts.   We have had no friction, and this has been
largely due to the tact and judgment of our Secretary.
We must try to secure this again, but the sphere of
work is much larger than when Mr. Bond came.

Bettws-y-Coed,
February 5th, 1911.

To Mrs. Edmund Maurice.

We think of leaving here on Thursday and
spending a night at Barmouth.   I want to see the
earliest possession of the National Trust, and perhaps
the donor, Ruskin's friend.

Bettws-y-Coed,
February 28th, 1911.

To Mrs. Edmund Maurice.

I heard from Mr. Bond[1] that a member of the Trust wished to give One Tree Hill, and now he writes that he has leave to tell me that it is Gertrude and Dr. Hurry; and that it is to be in memory of Arthur. I know you will be very glad. How glad Arthur would be that his children showed a large generosity for a public object.

November 25th, 1911.

On Wednesday there will be a gathering of the family at the opening of the bath at Reading, given by his children and grand-children in memory of dear Arthur.[2]

November 28th, 1911.

To Miss Louisa Marshall.

I cannot tell you what a relief your gift is to me. It enables me to purchase all the houses now purchasable there. . . . I think that, with all our misfortunes there, much good is being done. A lady, who works among the poor near, tells that, the other night, she saw a woman lying on the pavement and went up to see if she could help. A young Irish policeman was there, and helped most beautifully to get the poor woman to the hospital. She was ill, but was known to be one of the worst characters. The policeman opened out about his awe at the dreadful character of the district; then he went on "But do you know, there are some ladies who come down here? I have not an idea who they are; and I don't know their names; but they are

---

[1] Mr Nigel Bond, Secretary of National Trust.
[2] Her brother, Arthur Hill

Christians.   They get possession of the houses, and
they won't let any of this wrong go on there ; not, if
they know it.   And there isn't anything to be made
out of it." This last sentence even pleased me ; for I
have been rather unhappy, because, lately, it has been
so difficult to make things pay as they always used to do ;
and herein one realised how the empty rooms (empty
because the tidy people dread the wickedness) had
shown some men that a sacrifice was made by the
owners, rather than they would tolerate wrong doing
where they had power to keep order.

January 2nd, 1912.

(About the proposed sale of Freshwater Place.)

To Miss Lily Shaen.

Well, then comes the question, how far is what
we planned and your Father made possible, still wanted ?
And how far can you and I secure its being carried on ?
If not to be carried on, what should take its place ?

These three questions must be faced.

The first is to me the most difficult to answer.   I
have been so long out of touch with the work there
Are the houses, which are thoroughly healthy and so
cheap, still prized by the people ? or are the showier and
more elaborately fitted houses attracting tenants ? The
letting would show this. . . . Supposing these houses,
and the bright little playground still appreciated, I do
not think you would find it at all difficult to get a
trained lady to take the management. . . . Numbers of
ladies are learning managing now ; and I, or those who
hereafter may represent me, would know such.   And
tho' I do not feel the need of houses in London anything comparable to what it was in old days (indeed, in

P P

many districts there are quantities of unlet rooms), the need of wise management is as great, or greater than ever; and, personally, I should feel it a *great* responsibility to give up power of controlling the management of any houses, for which I had been responsible. So that, if the houses still let, I do think it would be very sad to let them go; for, tho' I quite see that you can't do the thing, I feel sure you could get it done.

Now as to No 3. Suppose you decide to sell and give up the continuing thro' others of the old work, would you look out for something for which you would care, to which this land could be devoted? Its possession in a densely covered area is a power. Think over it well, will you?

April 12th, 1912.

OCTAVIA TO MISS ALICE COCKERILL.

Will you give my sincere thanks to Mrs. ——,[1] and tell her I am sure that there is a blessing on such gifts. I do rejoice when people's hearts are set on giving, and what a joy it is to them; it seems to make their lives so happy and so full. Gifts which are a sacrifice to the giver impress and inspire others, and I am glad to report them to those engaged in this work.

190 Marylebone Road,
January 2nd, 1912.

MY VERY DEAREST FLORENCE,

Lily Shaen writes to ask me about a possible sale of Freshwater Place, and the house in Marylebone Road.

I am going to see Capell on Saturday. I have a

---

[1] The above letter refers to a gift from a servant, for Mariners' Hill.

kind of idea that he may be able to help about access to Ide Hill from the Toys Hill side.

We have gone on with Ruskin's Life; it is very interesting; but the writer esteems his political economy higher than I should do, in comparison with his art work.

The New Year opens for me in many ways very happily. It is wonderful to think that I have been able to secure the purchase of the seventeen houses at Notting Hill, all we feared to lose; and even *one* seemed impossible at one time.

Then the Wandle scheme promises well. I have a letter from Miss Tupper, which may lead to the preservation of an important view from Mariners' Hill, which is in danger. I think my new workers promise well; and certainly the old ones are growing in power. I have various schemes for the year which is beginning, and hope to carry them through. I have just come in from Redvers Street, the place in Hoxton which we took over for the Montefiores. It is a joy to note the wonderful progress there. Miss Christian [1] has just been here. She gets into such real touch with all whom she sees. And all her gifts are so full of sympathy with the recipient. To-morrow is Cosette's [2] wedding; it is to be very quiet.

Your loving sister,
Octavia.

[1] A very dear friend of Miranda's.

[2] General Maurice's daughter, who had been working in Notting Hill with Miss Yorke and Octavia

CONCLUSION

For more than a year before her death, Octavia had suffered from breathlessness, and at Easter of 1912, she became aware that her illness was serious   She at once began to plan the devolution of her work   She wrote to the Ecclesiastical Commissioners and to five other owners of house property, to ask if they would appoint certain of her trained workers to take over the direct management of the houses   And she was much gratified that all these owners were ready to fall in with her suggestions , and that her lady workers were willing to undertake the responsibility of management and direction

She decided to bequeath her own freehold property to her married nieces, the three daughters of Mrs Charles Lewes, in the belief that they would care for the work, and continue the good management which would ensure the welfare of the tenants. Her nieces had been associated with her in many ways from their early girlhood, and their love and reverence for her made it likely that they would respond to this trust

These arrangements entailed many letters and interviews, the looking over documents and accounts (she had no fewer than nine banking accounts for which she was personally responsible), and all this was a most arduous task in her weak state of health

In May she went with Miss Yorke to Larksfield to try what rest and fresh air would do for her   She greatly enjoyed the beauty of the spring, and sat in an easy chair on the lawn for hours delighting in the buds and flowers, and specially in the scarlet poppies and golden broom seen against the blue distance

However, she was fast losing strength, and when she returned to Marylebone Rd , on June 3rd, she never left the house again , but her energy never flagged   Up to within three days of her death she continued to see her friends and fellow workers, using to the utmost her failing strength, and endeavouring to arrange for the efficient carrying on of the many works in which she took such a keen interest   She was much cheered by the money sent to secure the purchase of Mariners' Hill, and she watched eagerly for letters or news of donations.

Miss Rosamond Davenport Hill had bequeathed £500 to her sister, Miss Florence Davenport Hill, on the understanding that the latter should leave it to Octavia.   When, however, Miss F. D. Hill heard how very ill Octavia was, she generously sent a cheque, which came the very day before Octavia died.   This £500 was more than enough to secure the purchase of Mariners' Hill, and Octavia's delight and thankfulness were great.   It was a specially precious gift, as coming from such an old and dear friend   Octavia was anxious that her illness should not attract public attention, but, as it became known, flowers and loving messages came pouring in, which touched her deeply.   She longed to see her relations and friends, and was delighted to welcome all, as far as her failing strength would allow.   One of her nieces, after visiting her, wrote, "It was like Heaven, to be with her", and others felt the same.   She seemed to glow with faith and unselfish love, and she had a sweet smile for anyone who rendered the least service.

All through her illness she was surrounded by love.   Miss Sim, who for many years had formed part of her household, was unfailing in her watchful care   Her sisters were constantly with her, and Miss Yorke was devoted to her day and night. She was most tenderly and carefully advised by Dr. Turnbull, who had previously attended her sister, Miranda.

When Octavia realised that she could not recover she said, speaking of her work, "I might have given it a few more touches, but I think it is nearly all planned now, very well." It was a great comfort to her to know that Miss Yorke, who had lived and worked with her for thirty years, would stay on in the dear home in Marylebone Road, and form a centre for fellow-workers, and old friends, and, above all, that she would take the responsibility of such a large amount of the work.

Octavia was also very happy at the arrangements made for the other house property; for she knew that each group of ladies would gather others round them.   She felt that she was handing on the torch to those who were animated by the right spirit, and in speaking of this future for her work she said, " When I think of all this, it does not seem like death, but a new life."

On the evening of August 12th, she gathered her household round her to say good-bye, and on the following night passed peacefully away.

She was laid by her sister, Miranda, in the quiet little church-yard at Crockham Hill, and, although no formal invitations to the funeral had been sent, friends and relations gathered from far and near, even one of her Dutch friends coming from Amsterdam for the occasion, and many representatives of public bodies with which she had been connected were present Among the many lovely wreaths sent, was one from H R H. Princess Louise, bearing the following inscription —

> " In deepest admiration and esteem for one who devoted
> her whole life and energy to the advancement
> and welfare of her fellow-countrymen "

Sir Robert Hunter had been deputed to represent the Princess as he was Chairman of the " National Trust for preserving places of beauty," of which H R.H was President

Suggestions had been made that Octavia should be buried in Westminster Abbey, but her relations were obliged to decline this honour, as her express directions had been that she should be buried at Crockham Hill

The desire for a more public recognition, however, was gratified by a memorial service which was held in Southwark Cathedral, in the centre of a district where so much of her later work had been done. This was largely attended, and a beauti-fully appreciative sermon was preached by Canon Rawnsley.

Many tributes were paid to her memory in newspapers both English and foreign, but perhaps the best summary of her life's work might be expressed in the words which she herself used in returning thanks for the portrait presented to her by her friends in 1898. " When I am gone, I hope my friends will not try to carry out any special system, or to follow blindly in the track which I have trodden New circumstances require various efforts, and it is the spirit, not the dead form, that should be perpetuated When the time comes that we slip from our places, and they are called to the front as leaders, what should they inherit from us? Not a system, not an association, not dead formulas We shall leave them a few houses, purified and improved, a few new and better ones built, a certain record of thoughtful and loving management, a few open spaces, some of which will be more beautiful than they would have been; but what we care most to leave them is not any tangible thing, however great, not any memory, however good, but the quick eye to see, the true soul to measure, the large hope to grasp the mighty issues of the new and better days to come—greater ideals greater hope, and patience to realise both"

INDEX

THE END

Richard Clay & Sons, Limited
Brunswick Street, Stamford Street, S.E.,
and Bungay, Suffolk

CPSIA information can be obtained
at www.ICGtesting.com
Printed in the USA
LVHW10*1325130818
586825LV00008B/87/P